THE INTERGOVERNMENTAL PILLARS
OF THE EUROPEAN UNION

THE
INTERGOVERNMENTAL
PILLARS OF THE
EUROPEAN UNION

EILEEN DENZA

OXFORD

UNIVERSITY PRESS

OXFORD
UNIVERSITY PRESS

Great Clarendon Street, Oxford OX2 6DP

Oxford University Press is a department of the University of Oxford.
It furthers the University's objective of excellence in research, scholarship,
and education by publishing worldwide in

Oxford New York

Auckland Bangkok Buenos Aires Cape Town Chennai
Dar es Salaam Delhi Hong Kong Istanbul Karachi Kolkata
Kuala Lumpur Madrid Melbourne Mexico City Mumbai Nairobi
São Paulo Shanghai Taipei Tokyo Toronto

Oxford is a registered trade mark of Oxford University Press
in the UK and in certain other countries

Published in the United States
by Oxford University Press Inc., New York

© Eileen Denza 2002

The moral rights of the author have been asserted

Database right Oxford University Press (maker)

First published 2002

British Library Cataloguing in Publication Data

Data available

Library of Congress Cataloging in Publication Data

Denza, Eileen, 1937–
The intergovernmental pillars of the European union/Eileen Denza.
p. cm.
Includes bibliographical references and index.
1. Constitutional law—European Union countries. 2. European Union. I. Title.
KJE947 .D46 2002   341.242 2—dc21   2002030847

ISBN 0–19–829935–4

1 3 5 7 9 10 8 6 4 2

Typeset by Hope Services (Abingdon) Ltd.
Printed in Great Britain
on acid-free paper by
Biddles Ltd., Guildford and King's Lynn

Contents

Acknowledgements

I should like to express my gratitude:

to the House of Lords Select Committee on the European Communities (now the Committee on the European Union), for firing my enthusiasm for the study of the Intergovernmental Pillars when they were first constructed, and to the Committee Office for a continuing supply of Reports after I ceased to be Second Counsel;

to Professor Marise Cremona of Queen Mary College, London, with whom I teach External Relations Law of the European Union, for intellectual companionship throughout the journey and for frequent help with access to source materials;

to Ian Hendry, Deputy Legal Adviser in the Foreign and Commonwealth Office, who read and commented helpfully on an earlier version of Chapter 5;

to Anthony Langdon, formerly Deputy Under Secretary of State, Home Office, and United Kingdom Representative on the K.4 Committee from 1993 to 1995, who discussed with me many of the arguments put forward in Chapter 6 and checked that Chapter for factual accuracy;

to Oxford University Press, for their continuing support for the project over the last three years;

and finally to Paul Denza, my son, for research assistance with the international relations materials used in Chapter 2, for preparing the draft Bibliography and for much-needed help on occasion with the idiosyncrasies of my computer.

Eileen Denza
April 2002

Table of Cases

Tables of Treaties and Legislation

TREATIES AND OTHER INTERNATIONAL INSTRUMENTS

EUROPEAN UNION SECONDARY LEGISLATION AND OTHER INSTRUMENTS

Council Common Positions

Council Decisions

Council Declarations

Council Joint Actions

Council Joint Positions

Council Recommendations

Council Regulations

Council Resolutions

United States

Abbreviations

ACP States	African, Caribbean and Pacific States
AJIL	American Journal of International Law
Bull EC/EU	Bulletin of the European Communities/European Union
CEPOL	European Police College
CFI	European Court of First Instance
CFSP	common foreign and security policy
CIREA	Centre for Information, Discussion and Exchange on Asylum
CIREFI	Centre for Information, Discussion and Exchange on the Crossing of Frontiers and Immigration
CIS	Customs Information System
CML Rev	Common Market Law Review
COARM	Conventional Arms Exports
COCOM	Coordinating Committee for Multilateral Export Controls
COREPER	Committee of the Permanent Representatives
COREU	Correspondence Européenne
COSAC	Conference of European Affairs Committees
CSCE	Conference for Security and Cooperation in Europe
CYELS	Cambridge Yearbook of European Legal Studies
EBRD	European Bank for Reconstruction and Development
EC	European Community
ECHR	European Convention on Human Rights and Fundamental Freedoms
ECtHR	European Court of Human Rights
ECJ	European Court of Justice
ECOMSA	European Community Observer Mission in South Africa
EEC	European Economic Community
EJIL	European Journal of International Law
ELR	European Law Review
EFTA	European Free Trade Area
EP	European Parliament
EPC	European Political Cooperation
EPL	European Public Law

ESDI	European Security and Defence Identity
EU	European Union
EUMM	European Union Monitoring Mission
EUPM	European Union Police Mission
Europol	European Police Office
FBI	Federal Bureau of Investigation
FRY	Former Republic of Yugoslavia
FYROM	Former Yugoslavia Republic of Macedonia
GATS	General Agreement on Trade in Services
GATT	General Agreement on Tariffs and Trade
GNP	gross national product
HL	House of Lords
ICJ	International Court of Justice
ICLQ	International and Comparative Law Quarterly
IFOR	Implementation Force
ILM	International Legal Materials
IMF	International Monetary Fund
Interpol	International Criminal Police Commission
JAT	Jugoslaevnski Aerotransport
JCMS	Journal of Common Market Studies
JHA	Justice and Home Affairs
KFOR	Kosovo Force
LNTS	League of Nations Treaty Series
NATO	North Atlantic Treaty Organization
NCIS	National Criminal Intelligence Service
NPT	Non-Proliferation Treaty
NYIL	Netherlands Yearbook of International Law
OAU	Organization of African Unity
OCSE	Organization for Security and Cooperation in Europe
OECD	Organization for Economic Cooperation and Development
OJ	Official Journal of the European Communities
PHARE	Pologne, Hongrie, Aide à la Reconstructuration Economique
RUSI	Royal United Services Institute
SFOR	Stabilisation Force
TACIS	Technical Assistance to the Commonwealth of Independent States
TEU	Treaty on European Union
UK	United Kingdom
UN	United Nations
UNHCR	United Nations High Commissioner for Refugees

US	United States
WEU	Western European Union
WTO	World Trade Organization

Introduction: The Pillars of the Temple

The European Union established by the Maastricht Treaty is a strange and complex structure. The Union is not an international organization having legal personality under the law of its Member States and its status and powers under international law are controversial. It has no property or financial resources which belong to it. It is not a federal State even of a highly devolved character, mainly because it does not have the necessary independence in the conduct of its external relations. Its foreign policy and its external relations are in the last resort controlled by its fifteen Member States. These Member States continue to regard themselves as independent sovereign States and are so regarded by the rest of the international community. European lawyers are given to saying that the European Union is *sui generis*—which is true but not helpful.

The structure of the Union was described thus in Article A of the Maastricht Treaty:

The Union shall be founded on the European Communities, supplemented by the policies and forms of cooperation established by this Treaty. Its task shall be to organize, in a manner demonstrating consistency and solidarity, relations between the Member States and between their peoples.[1]

The European Communities are international organizations in the accepted sense. The European Community (originally the European Economic Community), the European Coal and Steel Community, and the European Atomic Energy Community all have defined institutions and their own financial resources. All three organizations possess international legal personality, so that they have rights and responsibilities under international law, they can be Contracting Parties to international agreements with States all over the world and in certain circumstances members of other international organizations. This trinity of linked international organizations, whose nature is elaborated not only in the Community Treaties but also in decisions of the European Court of Justice, is the foundation of the European Union but not its totality. Essential to the Union are the 'forms of cooperation' outside the three Communities—the Common Foreign and Security Policy and what was under the Maastricht Treaty described as Cooperation in the Fields of Justice and Home Affairs.

These supplementary forms of cooperation take place under quite different institutional rules from those in the three Community Treaties. The practical results of negotiation and cooperation are, to a much greater

---

[1] Article 1 of the Amsterdam version of the Treaty on European Union adds words on transparency, but the words quoted are unchanged.

extent than with the Communities, political or administrative. The most salient difference is that instruments adopted where they are intended to be legally binding are binding only under international law. They cannot create Community law rights or obligations. The cooperation taking place among the Member States in these areas is intergovernmental in its nature and in its results.

The European Union, since its contemporary shape began to emerge towards the end of the negotiation of the Maastricht Treaty, is colloquially described as having the structure of a temple—or at least of the façade of a temple.[2] The central supporting pillar is formed by the three founding Communities. The two flanking pillars are the Common Foreign and Security Policy (the Second Pillar) and Cooperation in the Fields of Justice and Home Affairs (the Third Pillar). By the Amsterdam Treaty the Third Pillar was cloven in two. Asylum, immigration by nationals of non-Member States, and judicial cooperation in civil matters, were taken from the Third Pillar to form a new Title IV within the European Community Treaty. The residual Third Pillar is now titled Provisions on Police and Judicial Cooperation in Criminal Matters.

While the three pillars are precisely identifiable in both the Maastricht and the Amsterdam versions of the Treaty on European Union, the over-arching pediment of the temple is less easy to describe in institutional terms. The objectives of the Union—which are set out in Article B of the Maastricht Treaty and, in an expanded form, in Article 2 of the Amsterdam Treaty on European Union—are general in nature, and no distinction is drawn between objectives to be achieved through Community action and those to be achieved through intergovernmental cooperation. The second objective of the Union, for example, is 'to assert its identity on the international scene, in particular through the implementation of a common foreign and security policy including the progressive framing of a common defence policy, which might lead to a common defence, in accordance with the provisions of Article 17; . . .' The assertion of the identity of the European Union takes place through the European Community's implementation of its common commercial policy and of its powers on development cooperation as well as through Union action pursuant to its common foreign and security policy. In the eight years since the Union assumed legal shape in November 1993 it has made astonishing strides in building coherent policies and developing the resources needed to project them abroad.

Article C of the Maastricht Treaty[3] provides for the Union 'a single institutional framework which shall ensure the consistency and the continuity

---

[2] For an account of the formation of the structure see Dehousse (1994) Ch 1: 'From Community to Union', and Editorial Comments Post-Maastricht in [1992] CMLR 199. See also Vignes (1993) pp 1329–44.

[3] Amsterdam Treaty on European Union, Article 3.

of the activities carried out in order to attain its objectives . . .' The Union is in particular required to ensure the consistency of its external activities and the Council and Commission are charged with this responsibility and required (by the Amsterdam Treaty) to cooperate to this end. The European Council 'shall provide the Union with the necessary impetus for its development and shall define the general political guidelines thereof'.[4] A less sublime analogy might picture the European Council as the single rider of a three-speed bicycle. The rider has a clear destination and must choose the most appropriate gear for each part of the road to be travelled.

The establishment in successive Treaties of the flanking pillars came about because the governments of the Member States of the European Communities wanted to formalize multilateral cooperation and create law-making procedures in highly sensitive areas, but without making the larger transfer of national autonomy in these areas into European Community competence and institutional structures. The legal imperative was particularly strong in the case of foreign policy. All the Member States sought a coherent, principled, and effective foreign policy for Europe but they did not for the most part want the disappearance or merger of the nation States into a single State. Given that one crucial criterion of the statehood of an entity is independence in the conduct of its external relations, the Member States could not set up a single foreign policy while keeping their separate nation status. The new foreign and security policy could be common (implying an ultimate national autonomy) but not single. A single foreign policy within Community competence would have implied loss of the ultimate national power to stand apart or even to act concurrently with the Community. Justice and home affairs were not in the same sense central to continued nation status, but national policies were sensitive and diverse. Given how close to defeat the Maastricht Treaty came in the national parliaments of Denmark, the UK and Germany, there is little possibility that in 1992 a Treaty transferring to the European Community national powers over foreign policy, defence, police, and criminal justice cooperation would have secured ratification by all the twelve national parliaments.[5]

The intergovernmental pillars are not well understood even by Community lawyers. They are often presented as inferior to the European Community in their methods and results and as adulterating the pure liquid of the Community legal order. The reasons why the Member States chose to set them up and to maintain them in the way they did and the advantages which they offer need more explanation. The objective of this

---

[4] Maastricht Treaty, Article D, Amsterdam Treaty on European Union, Article 4.
[5] See on this *R v Secretary of State for Foreign and Commonwealth Affairs, ex parte Lord Rees-Mogg* [1994] 1 All ER 457, [1993] 3 CMLR 101; *Brunner v European Union Treaty* [1994] 1 CMLR 57; Denza (1994a); Schwarze (1994); Glistrup (1994).

book is to describe the evolution and the present institutional structure of the Second and the Third Pillars and to appraise their strengths and weaknesses in legal terms. It is possible that under future Treaties other flanking pillars might be created or that the content of the existing pillars—particularly the Third Pillar—might be altered. Cooperation in sensitive areas begun under one of the Pillars may intensify to a point where the Member States are ready to trade loss of national autonomy for the greater legislative speed, certainty, and efficiency of the Community legal method.

The Second and Third Pillars could without losing their intergovernmental character take on with advantage some of the institutional features which characterize the Community method—in particular transparency, legal certainty, and effective judicial control. They will however remain a vitally important feature of the legal order established by the Maastricht and Amsterdam Treaties. The Pillars of the Temple should be seen not as a sign of weakness or of compromise but as representing the growing political maturity and sophistication of the European Union.

1

Two Legal Orders: Distinguishing Features of the Intergovernmental Pillars[1]

The Intergovernmental Pillars are not a legal innovation. They were established and continue to function because of the acceptance by the majority of the Member States, parliaments, and peoples of the European Union that European Community law is not appropriate for all the areas where they wish to work together. If the only options available were the Community law method or no legal framework at all, the Member States would in some contexts choose to have no legal framework. A legal framework based on international law offers a third way which does not compromise national sovereign powers in the way that the European Community legal order does.

What is meant by the claim by the European Court of Justice (ECJ) that the EC Treaties have created 'a new legal order of international law'[2] or, more radically, 'a new legal order'?[3] Is European Community law to be regarded as a particularly effective system of regional international law, or has it been created as, or mutated into, an entirely new species of law? If there are indeed two legal orders, to what extent are they still capable of cross-fertilization? Have the Treaty on European Union and the Treaty of Amsterdam eroded the dichotomy between the two legal orders of public international law and European Union law? Is public international law itself taking on some of the characteristics which have made European Community law an attractive as well as an effective system for regulating relations between sovereign States? Are the two streams converging?

---

[1] This chapter is based on an article published in [1999] ICLQ 257 under the title 'Two Legal Orders: Divergent or Convergent'.

[2] Case 26/62 *NV Algemene Transport-en Expeditie Onderneming van Gend en Loos v Nederlandse Administratie der Belastingen* [1963] ECR 1. For an account of the significance of this case, and of earlier steps to distinguish the Community's legal order from that of international law, see Schwarze (1999), especially pp 230–5.

[3] Opinion 1/91(*First EEA Opinion*) [1991] ECR 6079, especially at para 211: 'In contrast, the EEC Treaty, albeit concluded in the form of an international agreement, none the less constitutes the constitutional charter of a Community based on the rule of law. As the ECJ has consistently held, the Community treaties established a new legal order for the benefit of which the States have limited their sovereign rights, in ever wider fields, and the subjects of which comprise not only Member States but also their nationals . . .'. See de Witte (1994) at p 300: 'The European Court of Justice, for its part, has never stated in so many words that EC law is entirely outside the scope of public international law but some of its dicta seem to point in that direction.'

This chapter will first set out the broad similarities between public international law and European Community law. Secondly, it will identify the most obvious ways in which the two legal orders are different. Thirdly, it will take most of these differences in turn and examine how recent developments—whether contained in new treaties or emerging from contemporary practice—are diminishing their extent or their importance. Finally, it will suggest answers to the questions posed in the previous paragraph.

The Similarities

(i) Both public international law and European Community law are essentially law between sovereign States.[4] Setting aside for the moment the question of their effect on the rights and obligations of individuals, and the way in which they may change national constitutions or national legal orders, the States which form and are governed by both legal orders remain separate sovereign States. In contrast to any national legal system, international law and European Community law are horizontal rather than vertical in nature. Although the European Community may claim to be 'supranational' and some at least of its people and its governments had or have clear political aspirations to drive 'ever closer Union among the peoples of Europe'[5] towards a single federal State, such a change has not happened. The Member States continue to satisfy the established criteria for recognition as independent sovereign States and to be recognized as such by the rest of the world. European Community law is based on the Community Treaties concluded between these independent States, not superimposed by any higher authority, and although these Treaties do not provide explicitly for withdrawal or termination of membership of the Union, it is accepted politically that in the unlikely event of a State wishing to leave, it could not ultimately be compelled to remain a Member. It should be noted that the UN Charter likewise makes no provision for deliberate withdrawal from membership (as opposed to expulsion) and it has never been suggested that the Members of the UN have thereby forfeited their character as independent sovereign States.[6] As the then Lord Chancellor, Lord Mackay of Clashfern, stated in the House of Lords, referring to the UN as well as to the European Union: 'Conventions operate by agreement of the parties. The process of entering into them is not irrevocable, however: it is open to a party to withdraw under conditions that may be specified.'[7]

---

[4] See Bethlehem (1998).   [5] Preamble to the TEU.
[6] See Higgins (1991); Louis (1990), ch II Section 1: The Treaties as the Constitution of the Community; Livingstone (1965); Blum (1967); Akehurst (1979).
[7] Hansard HL Debs. 3 July 1996 vol 573, cols 1450–1. See also, especially on the question of amendment, de Witte (1994).

(ii) The principal sources of European Community law, as with public international law, are treaties together with custom. Historically, international law began as a system based almost entirely on custom, while the role of treaties was relatively small and specific. Throughout the twentieth century, however, the relative importance in practice of custom and treaties has been radically changing as larger and larger areas of customary law have come to be regulated either by bilateral or by multilateral treaties and the role of custom has come to be mainly one of helping to interpret these treaties. Community law, on the other hand, began as an entirely treaty-based legal system, but this has been extensively supplemented by the custom and practice of the Member States and of the institutions. The current position is in practice not significantly different from that under modern international law, and in particular international institutional law. The ECJ has, however, usually given a more restricted function to custom or practice where they have taken the view that it conflicted with the terms or with the true object and purpose of a treaty commitment.[8] In both legal orders, decisions of international or European courts have played a major role in identifying or shaping the general principles of law which have emerged as supplementary sources of the law.

(iii) Outside new treaties or evolution of custom or practice, new law or new obligations can under both legal orders be created only by organizations or bodies having specific delegated power for that purpose. No organ of any of the European Communities and no international organization has the power to act, to make binding law or to conclude international agreements at large. This distinguishes them from a sovereign State which has an inherent general power of unilateral action, lawmaking, or treaty-making constrained only by customary international law and by commitments which it has voluntarily assumed in the past. In this context one may compare the approach of the International Court of Justice in its two *Nuclear Weapons* Advisory Opinions,[9] with the contemporaneous judgment of the European Court of Justice in the *Working Time Directive* case.[10] In the former cases the International Court had first, in order to establish its own jurisdiction, to enquire whether the World

---

[8] See, for example, Case 68/86 *United Kingdom v Council* [1988] ECR 855, at p 898; Case C-271/94 *European Parliament v Council* [1996] ECR I-1705 at para 24 and Case C-84/94 *United Kingdom v Council (Working Time Directive)* [1996] ECR I-5755 at para 29: 'It is settled case-law that what is merely Council practice cannot derogate from the rules laid down in the Treaty . . .'.

[9] *Legality of the Use by a State of Nuclear Weapons in Armed Conflict* [1996] ICJ Reports 66; *Legality of the Threat or Use of Nuclear Weapons* [1996] ICJ Reports 226. See also Osieke (1993) and Matheson (1997).

[10] Case C-89/94 *United Kingdom v Council of the European Union (Working Time Directive Case)* [1996] ECR I-5755. See comments in [1997] ELR 579 and in CELS Occasional Paper No 2 (1997).

Health Organization and the General Assembly of the UN were 'authorized by or in accordance with the Charter of the United Nations' to seek an Advisory Opinion from the International Court of Justice (ICJ) on the legality of the use of nuclear weapons. In the latter case the ECJ questioned whether the power of the Council of Ministers[11] to adopt directives in order to protect the health and safety of workers extended to the adoption of legislation to control the hours which could be required of workers, holidays and rest periods—legislation whose purpose, it was argued by the UK Government, was essentially social in character and whose link to health and safety was 'generalized, unspecific and unscientific'. Both judgments illustrate the way in which law-making or other action by international institutions in both legal orders is constrained by the precise terms as well as by the objective of the treaty powers conferred by the delegating sovereign States.

(iv) Both public international law and European Union law are ultimately enforceable only through the legal mechanisms of the constituent Member States. Although the UN Charter contains provisions for the collective military enforcement of Security Council decisions, it has never been politically possible to turn these provisions into reality. Judgments of the ICJ have been enforced by voluntary compliance, coordinated national sanctions and third country mediation (which followed the judgment in the *United States Hostages in Tehran case*),[12] Security Council Resolutions have been enforced through national civil and criminal penalties for breach of economic sanctions and—where use of force became necessary—by coalitions of willing Member States using national military forces under the authorization of the Security Council. In the case of the invasion of Kuwait by Iraq in 1990 all these methods were deployed.[13] The position is the same for the European Community. Although the Treaties confer a duty of the European Commission to 'ensure that the provisions of this Treaty and the measures taken by the institutions pursuant thereto are applied', this does not confer or imply powers to police or inspect independent of the authorities of the Member States. Enforcement against individuals or enterprises of Community rules on competition, fisheries, fraud against the financial interests of the Community takes place ultimately through national criminal proceedings and national bailiffs or police. Even

---

[11] Under the EC Treaty, Article 118A, as amended by the Single European Act.

[12] *Case concerning United States Diplomatic and Consular Staff in Tehran* [1980] ICJ Reports 3. Sanctions were agreed by EC Foreign Ministers within the framework of European Political Co-operation (with no explicit mention of Treaty base) and were implemented in the UK under the Iran (Temporary Powers) Act 1980 (c 28). The powers were expressly linked in s 1(1) to 'breaches of international law by Iran in connection with or arising out of the detention of members of the Embassy of the United States of America'.

[13] On the precise legal basis under the UN Charter for the use of force pursuant to Security Council Resolutions regarding Kuwait, see Higgins (1991) ch XV.

the Treaty of Amsterdam, in giving the Council and Commission strengthened powers to counter fraud and other illegal activities affecting the financial interests of the Community, is careful to add: 'These measures shall not concern the application of national criminal law or the national administration of justice.'[14] The provisions on Europol in the Treaty of Amsterdam—so far from building up Europol into a body with the kind of direct enforcement powers which the FBI has in the United States— merely enable the Council, within five years after the entry into force of the Treaty, to 'enable Europol to facilitate and support the preparation, and to encourage the coordination and carrying out, of specific investigative actions by the competent authorities of the Member States, including operational actions of joint teams comprising representatives of Europol in a support capacity; . . .'[15] Judgments of the ECJ, as well as decisions of the Council or Commission which impose a pecuniary obligation on persons other than States are enforceable, but again: 'Enforcement shall be governed by the rules of civil procedure in force in the State in the territory of which it is carried out.'[16]

The Differences[17]

(i) Proposal and Negotiation of Further Law

The near monopoly of the European Commission to propose legislation under the European Community Treaties and the need for unanimity among the Member States in order to formally amend the Commission's proposal is a feature which, at least on the face of it, sharply differentiates Community law from public international law. In no international institutional or other context is there such a precisely drawn channel for the preparation of new law, or any legislative body which both by treaty obligation and by professional training is so dedicated to the achievement of the wider and longer term objectives of the Community, as opposed to the national interests of the Member States. In the UN context, although the role of the International Law Commission in the preparation of draft conventions or codes has become increasingly formalized, it has no monopoly in the matter, and public consultation with the States who would ultimately negotiate and determine any rules was integral to the International Law Commission's process from its outset.[18] In practice, of

---

[14] EC Treaty Consolidated Version, Article 280 (ex Article 209a).

[15] TEU Consolidated Version, Article 30.2(a) (ex Article K.2).

[16] EC Treaty Consolidated Version, Article 245 (ex Article 188) and Article 256 (ex Article 192).

[17] For a somewhat different list of characteristics of the European Community Treaties which 'go far beyond classic international treaties' see Piris (1999) at pp 559–61.

[18] See Sinclair (1987) for an account of the Commission's role in codification and progressive development of international law.

course, the differentiation is less sharp. Member States devote much private effort to persuading the European Commission to make proposals which they themselves would find politically and legally attractive. Throughout the legislative process in the Council there is a continuous and fluid dialogue in which the Commission indicates readiness to respond in any amendment or new proposal to the views of the majority of the Member States, thus putting pressure on the recalcitrant minority.

In the purely international context the States are in a stronger position to advance their own interests. They may convene an international conference to negotiate on a proposal which they have themselves prepared, they may build up a network of bilateral treaties with other like-minded States where a general conference appears unlikely—at least at the time—to endorse rules acceptable to them. Protection of human rights and protection of foreign investments are two examples of areas where a regional or a bilateral approach to treaty-making was in the longer term a more successful route to the development of legal rules on the lines favoured by Western democracies. States can fail to attend, or walk away from negotiations whose outcome they believe would be uncongenial to them.

An important consequence of the Commission's powers of proposal has been that in general the negotiating process of Council legislation was more transparent than that of international treaties. The Commission's proposal was required to be published, as was any revised proposal, and shortly after the introduction of the cooperation procedure by the Single European Act it became practice to publish the Council's common position. All these documents were easily accessible in the Official Journal. The European Parliament's Opinion, its proposed amendments and its debates were also published. Council proceedings and documents were confidential, but in practice the protection given to them was limited and Ministers emerging from negotiations were ready to brief the Press and their own national parliaments. It was therefore not in practice difficult for the interested and informed outsider—whether lobbyist, special interest group, private citizen, or national parliament—to follow or to contribute to a process which in the case of important or controversial legislation was usually prolonged.

By contrast the negotiation of international treaties was generally a secret process. States were entitled to publish their own proposals, but it was highly unusual for them to do so. Other States were by international usage constrained from publishing documents which were not originally their own. The archives and documents of States and of international organizations were normally entitled by customary or treaty law to inviolability. Negotiations took place in confidential diplomatic meetings or conferences. Only after they resulted in a final text signed or at least initialled was this published, disclosed to national parliaments and, on entry into force, registered with the League of Nations or, later, the UN. There was virtually no opportunity for even the informed outsider to have any real input into the detail of the text. Each participating government could choose whether and whom to consult or to include as expert or adviser on its delegation to an international conference.

(ii) The Role of National Parliaments

Under the constitutions of most democratic States, the ratification of, or accession to, important international agreements at least requires the approval of the national parliament. Procedures vary widely, as does the degree of real parliamentary control over the decision, and the extent to which the executive can bypass its own parliament by choosing to negotiate a treaty in a form which avoids the need for any domestic constitutional procedure before its entry into force. The corollary of the absence of opportunity for the national parliament over the detail of the text of any treaty is the opportunity to determine—or at least influence—the decision whether or not to ratify, to require renegotiation or the making by the government of reservations or statements of interpretation.

Under the US Constitution, for example, the need for the President to have the 'Advice and Consent of the Senate' before ratification of treaties[19] has proved a weapon of great potential to undermine (as with the Covenant of the League of Nations) to delay (as with the UN Covenants on Human Rights) or to strengthen—most recently with the World Trade Organization Agreements—the making of new international law. But even the Senate may be bypassed where the executive casts new international commitments in the form of 'executive agreements'. Although occasionally the obstinacy of a national parliament—for example the Danish Folketing over the Maastricht Treaty or the US Senate over the 1982 Law of the Sea Convention—may bring about cosmetic or even substantive improvements to the commitments thought to be unacceptable, this is a very rare occurrence. Usually the decision is in fact whether to accept or to reject.[20]

The Community Treaties themselves of course require ratification by national parliaments under constitutional procedures, so that neither the membership of the European Union nor its powers or procedures may be changed without the specific consent of the parliaments of all the Member States. Subordinate legislation by the Council or European Commission is however quite different in this regard. Under the Community Treaties,

---

[19] Article II, Section 2: 'He shall have power, by and with the Advice and Consent of the Senate, to make Treaties, provided two-thirds of the Senators present concur.'

[20] For accounts of procedures on treaties in several national parliaments see Cassese (1980). For an account of the place of treaties under the German Basic Law of 1949 see Meyring (1997).

once the Council has adopted a regulation, directive or decision, the national parliaments have no discretion over the substance of the legal obligations to be carried out. With a directive there is choice only over the 'form and methods' by which the national authorities will achieve the result required[21] while a regulation is immediately directly applicable. There may again be some technical room for manoeuvre as to the precise method of giving the regulation the necessary teeth for effective national enforcement, but there is no room for debate over acceptance, far less over the detail of what the Council has determined. It was indeed this lack of parliamentary discretion which led the UK, Irish, and Danish Parliaments on their accession to the European Community to devise what have been perceived as relatively effective methods of scrutiny before Council adoption of legislation.

(iii) Speed and Predictability of Change

The corollary of more general democratic control over the acceptance by sovereign States of new international law set out in treaties is the generally longer period of uncertainty before it is known when, or indeed whether, it will become law. Procedures for the ratification of treaties seldom occupy a high priority on the agenda of national parliaments, and there is a general tendency for the executive authorities to postpone these procedures until it is clear that there will be widespread international support for the treaty to be examined and debated. There may be a long period during which the treaty may be provisionally applied (a device commonly used in the case of commodity agreements because of the need for precision over the date of application), applied on an informal basis at least by those States which have deposited instruments of ratification (as was the case with the 1990 Dublin Convention on Asylum),[22] applied subject to a complex network of reservations and statements of interpretation, or simply in limbo.

With Community law instruments on the other hand—apart from amendments to the Treaties themselves—there is much greater legal certainty as to when the new law will be applicable. Regulations, directives, and decisions set out on their face the date of entry into force or implementation. Delays and lack of uniformity due to laxity of national implementation of directives have been greatly reduced by more vigorous Commission policing through infraction proceedings, by the possibility of Court of Justice fines for non-compliance with judgments and by the tighter general discipline among the authorities of the Member States

[21] EC Treaty Consolidated Version, Article 249 (ex Article 189).

[22] Convention determining the State responsible for examining Applications for Asylum lodged in one of the Member States of the European Communities, Cm 1623.

induced by the *Francovich*[23] case and by the cases which subsequently clarified the liability of Member States for breaches of Community law.

(iv) Uniformity of the Law

Linked to the predictability of the application of new Community law was the very high degree of uniformity of that law among the Member States, at least on the face of things. The Community Treaties and Community legislation permitted no unilaterally determined reservations to their terms. The individual derogations which were permitted—particularly in Accession Treaties—were normally for a limited period. For a Member State with genuine problems with new legislation it might be possible to devise wording which gave it a let-out on apparently objective grounds, for example geographical configuration. Temporary derogations were however vigorously policed by the Commission to prevent abuse. Member States would often seek to append unilateral statements of interpretation to the Council minutes of the adoption of a new instrument, but while these might be politically helpful at the time they were given short shrift if the Member State sought to invoke them before the ECJ.[24] The Commission and the ECJ fought continually, and with increasing success, to control actual implementation within the Member States. The legal ideal was that the Member States marched in unison or not at all.

By contrast, classical international law was much more permissive. Even in the matter of customary international law, regional variations were sometimes judicially sanctioned. Attaching numerous reservations even to such instruments as the UN Covenants on Human Rights was common practice. Study of the voluminous and complex reservations attached by States on ratifying these Covenants suggests that their number correlates more to the conscientious approach of some States to national implementation of their obligations than to the likelihood of systematic abuses of human rights.[25] Reservations to treaties might be expressly permitted, and when they were specifically limited or forbidden by the terms of the treaty, States would seek to achieve the same objective by appending statements of interpretation to their instruments of

---

[23] Joined Cases C-6/90 and 9/90 *Francovich v Italy* [1991] ECR I-5357; Joined Cases 46/93 and 48/93 *Brasserie du Pêcheur v Germany* [1996] ECR I-1029; *R v Secretary of State for Transport, ex parte Factortame Ltd (No 4)* [1996] ECR I-2553, [1996] QB 404.

[24] On this see Nicoll (1993).

[25] See Multilateral Treaties Deposited with the Secretary-General, Status at 31 December 1996: Declarations and Reservations to the Covenant on Economic and Social Rights are at pp 111–16 and Objections to them at p 116; Reservations to the Covenant on Civil and Political Rights are at pp 121–30, Objections to them at pp 131–4 and Derogations from the Covenant at pp 137–56. The longest lists of reservations come from the UK and the US. See also British Institute of International and Comparative Law (1997).

ratification or accession.[26] Rules admitting reservations only where they were not incompatible with the object and purpose of the treaty were slow to develop.[27] On a basis of reciprocity these reservations could be relied on not only by the reserving State but by any other State which wished to take advantage of them as against the reserving State. In the interpretation of international agreements much more weight was given to the *travaux préparatoires* leading to their conclusion than was ever accepted by the ECJ when construing the Community Treaties or Community legislation.[28] To establish the international legal obligations between two States, apparently Contracting Parties to the same treaty, was therefore a much more subtle and complex exercise than to establish the effect of a European Community regulation or directive.

(v) Effectiveness within the national legal order

Effectiveness of Community rules for individuals seeking to rely on them before domestic courts was the greatest leap forward made by European Community law. In some of the domestic legal systems of the original Member States treaties intended to confer rights on individuals could be invoked by those individuals before domestic courts. The Permanent Court of International Justice in its Advisory Opinion in 1928 on the *Jurisdiction of the Courts of Danzig* case said of an Agreement between Poland and Danzig that its wording and general tenor 'show that its provisions are directly applicable as between the officials and the Administration . . . '.[29] So direct effect was not invented by those who drafted the original Community Treaties or by the ECJ. What was novel was that direct effect—where the necessary conditions were satisfied— was obligatory for all Member States regardless of their constitutional attitude to the incorporation of international treaties in general into their domestic legal order. International law, whether customary or resulting from a new treaty or from a binding decision of an international organization, required only the achievement of a specified legal result. National constitutional barriers of different kinds could be and were interposed between treaties and rights for the individual. The treaty might have to be gazetted or undergo some form of parliamentary approval in order to be

---

[26] See, for example, Articles 309 and 310 of the 1982 UN Convention on the Law of the Sea and comments on this practice made on behalf of the European Union in the General Assembly, printed in [1996] British Yearbook of International Law 754–5.

[27] See *Reservations to the Genocide Convention Case* [1951] ICJ Reports 23.

[28] Advocate-General Warner indeed once stated categorically that 'The Court never looks at travaux préparatoires as an aid to interpretation.' His position was made clear in Case 28/76 *Milec v HZA Freiburg* [1976] ECR 1639 at 1664 and in Case 136/79 *National Panasonic v Commission* [1980] ECR 2033 at 2066.

[29] [1928] Permanent Court of International Justice Reports Ser B No 15 at pp 117–18. The Opinion is discussed by Wyatt (1982) at pp 150–1.

accepted into the domestic legal system. In UK law, as a logical consequence of the supremacy of Parliament, a treaty was incapable of creating
rights or obligations enforceable by domestic courts, so that the UK was
unable to give effect to certain treaty commitments, in particular those
which altered the law of the UK, without transposing them into statutory
law. If treaties could be directly enforced under domestic law, it would
have been possible for the executive to bypass Parliament by concluding
them.[30]

The ECJ emphasized that under the European Community Treaties
such barriers were not permissible. Regulations must be capable of being
invoked by individuals or firms before national courts as soon as they
entered into force. Where a Member State had failed fully and correctly to
implement a directive by the end of the period allowed for that purpose,
individuals or firms could also invoke the directive against the defaulting
Member State—a result achieved by the Court notwithstanding some
protest on the part of a number of Member States.[31] The individual could
thus—at least where Community law was sufficiently clear—go straight
to a domestic court and obtain an instant and immediately enforceable
remedy. His position under the Community legal order may be sharply
contrasted with his position in seeking to enforce rights accorded under
the European Convention on Human Rights (ECHR). Under several of the
legal systems of the States Parties he could not rely directly on the rights
accorded to him under the Convention, In all States Parties he was
required to exhaust domestic remedies up to the highest level before even
beginning the long march to Strasbourg by exercising his right of individual petition to the European Commission of Human Rights.

Universal direct effect is thus the feature which most sharply contrasts
the Community legal order from public international law and has led to
the claims that it forms a 'new legal order' or even that it demonstrates that
the European Community has already become a federation.[32]

(vi) Effective Judicial Supervision

Next to universal direct effect within national legal systems, the compulsory jurisdiction of the ECJ was the second great leap forward by the
Community legal order beyond the classical system of international law.

[30] The role of Parliament in the UK conclusion of treaties is described in detail in Appendix
4 HL Select Committee on the European Communities (1990–91*b*) at p 56. On the effect of
treaties in UK domestic law see *J H Rayner (Mincing Lane) Ltd v Department of Trade and
Industry* [1989] Ch 72; *R v Secretary of State for the Home Department, ex parte Brind* [1990] 1 All
ER 469.

[31] See for example the UK submissions in Case 41/74 *Van Duyn v Home Office* [1974] ECR
1337 at 1343.

[32] See, for example, Barker (2001) at p 81, who argues that 'for international lawyers,
European Union is not international law'.

Submission of international legal disputes in advance of their arising simply did not occur before the twentieth century. Although there was a great
advance in adjudication of international disputes under the Permanent
Court of International Justice, this momentum was lost when the ICJ
began to operate in the shadow of the Cold War. The Communist States
were opposed in principle to the settlement of any international disputes,
even disputes among themselves, by judicial means. Other States
appeared unable to look to a longer term self-interest in the peaceful settlement of disputes and sought *ad hoc* arbitration or judicial settlement
only of cases where they were confident of victory. Most disappointing for
believers in the ICJ was the reluctance of the Permanent Members of the
Security Council to accept its compulsory jurisdiction, especially in the
context of an actual or an anticipated defeat. Following withdrawal by
France[33] and the US[34] of their acceptances of the compulsory jurisdiction
of the ICJ, the UK is left alone among the Permanent Members of the
Security Council in accepting the compulsory jurisdiction of the ICJ with
only very limited reservations.

By contrast the European Community was from an early stage a legal
order dominated and in many of its most important aspects shaped by the
ECJ. The wide jurisdiction given automatically to the ECJ by the
Community Treaties, together with the eagerness of the European Commission, and the readiness of the other Community institutions and of
individuals and enterprises directly affected by Community decisions to
submit disputes to legal adjudication soon made the ECJ the cohesive
force which welded the Member States, the institutions, and their citizens
into a true legal system. The increasing readiness of the national courts to
seek guidance on questions of Community law increased the permeation
of the national legal systems by a consciousness of the importance and
effects of Community law. The ECJ itself asserted strongly its role as a
constitutional court for the Communities and was ready whatever the
political sensitivities to guard the Treaties against any illegality by the
Member States or by the institutions. It came to be assumed that all issues
of legal importance would eventually be determined by the ECJ, and there
was seldom great national interest in deferring such determinations for
long. The problem for the ECJ soon came to be not one of building
confidence or attracting custom but of sensible allocation of its resources

---

[33] Following ICJ Orders for Interim Measures in the *Nuclear Tests* Cases [1974] ICJ Reports
253.

[34] Following assumption of jurisdiction by the ICJ in *Nicaragua v United States (Military and
Paramilitary Activities) (Jurisdiction)* [1984] ICJ Reports 602. For arguments on the issues raised
by the judgment and the US withdrawal see [1985] AJIL at pp 373, 379, 385, 423, 442, 652, 657,
682 and 992.

and of avoiding longer and longer delays in the delivery of judgments and opinions.[35]

(vii) Loss of Autonomy

A further significant distinction between international law and European Community law was that international law looked only to performance of the legal duty specified by custom, treaty, or general principle of law. Beyond this it did not limit the law-making or treaty-making power of the State. Under Community law on the other hand, in part as a logical consequence of the doctrine of direct effect, the existence of a Community rule will preclude even parallel domestic legislation (unless it is of a merely subordinate or implementing character).[36] It will also preclude the conclusion by Member States of international agreements capable of affecting the Community rule (even if in fact these agreements do not apparently affect the rule and share its objective). The exclusion of parallel legislative competence, and the development by the ECJ of the link between the internal Community rule and the external treaty-making capacity has been a major factor in achieving uniformity within the European Community legal order. But in some contexts States have been reluctant to agree to new Community rules, not because of the specific content of the rules themselves, but because of the consequential loss of related national law-making competence and external treaty-making capacity. Like the insistence on uniformity among Member States in the emergence of new rules, the restrictions imposed on national law-making and treaty-making powers have proved to be an inhibition on progress as well as a cohesive feature of the Community legal order.

The Convergence

Some of the differences which have just been outlined were apparent from the original text of the Community Treaties. But others became apparent only as the European Community institutions developed their practice and as the ECJ through its jurisprudence clarified the Treaties—or, in the opinion of at least some lawyers, created new law.[37] The increasing volume of European Community law and its direct application and direct

---

[35] On this, see British Institute of International and Comparative Law (1996). For comparison of the ECJ with the ICJ see N. D. White (1996) at pp 118–31.

[36] See, for example, Case 16/83 *Prantl* [1984] ECR 1299; Case 222/82 *Apple and Pear Development Council v Lewis Ltd* [1983] ECR 4083; Case 272/83 *Commission v Italy* [1985] ECR 1057; Case 216/84 *Commission v France* [1988] ECR 793.

[37] For example Sir Patrick Neill (as he then was) in his Memorandum on the European Court published and submitted to the House of Lords Select Committee on the European Communities said: 'The European Court of Justice has engaged in "creative jurisprudence" on many occasions': HL Select Committee on the European Communities, (1994–5*b)* at p 219.

effect within national legal orders meant that large numbers of adminis-
trators, businessmen and lawyers who had little or no previous experience
of public international law were obliged to learn and to work with
Community law. They approached it as a new legal system, not carrying
with them any assumptions derived from international law. While at
the outset public international lawyers took a keen interest in the newly
developing European Community legal order, and there were many who
taught or practised in both systems, increasing specialization and the
sheer volume of case law, practice and writing began greatly to reduce the
number of international lawyers claiming expertise in Community law.
Only those working in the developing area of the external relations of the
Communities required real understanding of both systems and of the differences between them as well as their interaction.[38] For thirty years after
the establishment of the European Communities divergence between the
two legal orders became increasingly apparent.

The reversal of this process of divergence may be said to have begun
with the Treaty on European Union, signed in February 1992. The Union
established by this Treaty was significantly different from the European
Communities which would now form the central pillar of a new and
enlarged political structure. The European Communities themselves
would be given important powers in new areas, most significantly to carry
forward European Monetary Union. Within the European Community
there were new law-making procedures established which to some extent
enhanced the specifically Community characteristics. In particular the
Treaty enlarged the pre-existing possibilities for the Council by majority
vote to adopt laws which would bind even those States which had voted
against their adoption[39] and greater involvement in the law-making
process by the European Parliament—which was accountable only to the
people of Europe who had directly elected it, and not to the governments
or the national parliaments of the Member States. On the other hand, this
Treaty marked the beginning of a greater tolerance of diversity within the
Community—notably in the opt-out permitted to the UK in the matter of
the Social Chapter and in the flexible arrangements for the establishment
of economic and monetary union.

The signatory governments also made clear in establishing the new
inter-governmental pillars of the Union that although they wished to formalize or extend cooperation and create law-making procedures in new
areas—foreign and security policy and justice and home affairs—they
were not ready to bring these areas within European Community compe-

[38] On interaction, see Bethlehem (1998).

[39] Some of the possibilities were in the Treaty from the beginning, but only after the entry
into force of the Single European Act in 1989 did it become practice to use or seriously to
threaten to use them.

tence.[40] Foreign policy, given that independence in the conduct of foreign relations remained a crucial test of the retention of individual sovereign statehood, was particularly sensitive. There was real doubt as to whether the Member States could retain separate sovereign status if they set up a single, as opposed to a common, foreign policy, losing the power of autonomous action. Justice and home affairs, though further from the heart of sovereign status, were also areas of great national diversity and political sensitivity. The Member States—collectively at least, for some were ready for closer integration—did not wish to give the European Commission the sole right of initiative with the publicity for negotiations which that entailed, or to give the European Court of Justice general judicial powers in these areas. The solution was to set up new structures, the Common Foreign and Security Policy (CFSP) and Co-operation in Justice and Home Affairs, which would operate using the methods and procedures of public international law.[41]

Under the Second and Third Pillars set up by the TEU, the Commission would be associated with the work but would have only limited powers to propose, and proposals by Member States would not automatically be published. The Council would have the power to create new obligations binding on the Member States under international law, but these would require endorsement by national parliaments only where (as was envisaged under the Justice and Home Affairs Pillar) these took the form of international conventions. The obligations would not be required to have direct effect within national legal systems. Under Article L[42] of the Treaty the ECJ would have no jurisdiction over the Second Pillar (the CFSP) and its jurisdiction over the Third Pillar (Justice and Home Affairs) would be limited to whatever was accorded by the Member States in negotiating individual conventions. This was to prove a highly divisive provision as conventions began to be drawn up under the framework of the Third Pillar. The European Union itself, the pediment above the three pillars, was not created as an all-embracing international organization having international legal personality. It remained largely political and supervisory in character. Since neither of the intergovernmental pillars was given international legal personality either, this created practical problems when agreements with third States became necessary, particularly within the context of the CFSP. It did however serve to emphasize the separate character of the inter-governmental pillars.

---

[40] Although the Single European Act concluded in 1986 (Cmnd 9758) placed European cooperation in the sphere of foreign policy (then known as European Political Cooperation) on a treaty basis, no law-making powers were at that stage given to the Council.
[41] Vignes (1993) at p. 1329; Meyring (1997) at pp 230–6; Wyatt and Dashwood (2000) ch 8.
[42] Later Article 46.

The pillars would not form part of the European Community legal order. There would be a limited role for the Commission, little transparency in negotiation of proposals, no effective judicial supervision of new instruments and—probably the most important factor for the Member States—no unforeseen loss of national autonomy. The UK, in amending the European Communities Act 1972[43] prior to ratification of the Treaty on European Union, did not include those parts of the Treaty which related to the inter-governmental pillars as 'Community Treaties', thus stressing that within the UK they would be regarded as merely inter-governmental in character.[44] But although some commentators regretted that the TEU had formalized further cooperation only under the much less intrusive order of public international law, this was not among the factors which caused the ratification of the Treaty on European Union to be so prolonged and difficult.[45]

As the intergovernmental pillars have evolved they have developed in some ways into law-making bodies having the advantages of both the European Community and the international legal orders. They made closer integration feasible where it would not otherwise have been accept-able to all the governments and national parliaments of the Member States. Where some of the characteristics of the Community legal order were necessary, for example in regard to the implementation of UN sanc-tions, it was easy for a decision taken within the CFSP to be given effect by a Community regulation.[46] The Council and Commission took seriously the duty imposed on them by Article C of the TEU to ensure the consis-tency of the external activities of the Union and to use appropriate powers for that purpose whether under the First or the Second Pillars.[47]

The Maastricht Treaty also emphasized that the First and Third Pillars were not rigidly separate compartments by providing in Article K.9 the 'passerelle' or bridge whereby the Council acting unanimously was given the power to transfer certain subjects placed within the Third Pillar into the First Pillar, and to determine appropriate voting conditions. This transfer could be made without Treaty amendment but subject, in effect, to ratification by all the Member States. Article K.9 was never used. Instead what was done by the Treaty of Amsterdam was to transfer into a

---

[43] c 68.

[44] The same approach had been followed by the U.K. with Title III of the Single European Act which in the European Communities (Amendment) Act 1986 (c 58) was not added to the definition of 'the Community Treaties'.

[45] For accounts of the ratification procedures in the various Member States see *Revue du Marché Commun* 1993 and 1994. Meyring (1997) is deeply critical of the assessment by the German Constitutional Court of the implications of the establishment by the Treaty of the Third Pillar.

[46] Under Article 73g (now Article 60) or Article 228a (now Article 301) of the EC Treaty.

[47] On consistency, see Chapter 8 below.

new title within the EC Treaty those areas of Third Pillar competence which relate essentially to free movement of people. It was clearly decided by the negotiating governments that the establishment of 'an area of freedom, security and justice' required swifter and more tightly integrated procedures and rules than the Third Pillar offered.

At the same time there have taken place changes in how international law is made and applied: more transparency in negotiation; a greater degree of uniformity; stronger effectiveness within national legal orders; and wider acceptance of judicial supervision. Some of these changes are natural to the evolution of international law into a more mature legal order, or they result from the ending of the Cold War. But the success of the European Community legal system may also have had some influence. The result is that as the European Union has to some extent embraced variable geometry,[48] and this has been carried forward by the Treaties of Amsterdam and Nice, the international legal order has in many areas at least become more cohesive.

(i) Negotiation of Further Law—Transparency

There are strong and increasing pressures towards greater transparency in the making of new law of all kinds. They have come from citizens and non-governmental organizations in many democratic States (in particular States such as Sweden and the Netherlands which have a tradition of freedom of access to national government information) from national parliaments and the European Parliament. Within the European Union there have been many attempts to respond: Declaration 17 to the TEU on the Right of Access to Information; the Code of Conduct adopted by the Commission and Council in 1993; the revised Council Rules of Procedure; publication in the Official Journal of common positions adopted by the Council where the co-operation or co-decision procedure was being followed; and publication of the record of formal votes taken within the Council.[49] In response to pressure from some national parliaments for negotiating proposals within the Justice and Home Affairs Pillar to be made public, they have to a significantly greater extent made documents available at least to those national parliaments. The House of Lords European Communities Committee, for example, in their 1993 Report on *House of Lords Scrutiny of the Intergovernmental Pillars of the European Union* asked UK Ministers to provide Parliament with drafts of conventions or proposals within the intergovernmental pillars where they were of

---

[48] See Usher (1997).
[49] See OJ L340/41 and OJ L340/43, 31.12.93; OJ C213/22, 17.8.95 and OJ C230/4, 4.9.95. See also Case T-194/94 *Carvel and Guardian Newspapers Ltd v Council* [1995] ECR and Case T-174/95 *Svenska Journalistforbundet v Council* [1998] ECR 2289.

significant importance—particularly where the rights or duties of individuals might be affected, where UK legislation might eventually be required, or where legally binding commitments might be imposed on the UK. The Government to a large extent agreed to meet this demand within the context of the Justice and Home Affairs Pillar.[50] The documents supplied under this undertaking enabled the Committee to carry out intensive examination and report on a number of significant Third Pillar proposals.[51]

The Amsterdam Treaty carried transparency forward in several ways. In a Declaration on Article K.6(2) (now Article 34) of the TEU:

The Conference agrees that initiatives for measures referred to in Article K.6(2) of the Treaty on European Union and acts adopted by the Council thereunder shall be published in the Official Journal of the European Communities, in accordance with the relevant Rules of Procedure of the Council and the Commission.

A new Article 191a[52] was added to the Treaty on European Union, under which:

1. Any citizen of the Union, and any natural or legal person residing or having its registered office in a Member State, shall have a right of access to European Parliament, Council and Commission documents, subject to the principles and the conditions to be defined in accordance with paragraphs 2 and 3.

General principles and limits to the right of access were to be determined by the Council, and the Council and Commission were to make specific provision for access in their Rules of Procedure.

If the international legal order is now to an increasing extent based on 'open covenants' they are far from being 'openly arrived at'. There are however encouraging signs of a greater readiness among democratic governments to carry out much wider consultation with specialist groups, such as trade and industry associations or environmental lobbying organizations, before concluding specialized multilateral agreements. The UN Conference on Environment and Development held in Rio de Janeiro in 1992 which adopted, *inter alia*, the Framework Convention on Global Climate Change and the Convention on Biological Diversity was preceded by massive preparation by governments to which non-governmental organizations made substantial contributions. Scientific and research groups directly assisted the Preparatory Committee for the Conference,

[50] HL Select Committee on the European Communities, 28th Report (1992–93b) paras 52–5, 66–8; Observations by the Secretary of State for Foreign and Commonwealth Affairs and the Secretary of State for Home Affairs, Cm 2471. See Chapter 10 below.
[51] A further Report of the Committee: HL Select Committee on the European Communities, 6th Report (1997–98b) contains an account of work under the new system as well as suggestions for extending it. HL Select Committee on the European Communities, 15th Report (1997–98e).
[52] EC Treaty Consolidated Version, Article 255.

and large numbers of representatives of non-governmental organizations attended the Conference in their own right and not merely as advisers to the participating governments.[53] Another example of the more open climate is the Multilateral Agreement on Investment, a proposed treaty designed to promote and protect foreign investment under negotiation within the framework of the Organization for Economic Cooperation and Development. A draft text circulated very widely among academic experts, lawyers and non-governmental organizations, was extensively debated by specialist conferences[54] and in national parliaments and was so strongly criticized that the negotiations were effectively brought to an end.[55]

(ii) The Role of National Parliaments

Linked to greater transparency which affords the possibility of input from interested outsiders is a systematic increase in the influence of national parliaments during the European Community law-making process. To some extent it was always possible for a national parliament to have a certain degree of input whether by private control through mandate of Ministers before Council meetings (the Danish method now also followed by Finland) or by public hearing of evidence and publication of pre-legislative reports (the method developed by the House of Lords but now followed to an increasing extent by the French and German Parliaments).[56] The Member States attached a Declaration to the TEU noting the importance of encouraging greater involvement of national parliaments in the activities of the European Union. There was to be closer contact between the European Parliament and national parliaments and, most importantly, the governments of the Member States were to 'ensure, *inter alia*, that national parliaments receive Commission proposals for legislation in good time for information or possible examination'.

Under the Treaty of Amsterdam this Declaration has an enhanced status. It becomes a Protocol on the Role of National Parliaments in the European Union and its terms are legally binding—to the extent that this was possible without interference in internal constitutional relations between national governments and parliaments—and is much more precise. All Commission consultation documents as well as legislative proposals are to be forwarded to national parliaments. Before a legislative proposal, or proposal for a measure under the Third Pillar, is placed on the

---

[53] Freestone (1994).

[54] Conferences in London were organized by the British Institute of International and Comparative Law in 1997 and by Oxfam in 1998.

[55] See also Sands (2000) at p 113.

[56] On UK system see Denza (1993*a*); Denza (1993*b*). For more general accounts see European Parliament (1994) and Weber-Panariello (1995).

Council agenda for decision there must be a six-week period following its being made available in all languages to the European Parliament and the Council. This compulsory six-week period (for which exception may be made only on grounds of explained urgency) ensures that the possibility of scrutiny by democratic national parliaments prior to the adoption of new European Community or European Union law in whatever form is a real one. It is, of course, for national parliaments to ensure that they take advantage of the opportunity to consider measures in draft, but at least the same opportunity as has always been open in regard to international treaties requiring ratification is now available to them in regard to European Community instruments, as well as intergovernmental measures adopted under the Third Pillar.

As for parliamentary scrutiny of international treaties, the UK—much influenced in this regard by the success of its system of scrutiny of European Community and Third Pillar documents—took a step forward when the House of Lords in 1996 persuaded the Government to supply, along with the text of a treaty signed subject to ratification, an Explanatory Memorandum describing the background to the treaty adopted and assessing its significance. The Government's undertaking followed the introduction in the House of Lords of a Bill by Lord Lester of Herne Hill which received wide support when debated. As in the case of European documents the Memoranda from the Government were expected to be of great assistance in enabling Parliament to decide whether to carry out its own enquiry and perhaps debate a particular treaty. Such debates had been possible since the introduction in 1924 of the Ponsonby Rule under which the Government already laid the text as a Command Paper before Parliament for twenty-one sitting days before proceeding to ratify under its prerogative powers, but little use had been made of the opportunity for debate by Parliament even in the case of important treaties unless an enabling domestic measure was required.[57]

(iii) Speed and Predictability of Change

The corollary of making law through international conventions requiring national ratifications is a loss of certainty as to when the instrument will enter into force, since the national parliaments cannot be required to assent or indeed to act within any particular time constraints. The Member States compounded this difficulty, in adopting individual conventions

---

[57] See debate on Treaties (Parliamentary Approval) Bill, Hansard HL Debs 28 February 1996 vol 569, cols 1556–62. The new arrangements are explained in Hansard HL Debs 16 December 1996 vol 576 WA 1101. The Minister's speech and reply are in [1996] British Yearbook of International Law 746 and 753. More generally, see Riesenfeld and Abbott (eds) (1994).

under the Third Pillar, by prescribing that they should enter into force only when ratified by all the Member States. The Dublin Convention on Asylum, which was agreed in 1990 before the formal establishment of the Third Pillar replaced earlier informal intergovernmental cooperation, took seven years to enter into force, though to a large extent it was implemented administratively in the interim period. Although several important conventions were agreed under formal Third Pillar procedures, only the Europol Convention has yet received the ratifications by all fifteen Member States necessary for entry into force. The delay in securing national ratifications came to be seen as one of the main weaknesses of the third pillar method of law-making.

In the context of treaty relations with non-Member States, the European Union is making efforts to speed or to coordinate national ratifications of international agreements. Where general multilateral agreements are, as is usually the case, mixed in character so that they require national ratifications as well as acceptance by the European Community, it is becoming usual for the Council to try to coordinate the deposit of national ratifications and the deposit of the Community instruments so far as this is constitutionally possible, so that the instrument will enter into force at the same time throughout the Union. This was done, for example, with the Montreal Protocol to the Convention on Substances that Deplete the Ozone Layer and with the World Trade Organization Agreements.[58]

The Treaty of Amsterdam introduced such an approach in the context of Third Pillar conventions. Under Article 34 (ex Article K.6) where the Council recommends a newly established convention to Member States for adoption in accordance with their constitutional requirements, 'Member States shall begin the procedure applicable within a time limit to be set by the Council.' Such a provision cannot of course oblige the national parliament to act, far less pre-judge the outcome of its consideration, but it should at least avoid the position whereby the executive for whatever reason does not even lay the convention before its national parliament.

(iv) Uniformity of the Law

In this area there is clear cross-fertilization between the Community and the international legal orders. International conventions to an increasing extent require a large number of ratifications before they can enter into force at all, and the number has tended to increase in recent years.[59] These

---

[58] See Close (1985); MacLeod, Hendry, and Hyett (1996) p 268.
[59] For example the 1958 Geneva Conventions on the Law of the Sea and the 1961 Vienna Convention on Diplomatic Relations required twenty-two instruments of ratification, the 1965 Convention on the Settlement of Investment Disputes required twenty, the 1968 Treaty

conventions are also tending to prohibit reservations entirely or to permit them in only limited areas. The 1982 UN Convention on the Law of the Sea, for example, provides that: No reservations or exceptions may be made to this Convention unless expressly permitted by other articles of this Convention.[60] In the case of codification conventions there appears to be greater reluctance to enter reservations, to enter them only in regard to very limited areas and not in practice to rely on the reservations. The Vienna Convention on Diplomatic Relations is one law-making Convention where substantive reservations have related only to two points where the Convention departed from previous customary law, and there is no evidence of their having been relied on in recent practice.[61] In addition there is evidence that the major law-making international conventions, such as the Vienna Convention on the Law of Treaties, are coming to acquire the status of customary international law so that even non-parties appear to accept their provisions as binding law.[62] Special regional approaches to questions of customary international law, for example the Latin American insistence on the foreign investor forfeiting any right to diplomatic protection, the approach of formerly dependent States to the nature of their rights over their natural resources, or the Communist States' approach to international settlement of disputes, seem to be fading in significance in the face of a stronger and more uniform global legal order.

The European Union, on the other hand, has recently been permitting a greater degree of diversity in the march towards an agreed objective. Progress, particularly in new areas of competence has come to resemble a marathon of runners rather than a military advance. Thus in the TEU in 1992, the device of a Protocol on Social Policy among eleven Member States and an Agreement on Social Policy attached to it in effect permitted the UK to opt out of provisions based on the 1989 Social Charter which their Government found unacceptable. By the Treaty of Amsterdam, signed in 1997 by a successor Government in office in the UK, it was agreed that these instruments should be repealed.[63] The arrangements permitting derogations from the provisions on the carrying forward of economic and monetary union were on the other hand not modified.

The Treaty of Amsterdam contains provisions integrating the Schengen acquis—the measures negotiated among a steadily increasing number of Member States within the framework of the Schengen Agreements on the gradual abolition of checks at common borders, and intended to imple-

on the Non-Proliferation of Nuclear Weapons instruments from all three Depositaries plus forty, the 1966 UN Covenants on Human Rights and the 1969 Vienna Convention on the Law of Treaties required thirty-five, the 1982 UN Convention on the Law of the Sea required sixty.

[60] Cmnd 8941, Art 309. [61] Denza (1998) at pp 5–6.
[62] See Aust (2000) at pp 9–13. [63] Article 2, amending the EC Treaty, para 58.

ment or compensate for the absence of border control of people. These provisions, however, take special account of the fact that the UK and Ireland are not parties to the Schengen Agreements as well as of the special position of Denmark, a member of the Nordic Passport Union together with Iceland and Norway. The UK was permitted to maintain its border controls on people, in particular to check their entitlement by virtue of Treaty rights to enter the UK. Ireland and the UK are not automatically bound by any of the Schengen acquis provisions, or even by decisions of the ECJ interpreting them; they do not automatically take part in the adoption of new measures under Title IV of the EC Treaty, but they may apply to take part in adoption and application of a new measure under that Title, or a measure already adopted under it. By way of further complication Ireland—more schizophrenic than the UK about internal border controls within the European Union—may by notification opt out of these special arrangements and decide to be covered by the ordinary provisions of the EC Treaty. A similar option was given to Denmark.[64]

The forward looking provisions on the sensitive issue of defence in Article J.7 (now Article 17) of the Treaty on European Union as revised by the Treaty of Amsterdam contained a remarkable acknowledgement of the differing positions of the Member States. Paragraph 1 provided:

The policy of the Union in accordance with this Article shall not prejudice the specific character of the security and defence policy of certain Member States and shall respect the obligations of certain Member States, which see their common defence realised in the North Atlantic Treaty Organisation (NATO), under the North Atlantic Treaty and be compatible with the common security and defence policy established within that framework.[65]

The 'specific character' of the defence policy of certain Member States was a veiled reference to the neutrality of Austria, Sweden, Finland, and Ireland. It was provided that the Western European Union (WEU) should provide the European Union with 'access to operational capability' in the defence context, mainly for humanitarian and rescue tasks, peacekeeping and peacemaking. All Member States of the European Union would be entitled to participate both in planning, decision-taking, and operational activities, but they would not all be obliged to do so. Two or more Member States might develop closer cooperation within WEuropean Union or NATO provided that this does not run counter to the defence provisions of the Treaty of Amsterdam. The formulation and development of a common defence policy under the Treaty (discussed in Chapter 11 below) accepts

[64] New Title IIIa added to the EC Treaty by the Treaty of Amsterdam (Title IV of the Consolidated Version), in particular Article 73q (now Article 69) and the related Protocols on the position of Denmark, the UK, and Ireland.
[65] TEU Consolidated Version, Article 17 (ex Article J.7).

the great diversity in the historical approaches among the Member States towards defence and permits flexibility in the matter of active contribution of military forces and equipment.

Article K as revised by the Treaty of Amsterdam also attempts, by permitting relaxation of the unanimity practice, to deal with the problem of delays in ratification of Third Pillar conventions. Having set out clearly the different instruments which the Council may adopt for purposes of Police and Judicial Co-operation in Criminal Matters, concluding with conventions to be recommended to the Member States for adoption in accordance with national constitutional requirements, Article 34.2 says: 'Unless they provide otherwise, conventions shall, once adopted by at least half of the Member States, enter into force for those Member States.'

The Treaty of Amsterdam also contains a general provision[66] envisaging closer cooperation between Member States, who are to be entitled to use the institutions, procedures, and mechanisms laid down by the Treaties subject to a number of conditions. The cooperation must be 'aimed at furthering the objectives of the Union and at protecting and serving its interests', respect the principles of the Treaties and the single institutional framework of the Union, concern at least a majority of the Member States, and save the rights, obligations, and interests of non-participants. The provisions integrating the acquis of the Schengen Agreements into the Treaty, referred to above, are an initial example of this new and more relaxed approach.

(v) Effective Judicial Supervision

Within the international legal order there has since the early 1980s been a great resurgence in the acceptance of judicial supervision at least of particular treaties or particular legal disputes. There has been a great increase in the actual use of the ICJ to settle disputes over boundaries, continental shelf demarcation, and the use of international waterways.[67] New tribunals have been established and begun active work under the International Convention on the Settlement of Investment Disputes and the 1982 Law of the Sea Convention. There has been a steady completion of ratification of the European Convention on Human Rights and Fundamental Freedoms by all Members of the Council of Europe, including such recent Members as Russia and the former Soviet Republics. Virtually all now accept the right of individual petition and there has been

[66] TEU Consolidated Version, Title VII Articles 43 to 45 (ex Title VIa, Article K.15–17).

[67] eg *Delimitation of the Maritime Boundary in the Gulf of Maine (Canada/USA)* [1984] ICJ Reports 246; *Tunisia v Libya* [1985] ICJ Reports 192; *Burkina Faso v Mali* [1986] ICJ Reports 554; *Case concerning the Land, Island and Maritime Frontier Dispute (El Salvador/Honduras)* [1992] ICJ Reports 351; *Libya v Chad* [1994] ICJ Reports 6; *Case concerning the Gabcikovo-Nagymaros Project (Hungary v Slovakia)* [1998] ILM 162.

a huge increase in the volume of cases. Shortly before the break-up of the Soviet Union, its Minister for Foreign Affairs made clear in a letter to the Secretary-General of the UN that it would no longer oppose the compulsory reference of international disputes to United Nations organs including the International Court of Justice. Where the Soviet Union had made reservations to provisions in international agreements requiring disputes to be submitted to international adjudication, the reservations would be withdrawn. Human rights agreements would be re-examined first. The letter stated that the Soviet Union in taking that decision was 'guided by the interests of strengthening the international legal order ensuring the primacy of law in politics'.[68]

The European Union, by contrast, with the establishment of the Second and Third Pillars took a step backwards by excluding the jurisdiction of the ECJ entirely from the Second Pillar and allowing it jurisdiction over the Third Pillar only in regard to specific conventions where the Member States agreed. The UK proved very reluctant ever to agree to give the ECJ jurisdiction over conventions, and this was one of the main factors which held up agreement on them. Other Member States, however, were not convinced that exclusion of the ECJ was necessary to the intergovernmental approach. In the case of the Europol Convention the Member States in the end agreed to differ, drawing up a Protocol under which the ECJ would have jurisdiction to give preliminary rulings on the interpretation of the Convention, but Member States would be entitled to choose whether to accept this jurisdiction.[69] All Member States except the UK made clear that they would accept the jurisdiction of the ECJ over the Convention. Under the Treaty of Amsterdam the ECJ is given a somewhat wider general jurisdiction over Third Pillar questions, but the 'optional approach' described above will apply to any preliminary rulings.[70]

(vi) Preservation of Autonomy

Fear of the loss of autonomy is the overwhelming reason for the preference of Member States for the intergovernmental mode of cooperation as the European Union moves into new areas. In the case of the CFSP such a method is essential in order to preserve a key element of the sovereignty of the nation States. In other areas extending or formalizing intergovernmental cooperation may be seen as a first step to ceding some degree of national power in a sensitive area, and may be regarded, in some areas at

[68] Letter of 28 February 1989 from Mr Shevardnadze, printed in [1989] AJIL 457.
[69] Europol Convention OJ C316/1, 27.11.95, Cm 3050; Protocol drawn up on the basis of Article K.3 of the TEU on the interpretation, by way of preliminary rulings, by the ECJ of the Convention on the Establishment of a European Police Office, Cm 3465. This precedent was followed by other Third Pillar Conventions.
[70] Article 35 (ex Article K.7).

least, as a halfway house. Under the Second Pillar, and even under the Third Pillar the making of binding laws having effects on individuals within the Member States is not seen as the main priority—sharing of information and facilities and developing common policies in the face of common threats, whether from international criminals or non-Member States, are perceived by those actually working within the relevant areas as the real point. The Member States while placing intergovernmental cooperation on a formal legal basis wish to preserve their national powers in such matters as criminal law, foreign and defence policy. They fear not so much majority voting on particular issues—though this is seen by some as essentially undemocratic—as the loss of the inherent power of concurrent or even conflicting action. This is what the Second and Third Pillars offer. Obligations under international law may be imposed, but if they are broken it is in fact unlikely that another Member State will rush to the International Court of Justice even if that Court had jurisdiction over the resulting dispute.

The provisions of the Amsterdam Treaty emphasize the safeguarding of national competence in a number of ways. The Council, for example, under the revised provisions on the Second and Third Pillars was given new powers to conclude international agreements with non-Member States or with international organizations. A Declaration attached to the relevant Articles of the TEU says however: 'The provisions of Articles J.14 and K.10 of the Treaty on European Union and any agreements resulting from them shall not imply any transfer of competence from the Member States to the European Union.'[71] It was becoming administratively necessary for the proper operation of the Pillars that agreements could be made on such matters as the status of fact-finding or humanitarian missions or on police cooperation with non-Member States, but Member States were determined that there should be no argument based on the *AETR*[72] jurisprudence that they would themselves by virtue of such agreements lose the competence to conclude similar agreements.

To the same effect is a Declaration on Article 63(3)(a) (ex Article 73k(3)(a)) of the European Community Treaty which gives the Council power to adopt measures on conditions of entry, visas, and residence permits. The Declaration specifies that Member States may negotiate and conclude agreements with third countries in these areas 'as long as such agreements respect Community law'. A Protocol annexed to the EC Treaty

---

[71] Now Articles 24 and 38 of the TEU Consolidated Version.
[72] Case 22/70 *Commission v Council (AETR)* [1971] ECR 263, especially para 17: 'In particular, each time the Community, with a view to implementing a common policy envisaged by the Treaty, adopts provisions laying down common rules, whatever form these might take, the Member States no longer have the right, acting individually or even collectively, to undertake obligations with third countries which affect those rules.'

and dealing with External Relations with regard to the Crossing of External Borders confers a similar external power on the Member States in regard to border checks, with the saving 'so long as they respect Community law and other international agreements'. Such provisions draw a clear line in the sand preventing the possibility of the Treaty of Amsterdam leading to further loss of the power of the Member States to conclude international agreements.

(vii) Human Rights

By way of coda to these examples of closer fusion between international law and European Union law it may be noted that the gradually closer attention paid over the last twenty-five years by the ECJ to the jurisprudence of the European Commission and Court of Human Rights,[73] and the significantly greater acknowledgement in the Treaty of Amsterdam of the human rights dimension of the European Union also serves to break down barriers between the two legal orders. Article 7 (ex Article F) of the TEU, stating that the Union is founded on the principles of liberty, democracy, respect for human rights and fundamental freedoms and the rule of law describes these as 'principles which are common to the Member States', but they are also principles which have in recent years been more highly developed through international legal agreements, procedures, and cases. The new power for the Council to determine the existence of a persistent and serious breach of human rights by a Member State and to suspend a Member found to be in breach of human rights from European Union rights[74] is in practice unlikely to be exercised except following disregard of a judgment of the European Court of Human Rights.

It is under the Treaty of Amsterdam a legal as well as a political requirement that applicants for membership respect human rights—and in practice this means that applicants must become Contracting Parties to the ECHR and also accept the right of individual petition and the compulsory jurisdiction of the European Court of Human Rights. Given that a large number of applicant States, including Russia and former Soviet Republics, have in this context become Members of the Council of Europe and Parties to the ECHR, the European Union by its policy, now explicit in the Treaty, strengthened a most important and successful part of the international legal order.

---

[73] On this see Clapham (1990); House of Lords Select Committee on the European Communities, 3rd Report, (1992–93a); Case C-260/89 *Elliniki Radiophonia Tileorassi AE (ERT) v Dimotiki Etairia Pliroforissis (DEP)* [1991] ECR I-2925.
[74] TEU Consolidated Version, Article 7 (ex Article F.1).

Conclusion

On the basis of this preliminary survey of the features which distinguish European Community law from classical international law, some answers will be given to the questions posed at the outset of this chapter.

1. European Community law is best regarded as a particularly effective form of regional international law.
2. Whether European Community law and international law form two legal orders or not, they are capable of cross-fertilization and they are cross-fertilizing to an increasing extent.
3. The TEU and the later revisions to it have eroded the dichotomy. In establishing and improving the intergovernmental pillars, the Member States have shown that there is still a place in their institutional relations for a specially designed method based on public international law.

2

Evolution of European Political Cooperation and Formation of the Second Pillar

The Legal Straitjacket

To understand the legal constraints on the formation of a common foreign policy between States one must bear in mind that independence in the conduct of external relations is an essential element of sovereign status in international law. Article 1 of the 1933 Montevideo Convention on Rights and Duties of States,[1] which is often taken as a starting point in examining the nature of a State, provides that: 'The State as a person of international law should possess the following qualifications: (a) a permanent population; (b) a defined territory; (c) government; and (d) capacity to enter into relations with other States.' The UK has stated that the criteria normally applied for the recognition of a State are 'that it should have, and seem likely to continue to have, a clearly defined territory with a population, a Government who are able to exercise effective control of that territory and independence in their external relations'.[2]

Although there have been, and continue to be, a few cases where entities not having full independence as sovereign States enjoy limited capacity to conduct some forms of external relations, such as entering into treaties or sending missions,[3] the general rule is that where an entity is newly admitted to independent sovereign status, it is accepted as having capacity to succeed, to conclude and to accede to international agreements, to send and receive diplomatic missions, to become a member of international organizations, and to defend itself from attack. Conversely, where a State loses independent sovereign status by entering into a union with another State or States, its separate treaty relations are integrated, its separate embassies are closed or become embassies of the new State, its separate membership of international organizations lapses, and it no longer has the right to call on other States to assist it in defending itself.[4] The United Kingdom of Great Britain, for example, resulted from the

[1] 165 LNTS 19; [1934] AJIL Supp 75.
[2] Hansard HC Debs Vol 55 col 226, WA (29 February 1984).
[3] See Weiler (1999*b*) (especially pp 136–68).
[4] See, generally, Oppenheim (1996), Vol I pp 121–46; *Austro-German Customs Union Case* 1931 PCIJ Reports Series A/B No 41; Crawford (1979); Denza (1998) pp 20–8.

Treaty of Union which fused the Parliaments of England and Scotland. In recent years the decolonization process and the break-up of the Soviet Union and Yugoslavia have led to the emergence of many new sovereign States.[5] Disappearances have been far fewer, but they include the fusion of North and South Vietnam, the union of the two Yemen States, and the re-emergence of Germany as a single State.

It was therefore clear that as the Member States of the three European Communities limited their sovereign rights in ever wider fields,[6] this limitation must stop short of integration of their foreign policies. The establishment of a single foreign policy would have the effect of turning a confederal Community into a federal Union. There were some who saw the future of Europe in these terms, but they did not include the ministers or the electors of the larger Member States.[7]

On the other hand, the Member States had with the original Treaties taken the bold step of providing for a common commercial policy. Providing international legal personality for the three Communities was not novel, and by the 1950s it was already common for international organizations such as the UN and its Specialized Agencies to conclude international agreements with individual States providing for the status, privileges and immunities of their headquarters, staff, representatives, and experts. Commercial agreements were an important element of a State's external powers, however, and the EC Treaty expressly delegated to the Community the power to conclude such agreements and specified procedures for their negotiation and conclusion. The delegation of power over trade agreements was a logical corollary of the commitment to free movement of goods within the Community, but some of the wider consequences for external policy were not fully appreciated at the outset. Gradually it became apparent through the development of the common commercial policy into wider and more politically sensitive areas, and the

---

[5] For a clear account of the division of Czechoslovakia into two States see Stein (1994).

[6] Opinion 1/91 *(First European Economic Area Opinion)* [1991] ECR 6079 at para 211.

[7] The House of Lords Select Committee on the European Communities, distinguishing the different meanings of 'sovereignty', said: 'sovereignty is used in international law to describe the characteristics of a State. A sovereign State must possess a settled population, a defined territory, a government having the power to maintain its internal legal order, and independence in the conduct of its international relations. A State recognized as sovereign enjoys under international law the right to send and receive diplomatic missions, to become a party to treaties and a member of international organisations such as the United Nations—which is "based on the sovereign equality of all its Members". Sovereign States may accept specific restraints on policy, such as those imposed by United Nations and NATO over defence or by GATT over trade relations, without loss of sovereign status. But it is possible that so much competence could be transferred from Member States to the Community that Member States would lose their status as sovereign States.' HL Select Committee on the European Communitites, 17th Report (1990–91*b*), at p 8.

growing jurisprudence of the ECJ that a substantial part of the armoury of national foreign policy tools had been irrevocably ceded.[8]

The role given to the European Commission in the negotiation of external commercial agreements placed them on the international stage.[9] Although the Commission negotiated within the framework of a Council mandate, might be supported or restrained at the negotiating table by delegates of the Member States, and was dependent on the Council for final approval of agreements with third countries,[10] its role as negotiator for the European Economic Community made it a significant figure in international trade organizations, in particular the General Agreement on Tariffs and Trade (GATT), and also in foreign capitals. The Commission began to establish delegation offices in important foreign capitals. These delegations were not embassies and could perform only functions related to trade and aid—the two areas of express Community competence. But on the basis of headquarters agreements, of commercial awareness or of courtesy they were often given an extensive range of diplomatic privileges and advantages. The areas of Community competence in external matters gradually pushed out as international commerce became increasingly intertwined with other matters such as environmental protection, animal welfare, human rights, and political sanctions. The Community began to adopt internal rules in a variety of contexts which, to be consistent and effective, would require the negotiation of parallel treaty rules with non-Member States. In a series of cases the European Court of Justice (ECJ) was soon to make clear that the adoption of internal rules not only gave the Communities the power to conclude treaties which might affect those rules, but excluded in these areas the treaty-making power of the Member States.

It was becoming anomalous, and little appreciated by non-Member States, that the Community lacked coherence of negotiating approach to situations which could not be firmly contained within the commercial sphere. As Lord Carrington put it when speaking as British Foreign Secretary in 1981 to the Foreign Policy Association in New York: 'Over the years the realisation has grown that economic policy and foreign policy are Siamese twins.'[11]

---

[8] Soetendorp (1999) suggests at p 5 that the benefits of economies of scale, making the Community a powerful trading bloc commanding the largest share of world trade, were the most important reason for creating a common external trade policy. This fails to explain the continued resistance of the Member States to expansion of the common commercial policy into areas beyond those covered in the original EEC Treaty.

[9] Article 113.3 (now Article 133) of the EC Treaty gave the Commission express negotiating powers for agreements with third countries implementing the common commercial policy.

[10] EC Treaty, Articles 113 and 114 (now Article 133).

[11] [1980] 57 *International Affairs* No 1 p 1, at p 3.

The First Links

In December 1969, the summit meeting of Heads of State and of Government at The Hague commissioned a study of how they could better coordinate information and foreign policy formation. The decision was the result of a proposal by President Pompidou, in the context of prospective enlargement of the Community, that regular meetings of Foreign Ministers should take place with a view to making progress on political unification. The Luxembourg Report of October 1970 formed the response to the summit commission. It codified early practices of consultation and consensus building on specific issues which were little more than good diplomatic practice between like-minded States with major common interests. Beyond this, it established principles and procedures for cooperation. The objectives were to match the implementation of external Community policies with action by its Member States in the political sphere and to exercise Europe's growing responsibilities in the wider world.

As to procedures, Foreign Ministers were to meet twice a year in the capital of the Member State holding the rotating Presidency of the Community, and Political Directors, senior diplomats from the foreign services of the Member States, were to meet four times a year. This Political Committee later became known as the Davignon Committee. To emphasize the firmly intergovernmental character of this travelling consultation, the Commission would be permitted to attend only if invited to express views on European Community aspects of the questions under discussion. Common positions would be formulated by consensus and there would be common action 'where it appears possible and desirable'.[12] A single objector could thus prevent adoption of a common position and any action. The two subjects which dominated early work by Foreign Ministers were the Middle East and the impending Conference on Security and Cooperation in Europe (CSCE). On the Middle East, in spite of fundamental differences and rivalries between France and the UK, Member States succeeded in forming a common approach towards the Arab–Israel conflict which was distinct from that of the United States and enhanced Europe's international identity even if it did little to bring peace to the area.[13] CSCE was later to adopt the Helsinki Principles on Relations between East and West[14] which were of great importance as a guarantee of security and as a catalyst for change during the later stages of the Cold War.

[12] de Schoutheete (1980); Hill (ed) (1983); Nuttall (1985a) pp 203–4; Meynell (1981) pp 368–70; Nuttall (1992) ch 2.
[13] See Soetendorp (1999) ch 6 pp 93–113; Nuttall (1992) pp 97–109, 158–68.
[14] Cmnd 6198; Review of the International Commission of Jurists No 35 p 45. See Nuttall: (1992) pp 110–18.

Shortly after the first enlargement of the Communities, the Nine Member States re-examined European Political Cooperation (EPC) and set out their conclusions in the 1973 Copenhagen Report. Neither the Luxembourg Report nor the Copenhagen Report was intended to create legal relations of any kind. This was emphasized by the Copenhagen Report, which said: 'The Political Co-operation machinery, which deals on the intergovernmental level with problems of international politics, is distinct from and additional to the activities of the institutions of the Community which are based on the juridical commitments undertaken by the Member States . . .'[15] Following exchanges of information, decisions and actions would be taken by national governments. Although there had been discussion of a secretariat, the Member States could not agree whether it should be in Brussels—too close for comfort to the European Community institutions—or in Paris, and so EPC continued without any collective back-up or institutional structure. As Simon Nuttall explained: '. . . the exercise was conducted by diplomatists for diplomatists, employing informal and highly flexible procedures'.[16]

The London Report on European Political Cooperation

The London Report approved by the Foreign Ministers of the Ten Member States in October 1981[17] contained an appraisal of eleven years of EPC operation and included some modest procedural improvements. The Ministers noted that EPC 'has steadily intensified and its scope continually broadened', but that 'the Ten are still far from playing a role in the world appropriate to their combined influence'. They renewed the basic commitments:

to consult partners before adopting final positions or launching national initiatives on all important questions of foreign policy which are of concern to the Ten as a whole. They undertake that in these consultations each member state will take full account of the position of other partners and will give due weight to the desirability of reaching a common position. They note that such consultations will be particularly relevant for important international conferences where one or more of the Ten are to participate, and where the agenda will include matters under discussion in European Political Co-operation or on which the Ten have a common position.

On procedures, great emphasis was laid on informality and confidentiality. At Ministerial meetings: 'There will be no formal agenda, official interpretation or officials present (except for a Presidency notetaker).' Below Ministers was a three-tier structure of the Political Committee, the

[15] Copenhagen Report, 23 July 1973.
[16] Nuttall (1985a). See also Nuttall (1992) at pp 11–25, 71–80; de Schootheete (1980); Gérard (1987).
[17] Cmnd 8424.

Correspondents' Group and the Working Groups. In future, as well as reacting to world events, the Political Committee were to commission longer-term studies on areas mentioned in the Copenhagen Report, and where their positions diverged. The Presidency would take the lead on behalf of the Member States in contacts with non-member countries. Heads of Mission in non-member countries were to meet regularly to exchange information and coordinate views, and could submit joint reports or recommendations for joint action to the Political Committee. Three Member States could convene the Political Committee, a Ministerial meeting, or a meeting of Ambassadors in a non-member country.

The London Report also made the first concessions towards integrating EPC with the Community institutions and providing it with an official infrastructure. The Ten were to:

provide, as appropriate, for Political Co-operation meetings on the occasion of Foreign Affairs Councils. The Presidency will ensure that the discussion of the Community and Political Co-operation aspects of certain questions is co-ordinated if the subject matter requires this. Within the framework of the established rules and procedures the Ten attach importance to the Commission of the European Communities being fully associated with Political Co-operation at all levels.

What this meant in practical terms was that Ministers could discuss EPC subjects not only in Brussels rather than in the Presidency capital, but even in the Council chamber as well as informally over a working lunch. On such occasions the Council Secretariat would withdraw from the chamber to make clear that the Ministers were not acting as the Council. The presence of the Commission was increasingly tolerated by foreign Ministers, though usually on the basis of some claim to Community competence on the issue being discussed or the need for coordination with related Community questions. Contacts between the Presidency and the European Parliament were also extended on a more informal basis, though this fell short of any requirement or regular practice of consulting or even informing the Parliament about specific issues being addressed by EPC.

To provide organizational support and continuity, the Presidency would be 'assisted by a small team of officials seconded from preceding and succeeding Presidencies. These officials will remain in the employment of their national Foreign Ministries, and will be on the staff of their Embassy in the Presidency capital. They will be at the disposition of the Presidency and will work under his direction.'[18] The limited numbers and divided loyalties of this 'small team of officials' were an important limitation at this stage on the possibilities of EPC. Given the proliferation of foreign policy events and issues, it would not be conceivable for any political

---

[18] This became known as the Troika formula.

entity or body to formulate policy in any meaningful way across the spectrum without a substantial body of experts guided by coherent intelligence and subject to some form of overall direction. Lack of continuity in the 'small team of officials' was also a serious limitation. The Troika formula, in which the current Presidency was supported by the previous and the next Presidencies, diminished, but did not eliminate the difficulty.

An important feature of EPC formalized in the Copenhagen Report was the Correspondence Européenne (COREU) system whereby cypher telex messages with information, proposals, and draft documents were exchanged between identified correspondents in the Foreign Ministry of each Member State. By 1981 5,000 messages a year—mostly procedural in character—were exchanged through this network.[19]

The Practical Results of European Political Cooperation

Given the structure and procedures just described, it is clear that it is very difficult, on the basis of published documents, to give an account of what EPC actually achieved in its early years. Even where there was agreement, there would usually be no published document or single record of proceedings. Exchanges took place, given the absence of official interpretation, in a mixture of English and French, so that there was little safeguard against misunderstanding. There was no Commission to act as guardian or watchdog of what had apparently been agreed. This obscured those occasions when a Member State later failed to comply with a common position, but it also obscured the extent to which shared information and analysis, together with the political pressures to conform, did influence national decisions, votes, and actions. As Meynell observed in 1981: 'But what secrecy means is that it is not possible to show for certain what (probably many) minor matters are successfully harmonised or coordinated, nor what major questions have been deadlocked into banalities, and by whom, and on what issues.'[20]

To insiders on the other hand, the impact of EPC was striking. Douglas Hurd, writing in 1981 when he was Minister of State for Foreign and Commonwealth Affairs, said:

Since I first joined the Foreign Office in 1952 the biggest change of diplomatic method stems from European Political Co-operation. In 1952 it was broadly speaking with the Americans only that we shared information and assessments; policy making was a national preserve. Now in some areas of diplomacy our policy is formed wholly within a European context; and in no area is the European influence completely absent. The flow of information between the Foreign Ministries of the Ten is formidable.[21]

---

[19] Meynell (1981), at p 370.　　　　[20] Meynell (1981), at p 371.
[21] Hurd (1981). Douglas Hurd was responsible for liaison with the European Parliament

In looking for practical results it must also be borne in mind that early attempts at a European foreign policy, like national foreign policies, were not for the most part aimed at the production of international legislation, public documents, or specific practical results or events. They were over-whelmingly reactive in character. The Member States as a general rule developed common positions or contemplated joint action only where a need was perceived to respond to a particular event, threat, or problem. The best known area of early cooperation of this kind was the Middle East, but there was also from an early stage consultation leading to joint statements, amendments, and votes in many international conferences and in institutions such as the UN and the Conference on Security and Cooperation in Europe. The sporadic nature of EPC was emphasized by Sir John Fretwell, formerly British Ambassador to France, who in evidence in 1993 to the House of Lords described it as:

incomplete both in time and space: some areas of the world may never have attracted attention at Council or Political Committee level; others may have been discussed only in relation to a specific problem or incident in the past. Unlike a national Government, which can be assumed to be exercising a foreign policy in relation to all parts of the world where it has interests, the Twelve collectively have a policy only to the extent that they have discussed a given situation and reached an agreed conclusion which is still relevant.[22]

Even at this stage, however, certain tools were available where the need was seen for the Member States to go beyond mere exchange of infor-mation and views to specific action. In response to a situation in a non-Member State there might be a joint démarche delivered by the Presidency, and some of these entered the public domain. In the context of international organizations or international negotiations there were increasing numbers of agreed statements and common responses to pro-posals. Many of these negotiations were for 'mixed agreements' where the European Community possessed external competence over part, but not all, of the subject matter of the negotiation. The lengthy negotiations for the UN Convention on the Law of the Sea were a striking example of such a negotiation. The Commission could take the lead insofar as exclusive Community competence was accepted by the Member States, but coordi-nation beyond this had to be agreed under EPC procedures.

during the 1981 UK Presidency and later became Foreign Secretary. See also Carrington (1981/82); Gérard (1987) at p 469: '. . . la cooperation politique étrangère a créé, dans les administrations des affaires étrangères des États membres, les conditions d'un réflexe d'échanges d'information et de concertation'.

[22] HL Select Committee on the European Communities, 28th Report (1992–93b), p 58.

Collective Sanctions

If Foreign Ministers looked for collective action beyond words or votes, this could be taken only by each of the Member States or by the European Community. Political cooperation had at its disposal neither law-making nor treaty-making powers, neither finances nor forces. An example in the first category—coordinated action by Member States—occurred in 1980 following the seizure by militant students of the US Embassy in Teheran. No majority could be secured in the UN Security Council for the imposition of economic sanctions on Iran in response to its complicity and support for this flagrant breach of the duty to protect a foreign diplomatic mission and the staff within. The US instituted legal proceedings against Iran before the ICJ and secured from the Court an interim order requiring Iran to release the hostages immediately, but Iran failed to comply.[23] European Community Ministers were anxious to demonstrate practical support not only for the US but also for the universal rules guaranteeing the inviolability of embassies and of diplomats. Following exploratory discussion in Brussels of the legal possibilities, a decision in principle was taken within the EPC framework that sanctions should be imposed on Iran and should extend not only to prohibiting import and export of goods but to banning the performance of construction and service contracts between nationals and companies of Member States and nationals and companies of Iran.

In some Member States, including the UK, new legislative authority was needed for this course in the absence of a mandatory Security Council resolution and of a mandatory EC Council of Ministers regulation. Community Ministers then met in Naples and determined the precise scope of sanctions. Reference was made at this stage to Article 224 of the EEC Treaty, though there was considerable doubt whether this was appropriate in the absence of any Security Council decision or of any 'serious international tension constituting a threat of war'. The agreed sanctions against Iran were then implemented at national level until the settlement in January 1981 which led to the release by Iran of the US hostages. The absence of a binding Community obligation did however cause some disarray, in particular because the UK Parliament declined to interfere with contracts which had been concluded between the seizure of the Embassy and the decision by European Foreign Ministers to impose sanctions.[24]

In contrast, action by the European Community was taken one year later in response to the role of the Soviet Union in the imposition of martial law

---

[23] *Case Concerning United States Diplomatic and Consular Staff in Tehran* [1980] ICJ Reports 3.
[24] Hurd (1981); Denza (1994*b*); at p 589; Nuttall (1985*b*) at pp 223–5.

in Poland and the subsequent repression. Again, the Soviet veto precluded any binding Security Council resolution, and there was at first considerable reluctance among the Member States to use Article 113 of the EC Treaty, the cornerstone of external commercial policy, as a basis for action which would be taken for a political rather than a commercial purpose. Following guidelines drawn up in December 1980 by the European Council on responses to the situation in Poland, the EC Council of Ministers made decisions enabling Community budget funds to be used for humanitarian purposes in Poland instead of for sales at special low prices of Community farm produce whose distribution would inevitably be controlled by Polish State buying agencies. The Council also decided, after prolonged legal argument, to use Article 113 of the EC Treaty to impose by regulation collective economic sanctions against the Soviet Union. The precedent thus set was followed in 1982 when economic sanctions were imposed against Argentina following its invasion of the Falkland Islands.[25]

The Single European Act

The Single European Act, concluded in February 1986, marked the origin of the pillar structure of the European Union.[26] The Preamble set out that the Contracting Parties were:

Moved by the will to continue the work undertaken on the basis of the Treaties establishing the European Communities and to transform relations as a whole among their States into a European Union, in accordance with the Solemn Declaration of Stuttgart of 19 June 1983; . . . [and] Resolved to implement this European Union on the basis, firstly, of the Communities operating in accordance with their own rules and, secondly, of European Cooperation among the Signatory States in the sphere of foreign policy and to invest this union with the necessary means of action; . . .

Until a late stage of the intergovernmental negotiation, revisions to the Community Treaties and negotiations for a new treaty instrument to codify EPC practices were kept entirely separate. Political Directors were in charge of the formulation of provisions which would for the first time place EPC procedures on a treaty basis, and they were not involved in the much more complex and difficult negotiations on the European Economic Community Treaty. The Commission in its formal Opinion on revision of the EEC Treaty argued strongly that the two areas of activity should be

[25] Council Regulations 596/82 [1982] OJ L72/15; 877/82, [1982] OJ L102/1; Meynell (1981) at p 378. See also Kuyper (1982); Kuyper (1993) at p 387; Koutrakos (2001) at pp 60–3.
[26] The metaphor was first used in the Tindemans Report: see de Schoutheete (1986): See also Neville-Jones (1983). An Appendix to this article at p 691 contains the text of the Solemn Declaration of Stuttgart, made on 19 June 1983.

combined. At a late stage, the European Council in December 1985 took the significant political decision to reunite the two draft treaties, so that the resulting instrument was named the Single European Act.[27]

Title I of the Single European Act—Common Provisions—contained a laconic three Articles. Article 1, echoing the Preamble, set out the legal bases of the European Communities and of Political Cooperation. The new treaty provisions on Political Cooperation were to 'confirm and supplement the procedures agreed in the reports of Luxembourg (1970), London (1981), the Solemn Declaration on European Union (1983) and the practices gradually established among the Member States'. It was however striking that the 'European Union', which featured in the Preamble as the objective of the new treaty, was not formally established by the Treaty itself. The embryonic Union was however, at least by implication, placed under the institutional supervision of the European Council. The Heads of State or of Government of the Member States and the President of the Commission of the European Communities had already been meeting at least once in each six-month Presidency for several years, but Article 2 of the Single European Act was the first acknowledgement in a treaty text of their existence as an institution. They were required to meet at least twice a year, but this was the full extent of the legal duties and functions imposed on them by Article 2.[28]

Article 3 of the Single European Act provided that while the institutions of the European Communities would exercise their powers and jurisdiction under the conditions of the Community Treaties as supplemented by Title II, the institutions and bodies responsible for EPC would exercise their powers and jurisdiction under the conditions of Title III and the earlier documents described above. Title III however, consisting of the single Article 30, created no new institutions, and gave very limited roles to the existing European Community institutions. The Council of Ministers had no formal role whatsoever, and all treaty obligations were laid on 'The High Contracting Parties'. The fundamental obligation, couched in obviously soft law terms, was to 'endeavour jointly to formulate and implement a European foreign policy'. The Commission had the right to be 'fully associated with the proceedings of Political Cooperation', in particular to be present at all meetings, and the duty, together with the Presidency, to ensure consistency between the external policies of the European Community and the policies agreed in EPC.[29] An esoteric distinction was thus drawn between 'external policy' relating to European Community rules and formulated by the Community institutions, and

---

[27] For accounts of the negotiations see Glaesner (1986) Jacqué (1986); Nuttall (1985*a*); Nuttall (1992) ch 7.

[28] For an account of their procedures see Nuttall (1992) p 14.

[29] Article 30.3(6) and 30.5.

'foreign policy' which to the extent that it would become European would be formulated by Foreign Ministers and governed by public international law. The Presidency of EPC would be held by the High Contracting Party which held the Presidency of the Council of the European Communities.[30]

The European Parliament was to be 'closely associated' with EPC—which meant that the Presidency was responsible for informing the Parliament of foreign policy issues under examination and ensuring that the Parliament's views were duly taken into consideration.[31] This gave the Parliament very little influence over EPC unless, as began increasingly to happen, there was some connection between a matter being discussed in EPC and a matter, such as budgetary provision for aid, or an external association agreement with a particular non-member country, where the Parliament had blocking or amending powers.

The European Court of Justice was given no advisory, interpretative, or dispute settlement role. Its total exclusion from EPC was emphasized in Article 31 of the Single European Act. Quite apart from this express exclusion of the Court, the terms of Title III were by their nature almost incapable of giving rise to justiciable rights and duties. Apart from bare procedural obligations to meet at specific intervals, all other obligations were deliberately cast in soft law terms. The High Contracting Parties were required, for example, to 'ensure that common principles and objectives are gradually developed and defined', to 'refrain from impeding the formation of a consensus', and to 'organize a political dialogue with third countries and regional groupings whenever they deem it necessary'. The new obligation to ensure consistency between external Community policies and EPC was cast in apparently hard law terms, but although it was politically innovative and in the longer term highly significant, it was by its very nature not easily justiciable by any international tribunal.

The procedures and practices set out in Article 30 were otherwise for the most part no more extensive than those already developed. An accompanying Ministerial Decision elaborated these procedures in greater detail and in particular placed the EPC Secretariat permanently in Brussels, in the Council of Ministers building.[32] The Secretariat would still consist of national diplomats on secondment, but drawn from five Member States instead of the three in the Troika structure set up under the London Report. One provision however which, at least in retrospect, can be seen

---

[30] Article 30.10(a).   [31] Article 30.4.

[32] Article 30.10(g) provided that: 'A secretariat based in Brussels shall assist the Presidency in preparing and implementing the activities of European Political Cooperation and in administrative matters. It shall carry out its duties under the authority of the Presidency.' The implementing Decision is printed as an Annex to Nuttall (1985*a*) in [1986] Yearbook of European Law at p 223. For description of the role and limited functions of the EPC Secretariat see Nuttall (1992) pp 19–23 and 255; Gerard (1987).

as significant was Article 30.6, in which the Parties 'consider that closer cooperation on questions of European security would contribute in an essential way to the development of a European identity in external policy matters' and expressed their readiness to coordinate positions more closely on political and economic aspects of security. They were to work both at national and international institutional level to maintain techno-logical and industrial conditions for security. This language, however, was not intended to impose any specific commitments in the field of defence or to undermine in any way the primacy of NATO. The limits to the new process of security cooperation were firmly set out in Article 30.6(c): Nothing in this Title shall impede closer cooperation in the field of security between certain of the High Contracting Parties within the frame-work of the Western European Union or the Atlantic Alliance.

In most Member States the ratification of the Single European Act pro-ceeded smoothly. In Denmark the new Treaty was submitted to a referen-dum which resulted in a comfortable majority. Denmark made a Declaration on signature stating that the new provisions on European Political Cooperation did not affect Denmark's participation in Nordic cooperation in the sphere of foreign policy.

In the UK it was necessary to pass primary legislation to extend the 'Community Treaties' which by the terms of the European Communities Act 1972, s 2[33] would be given legal effect in the United Kingdom. Under the European Communities (Amendment) Act 1986,[34] however, a careful distinction was drawn between those provisions of the Single European Act which extended the earlier Community Treaties (Title II and certain parts of Title I and Title IV) and the provisions which related to European Political Cooperation. The latter provisions were deliberately not given the status of 'Community Treaties', so that there could be no question in the UK courts of their provisions being invoked by individuals or prevail-ing over potentially conflicting domestic or Community rules.[35]

Ireland took the same view as the UK as regards the parts of the Single European Act which required incorporation into Irish law, and legislation was passed on similar lines. Before Ireland could ratify, however, an Irish citizen, Raymond Crotty, applied to the court for an injunction to restrain the Government. He argued, *inter alia*, that the provisions on European Political Cooperation went beyond the constitutional authority given to the executive when Ireland had joined the Communities and required a constitutional amendment to be approved by referendum. In the case of

---

[33] c 68.   [34] c 58.

[35] The Single European Act as a whole was, however, by s 3(4) approved for the purpose of the European Parliamentary Elections Act 1978—as was necessary because of the increased powers given under it to the European Parliament.

Crotty v An Taoiseach,[36] Henchy J, who formed part of the majority in the Irish Supreme Court held that under Article 30 of the Single European Act: 'each Member State will immediately cede a portion of its sovereignty and freedom of action in matters of foreign policy. . . . A purely national approach is incompatible with accession to this Treaty.'[37] Finlay CJ dissented from the majority, holding, more accurately, that the provisions 'do not give to the other High Contracting Parties any right to override or veto the ultimate decision of the State on any issue of foreign policy. They impose an obligation to listen and consult and grant a right to be heard and consulted.'[38]

The Supreme Court, by a three to two majority, held that constitutional amendment was indeed required. The necessary amendment was approved, but in view of the sensitivity of the inclusion of security in the provisions on EPC, the Irish Government attached a Declaration to their instrument of ratification stating:

that the provisions of Title III do not affect Ireland's long-established policy of military neutrality and that coordination of positions on the political and economic aspects of security does not include the military aspects of security or procurement for military purposes and does not affect Ireland's right to act or refrain from acting in any way which might affect Ireland's international status of military neutrality.

With the entry into force in 1987 of the Single European Act, European Political Cooperation may have seemed more like a fifth wheel on the coach than a flanking pillar. But its provisions were now set out, however tentatively, in a binding treaty rather than a series of inaccessible political reports and documents. Although the Council of Ministers had no institutional role, reference was made to the growing practice of the Ministers discussing foreign policy matters within the EPC framework on the occasion of the Council.[39] The Commission was given a formal if limited role and the European Council was placed in overall charge. It would no longer be possible to argue that political cooperation was institutionally entirely distinct from the European Communities and that it might be open to non-Member States to participate. In the Declaration on Article 30 made on the occasion of the signing of the Single European Act, the Parties

reaffirm their openness to other European nations which share the same ideals and objectives. They agree in particular to strengthen their links with the member-

---

[36] [1987] 3 CMLR 666. See critical comment by Temple Lang (1987) especially p 715: 'Few people in Europe could consider this judgment as a balanced description of Title III, or of its correct legal interpretation (as distinct from its possible future development).'
[37] Temple Lang (1987), at p 725.   [38] Temple Lang (1987), at p 730.
[39] Article 30.3(a).

countries of the Council of Europe and with other democratic countries with which they have friendly relations and close cooperation.

This did not, however, imply that these other countries would have any input into the formation of European foreign policy.

The Product of EPC: Words

Most of the statements which emerged from European Political Cooperation (EPC) following the entry into force of the Single European Act were directed to human rights violations. In April 1992, for example, the Community and its Member States expressed concern at continuing violations of human rights in Equatorial Guinea, which risked endangering the democratization process initiated by the recent review of the constitution. They reaffirmed 'the great importance they attach to the respect of human rights in accordance with Article 5 of the Fourth ACP–Lomé Convention and with the Resolution of the Council of Ministers of 28 November 1991 on human rights, democracy and development.'[40] In October 1992 they welcomed the results of the first democratic elections in Angola, confirmed by the Special Representative of the UN to be free and fair.[41] But in January 1993 they deplored the outbreak of widespread and fierce fighting in Angola which had led to a setback for the peace process which had led to those elections.[42] In February 1993 they deplored the violence in Zaire which had caused numerous deaths, including that of the French Ambassador in Kinshasa, and appealed for an end to the fighting, the maintenance of order in compliance with human rights, and an end to actions obstructing democratic transition.[43] On 25 March 1993 the Community and its Member States welcomed the submission and publication of the report of the Commission on the Truth in El Salvador. They claimed that implementation of its recommendations would be crucial for achieving national reconciliation and consolidation of peace in El Salvador and expressed concern at the possibility of an amnesty before this had been carried out.[44]

Given that all European Member States were Parties to the ECHR and the UN Covenants on Human Rights, there was not usually difficulty in formulating such statements of concern or exhortation. They did not have any direct legal effects, but the 'consistency' requirement in the Single European Act meant that they would be taken into account in the formulation of European Community offers of trade and aid as well as specific

[40] EPC Press Release P 48/92, 15 April 1992.
[41] EPC Press Release P 100/92, 22 October 1992.
[42] EPC Press Release P 7/93, 22 January 1993.
[43] EPC Press Release 10/93, 1 February 1993.
[44] EPC Press Releases 25/93, 25 March 1993 and 101/93, 28 October 1993.

national decisions. Thus the response elaborated within EPC to the annulment of the 1993 elections in Nigeria was a decision by the Community and its Member States to suspend military cooperation, deny visas to members of the army and security forces and their families, suspend military visits, and suspend development aid.[45] Action on all of these except for development aid would, in July 1993 (prior to the entry into force of the TEU) have been exclusively for the Member States.

Some common positions merely underlined obligations falling on the Member States or on others as Members of the UN. In a statement of 17 February 1992, for example, the Community and its Member States 'welcome the unanimous adoption by the Security Council Resolution 731', and recalling the statement on the bombing of flights Pan Am 103 and UTA 772 earlier issued by the European Council, they 'underline the great importance which they attach to compliance by Libya with Security Council Resolution 731 and they urge Libya to fulfil the requests to which the Resolution refers without delay'. The statement itself had no direct legal consequences, but paved the way to a later request by the UK and France to the Security Council to impose binding sanctions against Libya in response to its failure to comply with Resolution 731.[46]

The Product of EPC: Actions

In addition to the formulation of common positions in declarations or press releases, the Member States were by this stage using a range of other methods of giving practical effect to policies adopted within the framework of EPC—joint démarches made by the Presidency in the capitals of non-Member States, agreed statements in the UN and its specialized agencies, in other international organizations and in negotiating conferences on an increasing range of subjects. Active diplomacy began to take the form of sending observers and mediators into areas of conflict. In 1992 for example, the Member States decided to despatch a team of fifteen observers to South Africa—police officers, lawyers, and economists—with a mandate to try to defuse violence and to promote peace in areas of potential conflict. The European Community Observer Mission in South Africa (ECOMSA) was to work closely with South African authorities as well as with teams of observers from the UN and other international organizations such as the Organization for African Unity and the Commonwealth.[47] The observers' mandate was renewed at six-monthly intervals as

---

[45] EPC Press Release P 69/93, 13 July 1993.
[46] See Nuttall (1992) pp 27–9. Mandatory sanctions imposed by Security Council Resolution 748 (1992) were implemented by Council Regulation 945/92, OJ L101/53, 15.4.92.
[47] Declaration on South Africa, EPC Press Release 101/92, 27 October 1992.

the multi-racial elections drew closer.[48] In October 1993 a team of European Community observers, along with other groups, monitored the elections in Pakistan and concluded that they had in general been free, impartial, and transparent. The Community and its Member States accordingly congratulated Benazir Bhutto on her election as Prime Minister.[49]

Recognition within the EPC Framework

In December 1991, against the background of a complex and rapidly evolving situation resulting from the dissolution of the Soviet Union and Yugoslavia, and as negotiations for a new European Treaty were approaching their conclusion, the Member States moved into a significant new area of foreign policy. Ministers acting in European Political Cooperation adopted Guidelines on the recognition of new States in Eastern Europe and in the Soviet Union. Eleven years previously the UK had brought its national practice regarding the recognition of new *governments* into line with that prevailing in other Member States. It was announced in a statement to both Houses of Parliament:

We have conducted a re-examination of British policy and practice concerning the recognition of governments. This has included a comparison with the practice of our partners and allies . . . we have decided that we shall no longer accord recognition to governments. The British Government recognises states in accordance with common international doctrine.[50]

The consultation in 1980 was not exclusively with the other Member States, nor was the change expressed to be the result of European Political Cooperation, but the effect was that the UK, which had previously made formal statements or acts of recognition of new governments, fell into line with the low-key approach adopted elsewhere in Europe of leaving recognition to be inferred from the course of diplomatic or governmental dealings with a new regime.

The Guidelines on the recognition of new States adopted by European Ministers in 1991 were made public and laid before Parliament in the United Kingdom. Although they must be evaluated in the context of the efforts of the Member States to secure orderly and democratic transition once the break up of the Soviet Union and Yugoslavia became inevitable, they represented a clear departure from the previous practice of the United Kingdom on the recognition of States which had until then been based overwhelmingly on assessment of whether the new entity satisfied

---

[48] EPC Press Release P 102/93, 8 November 1993.
[49] EPC Press Release P 98/93, 20 October 1993.
[50] Hansard HC Debs 25 April 1980; WA 277; HL Debs 28 April 1980 WA 1121.

the factual criteria of sovereign statehood. Under the Guidelines of December 1991:

The Community and its Member States confirm their attachment to the principles of the Helsinki Final Act and the Charter of Paris, in particular the principle of self-determination. They affirm their readiness to recognise, subject to the normal standards of international practice and the political realities in each case, those new States which, following the historic changes in the region, have constituted themselves on a democratic basis, have accepted the appropriate international obligations and have committed themselves in good faith to a peaceful process and to negotiations.

Therefore, they accept a common position on the process of recognition of these new States, which requires:

—respect for the provisions of the Charter of the United Nations and the commitments subscribed to in the Final Act of Helsinki and in the Charter of Paris, especially with regard to the rule of law, democracy and human rights:

—guarantees for the rights of ethnic and national groups and minorities in accordance with the commitments subscribed to in the framework of the CSCE:

—respect for the inviolability of all frontiers which can only be changed by peaceful means and by common agreement:

—acceptance of all relevant commitments with regard to disarmament and nuclear non-proliferation as well as to security and regional stability:

—commitment to settle by agreement, including where appropriate by recourse to arbitration, all questions concerning state succession and regional disputes.

The Community and its Member States will not recognise entities which are the result of aggression. They would take account of the effects of recognition on neighbouring States.

The commitment to these principles opens the way to recognition by the Community and its Member States and to the establishment of diplomatic relations. It could be laid down in agreements.[51]

The language of this common position is clearly non-binding, but there is a curious innovation in the reference to 'recognition by the Community and its Member States' and not merely to recognition by the Member States. This was echoed in EPC Press Releases of 31 December 1991 and 15 January 1992[52] in which the 'Community and its Member States' in the light of assurances from ten of the former Soviet Republics said that they were 'ready to proceed with the recognition of these Republics'. Although the formula 'The Community and its Member States' was standard in EPC documents, it might have been open to question by lawyers whether the

---

[51] The Guidelines are in (1992) 31 ILM 1486–7 and in [1993] EJIL 72. The successive Opinions of the Arbitration Commission established by the Peace Conference (the Badinter Commission), which applied the Guidelines to individual republics within Yugoslavia, are also printed in (1992) 31 ILM. See also Harris (1998) at p 147 where texts of the Declarations and of Opinion No 10 are accompanied by commentary on their divergence from practice.

[52] P 137/91 and P 8/92.

competence ascribed to the European Community by the Treaties included the recognition of new State entities.

As in the case of sanctions against Iran described above, the words contained in the Guidelines had to be followed, to be effective in international law, by action on the part of the Member States. What was, however, of most significance in the context of the ongoing construction of European Political Cooperation was the decision to subject the important national foreign policy instrument of recognition of new States to collective discipline, and that, moreover, under rules which constituted a significant departure from those applying under the international practice of the time. The act of recognition differs from a statement of political approval or disapproval in that it involves important legal consequences such as entitlement to property, to participation in international agreements whether as a successor State or as an acceding State, and to self-defence. The merits of this step will be considered below in Chapter 4, but even in the highly exceptional political situation of 1991 the Guidelines were an important new restraint on national independence in the conduct of foreign relations.[53]

The case of Macedonia illustrated the non-binding character of the Guidelines on Recognition of New States, as well as the difficulties inherent in the practice of proceeding only on the basis of unanimity among the Member States. Greece had for some time objected to the use of the name Macedonia for a constituent part of Yugoslavia on the basis that this name was historically Greek and should not be used by an entity which was predominantly Slav. In response to this concern, the Guidelines for recognition of former Yugoslav republics required Macedonia to adopt constitutional and political guarantees ensuring that it had no territorial claims against a neighbouring Community State and would not conduct hostile propaganda 'including the use of a denomination which implies territorial claims'. The Government in Skopje made changes to their Constitution and undertook international commitments to meet this requirement, and Robert Badinter, Chairman of the Arbitral Commission attached to the Yugoslav Peace Conference which was to assess compliance with the Guidelines, concluded that European Guidelines for recognition were satisfied. The European Council meeting in Lisbon in June 1992—by which time Slovenia, Croatia, and Bosnia had all been recognized by EC Member States—nevertheless deferred to Greek sensitivities by expressing readiness to recognize the new Republic under a name which did not include the word 'Macedonia'. This solidarity with Greece continued for a further year, but fragmented after Macedonia was admitted to the UN in

---

[53] See Recognition: Recent Developments in State Practice, [1993] EJIL 36; Weller [1992] especially pp 586–96; Murphy (1999) at pp 557–60; Warbrick (1996).

April 1993 under the provisional name of 'The Former Yugoslav Republic of Macedonia'.[54]

Towards Political Union: 1990–92

The Intergovernmental Conference of the Member States convened in December 1990 was mainly driven by the decision to negotiate amendments to the Community Treaties to implement economic and monetary union. But as the Conference approached and negotiation began, proposals for political union began to assume greater importance. Some of these related to greater powers for the European Parliament and to wider possibilities for majority voting in the Council of Ministers. External events cast a growing shadow as governments and diplomats tried to grapple with the implications of the collapse of Soviet hegemony over Eastern Europe, the collapse of the Soviet Union itself and with disintegration in Yugoslavia. In June 1990 the European Council in Dublin acknowledged a link between German reunification, political union, and economic and monetary union.[55]

It was clear that, since the forthcoming treaty would create and not merely foreshadow a European Union, the constitutional structure of this Union was of great importance. The political choice offered to the Member States was between the form of a tree—in which European Political Cooperation and the new provisions on cooperation on justice, external immigration, and asylum would be integrated into the European Community though subject to different institutional rules—and the form of a temple. The temple structure would comprise a central pillar (the First Pillar) formed by the European Community and the two other existing Communities. The two flanking pillars would set out the objectives and procedures for political cooperation in foreign affairs (the Second Pillar) and for cooperation in justice and home affairs (the Third Pillar). The unifying pediment over the three pillars would be political in character, confirming the overall supervisory role of the European Council.[56]

Until April 1991 this debate on the future constitutional structure of the Union took place between the Member States, in secret. Since treaty amendment was required, the published proposals of the Commission and of the European Parliament had no special legal status. The Conference still clung to traditional methods of intergovernmental diplomacy whereby proposals and other negotiating documents from the

---

[54] Hansard HC Debs 30 November 1992 col 119; HL Debs 8 December 1992 col 90; Warbrick (1993) at pp 437–8; Denza (1994b) at p 581; European Report No. 1907, 4 December 1993. The degree of solidarity with Greece may be seen as remarkable, given that Greece had often emphasised that EPC Declarations were not binding—see Soetendorp (1999) pp 43–4.

[55] William Wallace and Helen Wallace (2000) p 467.   [56] See Vignes (1993).

Member States were kept secret from the European Parliament, from national parliaments, and from the general public. In April 1991, however, the Luxembourg Presidency sent to their national Parliament and to the European Parliament the draft text of a new Treaty on Political Union. This at once came into the public domain and was carefully and critically scrutinized by the European Parliament and by some at least of the national parliaments. A later consolidated draft text which was before the European Council in late June was also made public by the Luxembourg Presidency.

The House of Lords Select Committee on the European Communities carried out a careful scrutiny of the draft Treaty, following an earlier Report of 1990 prepared in advance of the intergovernmental negotiations.[57] The June version of the Treaty contained in its first Article words (later deleted on the insistence of the United Kingdom): 'This Treaty marks a new stage in a process leading gradually to a Union with a federal goal.' The Committee commented on this:

Whatever may be the meaning of the words 'federal goal', the implication of this text is that under a new Treaty the Member States would remain independent sovereign States—their 'ever closer union' based ultimately on treaty. Any further moves towards federation would require a further treaty.

The structure proposed in the Luxembourg draft Treaty was that of the three pillars. The flanking or supplementary forms of cooperation 'would not be brought into the system established by Community law, with its directly applicable and directly effective legislation and the correlative loss of the power of independent action by Member States. They would continue to be based essentially on international law.' The Committee had in their earlier Report underlined that to bring foreign policy into the Community structure would imply loss of ultimate national independence in the conduct of external relations and therefore of separate sovereign status for the Member States. They concluded however that the three pillar structure, although it would impose new constraints and lead to a strengthening of the external powers of the Community, would be compatible with indefinite retention by the Member States of separate sovereign status. Their views were in line with legal and political evidence given to them on behalf of the Foreign and Commonwealth Office, which emphasized that UK Ministers would not sign up to provisions which did not permit the retention of independence.[58]

In mid-1991 the Netherlands took over the Presidency of the Community, and shortly thereafter they placed before the Intergovernmental

---

[57] HL Select Committee on the European Communities, 27th Report 1989–90 (1990–91*b*).
[58] HL Select Committee on the European Communities, 17th Report (1990–91*b*) paras 105–10 and 130–1. FCO evidence on the common foreign and security policy is at pp 17–18.

Conference a redraft of the Treaty based on the unitary 'tree' model. It became clear, however, that this structure could not command the unanimous support of the Member States, and in December 1991 the Conference adopted in Maastricht a provisional text which was based on the earlier Luxembourg draft. On 7 February 1992, again in Maastricht, the Member States signed the Treaty on European Union and thereby established among themselves a European Union. The Union no longer had a 'federal goal'. Instead it had a structure which was clearly intergovernmental. Under Article A of the new Treaty:

The Union shall be founded on the European Communities, supplemented by the policies and forms of cooperation established by this Treaty. Its task shall be to organize, in a manner demonstrating consistency and solidarity, relations between the Member States and between their peoples.[59]

Among the objectives of the Union was: 'to assert its identity on the international scene, in particular through the implementation of a common foreign and security policy including the eventual framing of a common defence policy which might in time lead to a common defence'. The Union was to be served by a single institutional framework. Article E elaborated this with care:

The European Parliament, the Council, the Commission and the Court of Justice shall exercise their powers under the conditions and for the purposes provided for, on the one hand, by the provisions of the Treaties establishing the European Communities and of the subsequent Treaties modifying and supplementing them and, on the other hand, by the other provisions of this Treaty.

The 'other provisions of this Treaty' included Title V—Provisions on a Common Foreign and Security Policy. The powers and procedures assigned to the European Parliament and the Commission in Title V were very much more limited than those under the Community Treaties, while the European Court was to be totally excluded. The Commission, which had been an advocate of the unitary 'tree' structure, described the outcome of the Conference thus:

In the field of Political Union a major step was taken with the incorporation into the Treaty of provisions on a Common Foreign and Security Policy covering all aspects of foreign and security policy and establishing a system of routine cooperation between the Member States in the conduct of national policy.[60]

[59] See Durand (1992) pp 359–64; Dehousse (ed) ch 1; Hartley (1993) at pp 229–31; William Wallace and Helen Wallace (2000) p 472.
[60] Bull EC 1991 No 12, 1.1.1.

The Common Foreign and Security Policy

The Maastricht Treaty by Title V with its single Article J established a new common foreign and security policy (CFSP) which was to replace European Political Cooperation. The new CFSP was in the following legal respects significantly different from EPC:

1. Article J.2 set out specific objectives for the CFSP. These were to safeguard the common values, fundamental interests, and independence of the Union, to strengthen the security of the Union and its Member States in all ways, to preserve peace and to strengthen international security, in accordance with the principles of the UN Charter, the Helsinki Final Act and the objectives of the Paris Charter, to promote international cooperation and to develop democracy, the rule of law, and respect for human rights. This can be seen as providing a legal framework for common action which would now go beyond procedural and political cooperation and assume a binding character.
2. The carefully maintained institutional distinction between the Council and the Member States acting in political cooperation disappeared. The Council was given new powers to adopt two new kinds of instrument—common positions and joint actions.[61]
3. Both common positions and joint actions would be binding under international law.[62] Member States were required to 'ensure that their national positions conform to the common position' and to uphold the common position in international organizations and conferences.[63] The Council, under guidelines from the European Council, might also decide 'on the principle of joint action' and lay down the scope, objectives, and 'means, procedures and conditions for its implementation'. Joint actions would 'commit the Member States in the positions they adopt and in the conduct of their activity'. A limited escape clause allowed Member States to derogate in cases

[61] When the Treaty entered into force, the Council on 8 November 1993 decided that it would be called the Council of the European Union and so designated in all acts, including those under the Second and Third Pillars—'political declarations which the Council adopts under the common foreign and security policy will thus be made in the name of the European Union.' Council Decision 93/591 [1993] OJ L 281/18.

[62] See Macleod, Hendry, and Hyett (1996) at p 412: 'But the process remains intergovernmental, subject to international law, not Community law. Its product is instruments governed by international law, not Community legislation.' See also Douglas Hurd (1994), at p 425; Foreign and Commonwealth Office evidence, in House of Lords Select Committee on the European Communities 17th Report, (1990–91b), at pp 17–18.

[63] This applies only to formal common positions of the Council which are numbered, with the letters CFSP after the number, and published in the Official Journal: see Macleod, Hendry, and Hyett (1996) at p 417.

of imperative need and failing a Council decision. The Council was to be informed immediately.

4. The CFSP would include 'all questions relating to the security of the Union including the eventual forming of a common defence policy, which might in time lead to a common defence'. Western European Union was requested to implement Union decisions with defence implications. By the time that the Maastricht Treaty entered into force, all European Union Member States were either full Members or observers in WEU. Some Member States only were Members of NATO, while others—Austria, Ireland, Finland, and Sweden—were for varying historical reasons committed to a policy of neutrality. Article J.4(4) therefore provided that Union policy 'shall not prejudice the specific character of the security and defence policy of certain Member States and shall respect the obligations of certain Member States under the North Atlantic Treaty and be compatible with the common security and defence policy established under that framework'. The ten Member States which were members of WEU made a Declaration on signature of the Maastricht Treaty which made clear that 'WEU will be developed as the defence component of the European Union and as the means to strengthen the European pillar of the Atlantic Alliance'. The Declaration elaborated the procedural implications of this.

Most of the remaining provisions in Title V closely reflected the terms of the Single European Act or the practice developed in EPC. Thus, for example, the European Council, which had made its first formal appearance in the Single European Act, was given a specific duty to 'define the principles of and general guidelines for the common foreign and security policy'. Diplomatic and consular missions of the Member States were required to cooperate in non-member countries in implementing Council common positions and other measures. These missions were also—by amendment to the European Community Treaty—responsible for implementing the new entitlement for EU citizens to claim diplomatic protection from a mission of any Member State where his own Member State is not represented. Article C of the Treaty provided that the single institutional framework of the Union would ensure consistency and continuity of its activities, particularly in external relations, and the Council and Commission under their respective powers were to be responsible for this. The Commission under Article J.8 was given a power, along with the Member States, to refer any CFSP question or proposal to the Council. Any jurisdiction for the ECJ was firmly excluded by Article L.

The creation of the Second Pillar as a generator of action as well as binding legal instruments meant that it became necessary to make provision for its financing. Article J.11 provided that administrative expenditure of the institutions should be charged to the budget of the European Communities. More difficult was the new question of operational expenditure. The Council was given power to decide unanimously to charge this to the EC budget, where it would be subject to the budgetary procedure laid down in the Treaties. In the alternative the Council might determine that it should be charged to the Member States under a scale to be decided. These provisions, which contained no automatic fallback, were from the outset criticized as showing that the Union lacked any financial autonomy.[64] In practice they soon proved to be divisive and time-wasting.

On voting, unanimity remained the general rule, with the exception of procedural questions. In adopting a joint action, however, or at a later stage of its development, the Council was entitled to 'define those matters on which decisions are to be taken by a qualified majority'.[65] In the event the Council did not prove ready or eager to make use of this possibility. In a Declaration made on signature of the Treaty Member States agreed that where a qualified majority existed in favour of a decision, they would where possible avoid blocking a unanimous decision.

The Ratification of the Maastricht Treaty

It was almost two years before all twelve Member States ratified the Maastricht Treaty. The national sensitivities which so prolonged the process varied from State to State. In three Member States however—Denmark, the UK, and Germany—the nature of the new Second Pillar was of significant importance and was carefully considered at national level.

The first derailment of the ratification process occurred in Denmark, where on 2 June 1992 the people in a national referendum voted narrowly against Danish acceptance of the Treaty. Although there were a number of aspects of the Maastricht Treaty which aroused antagonism, it appeared that potential loss of national sovereignty was the most important. The Danish people were happy to belong to a European Community but unwilling to become part of the new Union. The possibility of the European Union acquiring a defence role aroused particular suspicion. Denmark was not a member of WEU, and Danish mothers opposed the idea that their sons might be called to die in a European army.

Renegotiation of the Treaty was not however on offer. In October Denmark submitted to the other Member States in a document entitled 'Denmark and Europe' an account of the points of particular difficulty to Denmark. A way was sought, short of amending the Treaty and thus

---

[64] Dehousse (ed) (1994) at p 8. See also Fink-Hooijer (1994) at pp 184–5.
[65] Articles J.3(2) and 8(2).

re-opening the ratification procedure in States where it was already complete, to gloss the text on these points of concern, which included the possibility of Union moves towards a defence policy. The European Council
meeting in Edinburgh in December 1992 issued a Decision concerning certain Problems raised by Denmark on the Treaty on European Union,
which was intended to form the basis for a 'fresh try' by Denmark to
secure the necessary popular assent. In Section C of this Decision, on
Defence Policy, the European Council noted that, although Denmark was
an observer to WEU, nothing in the Treaty committed Denmark to becoming a member: 'Accordingly, Denmark does not participate in the elaboration and the implementation of decisions and actions of the Union which
have defence implications, but will not prevent the development of closer
cooperation between Member States in this area.' The implication was that
the necessary unanimity would exist in the absence of any participation by
Denmark.

The European Council Decision was regarded as creating legal rights
and obligations among the Member States. Denmark later registered it
with the UN Secretariat as an international agreement. Under Article 31 of
the 1969 Vienna Convention on the Law of Treaties[66] it would qualify as
an 'agreement relating to the treaty which was made between all the parties in connection with the conclusion of the treaty'. Such an agreement
forms part of the 'context' of a treaty and must therefore be taken into
account in interpreting its terms.[67] The Decision—along with other documents adopted at the Edinburgh European Council—enabled the Danish
Folketing to vote by a seven-eighths majority in favour of the Treaty, and
in a second referendum the electorate approved ratification.[68]

The first referendum in Denmark, together with the very narrow majority in favour of the Treaty in the referendum in France, focused opposition
to the Maastricht Treaty in other Member States and prolonged ratification
procedures where they had not already been completed. In the United
Kingdom strong opposition to the Treaty led to months of heated debate
in the House of Commons. Most controversial were the provisions on economic and monetary union and the Social Chapter, and the latter came
close to bringing about the fall of the Conservative Government. There
was extensive discussion in both Houses of Parliament on whether it was

[66] UKTS No 58 (1980), Cmnd 7964.
[67] See Hansard HL Debs 3 June 1992 cols 938–45 (UK Government Statement and
responses); Bull EC 1992 No 12, 1.2; points 1.3 and 1.37; Hartley (1993) at pp 254–7; Glistrup
(1994): Curtin and van Ooik (1994); Gardiner (1997).
[68] Some years later, on 6 April 1998, the Supreme Court of Denmark delivered a Decision
concerning the Maastricht Treaty in response to a further challenge to its constitutional legality. This Decision, reported in [1998] Ugeskrift fur Retsvaesen H 800, did not however focus
on issues relevant to the Second Pillar. See comment by Harck and Palmer Olsen in [1999]
AJIL 209.

constitutionally proper to hold a referendum on the issue of UK ratification. The vote in the House of Lords which rejected the proposal for a referendum by 445 to 176 had the largest participation recorded in the seven-hundred-year history of the Chamber.[69]

After completion of the prolonged Parliamentary procedures however, a court action was brought by Lord Rees-Mogg claiming *inter alia* that the executive was incapable of transferring any of its prerogative powers in the fields of foreign policy, security, and defence without statutory enactment. The European Communities (Amendment) Act 1993, following the precedent of the statute which had given effect to the Single European Act, did not include among the proposed 'Community Treaties' Titles V and VI which established the new forms of intergovernmental cooperation. Ratification of those parts of the Maastricht Treaty would be carried out under the prerogative treaty-making powers of the executive. Counsel for Lord Rees-Mogg in submitting that this proposed procedure violated UK constitutional procedures relied on the Irish case of *Crotty* described above.[70]

In *R v Secretary of State for Foreign and Commonwealth Affairs ex parte Lord Rees-Mogg*[71] the English High Court held that the *Crotty* case had turned on the provisions of the Irish constitution and was therefore of no assistance. In the UK, the courts had no jurisdiction to consider the question raised. The High Court relied on the judgment of Lord Denning in *Blackburn v Attorney-General*[72] who had said in the context of the proposed accession by the United Kingdom to the European Community Treaties:

When her Ministers negotiate and sign a treaty, even a treaty of such paramount importance as this proposed one, they act on behalf of the country as a whole. They exercise the prerogative of the Crown. Their action in so doing cannot be challenged or questioned in these courts.

The High Court in the *Rees-Mogg* case said that, quite apart from the question of non-justiciability, Title V of the Maastricht Treaty did not entail an abandonment or transfer of prerogative powers but an exercise of those powers:

So far as we know, nobody has ever suggested that the Charter of the United Nations, for example, or of the North Atlantic Treaty Organisation, involves a transfer of prerogative powers. Title V should be read in the same light. In the last resort, as was pointed out in argument, though not pursued, it would presumably

---

[69] See Denza (1994a). The relationship between UK constitutional law and European Community law was explained in the White Paper published in May 1967 by the Labour Government, *Legal and Constitutional Implications of United Kingdom Membership of the European Communities*, Cmnd 3301.

[70] See n 36 above.   [71] [1994] 1 All ER 457, [1993] 3 CMLR 101.

[72] [1971] 1 WLR 1037, [1971] CMLR 784.

be open to the Government to denounce the Treaty, or at least to fail to comply with its international obligations under Title V.[73]

Germany was the last Member State to deposit its ratification and thus bring the Maastricht Treaty into force. The Bundestag and the Bundesrat decided to adopt a new Article 23 into the German Constitution as a basis for Germany's participation in the European Union. Public debate in Germany focused on possible threats from the Treaty to the constitutional rights of German citizens and on the need for greater involvement by national parliaments in the process of European integration. Even after the constitutional amendment became law, Germany delayed its ratification of the Maastricht Treaty until its Federal Constitutional Court in the case of *Brunner v European Union Treaty*[74] ruled on complaints by a German citizen that the Treaty would breach his constitutional rights and guarantees.

Brunner argued *inter alia* that the existence of Germany as an independent sovereign State would be under threat since the integration to be effected by the Treaty would bring about 'development towards the covert and irrevocable institution of a European federal state'. The Federal Constitutional Court drew a careful distinction between the central areas of competence to be exercised by the European Community—the customs union, free movement of goods, the internal market, coordination of economic policies, and the development of monetary union—and the areas where cooperation would remain on an intergovernmental basis, in particular foreign and security policy. The implication of this structure was that:

Germany is one of the 'Masters of the Treaties', which have established their adherence to the Union Treaty concluded 'for an unlimited period' (Article Q) with the intention of long-term membership, but could also ultimately revoke that adherence by a contrary act. The validity and application of European law in Germany depend on the application-of-law instruction of the Accession Act. Germany thus preserves the quality of a sovereign State in its own right and the status of sovereign equality with other States within the meaning of Article 2(1) of the United Nations Charter of 26 June 1945.[75]

As regards the argument that the Union might have powers to take action against holders of constitutional rights in Germany, the Court emphasized that the joint actions and measures which the Council might adopt under Title V or Title VI of the Treaty would have no effects of constitutional relevance on individuals. Such Council decisions would be binding in international law, but they would not have direct effect in Member States or be

---

[73] *Rees-Mogg* case (n 71 above) *per* Lloyd LJ at para [55].
[74] [1994] 1 CMLR 57. See also critical comments on the ruling: by Schwarze (1994) and Everling (1994).
[75] [1994] 1 CMLR 57, paras [54], [55].

capable of claiming precedence over national law. There was in the Treaty a clear separation between Community powers and the new intergovernmental policies and forms of cooperation: 'The Council therefore cannot rely on the supra-national forms of action under European Community law if it wishes to take measures in the areas of the foreign and security policy or justice and home affairs.'[76]

In dealing with the argument that the Union might autonomously increase its own powers, the Federal Constitutional Court stressed that the Treaty contained no evidence that the Contracting Parties intended to establish in the Union an independent legal subject which would be the holder of its own powers. It was clear that the Union possessed no independent legal personality. It would be the Member States acting jointly who would provide the Union with objectives and means. They had taken a conscious decision not to place the foreign and security policy and justice and home affairs into the supra-national decision-making structure, and this decision could not be altered without prior ratification by the Member States.[77]

Following the judgment of the Federal Constitutional Court, Germany ratified the Maastricht Treaty at once. The new three pillared constitutional structure became law on 1 November 1993. But the birth had been traumatic. In Weiler's words: 'At the popular level, Maastricht was a shock. Public opinion was more shocked to discover that which was already in place than that which was being proposed.'[78] Although the new Common Foreign and Security Policy was only one of the concerns, it was clear that there was no popular demand for a federal Europe. The Second Pillar—enabling the nation States to retain the ultimate independence in foreign policy which was a key test of sovereign status—reflected the mood of the people. Judge Mancini expressed it thus:

While the Maastricht Treaty has conquered a large and important territory, it has nevertheless not led the Union across the threshold wherein lies the federal state. I shall say more: it seems to me that the closer the Union moves towards statehood, the greater the resistance to the attainment of this goal becomes.[79]

[76] [1994] 1 CMLR 57, paras [16]–[18].   [77] [1994] 1 CMLR 57, paras [66]–[69].
[78] Weiler (1999*a*) p 8.
[79] Mancini (2000), ch 4, 'Europe: The Case for Statehood', 51 at p 53.

3

Evolution of Cooperation in Justice and Home Affairs and Formation of the Third Pillar

Political Constraints on Law-Making

In the case of foreign policy coordination—as explained in Chapter 2 above—the principal reason for avoiding Community methods was the legal importance of independence in the conduct of external relations as a defining element of statehood. This constraint did not apply to cooperation among law enforcers. But, for a variety of reasons, Member States were for many years reluctant to contemplate bringing cooperative procedures on justice and home affairs within the competence of the EC. While the European Community Treaty contained powers on the common commercial policy and on the formation of association agreements which had the potential to be stretched to cover external actions which were truly political in their objectives, provisions on intra-Community movement of people and even the notoriously elastic Article 235 could not be—or at least were not—extended in any similar way.[1]

The first reason for this was that common executive or legislative action against external immigrants, terrorists, drug smugglers, or international criminals raised issues of national jurisdiction and of differences among constitutional, civil, and criminal laws which were sensitive as well as extremely complex. In the criminal justice field in particular—in spite of the gradual unifying effect of the ECHR—there are fundamental differences in national laws as well as an assumption in each Member State that its own system clearly reflects natural justice. There were strong political arguments against ceding national competence in these areas which were usually more comprehensible to citizens and to national parliaments than were the remoter issues dealt with in European Political Cooperation. The international law method left national governments and parliaments with the final decision, which might be taken at leisure, on whether to ratify a new treaty. It offered greater possibilities for retaining the detail of

---

[1] On the controversies of this period over possible EC Treaty powers see Plender (1990). Plender concludes, at p 608: 'All this suggests that the Treaty as it stands is an inadequate basis for the control of immigration from non-member countries.'

national criminal laws and procedures, either through negotiation or by derogations or statements of interpretation. International agreements could not 'occupy the field' so as to deprive national legislatures of power in the relevant area.

Secondly, cooperation among law enforcers was not in its early stages seen as a law-making process. Rather it was a collaboration among like-minded enforcers to exchange information and compare methods in order to strengthen barriers against common enemies. For those who began the process of informal intergovernmental cooperation, democratic account-ability and legal safeguards for the individual were not at the forefront of their minds. National immigration policies and national criminal laws were jealously guarded and the objective was informal exchange of infor-mation and practical cooperation to make them more effective, not the construction of common policies or common rules. Drawing up inter-national conventions on questions such as extradition, transfer of prison-ers, and formal mutual assistance in the conduct of national criminal trials was generally regarded as the province of the Council of Europe.

Thirdly, while European Political Cooperation did seek to attain some form of visible common European identity and publicly articulated common approach, there was no similar objective for the process of coop-eration in law enforcement. The exchanges were by their nature secret. Police officers, counter-terrorists, and drug-busters met as unobtrusively as possible and neither the substance of their exchanges nor any successes in law enforcement which they brought about were announced. For this reason the transparency which flowed from Commission involvement, published Commission proposals, and published agreements or Council legislation held no attraction.

For these three reasons therefore—the sensitivity of the subject, the per-ceived need for avoiding legal relations, and the climate of secrecy—there was during the 1970s and early 1980s no willingness among the Member States to extend European Community powers into the fields of coopera-tion in law enforcement or migration control, or to create new powers by amending the Treaties.

The Early Links

Whereas the beginning of European Political Cooperation can be traced to a specific decision of the Heads of State and Government in 1969, it is more difficult to pinpoint the origin of secret collaboration between the law enforcers of the Member States. In general, ad hoc groups of Ministers or officials were set up as the need arose and without any overall structure, common procedures or practices of accounting to Heads of State and Government or to Ministers of Justice and Home Affairs. Whether the

Commission was permitted to 'observe' and whether the Council Secretariat or the European Political Cooperation Secretariat provided continuity and support varied from group to group.[2] The earliest and best known of these was the Trevi Group of Ministers of the Interior and of Justice, named after the fountain in Rome near which Ministers set it up in 1975.[3] The Trevi Group focused on practical ways of combating international crime, and terrorism in particular. Later its activities broadened to include other aspects of police training and methods of fighting international crime.[4]

The Solemn Declaration of Stuttgart, made in 1983, listed among activities which might be conducive to the attainment of European Union:

... legal instruments which can strengthen cooperation among the judicial authorities of the Member States, notably in civil and commercial matters, cooperation in the areas of the suppression of infringements of Community law, identification of areas of criminal and procedural law in which cooperation . . . might be desirable.[5]

The impetus towards more formal structures for intergovernmental cooperation grew with the commitment under the Single European Act to establish an internal market as 'an area without internal frontiers in which the free movement of goods, persons, services and capital is ensured in accordance with the provisions of this Treaty'. It was apparent to the Governments of the Member States that—whatever the extent of the obligation to remove internal Community border controls and however long it took in practice to achieve—the corollary of free movement of people throughout their territories was stricter 'flanking measures' to exclude or control drug traffickers, terrorists, and other criminals, as well as uninvited migrants.

A declaration attached to the Single European Act, relating to Articles 13 to 19, stated that:

Nothing in these provisions shall affect the right of Member States to take such measures as they consider necessary for the purpose of controlling immigration from third countries and to combat terrorism, crime, the traffic in drugs and illicit trading in works of art and antiques.

The Member States also attached to the Single European Act a political declaration on the free movement of persons stating:

[2] Nicoll and Salmon (2000) pp 385–7.
[3] The Naples Convention on the Provision of Mutual Assistance between Customs Authorities, signed in 1967, UKTS No 93 (1980), Cmnd 8080, may also be taken as the earliest example of intergovernmental collaboration for enforcement of Community rules—see Statewatch texts (1997) p 9.
[4] Anderson et al (eds (1995) pp 53–6.
[5] [1983] Yearbook of European Law 276, at pp 281, 284; [1983] CML Rev 691 (text of Solemn Declaration).

In order to promote the free movement of persons, the Member States shall cooperate, without prejudice to the powers of the Community, in particular as regards the entry, movement and residence of nationals of third countries. They shall also cooperate in the combating of terrorism, crime, the traffic in drugs and illicit trading in works of art and antiques.

The implication of these two declarations was that the matters listed were *prima facie* within national competence and that most of the cooperation envisaged would take place under the existing intergovernmental procedures. The Commission however maintained that a number of the compensatory measures envisaged—in particular a draft directive on the control of the acquisition and possession of weapons[6]—were within the powers of the European Community as enlarged by the Single European Act. As will be seen below, however, it did not press strongly its case for European Community legislation.

Even before the negotiation of the Single European Act, limited agreements between some of the Member States were foreshadowing the reduction or lifting of border controls. In 1960 systematic border controls were ended between the Benelux States—Belgium, the Netherlands, and Luxembourg. In 1985 these three States, together with France and Germany, signed at Schengen an Agreement on the Gradual Abolition of Checks at Common Borders.[7] This was little more than a negotiating framework for the elaboration of further intergovernmental agreements on such matters as police cooperation, extradition, approximation of laws, and exchange of personal data to enable the central objective of complete abolition of controls to be achieved. The Schengen Agreement was 'regarded by the Commission as a dress rehearsal for the total lifting of border controls in the European Community in 1992'.[8]

Following the entry into force of the Single European Act in 1987, intergovernmental work intensified in the Trevi Group (already mentioned), in the Working Group on Immigration, in the Working Group on Judicial Cooperation and in the Customs Mutual Assistance Group. In December 1988 the European Council in Rhodes set up a Group of Co-ordinators on free movement of persons. Six months later this Group submitted to the European Council in Madrid a Report which became known as the Palma Document.[9] The Co-ordinators set to one side the national differences over the extent of the obligation under the Single European Act to ease or eliminate border control of people and on the legislative or intergovernmental

---

[6] COM(87) 383 final.

[7] English translation in Plender (1988) at p 810, and in HL Select Committee on the European Communities, 22nd Report (1988–89), Appendix 3.

[8] HL Select Committee on the European Communities, 22nd Report, (1988–89) at para. 3.

[9] Printed in HL Select Committee on the European Communities, 22nd Report (1988–89) Appendix 5 and in Statewatch texts (1997) at p 12.

methods to be used. They drew up a catalogue of the measures to be adopted, distinguishing between those which were essential and others which were desirable, identified the appropriate forum for the examination of each and sought themselves to provide impetus to progress or agreement.

The Palma Document recognized that the creation of an area without internal frontiers would necessitate tighter controls at external frontiers—controls which should be highly effective since they would be valid for all Member States. The harmonizing of conditions of entry for nationals of non-Member States related particularly to visa policy: a common list of countries whose nationals would require visas, a common 'black list' of persons to be refused entry, some harmonization of criteria for granting visas and a European visa. Harmonizing asylum policy would be based on common obligations of the Member States under the 1951 Geneva Convention relating to the Status of Refugees[10] and the 1967 New York Protocol[11] to that Convention. Work would focus on ensuring identical commitments by Member States, determination of the State responsible for examining the application for asylum, procedure for examination of 'clearly unfounded requests', conditions for movement of applicants between Member States, and examination of a possible sharing of the economic burden of a common policy on asylum. Agreement had in fact already been reached on the principles which were to be adopted in Dublin in June 1990 as the Convention determining the State responsible for examining Applications for Asylum lodged in one of the Member States of the European Communities ('the Dublin Convention').[12]

The competent fora identified in the Palma Document for these various tasks were not limited to those controlled by the Member States—national legislation, intergovernmental cooperation including European Political Cooperation, and action under EC Treaty powers. They also included the Council of Europe which had already provided the framework for numerous international conventions on relevant subjects such as extradition, transfer of criminal proceedings, mutual assistance in civil and criminal matters, and illegal traffic in works of art.[13] The UN was responsible for the 1988 UN Convention against Illicit Traffic in Narcotic Drugs and Psychotropic Substances[14] as well as for continuing work on asylum and refugee status.

The extensive network of conventions already in force and under negotiation in other international organizations made it impossible for the

---

[10] UKTS No 39 (1954), Cmd 9171.   [11] UKTS No 15 (1969), Cmnd 3370.

[12] UKTS No 72 (1997), Cm 3806; [1997] OJ C254/1.

[13] For a list of Council of Europe Conventions on Criminal Matters up to 1990 see Schutte (1994) at p 187, n 18.

[14] UKTS No 26 (1992), Cm 1927, [1988] BYIL 527.

Member States simply to consider the best way of drawing up and implementing the compensatory measures to offset free movement within their territories. For each subject the starting point was the extent, nature, and effectiveness of existing international obligations. There was no point in duplicating, as among the Member States, international agreements which were more effective by reason of wider participation by non-member States and with which national enforcement authorities and courts were already familiar. For some subjects it might merely be necessary to ensure that all Member States and, where appropriate, the European Community were Contracting Parties without reservation to a particular agreement. Other international agreements might offer the possibility for the Member States to adopt, as among themselves, particular interpretations or enforcement mechanisms. Whether such differentiation between Member States and non-Member States was permissible would depend on the construction of the relevant multilateral agreement under the rules contained in the Vienna Convention on the Law of Treaties[15] or in customary international law.

The Position of the Commission

The overriding objective of the Commission at this period was the removal of border controls affecting the free movement of people in the internal market. Its position was that, as a matter of law, Article 8a of the EC Treaty as amended by the Single European Act required border controls to be dismantled by the Member States by 1992 in order to complete the internal market as 'an area without internal frontiers in which the free movement of . . . persons . . . is ensured in accordance with the provisions of this Treaty'. It accepted the need for effective compensatory measures as the corollary of its main objective, and also because it regarded frontier controls as ineffective.

In the Communication of the Commission to the Council made in December 1988,[16] the Commission accepted that 'in order to achieve the stated objective of completing the internal market as defined, decisions need to be taken both by the Community institutions and by the Member States in accordance with their respective powers, and that the Member States are called upon in particular to strengthen their co-operation in areas corrected with internal security'. Although the Commission in its 1985 White Paper on the completion of the Internal Market[17] had included

---

[15] UKTS No 58 (1980), Cmnd 7964. The most relevant provisions are Articles 31 to 33 on Interpretation of Treaties and Article 41 on Agreements to modify multilateral treaties between certain of the parties only.

[16] COM(88) 640 final, printed in HL Select Committee on the European Communities, 22nd Report (1988–89) Appendix 4.

[17] COM(85) 310 final.

in its work programme prospective measures on drugs legislation, on asylum and refugee status, on visas, on extradition, and on the status of
nationals of non-member countries, in 1988 it proposed:

... that Community legislation in this field be applied only to those cases where
the legal security and uniformity provided by Community law constitutes the best
instrument to achieve the desired goal. This would mean therefore that large scope
would be left, at this stage, to co-operation among Member States notwithstanding
the fact that the Commission should be permitted to participate, even on an informal basis, in this form of co-operation with a view to ensuring compliance with the
before-mentioned objectives.[18]

The Commission then reviewed the need for the directives listed in the
1985 White Paper in the perspective of the intergovernmental work
already in progress (its account overlaps considerably with that in the
Palma Document just described) and concluded that in most areas, successful conclusion of the steps contained in the intergovernmental programme would—at least for the time being—provide sufficient security to
enable internal frontier controls to be lifted. It did, however, press for
progress on the Directive already sent to the Council on the control of the
acquisition and possession of weapons.[19] In its 1988 Communication it
also argued in favour of a Council directive coordinating certain aspects of
asylum policy. But a few months later it was prepared to accept, in the
light of progress towards an intergovernmental agreement identifying the
Member State responsible for examining an asylum request, that a directive might not be necessary.[20]

The general approach of the Commission was well expressed in these
words: 'We would much prefer to see agreement on concrete measures,
adopted by whatever machinery people feel is best, rather than pursue
Community legislation for its own sake.'[21] Monar, however, suggests that
the Commission's real motive was the fear that by insisting further on the
use of Community powers it could lose the chance of increasing its
influence in the growing network of intergovernmental cooperation.[22]

[18] COM(88) 640 final, paras 9 and 14.   [19] COM(87) 383 final.
[20] Evidence to HL Select Committee on 25 April 1989 by Claus-Dieter Ehlermann and
Adrian Fortescue: see HL Select Committeee on European Communities, 22nd Report
(1988–89) at Q 51. The European Court had examined, in Joined Cases 281, 283–285, 287/85
Germany, France, Netherlands, Denmark, UK v Commission [1987] ECR 3203, the extent to which
the EC Treaty provisions on cooperation in the social field could be extended to cover
national migration policies in relation to non-member countries.
[21] HL Select Committee on the European Communities, 22nd Report (1988–89) at Q 1 (Mr
Fortescue).
[22] Monar (1994) 69, at p 71. See also de Lobkowicz (1994) 99, at p 108.

The Twin-track Approach to Compensatory Measures: Schengen

For the next two or three years, work between the Member States progressed on parallel tracks. In 1990 the original five States Parties (the
Benelux States, France, and Germany) concluded a Convention applying
the Schengen Agreement ('the Schengen Implementing Convention').[23]
The Preamble to the Implementing Convention referred back to the commitment in the Single European Act to 'an area without internal frontiers'
and stated: 'Whereas the aim pursued by the Contracting Parties coincides
with that objective, without prejudice to the measures to be taken to
implement the provisions of the Treaty.' The Parties thus presented the
Convention as a 'going beyond measure' designed to spearhead the way
towards an explicit Community objective.

The central commitment of the Schengen Implementing Convention
was that: 'Internal borders may be crossed at any point without any checks
on persons being carried out.'

The provisions forming the corollary to this obligation concerned the
strengthening of the external borders of the Schengen area, common
arrangements for issuing visas and harmonizing visa policies, and conditions on the movement and residence of aliens (nationals of States not
Members of the European Communities). There were rules on responsibility for determining a request for asylum and for returning an applicant
to the Member State responsible. There were extensive and detailed rules
for police cooperation in preventing and detecting criminal offences,
including hot pursuit of suspects across internal borders. Existing Council
of Europe Conventions and other rules on mutual assistance among
administrative and judicial authorities and on extradition were supplemented by more extensive requirements. National legislation on firearms
and ammunition was to be standardized.

The Contracting Parties agreed to set up a joint information system, the
Schengen Information System, to enable designated authorities to have
access to data on persons and objects gathered by another Party and
required for such Convention purposes as extradition, border control, and
the issue of a visa or residence permit. The Convention contained provisions for the protection and security of personal data held under the
Schengen Information System. The standards were to be based on the 1981
Council of Europe Convention for the Protection of Individuals with
regard to Automatic Processing of Personal Data.[24]

---

[23] (1981) 30 ILM 84; Plender (1988), 815; Statewatch texts (1997) 110. For a comprehensive
analysis and criticism of the Schengen Convention see Meijers (1991); Schutte (1991);
O'Keeffe (1991); Anderson et al (eds) (1995) pp 56–63.
[24] UKTS No 86 (1990), Cm 1329.

The Schengen Implementing Convention—containing 142 Articles—was clearly a very serious attempt to provide the cooperative framework which would permit border controls to be removed. It established an Executive Committee with the power to set up Working Parties—an entire secret system to elaborate even more detailed rules. Even so, the signatory States safeguarded themselves in the Final Act by stipulating: 'The Convention shall not enter into force until the prior conditions for its implementation are fulfilled in the signatory States and checks at external borders are effective.' It was to take almost five years before the Schengen Implementing Convention was actually brought into force.

The Convention however provided, in Article 140, that it was open to any other Member State of the European Communities, on the basis of an accession agreement. Gradually it began to exert a gravitational pull. Italy signed in 1990, Portugal and Spain in 1991, and Greece in 1992. Only the UK (resistant to any commitment to lift internal border controls), Ireland (linked to the UK by the common travel area), and Denmark (linked to non-member Scandinavian States in the Nordic Travel Area) still held aloof from Schengen in 1992.

The Twin-track Approach: the Coordinators' Group

By comparison with the considerable agreement, on paper at least, among the Schengen States, the ad hoc groups seeking to make further progress within the European Community on the basis of the Palma Document made slow progress. The main efforts were directed towards asylum policy, control of external frontiers, and establishing a European Information System.

The first of these subjects continued to be negotiated within the framework of the Ad Hoc Group on Immigration and its specialist subgroups. The Dublin Convention determining the State responsible for examining Applications for Asylum lodged in one of the Member States of the European Communities[25] was signed in June 1990. Its objective was, consistently with common obligations of the Member States under the 1951 Geneva Convention and the 1967 New York Protocol, to permit greater free movement of people within the internal market by guaranteeing that refugees would have their claims determined by one Member State and would not be referred from one to another or be entitled to shop around for the most favourable forum for their applications. It was applied administratively by immigration authorities, although due to the need for ratification by all the Member States it did not enter into force for seven years.[26] The Convention was a mechanism for determining jurisdiction. It

---

[25] UKTS No 72 (1997), Cm 3806; [1997] OJ C254/1. [26] In September 1997.

was based on a degree of mutual trust in the observance of common humanitarian obligations and did not attempt any further harmonization of national laws or procedures. The asylum seeker gained the legal security of a right to determination by one Member State, but otherwise nothing was added to, or taken from, his expectations under the 1951 Geneva Convention.[27]

On external frontiers, a large measure of agreement was reached within the Ad Hoc Group on Immigration on a draft Convention on the crossing of external frontiers. This was to cover common standards of border control, mutual recognition of visas, and exchange of information on persons excluded on grounds of national security or public order. Final agreement on the text (which remained secret) was however held up for several years by disagreement between the UK and Spain on how the Convention would apply to the border between Spain and Gibraltar. As to the proposed European Information System (also secret) there were differences as to the appropriate legal instrument, the rules on data protection to be applied and on the possible solution of extending the Schengen Information System (described above) to all Member States.[28] Negotiations on this Convention took place in a Horizontal Group on Data Processing.

Among other groups labouring in the dark with less tangible results were:

1. The Groups on Judicial Cooperation, civil and criminal, which were formally part of European Political Cooperation. Their work initially concentrated on securing ratification by all Member States of Council of Europe conventions on such matters as extradition, mutual assistance, and international child abduction.
2. CELAD (Comité européen pour la lutte anti-drogues)—reporting directly to the European Council.
3. Mutual Assistance Group—in which customs law enforcers collaborated with particular emphasis on drug smuggling within the single market.

---

[27] Hailbronner (1992), at pp 922–5. Several commentators take the position that the Dublin Convention removed the right of an asylum seeker to submit successive, or multiple applications for refugee status, but such 'rights' cannot realistically be deduced from the Geneva Convention.

[28] Some of this history emerged at a later date, after these negotiations were replaced by somewhat more accessible negotiations under the Maastricht Treaty. See also Note by the Portuguese Presidency on the Form of agreement on the European Information System, June 1992, in Statewatch texts (1997) p 21 and Report by the Coordinators to the European Council at Edinburgh in December 1992 in ibid p 17.

Exchange of Intelligence

While progress by the Coordinators, the Ad Hoc Group on Immigration and the other groups described above remained slow due to the need for multilateral agreement on legally binding instruments which would require ratification by national parliaments, the direct exchange of information and intelligence continually intensified. Documents setting out the acquis of the Trevi Group—prepared either in the context of enlargement or on the eve of entry into force of the Maastricht Treaty[29]—show how extensive were the subjects on which confidential information was exchanged bilaterally within a common framework. Some of these arrangements were publicly announced at the time. The exchange of information about hijackings, for example, recommended by Ministers meeting in Bonn in 1983 and in Rome in 1985, formed the basis for collective sanctions imposed (under national laws) on the aircraft of States failing to observe obligations under the 1972 Hague Convention on Hijacking.[30] In 1984, in the wake of the shooting of a policewoman from the Libyan People's Bureau in London, the United Kingdom Secretary of State publicly proposed to European Ministers of Justice an arrangement whereby a diplomat expelled on grounds of involvement in terrorism from any Member State should be regarded as unacceptable in any other.[31]

For less high profile wrongdoers on the other hand—drug traffickers, money launderers, and forgers—as well as on methods of detecting explosives, protecting witnesses, policing sporting events, Ministers whether by recommendation or non-binding decision came to secret arrangements under which information flowed freely. For police and customs officers these systems appeared to work well. There was however growing unease that the arrangements were unstructured and unknown, and that national safeguards on data protection, interception of communications, and accountability of law enforcement officers did not apply or were being evaded.[32] This concern was expressed by Glyn Ford, MEP, in the following words:

. . . the work of the Trevi Group and the Schengen Group is totally without any form of accountability at European level. Some of the issues raised there are highly contentious and require some Parliamentary oversight. We do not notice much

[29] See Statewatch texts (1997), Vol I pp 25–31.
[30] The Heads of State and Government at the Bonn Economic Summit in 1978 resolved that their governments should take immediate action to halt flights to a country refusing extradition or prosecution of those who had hijacked an aircraft, and would initiate action to halt incoming flights from that country or by its airlines. They urged other governments to join them. See Levitt (1988).
[31] *Guardian,* 1 June 1984 *Telegraph,* 1 June1984; Denza (1998) p 67.
[32] For detail on the work of the Trevi Group see Bunyan (1993) ch 1.

reporting going on to national Parliaments either, it is only in the United Kingdom. With respect to the Schengen Agreement, only one national Parliament has ever seen the text of that Agreement to date.[33]

Integration of Justice and Home Affairs into the Union

It was clear to the Member States meeting at the Intergovernmental Conference convened in December 1990 that these chaotic, overlapping, and unaccountable negotiating structures were incapable of delivering a coherent body of rules on external immigration and law enforcement. If internal border controls were to be lifted without creating an area of free circulation for illegal immigrants, drug smugglers, and terrorists, a better framework for law-making was required. As Guild expressed it: 'Out of this morass of policy with varying degrees of co-ordination but lacking a legal identity, enforcement mechanism or judicial interpretative authority to ensure consistency, the 1990 Intergovernmental Conference on Political Union was determined to introduce some order.'[34]

Germany, in the wake of reunification and the disintegration of the Soviet Union, was particularly concerned at the greatly increased burden of immigration and asylum seekers from non-Member States. It was Germany which first proposed that the ongoing intergovernmental activity on immigration, visas, asylum, and the fight against drugs and organized crime should in some way be brought within the ambit of the Union. The varied reasons for its approach were listed by Wallace:

Federal Germany had a particularly sensitive history and geographical position, a citizenship law based on ethnic descent rather than birth within the national territory, a liberal asylum law drafted in the aftermath of the Third Reich as the cold war divided Europe, a large gastarbeiter population attracted by its strong economy, and a structural ambivalence about sovereignty and nationhood.[35]

National sensitivities over criminal laws and immigration policies described at the outset of this chapter nevertheless remained a powerful obstacle to the extension of European Community powers.

The choice of political structures for the new European Union offered at the Intergovernmental Conference convened in December 1990 has already been described in Chapter 2 above. The Single European Act

[33] HL Select Committee European Communities, 17th Report, (1990–91b) Q 150. It was the Netherlands Parliament which had been given the Schengen Agreement for scrutiny. Similar concerns were expressed by the Immigration Law Practitioners' Association and the Joint Council for the Welfare of Immigrants in later evidence to the Committee: see HL Select Committee on the European Communities, 28th Report (1992–93b) at pp 60, 63–8.
[34] Guild (1998) p 67.
[35] William Wallace and Helen Wallace (2000) p 496. See also Nicoll and Salmon (2000) pp 388–9; Hailbronner (1992) at pp 926–7; de Lobkowicz (1994) 99 at p 117.

already provided the embryo of a structure which would combine the European Communities with European Political Cooperation operating under the distinct powers and procedures of international law. The United Kingdom—resistant both to the elimination of internal border controls and to the expansion of Community competence—took the lead in proposing that justice and home affairs, like foreign and security policy, should be taken forward under a stronger and more coherent structure, but using intergovernmental methods.[36] This approach was preferred by the majority of Member States over the unitary model proposed by the Netherlands when it assumed the Presidency in mid-1991. The Commission by this time had somewhat lost faith in the potential of the intergovernmental method and favoured the unitary model, while accepting the need for different law-making procedures. Its views however carried little weight in the context of the Intergovernmental Conference.[37]

The UK position was elaborated in evidence given on behalf of the Foreign and Commonwealth Office to the House of Lords Select Committee on the European Communities on the earlier Luxembourg Presidency version of the draft Treaty on European Union. Although the UK believed that benefits would accrue from widening and deepening the existing cooperation, this was 'best done in a framework which remains as it is now outside the EC Treaty'. They were opposed to giving the Commission any right of initiative, to any majority voting even for implementing measures and to any automatic jurisdiction for the European Court of Justice.[38]

Justice and Home Affairs form the Third Pillar

The Maastricht Treaty by Title VI with its single Article K replaced the previous ad hoc arrangements by a new structure forming part of the Union. The new Pillar differed from the existing intergovernmental cooperation in the following ways:

1. Article K.1 provided that cooperation should be 'For the purposes of achieving the objectives of the Union, in particular the free movement of persons'. This was much less detailed than the corresponding Article J.2 which set out extensive objectives for the CFSP. Nine areas—all of them already subjects of cooperation among Member States—were listed as 'matters of common interest'. These included

---

[36] Hendry (1993); Gillespie (ed) (1996) pp 161, 163.
[37] See Dehousse (ed) (1994) pp 5–14; Vignes (1993) pp 1329–44; Bann (1996) p 90; den Boer (1998) pp 3–4.
[38] HL Select Committee on the European Communities 17th Report (1990–91*b*) Q 71 (Mr Eaton).

asylum policy, control of external borders, migration by nationals of non-member States, judicial cooperation in civil and criminal matters, customs and police cooperation.[39]

2. As well as the saving for the powers of the European Community in Article K.1, there was an express constraint in Article K.2 requiring any action to comply with the European Convention for the Protection of Human Rights and Fundamental Freedoms and the Convention relating to the Status of Refugees.

3. The Council—previously excluded from any role in justice and home affairs—was given the central role in the new legal framework. This reflected the 'single institutional framework' which under Article C of the Treaty of Maastricht was to ensure the consistency and continuity of Union activities. As well as becoming the forum for consultation and collaboration among Member States and having the power to draw up conventions which would continue to require national ratification, the Council could adopt two new kinds of instrument— joint positions and joint actions. 'Joint positions' might appear to be similar to 'common positions' under the CFSP—and indeed Article K.5 uses the term 'common positions'. Article K instruments did not however have the same clear legal status as CFSP instruments.

4. Article K.4 set up a Co-ordinating Committee of senior officials. This was in fact the old Group of Co-ordinators on free movement of persons with a new name and new powers. It was the equivalent for justice and home affairs of the Political Committee for the Common Foreign and Security Policy and became known as the K.4 Committee. As well as supervising and coordinating, the K.4 Committee was to prepare the work of the Council in its areas of responsibility and could deliver opinions at the request of the Council or on its own initiative.

5. Article K.4 also provided for the Commission to be 'fully associated' with work in justice and home affairs. This added to the intergovernmental work an element of continuity and objective expertise. The Commission was given by Article K.3 a right of initiative—shared with the Member States—in six of the nine areas of work.[40] Probably

---

[39] See Hendry (1993) at p 298: 'Title VI does not contain substantive rules of law regulating the matters of common interest. It is rather a legal framework for intergovernmental cooperation between the Member States in these policy areas.'

[40] The Commission took advantage of this new power immediately after the entry into force of the Maastricht Treaty with new proposals for a Convention on the crossing of the external borders of the Member States and for a regulation, based on the new Article 100c of the EC Treaty, determining the third countries whose nationals must be in possession of a visa crossing the external borders of the Member States. These proposals, in COM(93)684 final, replaced the convention under negotiation within the framework of the Palma document. A Communication on Immigration and Asylum Policies, in COM(94) 23 final, followed very soon afterwards.

the greatest benefit from this change was that Commission proposals were immediately made public, which led to demands for more general transparency in the Third Pillar. Only for judicial cooperation in criminal matters, customs cooperation, and police cooperation on serious international crime was the right of initiative reserved exclusively to the Member States.[41]

6. Article K.6 required the Presidency and the Commission to keep the European Parliament regularly informed, to consult the Parliament and to ensure that its views were taken into consideration. The Parliament was to hold an annual debate on progress on justice and home affairs.

7. Article K.8—which is identical to Article J.11— provided that administrative expenditure of the institutions on the Third Pillar should be charged to the budget of the European Communities. Operational expenditure, on the other hand, could be charged by Council decision to the EC budget, where it would be subject to the budgetary procedures laid down in the Treaties. In the alternative the Council might determine that it should be charged to the Member States under a scale to be decided. Instruments agreed under the Third Pillar were in practice likely to be implemented by national police or immigration authorities, and so the provisions for financing were less troublesome than the identical ones in the Second Pillar.

8. On voting, the rules in Articles K.3 and K.4 were also similar to those for the Second Pillar. Unanimity was the general rule, except for procedural matters. The Council could decide that measures implementing a joint action were to be adopted by a qualified majority. Measures implementing conventions on the other hand would automatically be adopted by a majority of two-thirds of the Contracting Parties, unless the Convention otherwise provided.

Differences from the Second Pillar

The Third Pillar resembled the Second Pillar in that the characteristic features of the Community method were excluded and the Council was given institutional primacy in the development of new laws and policies. Quite apart from the different subject matter, however, there were some significant legal differences between the Second and the Third Pillars, in particular:

---

[41] Morgan identifies as the main advantages of Commission involvement 'that it can bring an added value by its expertise, by its objective point of view, by its detachment from national interests, and possibly by its control of Community means of action.' Monar and Morgan (eds) (1994) at pp 16–17. See also Müller-Graff (1994) at p 27.

1. While for the Second Pillar it was made clear by Article J of the Treaty that both common positions and joint actions would be binding under international law, it was not clear from Article K whether joint (or common) positions and joint actions on justice and home affairs matters were legally binding or not. Article K.5 says that Member States within international organizations and at international conferences 'shall defend the common positions adopted under the provisions of this Title'—which suggests legal commitment in these contexts at least—but there is in Article K no requirement to ensure that national policies conform to any joint position. Nor is there any express provision making joint actions binding on the Member States. In the light of the clear contrast with the terms of Article J, it seems probable that only conventions—all subject to national ratification—were capable of being legally binding on the Member States so as to override inconsistent national laws or require their amendment.[42] Hendry suggests that the legal effect was to be inferred from the drafting of each instrument.[43] Given, however, that joint positions and joint actions were not free-standing resolutions or agreements by the Member States but instruments to be made by the Council under delegated powers, it is difficult to attribute to them a potential legal force which is not clearly envisaged in the enabling Treaty provision. This difference between the Pillars reflects the reluctance of Member States to see areas of sensitive national legislation such as immigration, asylum, and data protection, capable of being overridden without express approval by each national parliament.

2. While the jurisdiction of the ECJ was excluded entirely from the Second Pillar, Articles K.3(2)(c) and L permitted the Member States in drawing up conventions to give the Court jurisdiction over their interpretation and application 'in accordance with such arrangements as they may lay down'. Most Member States probably saw this provision as opening the way to extensive European Court jurisdiction over Third Pillar law, but it was to open up a serious rift between the UK and the other Member States. It may be taken as supporting the argument that joint positions and joint actions were not intended

---

[42] This is the view of Müller-Graff (1994) at p 509.

[43] Hendry (1993) at p 311. The Council itself did not appear to be clear on the question: in drawing up a list of the 'acquis' of the Union and its Member States in the field of Justice and Home Affairs in 1998, they decided not to indicate whether particular instruments were legally binding. The wording of the document however indicates that the Member States believed joint actions were capable of legal effect. List taken from http://ue.eu.int/jai/article.asp. Joint actions and some JHA decisions were also published in the L series of the Official Journal, again indicating the view of the Council that they had binding effect. See also den Boer (1999) at pp 304–5.

to create international legal obligations, since it would be difficult to justify a general distinction as regards the jurisdiction of the Court between obligations arising under a binding joint action and obligations arising under a convention.

3. Article K.7 expressly authorized 'the establishment or development of closer cooperation between two or more Member States in so far as such cooperation does not conflict with, or impede, that provided for in this Title'. There was no equivalent provision for the Common Foreign and Security Policy. It is of course characteristic of the international method of forming law that two, or only a few, States may lead the way by entering into commitments which gradually develop into general or even universal law.[44] The express provision in Article K.7 however reflected the importance of the Schengen Agreement and Implementing Convention, completing the link which had already been suggested in the Preamble to the Convention, described above.[45]

4. Article K.9—which became known as the passerelle (bridge) provision—authorized the Council to transfer any of the first six of the nine areas of competence described in Article K.1 into the First Pillar. Transfer would be into Article 100c of the EC Treaty which contained a corresponding 'receiving link' for the other end of the passerelle. The three areas excluded as too sensitive for this possibility were judicial cooperation in criminal matters, customs cooperation, and police cooperation—the same areas where any Commission right of initiative was excluded. Although Article K.9 required not only unanimity in the Council but also national ratification for any decision, it showed that the Third Pillar—unlike the Second—was seen to some extent as a halfway house. The Member States, having dabbled in the shallow water of intergovernmental cooperation, might find it politically easier and perhaps necessary for reasons of effectiveness to move into the deeper waters of European Community law.

5. The permeable nature of the barrier between the Third Pillar and the First was also apparent from the number of areas where legal competence was split between them. Visas, drug abuse, international fraud, and treatment of migrants were all subjects where the European Community had some competence. For some of these the division was the result of a compromise deal during the Intergovernmental Conference. For all of them the dividing line would give rise to legal

[44] See Chapter 1 above.

[45] Nicoll and Salmon (2000) p 390. For some at least of the Member States, the Schengen arrangements were, in the words of Carlos Westendorp, Spanish Minister for European Affairs, a 'self-destructing mechanism' which would disappear once the European Union took over the field—see *Agence Europe*, 2 July1993 at p 8.

difficulties in preparing implementing legislation, as well as to calls for the area in its entirety to be brought within Community competence. The primacy of the First Pillar was emphasized in Article K.1 where the areas of Third Pillar activity are qualified by the words 'without prejudice to the powers of the European Community', and by Article M, providing that nothing in the Maastricht Treaty should affect the European Community Treaties.

It can be seen from these last three differences that the Third Pillar was established on a somewhat temporary or experimental basis. Powers could be transferred from the Third to the First Pillar either by deliberate decision of the Council ratified by all national parliaments, or through the tendency of the European Community powers to be gradually enlarged. But any such transfer would be entirely one way.[46] The European Commission and the ECJ would be able to police the boundaries of the First Pillar and—as will be seen in Chapter 9 below—they have done so to good effect.

Declarations on Future Work

In a Declaration on Asylum attached to the Maastricht Treaty. the Member States stated that a priority for Third Pillar activity would be common action to harmonize aspects of asylum policy, in the light of the report on asylum drawn up at the request of the European Council meeting in Luxembourg in June 1991. They also declared that the Council would consider by the end of 1993, on the basis of a further report, whether to apply the passerelle provision in Article K.9 to asylum policy.

A further Declaration on Police Cooperation elaborated the somewhat general reference in Article K.1 (9) to 'police cooperation for the purpose of preventing and combating terrorism, unlawful drug-trafficking and other serious forms of international crime . . . in connection with the organization of a Union-wide system for exchanging information within a European Police Office (Europol)'. Chancellor Kohl of Germany had launched a proposal in 1990 for a European Police Office, able to respond to the increase in transborder crime which followed the collapse of the Soviet Union and the easing of border controls. He had hoped that the Maastricht Treaty would itself contain a commitment to the establishment of Europol. The Conclusions of the European Council in Luxembourg in June 1991 show an astonishing level of commitment at that stage to the project, recording a mandate for a

Treaty commitment to full establishment of a European Central Criminal Investigation Office (Europol) for those areas by 31 December 1991 at the latest.

[46] See Bieber (1994) at p 45.

Details to be laid down by unanimous decision of the Council. Gradual development of Europol functions: first of all only stations for exchange of information and experience (up to 31 December 1992), then in the second phase powers to act also within the Member States would be granted . . .[47]

It soon became clear, however, that the other Member States were not prepared to accept Europol except on the basis of a further round of intergovernmental negotiation on the detail of a convention which would clearly define the purposes, powers, and structure of the proposed agency.

In the meantime, the Declaration attached to the new Treaty set out areas where practical measures might be examined—coordination of investigations by national criminal and security authorities, common data bases, central analysis and assessment of police information, and further training. Many of these areas in the event had to await the Europol Convention, but the Declaration highlighted police cooperation as an urgent and important aspect of Third Pillar work.

New Working Structures for the Council

The new K4 Committee, described above, was parallel in terms of seniority and function to the Political Committee in the Second Pillar. It had the same relationship with COREPER, whose general responsibility to prepare the work of the Council was expressly safeguarded by the reference in Article K.4(1) to Article 151 of the European Community Treaty. In practice, the K4 Committee tried to resolve technical issues before a question passed through COREPER to the Council of Interior and Justice Ministers. COREPER would not generally reopen technical aspects, but might raise cross-pillar problems or political aspects before submitting the dossier to the Council for decision.

Below the K4 Committee, the Council reorganized work into three sectors: immigration and asylum; police and customs cooperation; judicial cooperation. For each of these sectors a Steering Group was appointed to monitor progress and each year to propose a work programme to the K4 Committee. These Steering Groups replaced the old Working Groups (Trevi, Immigration, Judicial Cooperation, and Customs Mutual Assistance). Each Steering Group had five or six Working Groups under it.[48] Further to complicate this five-tier structure of authority, a few of the old groups, such as CIREA (Centre for Information, Discussion and Exchange on Asylum), CIREFI (Centre for Information, Discussion and Exchange on the Crossing of Frontiers and Immigration) and the

---

[47] Bull EC 1991-6 point 1.38 (Annex I to Conclusions); Anderson et al (eds) (1995) pp 48–9·
[48] For a more detailed account of what is described as 'layered centralisation' see den Boer (1998) at pp 8–16.

Horizontal Group on Data Processing continued in an independent orbit. When CIREA was first proposed in 1991, it was argued that as a clearing house carrying out administrative functions for exchange of information on national laws, cases, policies, and statistics which would not itself take decisions, 'it should not be anchored in a formal legal way within the EC organisation.'[49] In setting up CIREFI in December 1992, Ministers also took the view that it should be a free-standing mechanism for exchange of information and should not be absorbed into the Council bodies to be set up when the Maastricht Treaty entered into force.[50]

The new structures were to some extent an improvement on the old, but by comparison with the well-understood three-layer system within the First Pillar (Council, COREPER, Working Groups) they formed an impenetrable labyrinth.

The Ratification of the Maastricht Treaty

The national parliamentary and judicial procedures which led, after nearly two years' delay, to the ratification of the Maastricht Treaty were described at the end of the previous chapter, with particular emphasis there on consideration of the Second Pillar. It may be regarded as a tribute to the political sensitivity of those who constructed the Third Pillar on a basis which did little more than formalize and restructure existing intergovernmental practices that during those prolonged and bitter debates and litigation in several Member States little was said about the new Third Pillar.

In the United Kingdom the European Communities (Amendment) Act 1993 excluded Title VI of the Treaty on European Union which formed the new Third Pillar, along with Title V forming the Second Pillar, from the provisions to be given the status of 'European Community Treaties'. This made clear their purely international character. Those parts of the Treaty would be ratified by the executive branch of the Government under prerogative powers and, together with any new obligations which might be generated under their provisions, would have in UK law only the status of any other unincorporated treaty. The position was explained to the UK Parliament and aroused no particular controversy.[51]

The German Constitutional Court in *Brunner v. European Union Treaty*[52] also stressed that cooperation in home and justice affairs would remain on

---

[49] Presidency Memorandum to Asylum Group, 7 October 1991, printed in Statewatch texts (1997) p 67. The decision to establish CIREA was taken in June 1992: see Statewatch texts (1997) pp 68–9.

[50] Memorandum by Ad Hoc Group on Immigration to Ministers, printed in Statewatch texts (1997) p 83.

[51] See Denza (1994a).   [52] [1994] 1 CMLR 57.

an intergovernmental basis. Any acts which the Council might adopt under the Third Pillar would not have direct effect in Member States or take precedence over national law and so could not undermine the constitutional rights of German citizens. Justice and home affairs had not been placed within the supranational decision-making structure of the European Communities. It followed that:

the protection of basic rights provided by the Constitution is not displaced by supra-national law that could claim precedence . . . In this respect the position is no different from that with a traditional international convention: in so far as its internal implementation would infringe constitutional rights it is prohibited by constitutional law.

It was clear from Article K.9 that even simplified transfer of parts of Justice and Home Affairs to European Community jurisdiction was dependent on prior ratification by Member States.[53]

If the Chancellor of Germany was in the vanguard of proposals to place police cooperation, as well as immigration and asylum policy, within the Community legal order, the German Constitutional Court was at the rear. It was an important consideration in the collective decision to develop the intergovernmental methods that individuals would not thereby be deprived of recourse to national courts and authorities or indeed of their remedies under the European Convention on Human Rights. Of major importance in this context was Article F of the Maastricht Treaty, which began:

1. The Union shall respect the national identities of its Member States, whose systems of government are founded on the principles of democracy.
2. The Union shall respect fundamental rights, as guaranteed by the European Convention for the Protection of Human Rights and Fundamental Freedoms signed in Rome on 4 November 1950 and as they result from the constitutional traditions common to the Member States, as general principles of Community law.'[54]

First Appraisals

Even before the Third Pillar was formally unveiled on the entry into force of the Maastricht Treaty, its architecture had been heavily criticized. By comparison with the Second Pillar, which codified practices refined over two decades, the Third Pillar bore signs of some hasty jerry-building.

[53] [1994] 1 CMLR 57, paras [16]–[22], [66]–[69]. For strong criticism of the judgment see Meyring (1997).
[54] See Twomey (1994) p 49.

Areas where competence was split between the First and the Third Pillars too often reflected political compromise rather than principle, there was uncertainty over the crucial question of the legal effect, and even the correct title, of the new instruments and an excessive reliance on international conventions which would require twelve—and soon fifteen—national ratifications to become legally binding. Judicial control, even of those conventions, was made dependent on uniformity of political commitment to the ECJ. As with the Second Pillar, however, it was clear by the end of the process of ratification of the Maastricht Treaty, that the Third Pillar broadly reflected the extent of public and parliamentary readiness at that stage to integrate asylum, immigration, police, and judicial cooperation into the EU.[55]

---

[55] For a contrary view from the Netherlands Parliament see Curtin (1993) at p 20.

4

CFSP Achievements and Weaknesses

The Conduct of the External Relations of a State

Before trying to evaluate the CFSP it is first necessary to describe what it is. It must be sharply contrasted with the foreign and security policy of a single State. A sovereign State is by definition responsible for the conduct of the totality of its external relations. It is legally constrained only by customary international law and by treaty obligations which it has inherited or assumed. It is not required to have objectives for its foreign and security policy. States have generally regarded the principal purpose of their foreign policy as being the pursuit of enlightened self-interest. Lord Palmerston, writing in 1856 to Lord Clarendon, explained British policy thus: 'When people ask me . . . for what is called a policy, the only answer is that we mean to do what may seem to be best, upon each occasion as it arises, making the Interests of Our Country one's guiding principle.'[1]

Defence of the physical, political, and religious character, of the State has been the first imperative. Spreading the political, religious, or cultural values of the State, in the case of the more powerful or enterprising States came second. Achievement of a stable world order—whether based on balance of power, on empire, or on collective security—has become a primary purpose of foreign policy for most States only relatively recently. It is probably correct to regard the pursuit of a stable world order as a particularly enlightened form of self-interest.

The formation of a State's foreign policy comes about as a result of a vast and continuous human enterprise. Even a small State with limited external interests will have at its disposal experts in diplomacy, history, economics, trading relations, and international law. From its overseas diplomatic and consular missions and its representations to international organizations there arrives every day a flood of information, analysis, demands for action or reaction to situations, events, and problems in dozens of other capitals. Precedents and advice are supplied when a foreign minister is asked for a decision. Decisions—even if they are decisions to abstain or to remain silent—must be taken across the board.

The foreign and security relations of a single sovereign State, moreover, are not merely a matter of attitudes, expressions of opinion and intent.

[1] Quotation from Temperley and Penson (1938) p 88. See also Kissinger (1994) pp 95–7.

These may constitute the 'policy', but they are supported by a range of powerful instruments. The State by its nature has international legal personality; it may conclude treaties, become a member of international organizations, send and receive diplomatic and consular missions, defend its external interests by domestic legislation and its physical and political integrity by armies and weapons. By exploiting its natural and human resources it has money at its disposal which may be used for external as well as internal purposes.

Satow, distinguishing diplomacy from the conduct of foreign policy, says:

But foreign policy is formulated by governments, not by diplomatists. In order to carry out its policy, a government will need to manage and adjust its international relations by applying different forms of pressure. How successful these pressures prove will greatly depend on the real power behind them.[2]

Allen, defining national foreign policy, says:

Foreign policy is not just about diplomacy and negotiation, which are best seen as means. Foreign policy is primarily about the definition of ends, or objectives, and only then about deciding how to pursue them . . . Foreign policy, therefore, is best seen as an attempt to design, manage and control the external activities of a state so as to protect and advance agreed and reconciled objectives.[3]

The position of a State conducting its foreign relations may thus be summed up in the words of the British music hall song of the Boer War era:

> We don't want to fight, but by jingo if we do
> We've got the ships, we've got the men, we've got the money too.

What is the Common Foreign and Security Policy?

The CFSP is not an attempt to replace the conduct by the Member States of their foreign relations. It has already been stressed and must be repeated that such a replacement would imply the end of the existence of the Member States as separate sovereign States. The CFSP is a *common* foreign policy and not a *single* foreign policy. It is a *policy* only, and when first established it was supported by hardly any of the tools for its formation and for its implementation which have been described above.

First, the European Union, not being a sovereign State, can act only under the powers conferred on it by treaty. It has no general or inherent power to conduct its own external relations. The common foreign and security policy was given objectives by Article J.1 of the Maastricht Treaty. These are wide-ranging and remarkably similar to those which it is suggested above

---

[2] *Satow (1979)* 1.3.   [3] Allen (1998) at p 44.

are the objectives of a State's foreign policy. They begin with the defensive objectives—to safeguard the common values, fundamental interests, and independence of the Union and to strengthen the security of the Union. They continue with the objectives concerned with the export of Union values—preserving peace and security in accordance with the UN Charter, the Helsinki Final Act, and the Paris Charter. They conclude with the objectives directed to a stable world order—promoting international cooperation, developing democracy, the rule of law, and respect for human rights.[4]

Secondly, when one turns to the instruments which may support an agreed Union policy the contrast becomes very sharp. The Union was not given international legal personality or treaty-making power by the Maastricht Treaty. Whereas the European Community, the European Coal and Steel Community, and the European Atomic Energy Agency may under prescribed procedures conclude treaties within their areas of competence and be admitted as members of international organizations where constitutional procedures and political circumstances permit, the Member States at the Intergovernmental Conference in 1991 rejected specific proposals that the Union should be given international legal personality. The Union was said to have an international identity—a political personality which did not however open the way to the assumption in its own right of new bilateral or multilateral rights and obligations.[5] The Council acting under CFSP powers may since the entry into force of the TEU impose new internal obligations on the Member States, but these are international legal obligations of limited scope and efficacy and they are not enforceable through the European Court of Justice.

The Union did not as such maintain diplomatic and consular relations. The European Community sends and receives numerous delegations with powers of representation and negotiation limited to the competence of the three Communities. On foreign policy matters outside these areas the Member States—though increasingly sharing premises, information, and functions—continue to maintain separate diplomatic and consular representation. The Presidency acted on behalf of the Union in non-member countries where this was necessary to implement agreed policies.[6] The Union has no Secretariat. The officials working to serve the objectives of the CFSP are employed by one of the institutions of the Union: the Council, the Commission, or the European Parliament. Their numbers and their status were substantially increased with the entry into force of the

---

[4] Koskenniemi (1998) at p 28, is critical of the formulation of the objectives of the CFSP in the Maastricht Treaty as being abstract and requiring more precise definition by the Member States.

[5] See Wessel (1997); Neuwahl (1998); Cremona (1998). This question is further considered in Chapter 5 below.

[6] See Hansard HC Debs 23 March 1994, WA col 290–1.

Maastricht Treaty,[7] but their numbers as well as the information at their collective disposal still fall well short of what is available to the larger Member States individually. Their role is in effect to contribute to the formation and implementation by the separate institutions of the common foreign policy. They cannot yet aspire to the cohesion, tradition, and single-minded loyalty which in the case of a national diplomatic service has been forged over many years of working in the interest of a single nation.[8]

There are no ships or men to defend the physical integrity of the Union. Not only was the control of military ships, aircraft, arms, munitions, and war material left firmly in the hands of the Member States, but Article 223 of the EC Treaty expressly permitted a Member State to 'take such measures as it considers necessary for the protection of the essential interests of its security which are connected with the production of or trade in arms . . .'. The Maastricht Treaty when it admitted into the CFSP 'all questions related to the security of the Union' left a common defence policy as a mere eventuality for the Union. Western European Union was 'requested' to elaborate and implement Union decisions with defence implications.[9] A common defence was envisaged as something for the future.

As to money, the European Union was not by the Maastricht Treaty given its own financial resources or even a separate budget made up of obligatory contributions from the Member States. To finance actions agreed under its common policy it had to borrow either from the budget of the European Communities or from the Member States. Under Article J.11 of the Maastricht Treaty, administrative expenditure was to be charged to the budget of the European Communities. As regards the much more significant matter of operational expenditure, the Council could decide to charge it to the European Communities' budget, but only by unanimous vote. Failing such a decision, the Council could decide to charge the Member States. France, for example, paid the expenses of the Inaugural Conference on the Stability Pact which resulted from an initiative by the French Prime Minister, M. Balladur.[10] Charging costs to the Member States did not require unanimity, but where several Member States were involved it did require agreement on the scale of contribu-

---

[7] See Declaration on Practical Arrangements in the Field of the Common Foreign and Security Policy, attached to the Maastricht Treaty; Morgan (1994). Following the entry into force of the Maastricht Treaty the EPC Secretariat was formed into a CFSP Unit of the Council Secretariat. A seconded Ambassador was supported by twelve seconded diplomats and by twelve permanent Council Secretariat staff. Hansard HC Debs 14 February 1994 WA col 556.

[8] See Cameron (1998*a*) at p 56: 'Member States inevitably approach problems from a national perspective whilst the Council has neither the experience nor the critical mass of officials to undertake new tasks in CFSP.'

[9] Article J.4 and Declarations on Western European Union by the States Members of the Western European Union and also of the European Union, attached to the Maastricht Treaty.

[10] See Edwards (1993) at p 500.

tions. This formula for financing in Article J.11 proved to be highly divisive. The lack of automatic financial cover for decisions taken under the Second Pillar either led to prolonged wrangling in the Council before a decision could be finalized or even prevented action within an appropriate timescale. Member States were aware that it was constitutionally inappropriate that intergovernmental action should be financed from the European Community's resources, but on the other hand they were unwilling or unable to find the money from national resources.

Even agreement in principle did not mean that actual funds would be readily available. If the decision was in favour of recourse to the Communities' budget, funds would require to be voted by agreement between the European Parliament and the Council of Ministers under the lengthy procedure set out in the EC Treaty. This had the advantage of involving the European Parliament, but might risk reopening compromises agreed in the Council if the Parliament sought to use its budgetary powers with the real object of challenging the policy. Recourse to financing by Member States implied that funds would have to be approved through national budgetary procedures. National parliaments were equally likely to question the policy or the method of allocating the financial burden between the Member States, or simply to delay the provision of funds. Monar gives a devastating account of the wrangles and improprieties over financing which clouded the first CFSP actions undertaken under the Maastricht Treaty provisions. He concluded that: '. . . while the member states are still reluctant to use the EC it has become obvious that as a collective they are not able to provide adequate financing for any CFSP action going beyond normal diplomatic means.'[11]

The CFSP, in addition to lacking most of the tools available to a State for the elaboration and implementation of its foreign relations, lacks any international legal basis for imposing order, democracy, or sound government practices on non-Member States. It is constrained by the general rules of customary international law, in particular the prohibition of intervention in the internal affairs of other sovereign States. It has no treaty-based powers to mediate or arbitrate in the settlement of disputes involving non-Member States. Because it has at present no military enforcement capacity, unlike NATO or similar organizations for regional collective security, it cannot take collective action, whether under the inherent powers of self-defence of the Member States or under authority delegated by the Security Council of the UN.[12]

---

[11] Monar (1997) at p 48. See also Fink-Hooijer (1994) at pp 184–5; Ryba (1995) at pp 19–21; Macleod, Hendry, and Hyett (1996) p 423; Regelsberger and Wessels (1996) at pp 40–1; Hill (1998) at pp 25–6.

[12] See Sarooshi (1999) ch 6.

Finally, the CFSP must be contrasted with the First Pillar of the EU and, to a lesser extent, with the Third Pillar in that the adoption of legal instruments—whether common positions, joint actions, European Community or national measures—is not the primary objective. The sharing of information and analysis and the development of shared understanding and a shared approach among the Member States may be of great value in a particular context. The outcome may not be capable of evaluation in terms of pages in the Official Journal and it may indeed take the form of a masterly inactivity.[13] If the outcome of a particular approach or initiative is successful, the situation may disappear from public attention without any credit being given to the CFSP. Failure may be due to obstinacy or intransigence of governments or persons outside the control of the European Union. The blame may then be laid on the inadequacy of the CFSP even though it cannot be shown that a different or even a more effective policy would have altered the situation.

To sum up the nature of the Second Pillar formed by the Maastricht Treaty before attempting evaluation, it is a unique experiment by EU Member States in forming a harmonious approach to the wider world. The voices of the Member States are to sing in harmony but not necessarily in unison. Where sweet singing in the choir is not enough, the necessary tools, whether carrot or stick, must be borrowed from the European Community or from the Member States.[14] While the music itself—the common policy—has to be agreed unanimously, there is room for solo singing—delegated action—by some voices only and even for qualified majority voting in taking implementing decisions. The Member States take it in turns to conduct the choir, but the powers of the conductor are very limited. No singer can be forced to sing, and a determined singer can put a stop altogether to a song whose tune he dislikes.

Specific Actions: Russia

The conduct of relations between the European Union and Russia in the early years of its newly-established and fragile democracy was a critical test of the CFSP. During the crisis in Moscow in September and October 1993—shortly before the entry into force of the Maastricht Treaty—two statements were issued by the Community and its Member States acting

[13] On this see Regelsberger and Wessels (1996) at p 31: 'Unlike internal market legislation foreign policy is also discretionary: action has to be decided on quickly according to specific situations, not by a long deliberation for systematic cases.'

[14] See Article C of Title I of the Maastricht Treaty: '. . . The Union shall in particular ensure the consistency of its external activities as a whole in the context of its external relations, security, economic, and development policies. The Council and the Commission shall be responsible for ensuring such consistency. They shall ensure the implementation of these policies, each in accordance with its respective powers.'

under European Political Cooperation expressing support for the process of democratic reform, upholding the authority of President Yeltsin and underlining the importance of the elections which were to take place in December. Free elections, the statements made clear, would allow the Russian people clearly to determine their own future.[15]

The Maastricht Treaty entered into force on 1 November 1993, and within a few days the Council of Ministers adopted the first CFSP joint action—on the despatch of an EU mission to observe the forthcoming parliamentary elections in Russia. The principle of this joint action had already been agreed at a special European Council meeting on 29 October. By the elections the Russian people adopted a draft Constitution offering a legal framework for political and economic reform. In December 1993 an EU statement recorded that the observers had confirmed that voting in the first Russian general elections held on the basis of a multiparty system and universal suffrage 'took place by and large in accordance with democratic principles'. This statement also set out the various other strands of the Union's efforts to assist reforms in Russia: the proposed Partnership and Cooperation Agreement (a mixed agreement between the European Community and its Member States on the one hand and Russia on the other), the technical assistance programmes (TACIS) funded through the European Community budget, and assistance for the new democratic Russian institutions.[16]

Over the following months various actions by the European Community acting under First Pillar powers, by the Member States, and by the European Bank for Reconstruction and Development (EBRD) took forward this policy approach by all possible means. A Joint Declaration agreed on 9 December 1993 by the European Community and Russia stressed Europe's backing for democracy and economic reform in Russia and set out a framework for continuing political dialogue.[17] The EBRD set up a credit line totalling $15 million with the International Moscow Bank to finance joint ventures and, together with the International Finance Corporation, set up an investment fund for private sector investment. The European Community allocated aid for displaced persons and for medical aid and poverty relief in Moscow.

On 24 June 1994 the Partnership and Cooperation Agreement between the European Community and its Member States and Russia was signed in Corfu. The Agreement set out a comprehensive and long-term framework for political, economic, and trade relations between Russia and the European Union. Because of the long delay due to the need for ratification

[15] EPC Press Releases 92 and 96/93 of 22 September and 4 October 1993.
[16] Council Decision 93/604/CFSP, OJ L286, 20.11.1993; EU Press Release P 114/93, (16 December 1993).
[17] Bull EC 12-1993 point 1.4.13.

by all the national parliaments, it was envisaged that there should be an interim agreement between the EC and Russia containing the trade provisions which were within exclusive Community competence.[18] In the event this was delayed because of the situation in Chechnya, where European Ministers continued to call for a ceasefire and efforts towards a political solution, and to complain of breaches of humanitarian law during the fighting.

Elsewhere however there were more positive developments—a Presidency press statement on 31 August 1994 welcomed the withdrawal of Russian troops from Estonia and Latvia, in accordance with the Helsinki Final Declaration of 1992.[19] For the first time President Yeltsin was fully involved in political discussions at the 20th Western Economic Summit. In this context Russia agreed to cooperate with international financial institutions, stabilize its currency, consolidate economic reform and to improve the legal and institutional framework for investment. The flow of money from Europe continued with EBRD loans granted for clean-up of oil slicks and repair of a damaged pipeline, and from the European Community Humanitarian Office humanitarian relief following the earthquake on Sakhalin island.

The Stability Pact

Concurrently with these bilateral actions aimed at consolidating democracy and economic reform in Russia, the European Union was working on the basis of a proposal by the French Prime Minister, M. Balladur, towards a multilateral security and stability pact involving European republics of the former Soviet Union as well as the US and Canada. The objective was to provide a negotiating framework and guarantees for more limited and specific agreements on the status of minority populations, ethnic problems, and border disputes. The European Council on 21 and 22 June, 29 October and on 10 and 11 December 1993 endorsed the plan and called for adoption of a joint action to implement it. The joint action adopted by the Council on 20 December 1993 provided that the European Union would convene a conference in Paris in 1994 and would invite 'the countries principally concerned by the initiative, the countries immediately neighbouring the countries principally concerned, States likely to make a particular contribution to the initiative, countries with an interest in stability in Europe by virtue of their defence commitments and countries which have association agreements with the Union . . .'.

[18] Bull EC 6-1994, point 1.3.30.
[19] Bull EC 7/8-1994, point 1.3.8; Edwards (1994) at p 550; Freestone (1993) at p 417. A timetable for Russian troop withdrawal from Lithuania had already been agreed in 1992, and withdrawal was completed in August 1993.

The Conference on Security and Cooperation in Europe (CSCE), the Council of Europe, WEU, NATO, and the UN were also invited to participate. This helped to dissipate some of the earlier anxieties about the European Union initiative expressed on the one hand by the US, which maintained that it should be for NATO to take the lead in issues relating to European security, and on the other hand by Russia, which argued that the opportunity should be taken to build up CSCE capabilities.[20]

Article 2 of the joint action set out the object of the conference and provided that the agreements and related complementary arrangements would constitute the basis for a stability pact to be forwarded to the CSCE which would act as its guardian. More detailed arrangements on procedure and the negotiating process were in reports approved by the European Council a few days earlier.[21]

The European Union played a central role in the negotiations which took place within the framework of the Paris Conference, chairing regional round tables of Baltic, and of Central and East European States. In March 1995 the Stability Pact was adopted in Paris, together with about one hundred bilateral agreements which formed its substantive core. Perhaps the most significant was a new Treaty on Good Neighbourliness and Friendly Cooperation between Hungary and Slovakia. The Council of Ministers noted that this was the 'successful culmination of the joint action by the Union under the CFSP. This initiative should help encourage the putting into practice of the principles and undertakings laid down at the United Nations, the OCSE and the Council of Europe.'[22] For those States which had aspirations towards European Union membership, the process of regional collaboration set in motion would greatly help them to fulfil the political conditions for accession which the European Council had laid down. Although the political responsibility for supervising the Stability Pact passed to the CSCE as planned, the European Community through the PHARE programme continued to support many projects which contributed to its aims. As Ueta expressed it: 'No diplomatic exercise other than the Stability Pact evolved so dramatically from scepticism to success.'[23]

The adoption of the Stability Pact and the end of the fighting in Chechnya opened the way for signature in July 1995 of the interim agreement between the EC and Russia. This gave most favoured nation treatment to imports from Russia (other than textiles, steel, and nuclear

---

[20] Ueta (1997) at pp 95, 97–8.

[21] Council Decisions 93/728/CFSP, OJ L339/1, 31.12.1993, 94/158/CFSP OJ L70/1 12.3.1994 and 94/367/CFSP, OJ L165/2, 1.7.1994; Edwards (1993), at p 504; Cook and Sands (1995) at p 227.

[22] Council Conclusions 29 May 1995; Bull EC 3-1995 point 1.4.4 and point 2.2.1, 5-1995 point 1.4.70.

[23] Ueta (1997) at p 92.

materials). Russia assumed the obligation to phase in national protection of intellectual property rights and to give protection from distortion arising from state aids.[24]

In November 1995 the Council of Ministers adopted a Strategy on EU/Russian Relations. This emphasized that

Good relations between the EU and a democratic Russia are essential to stability in Europe. The EU is therefore committed to establishing a substantial partnership with Russia in order to promote the democratic and economic reform process, to enhance respect for human rights, to consolidate peace, stability and security in order to avoid new dividing lines in Europe and to achieve the full integration of Russia into the community of free and democratic nations. The PCA provides a firm basis on which to build such relations with Russia.

The Strategy set out practical measures towards these objectives. The European contribution to Russia's democratic reforms was to include promotion of an independent judicial system, reinforcement of freedom of the media, monitoring of parliamentary and presidential elections, and support for Russian accession to the Council of Europe. Economic cooperation would aim at integration of Russia into the international economy and its admission to the World Trade Organization as soon as possible, application by Russia of internationally formulated safety principles for nuclear installations, improvement of environmental protection, consolidation of the legal framework concerning economic activities, and approximation of legislation with a view to possible establishment of a free trade area between the EU and Russia. There would be increased cooperation in Justice and Home Affairs. The Union would 'ensure transparency in Western European security decisions, especially those involving enlargement, in order to take into account Russia's concerns'. Russia was to be encouraged to exploit evolving channels for dialogue with NATO and WEU and to develop regional cooperation arrangements with Central and East European countries while the EU would contribute to this in the framework of the Stability Pact. Foreign policy measures would include political consultation at the highest political level, exchanges on foreign policy formulation and between legal departments, and enhancement of the Organization for Security and Cooperation in Europe (OCSE)[25] as a forum for political dialogue with Russia.

The European Council in December 1995 endorsed this strategy and confirmed their support for Russia's accession to the Council of Europe. They noted that the elections held in Russia that month were a 'major step

---

[24] European Council Conclusions in Bull EC 6-1995 point 1.14. Text of agreement in OJ L68/1, 15.3.1990. Smith (1998a) at p 77, argues that the decision was premature.

[25] In 1995 the Conference on Security and Cooperation in Europe (CSCE) was established on a more formal basis as the Organization for Security and Cooperation in Europe (OSCE).

towards consolidating constitutional institutions and anchoring democratic principles in the country's political life'.[26]

Evaluation of Policy towards Russia

In June 1992, during the ratification of the Maastricht Treaty, the European Council in Lisbon approved a report on general guidelines for joint action under the Treaty. The specific objectives were to be

—strengthening democratic principles and democratic institutions, and respect for human and minority rights;
—promoting regional political stability and contributing to the creation of political and/or economic frameworks that encourage regional cooperation or moves towards regional or sub-regional integration;
—contributing to the prevention and settlement of conflicts;
—contributing to more effective international coordination in dealing with emergency situations;
—strengthening existing cooperation in issues of international interest such as the fight against arms proliferation, terrorism and traffic in illicit drugs;
—promoting and supporting good government.[27]

The various instruments which have been described above—strategy, common positions, joint actions—adopted in the early years of the CFSP to deal with relations with Russia were clearly aimed at all of these specific objectives. They paid due regard to the principle of subsidiarity—which, in this context, may mean choosing another international organization as the most appropriate forum for implementing action. They showed respect for the proper functions of NATO, WEU, the Council of Europe, and the CSCE (later the OSCE).

The principal CFSP texts were clear and precise in setting out the obligations of the Member States and, unlike European Political Cooperation declarations, they were published in the Official Journal. Because common positions and joint actions would now impose international legal obligations on the Member States, legal advisers to the Council and to Member States became more closely involved with their drafting and this led to greater precision in the texts. Although Article J of the Maastricht Treaty was rightly criticized for failing to draw a clear distinction between common positions and joint actions, the distinction soon became clear in the light of Council practice.[28] There was effective coordination between

---

[26] Council Conclusions of 20/21 November 1995 in doc 11716/95 (Press 328-G). European Council Conclusions in Bull EC 12-1995 point 1.30 and Annex 9.
[27] Bull EC 1992-6, point 1.18.
[28] See Edwards (1994), at pp 546–7; Koskenniemi (1998) at pp 31–5; Ryba (1995) at p 17;

Second Pillar determination of policy and First Pillar measures such as the Partnership and Cooperation Agreement. By the end of 1995 the European Community had concluded Partnership and Cooperation Agreements with ten of the Republics of the Commonwealth of Independent States and Europe Agreements with Estonia, Latvia, and Lithuania.

On these objective criteria the European Union's implementation of the provisions and the deployment of the legal instruments made available under the Maastricht Treaty can be regarded as a success. Russia, during these dark and difficult days of transition, did not further fragment, lapse into anarchy, or revert to Communism, and the sustained, constructive, and critical support from the European Union must to some extent have contributed to this outcome. The European Parliament, however, in evaluating overall progress in implementing the common foreign and security policy in 1995, applied both institutional criteria such as the continued application of consensus in decision-making and subjective criteria such as whether the objective of asserting the Union's identity on the international scene was being met. They concluded that the progress sought by the authors of the Maastricht Treaty had not been achieved, although they acknowledged that 'as far as conventional bilateral external relations are concerned, the results have clearly been positive'. But it can hardly be regarded as a mark of the success of CFSP action that some Member States feel themselves obliged to vote against it. Nor should the assertion of the Union's identity on the international scene be regarded as a major objective in its own right. The assertion of Union identity should rather be seen as a means to more effective defence and assertion of common European interests.[29]

Specific Actions: Landmines

The European Union action on landmines is an excellent example of a foreign policy initiative with clear and precise objectives and in which the Council, acting under the Second Pillar, made effective use within the international context of the various legal tools available to them. In 1995 a UN Review Conference was planned to amend the 1980 Geneva Convention on Prohibitions or Restrictions on the Use of Certain Conventional Weapons which may be Deemed to be Excessively Injurious

---

Peers (1996c) at p 615: '. . . Joint Actions have consistently been used to organize the physical presence of EU staff, whether convoying aid, acting as envoys, administering towns or overseeing elections. Common Positions have consistently been used to establish general policy guidelines.'

[29] EP Doc EN\PR\291\291192, Report of the Committee on Foreign Affairs, Security and Defence Policy, 5 February 1996; Fink-Hooijer (1994), especially pp 178–84; Crowe (1998); Lang and Weber (2000). Lisbon European Council Conclusions in Bull EC 1992–6, point 1.18. A more negative assessment of policy is provided by Zielonka (1998a) at p 131. Contrast with Binyon in *The Times*, 7 January 2002, 'Booming Russia has a happy Christmas'.

or to have Indiscriminate Effects.[30] The EU Member States, who would be separately represented at the UN Conference, coordinated their overall approach within the Political Committee. There were to be three aspects: first, a European Union moratorium on export of anti-personnel mines; secondly, diplomatic efforts to secure changes to the 1980 Convention to extend it to armed conflicts within a country and to strengthen the prohibition on transfer of mines; thirdly, practical and financial assistance for international mine-clearance efforts.[31]

On 12 May 1995 the Council adopted a Decision on a joint action under Articles J.3 and J.11 of the Maastricht Treaty. Article 1 reflected the three agreed objectives set out in the previous paragraph. Article 2 required Member States to impose a moratorium on exports of anti-personnel mines in the light of the UN General Assembly resolutions. Control on exports of mines, which are clearly military in character, could not have been imposed under EC Treaty powers, but in Article 2 the Council laid directly on the Member States international law obligations which had to be given effect under national legal powers. Member States were permitted to apply moratoria broader in scope. Article 3 required Member States not yet bound by the 1980 Convention and its Protocol 2 (the Landmines Protocol) to 'take the necessary steps to become parties'. Whether the effect of this obligation was to remove the discretion normally permitted to a national parliament in domestic ratification procedures might be arguable. The Article also set out a binding common position on the lines described above for Member States to follow in the Review Conference, and required the EU (that is, all its institutions) to work actively to promote the universal nature of the Convention. The Presidency in particular was required to carry out démarches to advocate the common approach. Article 4 required Member States to participate in the Conference. The Union was to contribute funds for the organization of the Conference and also to the UN Voluntary Trust Fund for Assistance for Mine Clearance. Both contributions were to be charged to the European Communities' budget. Article 5 referred to European Community activities in mine clearance, but the Council could not of course impose any obligation in the context of a CFSP decision on the EC or on the Commission. Article 6 envisaged further mine-clearance assistance to specific third countries, and set out parameters for further Council decisions—which were to be taken by unanimity. There was a reservation of the right to ask the WEU to contribute to the implementation of specific actions of this kind.[32]

The European Parliament Committee on Foreign Affairs, Security and Defence Policy in a Report adopted a few days later welcomed the

[30] UKTS No 105 (1996) Cm 3497.
[31] Written Question E-421/95 to the Council, 20 February 1995, [1995] OJ C175/41.
[32] Council Decision 95/170/CFSP, [1995] OJ L115/1.

Council's joint action, but considered that it did not go far enough. The Parliament argued that the joint action should have gone further by imposing a Europe-wide ban on production, stockpiling, and internal transfer and that Member States should in the Review Conference be calling for even stronger controls, in particular a new Protocol on blinding laser weapons.[33] On 10 September 1995, shortly before the opening of the Review Conference, the Council adopted a supplementary common position requiring the Member States to promote 'the adoption of an additional protocol to the 1980 Convention concerning blinding lasers which satisfies the humanitarian concern to avoid unnecessary suffering without limiting the legitimate military use of lasers'. A group of government experts had prepared a proposal on those lines which had been submitted to the Conference.[34]

An amended version of the Mines Protocol (Protocol II) was adopted by the Review Conference on 3 May 1996. The amended Protocol met the objectives set out in the EU's Joint Action: it applied to armed conflicts which were not of an international character; it strengthened the prohibition both on the use and on the transfer of anti-personnel mines; it made new provision for appropriate assistance in mine clearance.[35] Later international actions, including the Ottawa Declaration of 5 October 1996 and the Brussels Declaration of 27 June 1997, led to the adoption in September 1997 of the Oslo Convention on the Prohibition of the Use, Stockpiling, Production and Transfer of Anti-Personnel Mines and on their Destruction.[36] This imposes a total ban on anti-personnel mines and requires States Parties to destroy all mines in areas under their jurisdiction within ten years. The Convention entered into force in 1999 and all European Union Member States are Parties. By September 2000 there were over one hundred Parties to the Convention, though they did not include Russia, China, or the US.

There have been later Joint Actions by the Council to update the legislation on landmines.[37] Specific decisions have authorized the coordination, supervising, and training of mine clearance experts in Croatia, and requested the assistance of the WEU in implementing this particular action.[38]

Weapons Proliferation and Arms Control

A crucial objective of EU policy in the period following the end of the Cold War was the strengthening of the safeguards against proliferation of

[33] EP session document A4-0119/95 of 24 May 1995.
[34] Common Position 95/379/CFSP OJ L227/3, 22.9.1995.
[35] Misc No 2 (1997) Cm 3507.   [36] UKTS No 18 (1999), Cm 4308.
[37] Joint Action 96/588/CFSP OJ L260, 12.10.1996; replaced by Joint Action 97/817/CFSP, OJ L338 9.12.1997.
[38] Decisions 98/627/CFSP and 98/628 OJ L300/1 and OJ L300/2, 11.11.1998.

nuclear weapons. This involved encouraging and assisting Republics of the former Soviet Union which possessed nuclear weapons on their territories (Kazakhstan, Belarus, and Ukraine) to give them up to Russia to be disabled and decontaminated, and to accede to the Non-Proliferation Treaty[39] (NPT) as States not possessing nuclear weapons. It also meant lobbying in preparation for the Non-Proliferation Treaty Review and Extension Conference for indefinite extension of the Treaty.[40] There was a rational division of labour in organizing this lobbying exercise—Member States were allocated third countries with which they enjoyed special relations, though all diplomats used the same agreed arguments.

In September 1993 the European Community and its Member States congratulated Belarus on its accession to the NPT as a State not possessing nuclear weapons, and they urged Ukraine and Kazakhstan to follow its example, arguing that this was essential for their full integration into the international community.[41] Soon after the entry into force of the Maastricht Treaty the EU welcomed the decision by the Parliament of Kazakhstan to fulfil commitments regarding accession to the NPT as a non-nuclear State. In July 2000 it was reported that an international team of scientists detonated a controlled explosion which destroyed the last of Kazakhstan's test sites and effectively removed it from the list of nuclear weapon States.[42] For the Ukraine, the European Union in January 1994 welcomed the signing of a tripartite agreement between the US, Russia, and the Ukraine on the removal of all nuclear arms from Ukrainian territory, describing this as 'an important contribution to international security and stability'. They welcomed also President Kravchuk's reaffirmation in this context of Ukraine's commitment to accede to the NPT. The Common Position on objectives and priorities of the European Union towards Ukraine which was defined by the Council later in 1994 was in many respects—such as political dialogue and support for democratic development, economic stabilization, and reform and integration of Ukraine into the world economic order—closely similar to the strategy on relations with Russia. It differed, however, in including important provisions on assistance for the process of nuclear disarmament and accession to the NPT as a non-nuclear weapons State, development of a Partnership for Peace programme and dialogue with WEU, support for CSCE efforts to resolve tensions in the Crimea and early implementation of an action plan

---

[39] Treaty on the Non-Proliferation of Nuclear Weapons, signed in London, Moscow, and Washington in 1968, UKTS No 88 (1970), Cmnd 4474.

[40] For a sense of the concern over proliferation following the disintegration of the Soviet Union and the efforts of the UK together with its EC partners to counter the dangers, see House of Lords debate on Weapons of Mass Destruction, Hansard HL Debs 12 February 1992 col 731, especially Lord Arran winding up for the Government at cols 756–62.

[41] EPC Bull Doc. 93/383.

[42] EU P 116/93; *The Observer*, 30 July 2000; *The Times*, 31 July 2000.

on nuclear safety and reform of the energy sector which would lead to the closure of the Chernobyl nuclear reactors.[43]

The outcome of the NPT Review and Extension Conference was an indefinite extension—agreed without a vote—of the Non-Proliferation Treaty. The Conference agreed on Principles and Objectives for Nuclear Non-Proliferation and Disarmament which stated *inter alia* that universal adherence to the Treaty was an urgent priority. They also agreed on tighter monitoring of disarmament and strengthened the Treaty review process. The French Ambassador to the Conference welcomed the outcome as a major contribution towards international non-proliferation.[44] The assessment of Muller and van Dassen was that: 'The joint action was an outstanding success in that it first of all combined the efforts of member states towards a common goal, provoked activities that would otherwise most likely not have been undertaken, and made a discernible, significant contribution to the successful extension outcome.'[45]

The European Union has continued effective coordination on policy and tactics regarding non-proliferation of nuclear weapons. In 1997 it adopted a Joint Action on the Union's contribution to the promotion of transparency in nuclear-related export controls.[46] Under First Pillar powers, Euratom concluded additional Protocols to Agreements on Verification and on Safeguards. A new Common Position adopted in April 1998 set out agreed objectives in terms of lobbying and coordinating substantive policy for the preparatory work for the 2000 Review Conference of the Treaty.[47]

This recent successful coordination under CFSP powers may be contrasted with the outcome of the 1992 European Political Cooperation (EPC) decision to extend recognition as a State to North Korea in terms which assumed full compliance by North Korea with its commitments under the Non-Proliferation Treaty (to which it had acceded in 1985). As pointed out above in Chapter 2, the extension of recognition on terms going beyond the satisfaction of the criteria for statehood was a novel departure at least for the UK, and was open to the criticism that the recognizing States had no sanction in the event of failure to fulfil promises made by the new State in the context of recognition. In March 1993 North Korea

[43] EU Presidency Communique of 18 January 1994, P3/94; Council Decision 94/509/CFSP, OJ L205/1, 8.8.1994; Common Position 94/779/CFSP of 28 November 1994 [1994] OJ L313/1.

[44] European Report, 13 May 1995 p 10; Observations by the Secretary of State for Foreign and Commonwealth Affairs on the Report from the Foreign Affairs Committee on UK Policy on Weapons Proliferation and Arms Control in the Post-Cold War Era, Cm 2895.

[45] Muller and van Dassen (1997) at p 65. The Paper explains the great difficulties which were overcome in forging a common policy, given the wide variety of national positions among the Member States on nuclear weapons,

[46] Joint Action 97/288/CFSP, OJ L120/1, 12.3.1997.

[47] Common Position 98/289/CFSP OJ L 129/1, 30.4.1998.

withdrew from the NPT, to the dismay of EC Member States. The withdrawal was later reversed in the context of an Agreement with the US intended to lead to the supply of reactors to North Korea. Although North Korea attended the Conference on Review and Extension of the NPT, it withdrew before the end and announced that it had 'suspended' its participation in the Treaty.[48]

Dual-Use Goods

In pursuance of the same objective of preventing proliferation and diversion of weapons, particularly weapons of mass destruction, the EU elaborated parallel instruments under the First and Second Pillars to control the export of dual-use goods. Dual-use goods are items which may be used either for civil or for military purposes. These parallel instruments made use of all powers available under the TEU and were designed to ensure that Member States complied with wider international obligations regarding control of weapons.[49]

The ECJ had confirmed that the export of dual-use goods fell within the scope of the common commercial policy established under Article 113 of the EC Treaty. The Court however also accepted that Member States, who were ultimately responsible for the protection of their national security, were entitled to restrict intra-Community movement of dual-use goods under the public security provisions of Article 36 of the EC Treaty[50] and were also entitled to restrict export to non-Member States under the analogous exception contained in Article 11 of Regulation 2603/69[51] which established common rules for exports from the Community.[52] Article 223.1(b) entitled Member States to take necessary measures 'for the protection of its essential interests of its security which are connected with the production of or trade in arms, munitions and was material'. A list of items was drawn up for the purposes of Article 223.1(b), but it was never updated. In practice, uniformity regarding exports from Member States to non-Community countries was for many years the result of the COCOM system[53]

The COCOM system was terminated following the end of the Cold War. Member States continued however, to maintain national restrictions

---

[48] EPC Press Release P 56/93, 16 June1993; European Report 13 May 1995, p 10; Cm 2895 paras 1 and 7.

[49] Cm 2895, at para 23.   [50] Case C-367/89 *Aimé Richardt* [1991] ECR I-4621.

[51] [1969] OJ L324/25, amended by Council Regulation 3918/91, [1991] OJ L372/31.

[52] Case C-70/94 *Werner Industrie-Ausrüstungen v Germany* [1985] ECR I-3189; Case C-83/94 *Leifer* [1995] ECR I-3231.

[53] COCOM stood for the Co-ordinating Committee for Multilateral Export Controls. Because of the need for secrecy and rapid updating, the list of items whose export was controlled was not set out in a formal international agreement which would have required registration with the United Nations and publication.

which might be based on the threat of international terrorism, on commitments on non-proliferation of nuclear materials, or on sanctions imposed by the UN Security Council as well as on perceived military threat. The completion of the Community internal market and the end of systematic inspection of goods crossing internal Community borders made divergence between national restrictions highly unsatisfactory. It was discovered that precursors for chemical weapons had been exported from Germany to Libya and a dual-use item was discovered being exported from the UK to Iraq. One possible basis for coordination of controls among the Member States might have been Article 224 of the EC Treaty, which provided that:

Member States shall consult each other with a view to taking together the steps needed to prevent the functioning of the common market being affected by measures which a Member State may be called upon to take in the event of serious internal disturbances affecting the maintenance of law and order, in the event of war, serious international tension constituting a threat of war, or in order to carry out obligations it has accepted for the purpose of maintaining peace and international security.

This Article was, however, never regarded as constituting an adequate basis for Community legislation, or even as a justification for the systematic continuation of national export controls on strategic exports.[54]

Under the legislative scheme adopted in December 1994, a Council Regulation setting up a Community regime for the control of export of dual-use goods established the requirement of an authorization for export of dual-use goods on a list. Goods not on the list also required export authorization where the national authorities or the exporter had grounds for suspecting that they might be used for the development, production or maintenance of chemical, biological, or nuclear weapons. Member States were entitled to maintain or to introduce stricter measures, subject to notifying them to other Member States and to the Commission. Export authorizations were to be valid throughout the Community. Detailed rules for customs procedures, administrative cooperation, and control measures were also prescribed in the Regulation. A Coordinating Group of national representatives was to monitor the application of the Regulation, and Member States were to impose national sanctions by means of 'effective, proportionate and dissuasive penalties'.[55]

In response to sensitivities in a number of Member States about extension of Community competence, however, the actual list of dual-use goods, as well as permitted destinations and guidelines to be applied in

[54] See Stefanu and Xanthaki (1997), Emiliou (1996) at pp 57–9.
[55] Council Regulation 3381/94 OJ L367/1, 31.1.94, amended by Concil Regulation 837/95 OJ L90/1, 21.4.95.

issuing authorizations, was set out in a linked Council Decision on the basis of Article J.3 of the TEU. The Decision took the form of a CFSP joint action. Article 1 of the Decision provided, *inter alia*: 'This Decision and Council Regulation (EC) No. 3381/94 of 19 December 1994 setting up a Community regime for the control of exports of dual-use goods, constitute an integrated system involving, in accordance with their own powers, the Council, the Commission and the Member States.' Annex III to the Decision set out guidelines for issuing export authorizations. Member States were to take into account their commitments under international agreements on non-proliferation, their obligations under Security Council or other international sanctions, as well as considerations of national foreign and security policy, including criteria on export of conventional arms agreed by the European Council.[56]

This joint action prescribing guidelines for control of exports of dual-use goods brought some degree of uniformity into an important area of the Community's common commercial policy and underlined the determination of the EU to give effect to common international obligations and to implement an agreed approach to export of sensitive goods to destinations where they might pose a threat to European security. There was, however, strong criticism that the cross-pillar nature of the related measures undermined their purpose of effective control, and that the joint action added nothing to the existing legal commitments of the Member States. Koutrakos argued that the CFSP joint action, by failing to incorporate common criteria, deprived the Community measure of any degree of control of national authorities. 'National authorities are hence enabled to manipulate the control system established by Regulation 3381/94 to protect national exports and hence accommodate national concerns of an essentially economic nature. It follows that the legal protection of the individual exporter is at risk.'[57] The cross-pillar approach was also inconsistent with the clear statements of the ECJ that the foreign and security policy objectives of a trade measure do not exclude it from the scope of the common commercial policy. In June 2000 the Council—citing the Court's decisions among their reasons—adopted a new Regulation based on Article 133 of the EC Treaty which replaced the Regulation and the Joint Action of 1994.[58] Given the national sensitivities on the export of dual-use goods, the use of a Second Pillar measure in 1994 may, however, have had transitional value in enabling confidence to be established among export authorities and so paving the way for general acceptance of a more effective Community regime.

---

[56] Council Decision 94/942/CFSP, OJ L367/8, 31.12.94, amended by Decisions 95/127 [1995] OJ L90/2; 95/128 [1995] OJ L90/3; 97/419 [1997] OJ L178/1; 97/633 [1997] OJ L266/1. See Emiliou (1996) at pp 61–4; Cornish (1997) at pp 81–8.

[57] Koutrakos (2001) ch 6 and 7, at p 105.   [58] See Chapter 8 below.

Arms Exports

In May 1998 the Member States reached political agreement on a Code of Conduct on arms exports. The Code, which was formally adopted by the Council on 8 June 1998, set out common criteria to be used by national authorities determining applications for export licences. The central principle to be applied was 'to prevent the export of equipment which might be used for internal repression or international aggression, or contribute to regional instability'. The Code explicitly recognized that States had a right to transfer the means of self-defence, consistent with the right of self-defence in the UN Charter.

The seven detailed criteria elaborated earlier criteria agreed at the Luxembourg and Lisbon European Councils in 1991 and 1992.[59] They included:

1. respect for international commitments of Member States (for example the UN Charter and the NPT);
2. respect for human rights in the country of destination, having regard to the risk of internal repression and to serious violations of human rights established by the UN, the Council of Europe, or the EU;
3. the existence of internal tensions or armed conflicts in the country of destination;
4. preservation of regional peace, security, and stability;
5. national security of the Member States and of their allies and friends;
6. the attitude of the destination country to terrorism, the nature of its alliances and its respect for international law;
7. the risk of diversion or re-export and compatibility of the weapons with the technical and economic capacity of the country of destination.

Where a Member State refused an application, it was to notify other Member States. If a second Member State wished to grant a licence for an identical transaction, it should first consult with the Member State which had already refused one. A decision by the second State to grant a licence following consultations was to be notified to the first Member State, with detailed reasons. Each year there would be a review of the Code and a Report on its operation. The criteria and the consultation procedure would apply to dual-use goods specified in the relevant Council Decision where the end-user might be the armed forces or internal security forces of the

---

[59] For an account of the background to the formulation of these principles, which can be traced in particular to the concern expressed after it emerged that European States had supplied Saddam Hussein with weapons used against them during the Gulf War in 1991, see Cornish (1997).

recipient State. Member States were entitled to operate more restrictive national policies. The Code was drafted in non-binding language, and was not published in the Official Journal.[60]

It cannot, of course, be claimed that the adoption of the EU Code of Conduct has removed from political controversy the supply of arms to non-Member States. In January 2000, for example there was bitter recrimination over the supply by the UK of Hawk spare parts to Zimbabwe,[61] and in February 2001 controversy as to whether supply by the UK of spare parts for Moroccan heavy artillery breached the requirement not to export equipment which might be used for aggressive territorial gain (in the context of the struggle for independence in Western Sahara).[62] But the formulation of explicit and detailed criteria is an important step towards transparency and helps to counter the cynical argument that refusal of a licence merely diverts a valuable export order to a competitor State.

The first annual report on the implementation of the Code concluded that the system had been effective and had increased understanding among the Member States on their policies on supply of conventional arms. A Working Group on Conventional Arms Exports (COARM) had examined issues such as the legal status of the Code and the possibility for non-Member States declaring adherence to its principles to gain access to their evolving interpretation. The annual report also provided information on refusals to authorize, the most frequent being from France (fifty) and the UK (forty-three).[63] A second annual report stated that there had been further strengthening of the Code, with considerable increase in notified denials and consultations among Member States. The associated countries of Central and Eastern Europe, the members of the European Economic Area, Cyprus, Malta, and Canada had declared that they subscribed to the principles of the Code and would adjust their national policies and rules accordingly. The report noted the adoption by the US Congress of a law on 'promotion of an international code of conduct for arms exports' and 'welcomed the fact that the United States has thus embarked upon a path where the European Union has played a pioneering role'.[64]

In December 1998 the Council built on the Code of Conduct initiative by adopting a further Joint Action on combating the destabilizing accumulation and spread of small arms and light weapons. The Preamble to the Joint Action noted:

[60] Europe, 25/26 May 1998, p 4 and text of Code in Docs N 2092, 12 June 1998; Bull EU 5-1998 points 1.3.5, 1.3.6, 6-1998 point 1.4.7; Conclusions of the Council of 25 May 1998, Press 162-8687/98. For a critical assessment of the Code see Peers (1998a) at p 673.
[61] See *The Times*, 28 January 2000.   [62] *Observer*, 4 February 2001.
[63] OJ C315/1, 3.11.1999; *Europe*, 2 October 1999, pp 5–6.
[64] OJ C379/1, 29.12.2000; *Europe* 3 and 4 January 2001 p 4; 16 September 2000 p 5 (Titley Report of European Parliament on the Code).

Whereas the excessive and uncontrolled accumulation and spread of small arms and light weapons . . . has become a problem of great concern to the international community and the phenomenon poses a threat to peace and security and reduces the prospects for sustainable development in many regions of the world; . . .

The initiative followed the adoption of a Security Council Resolution on illicit arms flows to and within Africa, as well as consequential actions by UN bodies and by Interpol. The key commitments in Article 3, to be pursued by the European Union in international and regional fora, were:

(a) a commitment by all countries to import and hold small arms only for their legitimate security needs, to a level commensurate with their legitimate self-defence and security requirements, including their ability to participate in UN peacekeeping operations;
(b) a commitment by exporting countries to supply small arms only to governments either directly or through duly licensed entities authorised to procure weapons on their behalf) in accordance with appropriate international and regional restrictive arms export criteria, including officially authorised end-use certificates or, when appropriate, other relevant information on end-use; . . .

Other commitments to be pursued by the Union related to production, inventories for purposes of control, national confidence building measures, combating illicit trafficking of small arms, and public education programmes. The Union would provide financial and technical assistance to programmes and projects making a contribution to the objectives of the Joint Action. The Presidency would ensure liaison with the UN, regional arrangements, and third countries, keeping the Council informed. The Council and the Commission were to be responsible for the consistency of the Union's activities in the field of small arms, 'in particular with regard to its development policies'.[65]

Defending the European Union from Exorbitant Jurisdictional Claims: Helms-Burton and d'Amato

In 1996 the US Congress, in an attempt to isolate Cuba by penalizing those who traded with or invested in the country, adopted the Cuban Liberty and Democratic Solidarity Act which became known from its sponsors as the Helms-Burton Act.[66] Later in the same year Congress also adopted the Iran-Libya Sanctions Act, known as the d'Amato Act, which used similar techniques with the object of isolating Iran and Libya in response to their support for terrorism and attempts to develop weapons of mass destruction. These Acts were vigorously opposed by the international community on the grounds that their extraterritorial effects violated international law

[65] Joint Action 1999/34/CFSP of 17 December 1998, OJ L9/1, 15.1.1999.
[66] Public Law No 104-114, printed in (1996) 35 ILM 357.

limits on jurisdictional claims and thereby infringed the rights of other sovereign States and their nationals as well as established rules on free trade, investment, and diplomatic protection.[67] In the words of Lowe:

There seems to be no attempt whatsoever to tie the power to impose penalties upon violation of the law to any link between the United States and the alleged offender; no attempt to show even the semblance of respect for the principles of international law concerning the allocation of jurisdiction between States . . . It does little to reassure those who think that many members of the US Congress do not understand international law at all, but see the world as one great federal State with the United States filling the role of the federal government.[68]

There was already a long history of disputes between Europe and the United States resulting from the latter's claims to regulate the conduct of foreign nationals in foreign States. In 1982 in particular, the US—responding to the Soviet invasion of Afghanistan—had attempted to stop several European contractors from performing their contractual obligations to help in the construction of the natural gas pipeline from Siberia to Western Europe. The Member States of the European Community, working within the EPC framework and with the assistance of the Commission, elaborated the detailed legal terms of a diplomatic protest delivered in Washington by the Ambassador of the Presidency Member State and the acting Head of the Commission Delegation. The Note claimed that the US measures contained 'sweeping extensions of US jurisdiction which are unlawful under international law'.[69] The UK subsequently adopted national measures under the Protection of Trading Interests Act 1980,[70] prohibiting compliance with United States orders, but this example was not followed by other Member States.

In 1996, however, the TEU presented more effective possibilities of collective legal defence. On 22 November 1996 the Council adopted a Joint Action based both on Article J.3 and Article K.3 of the Treaty. The Joint Action referred to guidelines from the European Council in Florence in June 1996 and gave its reasons for resisting the United States legislation in these terms:

Whereas a third country has enacted certain laws, regulations, and other legislative instruments which purport to regulate the activities of natural and legal persons under the jurisdiction of the Member States of the European Union;

---

[67] See, for example, Opinion of the Inter-American Juridical Committee responding to the General Assembly of the OAS, CJI RES II-14/96, (1996) 35 ILM 1322; UN Security Council statement in (1996) 35 ILM 493. For a detailed account of the provisions of the US legislation and the responses to it from governments and academic writers, see Lowe (1997) and Smis and Van der Borght (1999).
[68] Lowe (1997) at pp 385–6.
[69] Text in XXI ILM (1982) 891. See Lowe (1984); Lowe (1985); Kuyper (1984).
[70] c. 11.

Whereas by their extra-territorial application such laws, regulations and other legislative instruments violate international law;

Whereas such laws including regulations and other legislative instruments and actions based thereon or resulting thereon affect or are likely to affect the established legal order and have adverse effects on the interests of the European Union, and the interests of the said natural and legal persons; . . .

Concurrently with the Joint Action the Council adopted a Regulation under Articles 73c, 113, and 235 of the EC Treaty which, in addition to the reasons set out above to justify the Joint Action, recalled specific Community objectives—harmonious development of world trade, progressive abolition of restrictions on international trade, free movement of capital between Member States and third countries including removal of restrictions on direct investment. The Community Regulation was of course directly applicable throughout the European Union. It required nationals of Member States as well as companies and others under their jurisdiction to inform the Commission whenever their economic or financial interests were affected by the US legislation. It provided that judgments and decisions based on that legislation would not be recognized or enforceable within the European Union, prohibited compliance with the terms of the legislation, and gave European persons and companies a right to recover damages. The related Joint Action required Member States to take complementary protective national measures insofar as the interests of their nationals and others within their jurisdiction were not protected by the Regulation.[71]

These sweeping defensive provisions made it pointless for any US person or company with assets anywhere in the European Union to invoke the Helms-Burton or d'Amato provisions against European interests. Similar blocking legislation was later adopted in Mexico and Canada. The measures gave the European Union an extremely powerful negotiating weapon in seeking to persuade the US to abandon its confrontational course of action and to bring its legislation within internationally accepted limits. The EU also pursued legal remedies under the World Trade Organization (WTO) dispute settlement procedures, while Canada took the lead in the North American Free Trade Association.

By April 1997 the European Union and the US concluded a Memorandum of Understanding under which they would work together 'to develop agreed disciplines and principles for the strengthening of investment protection'—the objective of the Helms-Burton Act—and 'to counter the threat to international security posed by Iran and Libya'—the objective of the d'Amato Act. The US would continue its suspension of the

---

[71] Council Regulation (EC) 2271/96 of 22 November 1996, OJ L309/1; Joint Action 96/668/CFSP of 22 November 1996 OJ L309/7, 29.11.1996; Cremona (1998) at pp 90–4.

internationally offensive provisions of the Helms-Burton Act, and would apply the d'Amato Act in a way which took into account its international obligations.[72] At the EU/US Summit on 18 May 1998 a political settlement was agreed which extended and built on the 1997 Memorandum of Understanding. In return for continued suspension of any implementation of the two Acts affecting European interests, the European Union agreed to freeze action in the WTO against US violation of the organization's rules. The establishment of a Transatlantic Partnership on Political Cooperation would set up procedures to avert friction on issues of stability and security and in particular the imposition of unilateral economic sanctions. In a unilateral statement accompanying the Summit Conclusions the EU said that the decisions and statements 'form a single package and, taken together, offer the prospect of a lasting resolution of our differences with the US over these Acts'.[73]

Thus there was effective linkage of the defensive and negotiating weapons made available by the First, Second, and Third Pillars of the Treaty on European Union in order to achieve a strong position on an issue with major implications for foreign policy and for international law as well as for the economic interests of Europe. While Europe did its best to resolve the dispute in a manner which stressed the elements common to US and to European foreign policy, it also succeeded in defending its own economic interests against violations of international law by the United States.

South Africa

Throughout the early years of European Political Cooperation there were protracted efforts by European Foreign Ministers to determine a common approach to South Africa which went beyond words condemning apartheid. Differing historical and political links as well as the important commercial interests of the larger Member States prevented agreement on sanctions. In 1977 Ministers agreed on a non-binding Code of Conduct for Community Companies with Subsidiaries in South Africa, on working conditions for employees there. Stronger measures were not taken until the declaration of a state of emergency by the South African Government in 1985. Following a visit to South Africa by Troika Ministers, Member States agreed on an arms and security equipment embargo, withdrawal of military attaches, and freezing of sporting and other contacts. These measures were implemented nationally. Positive measures included assistance to anti-apartheid organizations, social and educational assistance to

[72] The Memorandum of Understanding is printed in (1997) 36 ILM 529 and in [1997] AJIL 498.
[73] General Affairs Council Conclusions May 1998; Smis and Van der Borght (1999).

the non-white community, and programmes to assist the Front Line States. A few months later Community measures were used to implement a ban on import of gold coins and of iron and steel, together with a ban on new European investment in South Africa. Although by 1985 a precedent had been set for the use of EC powers to implement more general sanctions against third States, there was no majority in favour of taking this course against South Africa.[74]

As the peace process in South Africa developed in the early 1990s, the European Community tried to assist in facilitating dialogue and defusing conflict. It deployed an Observer Mission in South Africa (ECOMSA) which operated along with missions from the United Nations, the Organization for African Unity and the Commonwealth. The conclusion of the Multi Party Negotiating process and the decision to create a Transitional Executive Council enabled the EC to develop a new approach. On the eve of the entry into force of the Maastricht Treaty the European Council in Brussels stated that this would consist of: 'Support for the transition towards multiracial democracy in South Africa through a coordinated programme of assistance in preparing for the elections and monitoring them, and through the creation of an appropriate cooperation framework to consolidate the economic and social foundations of this transition.'[75]

Implementing these Conclusions, one of the first Joint Actions adopted after the entry into force of the Maastricht Treaty set up detailed mechanisms for assistance and technical training from the European Union. A European electoral unit was established within the overall UN framework, and the details of its composition, objectives, and operations were set out in an Annex. Financing of assistance measures would come from the budget of the European Communities, but Member States sending observers would bear their expenses. In the run up to these first multiracial elections the European Union worked along with UN, Commonwealth, and Organization of African Unity teams.

Nelson Mandela was elected with 67 per cent of the vote. The Transitional Executive Council held its first meeting on 7 December 1993, and immediately afterwards the EU, responding to an earlier request by Mandela, lifted the sanctions which had been imposed by Member States since 1985.[76] The Union was then able to use first pillar instruments to cooperate fully with the newly democratic South Africa—extending cred-

---

[74] Nuttall (1992) pp 132–5, 230–7, 263–5.

[75] EPC Press Releases of 30 March 1983 and 25 September 1983; Conclusions of European Council of 29 October 1993 in Bull EC 10-1993 point 1.4; Edwards [1993] Yearbook of European Law 506.

[76] Council Decision 93/678/CFSP of 6 December 1993 OJ L316/45, 17.12.1993; Bull EC 12-1993 point 1.4.11; Holland (1995) and Holland (1997a) at pp 174–83; Ryba (1995) at pp 30–1.

its, trade preferences, and an early interim agreement as a framework for bilateral relations. By early 1996 relations had developed to the point where the European Community and South Africa could begin negotiations for a free trade area compatible with WTO rules.

While it could not be said that the actions by the European Community and later by the Union were critical to the outcome, the successive measures clearly contributed—as was envisaged by the guidelines on joint actions set out by the European Council in Lisbon in June 1992—to strengthening democratic principles and institutions, promoting regional stability, the settlement of conflicts and to supporting good government.[77] The history also shows that European Ministers found it easier to reach agreement on positive measures than on deterrent sanctions. There were, quite apart from differing political and commercial relations among Member States, real differences as to whether the isolation of South Africa during the apartheid years would be conducive to peaceful change towards multiracial democracy.

Sanctions

The early history of collective European Community sanctions has already been described in Chapter 2. The decision by the Council in 1982 to use Article 113 of the EEC Treaty as a legal basis for sanctions against the Soviet Union following the invasion of Afghanistan was followed a few months later by the imposition of sanctions against Argentina—implementing a Security Council decision relating to its invasion of the Falkland Islands. Article 113 EEC was also used in 1986 for some of the measures against South Africa which were described above.

The comprehensive sanctions imposed on Iraq following its invasion of Kuwait in 1990 illustrate the pre-Maastricht legislative procedure in its classic form. In this case there was a binding Security Council decision. Aspects of the embargo within Community competence were implemented by Council Regulations,[78] while other aspects were implemented at national level. A later Regulation[79] made under Article 235 of the EEC Treaty (presupposing the absence of other Treaty powers) prohibited the satisfying of any claims barred by sanctions against Iraq. The Council's legislative practice was for the Regulation to set out the parent Security Council resolution to be implemented and the decision within the EPC framework (which might elaborate, clarify, or even go beyond the Security

[77] See Fink-Hooijer (1994) at p 182.
[78] Council Regulations 2340/90 [1990] OJ L213/1 and 3155/90 [1990] OJ L304/1.
[79] Council Regulation 3541/92, [1992] OJ L361/1. The operation of the Regulation was illustrated in the case *Shanning International Ltd v Lloyds TSB Bank plc, Lloyds TSB Bank plc v Rasheed Bank* [2001] UK HL 31, [2001] 1 WLR 1462, HL (E).

Council resolution). Aspects of the EPC decision outside the competence of the EEC (such as freezing financial assets of the target State) were implemented by national measures. Similar legislation was adopted by the Council for sanctions against Libya,[80] and against Serbia and Montenegro.[81] There were however residual uncertainties, for example whether transport sanctions could properly be based on the commercial policy provisions of Article 113 EEC.[82]

The Maastricht Treaty provided specific new powers for the EU to impose sanctions. The Council may now adopt a common position under CFSP procedures on sanctions which will be in itself legally binding on Member States whether or not there is already a binding Security Council decision. Those parts of the Council decision which are outside Community competence—for example an embargo on supply of arms—may require implementation at national level, possibly including criminal sanctions. The parts of the Council decision within Community competence must immediately be implemented at Community level under the new powers given by the Maastricht Treaty. Under Article 228a of the EC Treaty (later Article 301):

> Where it is provided, in a common position or in a joint action of the Treaty on European Union relating to the common foreign and security policy for an action by the Community to interrupt or to reduce, in part or completely, economic relations with one or more third countries, the Council shall take the necessary urgent measures. The Council shall act by a qualified majority on a proposal from the Commission.

Article 73g (later Article 60) gave the Council parallel powers to take necessary urgent measures on the movement of capital and on payments. This Article also allowed Member States—where the Council had not acted—to take unilateral measures on capital movements and payments 'for serious political reasons and on grounds of urgency'. The Council however could decide that the Member State must amend or abolish such measures.

These powers certainly opened the way to swift action by the Union to implement obligations of the Member States under the UN Charter. The powers are not however limited to such cases—the Council can impose, and has imposed, sanctions more extensive than those required by Security Council resolution, and may also impose sanctions independently of the UN. Neither the common position or joint action behind the Community measure, nor the Community measure itself is open to meaningful scrutiny either by the European Parliament (which is not even consulted) or by national parliaments (who are generally informed of the

---

[80] Council Regulation 945/92, [1992] OJ L101/53.
[81] Council Regulations 1432/92, [1992] OJ L151/4 and 990/93, [1993] OJ L102/14.
[82] See Pavoni (1999) at pp 587–92.

measures after they are already in force). Both the CFSP common position or joint action and the European Community Regulation normally require national measures to prescribe criminal penalties, but there is by this stage no possibility for national authorities to question the principle of the sanctions already imposed by the Council. The powers to impose sanctions on third countries are now both draconian and effective.

Use of the New Sanctions Powers

The Council first used its new powers in order to reduce economic relations with Libya. On 22 November 1993 it adopted a Decision on the basis of Article J.2 of the TEU, implementing Security Council Resolution 883 (1993). Seven days later the Council implemented its own Decision by adopting Regulations which prevented the supply of certain goods and services to Libya.[83] On 15 March 1994 the Council adopted a common position on the basis of Article J.2 of the Treaty on European Union imposing an embargo on arms, munitions, and military equipment on Sudan. Article 2 of the common position provided: '1. This Decision shall take effect on 16 March 1994. Member States shall take the necessary steps to ensure that the embargo referred to in Article 1 is applicable from 16 March 1994.'[84] As the embargo to be imposed on Sudan related only to arms and military equipment, which were outside European Community competence, no Community implementing action was required.

Common positions relating to arms export might, however, be much more complex than the straightforward general embargo imposed on Sudan. One such case was the common position which followed Security Council Resolution No. 1021 of 22 November 1995, lifting the arms embargo applicable to the former Yugoslav Republics but with a number of provisos pending signature of the Peace Agreement. The common position not only required Member States to distinguish by reference to whether the arms were destined for Slovenia or the former Yugoslav Republic of Macedonia (FYROM) or for other former Yugoslav Republics, but also required them to 'show restraint in their arms export policy' towards Slovenia and Macedonia and to take into account in this context the common criteria in the Luxembourg and Lisbon European Council conclusions.[85]

The Council in imposing sanctions may at the same time provide a carrot, by way of incentives or procedures designed to facilitate a return to normal constructive relations. Thus, in November 1995 the Council

---

[83] Council Decision 93/614/CFSP, OJ L295/7, 30.11.1993 and Council Regulations 3274/93 and 3275/93 of 29 November 1993, OJ L295/1, OJ L295/4, 30.11.1993.

[84] Council Decision 94/165/CFSP of 15 March 1994 OJ L75/1, 17.3.1994.

[85] Common Position 96/184/CFSP of 26 February 1996 OJ L58/1, 7.3.1996.

condemned the human rights abuses by the military regime in Nigeria 'including capital punishment and harsh prison sentences, implemented after flawed judicial process and without granting the possibility of recourse to a higher court. In this context, it expresses its particular concern at the detention without trial of political figures and the suspension of habeas corpus.'

The European Union also expressed concern at the annulment of free and fair elections and the installation of a military dictatorship which showed no intention of returning Nigeria to democratic rule within a credible time frame. The sanctions measures reaffirmed by the Council were suspension of military cooperation, suspension of visits, visa and movement restrictions for members of the military and security forces, and cancellation of training contracts for Nigerian military personnel. All of these would be implemented at national level. The Council also agreed on suspension of development cooperation with Nigeria—this being an area where competence is shared between the European Community and the Member States. In this context, however, the Common Position provided: 'Exceptions may be made for projects and programmes in support of human rights and democracy as well as those concentrating on poverty alleviation and, in particular, the provision of basic needs for the poorest section of the population, in the context of decentralized cooperation through local civilian authorities and non-governmental organizations.'[86]

At the end of 1998 the Council was able to adopt a Joint Action setting out positive measures to be taken in support of the democratic process in Nigeria.[87]

There have been numerous other occasions on which the Council has used its CFSP powers to determine with uniform and binding effect the scope of sanctions to be imposed on a non-member country. The problems arising from the interrelation with the First Pillar will be more fully considered in the context of Chapter 8 below. At this stage four conclusions may be drawn:

---

[86] Common Position 95/515/CFSP, OJ L298/1, 11.12.1995. See also Common Positions 95/544/CFSP, 1995 OJ L309/1; 96/677/CFSP 1996 OJ L315/3; 97/358/CFSP 1997 OJ L153/6; 97/821/CFSP 1997 OJ L338/8; 97/820/CFSP, 1997 OJ L338/7. The importance of financial backing for the EU human rights policy was emphasized by Commissioner Patten in a speech on 3 March 2000 to the Council of Europe Conference on The Protection of Human Rights in the 21st century, where he said: 'Strengthening the rule of law, democratisation, and the prevention of conflict are objectives of spending too. Whether we are supporting electoral reform in Kazakhstan, water supply projects in sub-Saharan Africa, or training lawyers in China, we want our external assistance in whatever form to contribute *positively* to the promotion of human rights, including the right to development.'
[87] Joint Action 98/735/CFSP OJ L354/1, 30.12.1998.

1. The powers given by the Maastricht Treaty have been of significant help in enabling Member States to impose sanctions swiftly and on a uniform basis.
2. Although the European Union has generally been more successful in influencing the behaviour of non-Member States through the use of carrots (potential membership, closer forms of partnership or association) than through the use of sticks, there have been some cases (for example Haiti) where the threat or use of sanctions has had a salutary effect.[88]
3. There is no real democratic debate either at European or at national level and very little publicity before sanctions are imposed.
4. The pillar structure, together with the need for some national implementing measures, bring about an extremely complex and multi-layered regime. This is particularly unsatisfactory in that traders may be unwittingly ensnared and exposed to criminal penalties.[89]

Bosnia

The war in Bosnia had been under way for nearly two years before the Maastricht Treaty came into force, and was to last for another two years before it was brought to an end with the conclusion of the Dayton Agreements and their formalization in Paris in December 1995.[90] The length and ferocity of the conflict could be regarded as a failure for the UN, for the Organization for Security and Cooperation in Europe and for NATO—all of whom tried in various ways to bring it to an end. But the failure was particularly laid at the door of the newly created Common Foreign and Security Policy of the European Union, even to the extent of suggesting that it showed that the whole system was futile. Insiders however maintained that Europe did have an agreed policy, and that its contribution to the eventual outcome was constructive. The British Foreign Secretary Douglas Hurd, for example, argued:

But the fact that twelve countries of Western Europe have not been able to stop a civil war outside their own borders, albeit a civil war supported and abetted from outside, is hardly an argument for bringing the coordination of European foreign policy to an end. We have at each stage of the post-Yugoslav crisis agreed on what we should do—that is, we Europeans have avoided the disastrous rivalries of western powers in the Balkans which caused such harm in the first years of this century. We have provided a framework, negotiators and proposals for the negotiated settlement which will eventually end this war. We have agreed on sanctions, we have (most of us) deployed troops on the ground in support of a humanitarian

---

[88] See Smith (1998a), pp 76–8.   [89] See Canor (1998); Pavoni (1999).
[90] By the General Framework Agreement for Peace in Bosnia and Herzegovina signed at Paris on 14 December 1995, Cm 3154.

effort in which Europe has taken the lead. That adds up to a substantial, though not a decisive effort. The decision to end the war will be taken by those doing the fighting.[91]

The decision by Member States to recognize as States the constituent republics of Yugoslavia, and the context in which that decision was taken, were explained in Chapter 2 above. The Guidelines of December 1991 and the subsequent decisions to proceed to recognition which were taken within that framework can as a matter of policy be faulted. In adding a number of criteria on readiness to fulfil legal and human rights obligations which went well beyond the requirements of international law the Member States laid insufficient emphasis on fulfilment of the traditional criteria which focused mainly on the stability and viability of a new entity claiming to be a State. In addition, recognition of Bosnia as a State gave rise to expectations of external support in defending itself which in the event were not forthcoming.[92]

Following the breakdown of the constitutional talks between Serbs, Croats, and Muslims in Bosnia, the Community and its Member States acting in European Political Cooperation issued in May 1992 a Declaration in the following terms:

Although all parties have contributed, in their own way, to the present state of affairs, by far the greatest share of the blame falls on the JNA and the authorities in Belgrade which are in control of the army, both directly and indirectly by supporting Serbian irregulars. The killings and expulsion of populations in Bijeljina, Zvornik, Foca and other towns and villages, the siege and systematic shelling of Sarajevo, the holding of Sarajevo airport preventing even the safe passage of humanitarian relief from the ICRC are actions deserving universal condemnation.

The Declaration made specific demands for withdrawal of Yugoslav forces from Bosnia, the reopening of Sarajevo airport and commitments from Belgrade to respect for borders and minorities, in accordance with the draft Convention negotiated through the mediation of Lord Carrington as European negotiator. The Community and the Member States further decided to recall their Ambassadors from Belgrade for consultations, demand suspension of the Yugoslav Delegation from the CSCE and its increasing isolation in other international fora and to ask the Commission to study the modalities of economic sanctions.[93]

---

[91] Hurd (1994). See also Crowe (1998) at p 321: '. . . one thing the EU cannot be accused of is not having a policy. You may not have liked it, although given the constraints (no willingness to use force or to walk away) it may have been the best available (humanitarian aid and protection combined with brokering a political solution).'

[92] See in particular Weller (1992); Pellet (1992). For the decision on 7 April 1992 by the EC and the Member States to recognize Bosnia see Bull EC 1992-4 point 1.5.4.

[93] Foreign Affairs Council 11 May 1992, EPC Press Release P 56/92; Bull EC 1992-5 point 1.3.5; Hansard HL Debs 19 May 1992 WA col 30.

The European Community had already imposed sanctions on Yugoslavia before recognition of the separate Republics—suspending the Cooperation Agreement between the Community and Yugoslavia, withholding certain trade concessions and preferences, and imposing import controls. In February 1992 these economic benefits were restored to those republics and territories (including Montenegro) cooperating in the peace process.[94] On 27 May 1992, however, the Council imposed a total trade embargo on Serbia and Montenegro, including oil and oil products and activities (such as air services) likely to promote commercial transactions or benefit the economy of Serbia and Montenegro. A few days later the scope of the sanctions was broadened even further to bring it into line with Security Council Resolution 757 of 30 May. The European Community refused to accept Serbia-Montenegro as the sole successor to Yugoslavia.[95]

Concurrently with all these penal measures the European Community Peace Conference on Yugoslavia—originally convened in August 1991 under the chairmanship of Lord Carrington and chaired later by Lord Owen—was trying to work with the UN and with the CSCE to promote a peaceful solution and to limit the scale of human suffering. The Community gave extensive emergency aid to Bosnia and repeatedly demanded that the authorities in Belgrade should facilitate access to refugee camps and comply with their obligations under humanitarian law, especially the Geneva Conventions. At the European Council in Edinburgh in December 1992 the Heads of State and of Government expressed support for Security Council Resolution 787 which authorized the use of military measures for the delivery of humanitarian aid, as well as for NATO and WEU action to enforce sanctions and the arms embargo on the republics of the former Yugoslavia. They made clear however that, although there was then little to show for the effort they had expended, they continued to give 'priority to political means in order to resolve the crisis in Yugoslavia'.[96]

By April 1993 the peace plan devised by Cyrus Vance, the US Representative, and Lord Owen had been accepted by the Bosnian Government and by the Croats in Bosnia. The plan was based on the sovereignty of Bosnia-Herzegovina, the inviolability of its territorial integrity, respect for its pluralist character, and the inadmissibility of the acquisition of territory by force. These four elements remained constant throughout the war as the European preconditions of any acceptable settlement. In order to put pressure on the Serbs, the European Community persuaded the Security Council to tighten sanctions still further unless the Serbian

---

[94] Bull EC 1991-11 points 1.4.4, 1.3.20-22.
[95] Bull EC 1992-5 point 1.2.19–20 and 1992-6 point 1.4.12–13; OJ L151, 3.6.1992.
[96] Bull EC 1992 7/8 points 1.5.5–6, 1992-12 point 1.85 (Conclusions of the Edinburgh European Council).

attacks were stopped and a political settlement agreed within a few days. More drastic alternatives, such as the removal of the UN arms embargo in respect of the Bosnian Government and air strikes against selected Serb targets, were considered but rejected on the basis that such actions would have limited chances of success, would greatly increase civilian casualties and would jeopardize the continuing humanitarian action. The United States President, however, expressed support at this time for allied air strikes and permitting arms supplies to the Bosnian Government, thus undermining attempts to forge a united international response.[97]

In the summer of 1993 agreement was reached in the Geneva Conference chaired by Lord Owen and Thorvald Stoltenberg (who had replaced Vance) for partition of Bosnia into three republics—Muslim, Serb, and Croat—within the framework of a demilitarized Union of Republics of Bosnia-Herzegovina. In September the proposed partition was overwhelmingly rejected by the Bosnian Parliament. This effectively ended the Vance-Owen Peace Plan.[98]

The entry into force of the Maastricht Treaty in November 1993 did not lead to any significant changes in European policy or action in Bosnia. The Council quickly adopted a joint action as the legal basis for continuing support of the convoying of European humanitarian aid and increased the European contribution to the UN High Commissioner for Refugees. Half the cost of this contribution was charged to the European Communities' budget.[99] Sanctions against Serbia and Montenegro were in due course placed on the new legal bases—Article 228a and Article 73g—set out in the Treaty, but they continued to reflect closely the terms of Security Council Resolutions.[100] As the situation of the Muslims deteriorated with the siege of Sarajevo and the shelling of the market there, there were some governments in favour of military action to lift the siege. They did not constitute a majority, and the various initiatives by the US, by Russia, and by the European Union continued with little coordination. In April a Contact Group of Russian, US, French, German, and British representatives was formed to coordinate policies, and to produce plans which were applied in detailed maps.[101]

---

[97] EPC Press Releases 26/93 of 26 March 1993, 47/93 of 18 May 1993 and 53/93 of 8 June 1993; Bull EC 1993–4 point 1.4.3; Hansard HC Debs cols 21–36 (19 April 1993); *The Times*, 21 April 1993.

[98] *Guardian*, 30 September 1993.

[99] Decisions of 8 November 1993 OJ L286/1, 20.11.1993; 20 December 1993 OJ L339/3, 31.12.1993, extended by Decision of 7 March 1994, OJ L70/1, 12.3.1994; Bull EC 1993-11 point 1.4.1. Later decisions adapted and extended the Joint Action.

[100] Council Regulations 2471/94, implementing SC Resolution 942/1994 (freezing of funds) and 2472/94, implementing SC Resolution 943/1994 [1994] OJ L266/8 (general trade restrictions).

[101] Freedman (1994).

In May 1994 the European Council in Corfu accepted an invitation to set up for a period of two years a European Union administration of the town of Mostar in Bosnia. The Council of Ministers approved conditions for this enterprise which were set out in a Memorandum of Understanding signed in Geneva on behalf of the Troika, the Commission, the WEU, and the Government of Bosnia. The WEU contributed police resources to the project, and the cost of the administration was borne by the European Communities' budget. The Council later adopted a Joint Action to constitute an appropriate legal basis for European Union action and expenditure, specifying that the object was to contribute 'to the establishment of a single, multi-ethnic and lasting administration of the town'.[102] A European Union Administrator—Hans Koschnick—was appointed, with wide responsibilities in such fields as rebuilding, restarting local industries, health and social services, strengthening municipal administration, including a unified police, and resettlement of displaced persons. An independent European Union Ombudsman was appointed to hear claims of violation of rights by the Administrator. The European Union Administration in Mostar remained in being until April 1997—well after the end of the fighting in Bosnia—and was generally regarded as having contributed to stability in an area of inter-racial tension between Croats and Muslims.[103]

Assessment of Action on Bosnia

The Member States of the European Union were for the most part not seriously divided over how they should try to stop or limit the fighting in Bosnia. Douglas Hurd, on the basis of the comments quoted above, clearly regarded it as a sign of success that continuous dialogue and common action at the least prevented divisions within the Member States which might have led to a catastrophic escalation of the war. The Community and later the Union deployed all the sticks and the carrots which were legally within their power. They convened peace conferences and appointed diplomatic representatives who brokered agreements which were not respected by Serbia or by the Serbs in Bosnia and proposed peace plans similar to the terms on which a peace was ultimately built. They gave money and men who averted starvation and saved lives. They worked in close conjunction with other international organizations such as WEU, NATO, and the UN which did have more powerful weapons at their disposal but which also failed to force the Serbs into a peaceful settlement.

[102] European Council Conclusions in Bull EC 1994-6 point 1.22; Council Decision 94/790/CFSP of 12 December 1994 OJ L326/2, 17.12.94.

[103] Bull EC 1994–7/8 point 1.3.2; Council Decisions 94/308/CFSP, OJ L134, 30.5.1994; 94/790/CFSP, OJ L326/2, 17.12.1994; 94/776/EC OJ L312/34, 6.12.1994; 95/23/CFSP, OJ L33/1, 13.2.95. Later Decisions extended the joint action and dealt with budgetary implications. See Ryba (1995) 28–9 and Peers (1996c) 631.

Even if the Union had had more powerful tools at its disposal it is unlikely that they would have been deployed in the absence of a clear mandate from the national parliaments and the peoples of Europe for serious involvement. There was never any sustained popular pressure in Europe for the deployment of an intervention force in Bosnia. Perhaps the failure of European efforts shows only the great difficulty of stopping a war whose causes were complex and little understood by the general public as well as unrealistic expectations as to what the Common Foreign and Security Policy could achieve.[104]

The Balance Sheet of the CFSP after Maastricht

The specific initiatives described above were selected because they all involved the use of legal powers—in particular joint actions—which became available only with the entry into force of the Maastricht Treaty. In each case there was a consistent course of action by the European Union and an outcome which can now be evaluated. In most cases—the exception being Bosnia—that outcome was clearly positive. The Union successfully defended its security and its political character and to a certain extent spread its political and economic character in geographic areas of importance to it.

A more general evaluation of the CFSP in the period between the entry into force of the Treaty of Maastricht in November 1993 and the entry into force of the Treaty of Amsterdam in May 1999 might list the following achievements:

1. The structures, powers, procedures, and legal instruments which formed the foundation for the CFSP maintained the independent sovereign status of the Member States of the Union. In spite of extensive cooperation and joint action it has not been seriously maintained that the Member States have lost that ultimate independence in the conduct of their foreign relations which defines them as separate States. In this context the use of international law methods and structures has been important.
2. The use of instruments which are binding in international law was a significant step forward from European Political Cooperation in imposing discipline on the Member States. The instruments themselves, drafted at least in part by lawyers, were more precise than the loose declarations and press releases of earlier years and the practice began of printing them as binding legislation in the Official Journal. It appears that they were generally observed.

---

[104] See the assessments by Smith (1998a) at p 78; by Hill (1998) at p 35; and by Crowe (1998) at p 321; Nuttall (1994); Kintis (1997) at pp 148–73; Cafruny (1998).

3. Article J (2) of the Maastricht Treaty made a positive contribution to international diplomacy by its explicit formulation of policy objectives for CFSP. Even actions which had little effect (as in Rwanda) or were unsuccessful (as in Bosnia) were clearly aimed at preserving peace and security under international law and at developing democracy, the rule of law, and respect for human rights.

4. The extensive discussion and negotiation which preceded the adoption of a common position or joint action meant that it was solidly based on wide understanding of the issue and of the advantages and risks to the European Union. The decision carried more conviction abroad because it was unanimous. Joint actions had first to be authorized in principle by the European Council—giving them great political authority. In foreign relations, the power to shoot from the hip is not always an advantage.

5. Following from this extensive discussion is the value to individual governments and foreign ministries of the CFSP process. The greatest admirers of the CFSP are the professional diplomats who, far from fearing that their autonomy is under threat, argue that their national policies are supported and enriched by the operation of CFSP. Over the last twenty years the habit of solidarity among the Member States towards the outside world has shown a remarkable development. The consequence is that issues such as nuclear testing and the disintegration of Yugoslavia which might have provoked rivalries and public disputes among certain Member States did not do so. CFSP was not meant to be a mechanism for settlement of disputes among Member States, but by happy chance it has proved to be one.[105]

As to the weaknesses of the CFSP, they go to its limited character and powers, which were described at the beginning of this chapter.

1. Apart from imposing legal obligations on the Member States in areas where the European Communities do not have competence, the CFSP has no direct powers of action or enforcement. Policy decisions, such as the imposition of sanctions, must be followed by national or by European Community action. Though there is little indication that these powers are not being made available, the position leads to delay and to a confusing plethora of legal instruments.

2. Because the Union was not endowed with legal personality, it could not directly conclude international agreements. The Presidency might conclude instruments such as the Memorandum of

---

[105] See Peterson and Sjursen (eds) (1998) at pp 177–9: 'The point is that the CFSP constitutes a pivotal dimension in all EU Member States' foreign policies.'

Understanding on the administration of Mostar, but did so on behalf of the Member States, and any legal obligations thereby created were obligations of the Member States. This might not be a substantial problem, but again it caused confusion.

3. Even after the entry into force of the Maastricht Treaty the manpower available to formulate and to implement CFSP—as explained above—was too small and shifting to enable strategic planning to be carried out effectively across the spectrum of foreign policy issues.

4. The absence of independent financial resources—also explained above—was often divisive and was a serious constraint on speedy action.

Lack of powers, lack of money, and lack of men therefore were the constraints on CFSP under the Treaty of Maastricht. As will be seen in Chapters 5 and 11 below, however, the Treaty of Amsterdam and later developments on defence have gone some way to address the problems.

5

The Second Pillar under the Treaty of Amsterdam

Calls for Reform

The Maastricht Treaty contained in Article N(2) an automatic review mechanism in the following terms: 'A conference of representatives of the governments of the Member States shall be convened in 1996 to examine those provisions of this Treaty for which revision is provided, in accordance with the objectives set out in Articles A and B.' It was clear from Articles J.4 and J.10 of the Treaty that the Common Foreign and Security Policy was among the provisions to be reviewed. Although the Maastricht Treaty because of the delays in national ratification had come into force only in November 1993, advance work for the 1996 Review Conference was in full swing by mid-1994. The European Council meeting in Corfu in June 1994 set up a Reflection Group composed of representatives of the fifteen Member States, of the European Commission, and of the European Parliament and invited the institutions of the Union to draw up reports on the operation of the Treaty. The institutions responded with more enthusiasm than experience.

The European Parliament made radical suggestions for 'a more effective EU foreign policy within the framework of the Community pillar, integrating the common commercial policy, development cooperation policy, humanitarian aid and CFSP matters, and achieving better defined security and defence policies at EU level'. Specifically they suggested that:

It should be possible for a qualified majority of Member States to undertake humanitarian, diplomatic or military action which would qualify as a 'joint action', with guarantees that no Member State should be forced to take part if it does not wish to do so, nor should it be able to prevent the majority from taking such action.

The European Commission should have a right of initiative and implementing power. Consultation of the European Parliament should be obligatory before adoption by the Council of a joint action. Finally, as a contribution to conflict prevention a European Civil Peace Corps—training monitors, mediators, and specialists in conflict resolution—should be established.[1]

---

[1] EP Resolution A4-0102/95 on the functioning of the Treaty on European Union with a view to the 1996 Intergovernmental Conference—Implementation and development of the Union (Bourlanges-Martin report), para. 3.

The European Commission in its original opinion on the holding of an intergovernmental conference in 1996, 'Reinforcing Political Union and Preparing for Enlargement', had argued that in order to give the Union a clear identity on the world scene the objectives of the Conference should be:

—to bring together various strands comprising foreign relations into a single effective whole, with structures and procedures designed to enhance consistency and continuity;
—to improve the common foreign and security policy at all stages of its operation;
—to establish a proper European identity with regard to security and defence, as an integral part of the common foreign and security policy.'[2]

In its Report for the Reflection Group the Commission suggested that the coexistence in the Treaty of the Community approach and the intergovernmental approach was a source of incoherence. The institutional machinery which was to ensure harmony between the pillars of the Union had not functioned properly. In specific terms, there was unnecessary duplication of legal instruments, and the budgetary system led to procedural debates instead of debates on substance. The continued reliance on unanimous voting within the Second Pillar was one reason why the CFSP was so ineffective. There had been very limited use of the Western European Union (WEU). The coexistence of the Union without legal personality and the Community, and the complex and shifting nature of external representation led to confusion in international negotiations and alienation on the part of the public.[3]

The Council, predictably, was the most positive of the institutions in its Report for the Reflection Group. In its initial assessment of the performance of the common and security policy (CFSP) it stressed that: 'Both the expectations and the criticisms were, no doubt, sometimes exaggerated; the provisions of the Treaty cannot alone provide ready-made solutions to problems, but only the means to tackle them.' Experience of the common foreign policy must be analysed under its three successive stages—policy formulation, decision-making, and implementation. At the policy formulation stage, the Council lacked direct access to information, and processing even of indirect information was inadequate. There were legal doubts whether overall planning of policy towards a particular country could take account of aspects falling within Community competence. At the decision-making, stage there was a need for a clearer structure of Council bodies. On implementation, the failure to give legal personality to the Union had caused difficulties. Financing the CFSP—where there was a

[2] Paras 23–35 of Opinion.
[3] Intergovernmental Conference 1996—Commission report for the Reflection Group 1995, Preface, Part Two, ch II and Conclusion.

discrepancy between the European Parliament's powers of political control and its budgetary powers—also gave rise to controversy thus far unresolved.[4]

The Reflection Group's Report

The Reflection Group's Report to the European Council, the product of six months' labour from June until December 1995, identified as one of the three key areas for the 1996 Conference giving the Union a greater capacity for external action. While the Group accepted that CFSP as established under the Maastricht Treaty had produced positive results, it needed the means for more effective external action: 'It must be capable of identifying its interests, deciding on its action and implementing it effectively.'

On the first aspect, the Group proposed the establishment of a common foreign policy analysis and planning unit. Decision-making and financing procedures needed to be reviewed to adapt them to the nature of foreign policy 'which must reconcile respect for the sovereignty of States with the need for diplomatic and financial solidarity'. As to what this meant, however, the Reflection Group was divided. Implementation of external actions required a high profile, and there was support from some for the appointment by the European Council of a High Representative for the CFSP. Others advocated placing this new function within the Council Secretariat and raising the status of the Secretary-General.

The Reflection Group recommended further development of the European identity in security and defence—to be carried out in such a way as to strengthen the European pillar of the Atlantic Alliance and at the same time to respect the right of non-members of that Alliance to take their own defence decisions. These non-members of military alliances were eager to contribute to European security through participation in humanitarian, peacekeeping, and crisis management operations (the 'Petersberg tasks'), but the Reflection Group agreed that such participation should remain a matter for national decision. There was support for the arrangement also favoured by the European Parliament under which no State could be obliged to take part in military action by the European Union, but nor could any State prevent such action by a majority group of Member States. This device was soon to be described as 'coalitions of the willing'. There was general agreement on strengthening institutional and operational links with WEU, as well as WEU operational capabilities.[5]

[4] Report of the Council of Ministers on the Functioning of the Treaty on European Union, May 1995, Cm 2866, paras 54–73.
[5] Reflection Group's Report, SN 520/95 (REFLEX 21), First Part II Giving the Union greater capacity for external action and Second Part: An Annotated Agenda, Part IV paras 146–77. For views of some individual members of the Group, see La CIG 96: Réponses à Quelques Questions, 1995 Revue du Marché Commun 8.

The House of Lords Report

The House of Lords Select Committee on the European Communities, whose Reports on the negotiations leading to the Maastricht Treaty were described in Chapter 2 above, published its later Report, *1996 Intergovernmental Conference*, in the light of the Reports from the institutions to the Reflection Group. The vast array of documents and evidence considered by the Committee included submissions from UK Ministers, Commissioners, Ambassadors, and Members of the Reflection Group. The House of Lords Committee continued to support the intergovernmental approach for CFSP on the basis that: 'It deals with issues where constitutional accountability is to national parliaments and where the ultimate power of independent action is a critical test of nationhood.' They were opposed to majority voting on policy decisions while accepting it for implementing decisions and endorsing the possible delegation of authority to one or more Member States in order to carry out agreed policy. Clear principles for financing CFSP actions were needed in the new Treaty.

On defence, the Committee endorsed the approach set out by the UK Government in its Memorandum for the Intergovernmental Conference. Two key elements in the British approach were arrangements designed to enable Europe, consistently with NATO obligations, to shoulder a greater share of the burden of promoting security and stability, and equitable sharing of the increased burden among European nations.[6]

Changes Made by the Treaty of Amsterdam

The Intergovernmental Conference, meeting at the level of Heads of State or Government, reached agreement in Amsterdam in June 1997 on the substance of a Treaty amending the Treaty on European Union and the European Community Treaties. Following the legal revision of the text, the new Treaty was signed in Amsterdam on 2 October 1997. The ratification process, though it required referenda in several Member States, was much less fraught than that of the Treaty of Maastricht. The Treaty entered into force on 1 May 1999.

Title V of the Treaty on European Union was completely recast. The following points summarize the more significant changes of substance made to the Common Foreign and Security Policy:

[6] 21st Report, 1994–95, HL Paper 105 and HL Paper 88, Minutes of Evidence. Evidence on CFSP and Defence is summarized in paras 166–87 and the Committee's Opinion on them is in paras 268–75. Appendix 3 lists previously published documents considered. For debate on the Report see Hansard HL Debs 12 December 1995 cols 1171–1256. For a selection of the literature generated by the approaching IGC see the European Parliament publication CIG 96: Selection de références bibliographiques: articles de périodiques 1/96.

1. On cohesion: new provision in Article 11 strengthened the legal commitment on Member States to support the Union's external and security policy 'actively and unreservedly'.

2. Consistency between the Pillars was enhanced by giving the European Council in Article 13 specific duties to decide on common strategies in areas where the Member States have important interests in common and to 'ensure the unity, consistency and effectiveness of action by the Union'. The Council and Commission were also placed by Article 3 (ex Article C) under an express obligation to cooperate to ensure consistency.

3. The instruments available to the Union for implementing CFSP—common strategies, joint actions, common positions, systematic cooperation—were clearly differentiated, both as to decision-making procedure and as to the extent of legal commitment.

4. The Council was given express power under Article 18 to appoint a special representative with a mandate in relation to particular issues.

5. Voting procedures were gathered together in a new Article 23. Unanimity remains the rule for basic policy decisions. But there are two exceptions:

   (a) 'Constructive abstention'. If an abstaining Member State makes a formal declaration, it is not obliged to apply the decision but must accept that the decision commits the Union. If 'constructive abstainers' amount to more than one-third of weighted votes, the decision is not adopted.

   (b) 'Implementing decisions'. The Council acts by qualified majority vote when adopting any decision on the basis of a common strategy and when adopting any decision implementing a joint action or common position. A 'Luxembourg compromise' or 'emergency brake' safeguard entitles a Member State to oppose adoption of a decision by qualified majority 'for important and stated reasons of national policy'. Qualified majority voting may never be used for decisions with military or defence implications.

6. The Council was given a new power under Article 24 to conclude CFSP implementing agreements with States or international organizations. The Agreements are to be negotiated by the Presidency and concluded by the Council. The agreements bind the Member States, since neither the Council nor the European Union was given international legal personality.

7. On manpower, the Political Committee was given by Article 25 responsibilities to monitor the international situation, advise the Council, and monitor implementation of agreed policies. Article 18 named the Secretary-General of the Council High Representative for the common foreign and security policy and Article 26 required him

to formulate, prepare, and implement Council policy decisions as well as to conduct dialogue with third parties. The High Representative for the CFSP would head a Policy Planning and Early Warning Unit in the General Secretariat of the Council. A Declaration adopted by the Conference set out its functions and composition. The role of the Commission—both in forming policy and in representing the Union—was enlarged.

8. On financing CFSP action, Article 28 set out clear provisions. Both administrative and operational expenditure were to be charged to the European Communities' budget, but for operational expenditure there would be two exceptions—expenditure on operations with military or defence implications and cases where the Council acting unanimously decided otherwise. Expenditure not charged to the Communities' budget would be charged to the Member States in accordance with the gross national product scale unless the Council acting unanimously decided otherwise. A Member State making a 'constructive abstention' would not be obliged to contribute to financing the operation in question.

9. On defence, Article 2 referred more positively to 'the progressive framing of a common defence policy, which might lead to a common defence, in accordance with the provisions of Article 17'. Article 17 made clear that such a step would require a European Council decision which would in turn be subject to national ratification procedures. WEU became 'an integral part of the development of the Union providing the Union with access to an operational capability'. There would be closer institutional relations between WEU and the European Union. Full integration would require a European Council decision and national ratification. The Petersberg tasks—humanitarian and rescue tasks, peacekeeping and crisis management, including peacemaking—were explicitly listed as tasks within the security policy. When the Union used WEU to carry out such tasks, all Member States of the European Union would be entitled to participate. The special position of the neutral Member States and of the NATO Member States continued to be acknowledged. Details of collaboration between WEU and the EU were set out in a Protocol and in Declarations adopted by the Conference.[7]

---

[7] A summary of the changes made by the Treaty of Amsterdam to the CFSP, comparing them with the earlier recommendations of the House of Lords Select Committee on the European Communities, is in Appendix 2 to the 3rd Report, 1997–98, *The Amsterdam Treaty*. See also Cameron (1998*b*) at pp 68–74.

CFSP UNDER THE TREATY OF AMSTERDAM: TEXT AND COMMENTARY

TITLE V

Provisions on a Common Foreign and Security Policy

ARTICLE 11 (EX ARTICLE J.1)

1. The Union shall define and implement a common foreign and security policy, the objectives of which shall be:
   —to safeguard the common values, fundamental interests, independence and integrity of the Union in conformity with the principles of the United Nations Charter;
   —to strengthen the security of the Union in all ways;
   —to preserve peace and strengthen international security, in accordance with the principles of the United Nations Charter, as well as the principles of the Helsinki Final Act and the objectives of the Paris Charter, including those on external borders;
   —to promote international cooperation;
   —to develop and consolidate democracy and the rule of law, and respect for human rights and fundamental freedoms.
2. The Member States shall work together to enhance and develop their mutual political solidarity. They shall refrain from any action which is contrary to the interests of the Union or likely to impair its effectiveness as a cohesive force in international relations.

   The Council shall ensure that these principles are complied with.

Objectives of the Common Foreign and Security Policy (CFSP)

To set out specific objectives for the CFSP was an innovation at the time of its formal establishment by the Maastricht Treaty. As explained at the beginning of Chapter 4 above, sovereign States—responsible by definition for the conduct of the totality of their external relations—do not as a general rule formulate long-term objectives for this activity. A very high proportion of the conduct of foreign affairs by a sovereign State consists in reactions to external and unpredictable events. Before the Maastricht Treaty, no international organization had been given such extensive responsibilities in the field of foreign policy. To accompany such an extensive delegation of powers with a statement of objectives served the purpose of placing it within a constitutional framework. Even though most CFSP activity does not take a legislative form, the exercise was similar to what is normally done when law-making power is delegated to an international organization. The statement of objectives limits the extent of delegation by reference to the purposes set out. Although the CFSP may be defined and implemented in 'all areas of foreign and security policy', the Member States have not thereby ceded their ultimate sovereign authority to conduct their own foreign and security policy. CFSP creates for the Member States an additional layer of foreign policy formation and joint implementation for common and specific purposes.

The objectives listed in Article 11 are parallel to those which, it was suggested at the beginning of Chapter 4, are the usual objectives of a State's foreign policy—defence of the physical and political character of the State, spreading its fundamental values and pursuit of a stable world order. Of central importance is the emphasis on the principles of the UN Charter—even stronger in the Amsterdam than in the Maastricht Treaty. The UN Charter, binding on all Member States of the EU, is made clearly central to the conduct of all their foreign policy objectives.

Also central to the pursuit of a stable world order are the principles of the Helsinki Final Act[8] and the Charter of Paris.[9] Coordination of policy throughout the CSCE process was one of the early successes of European Political Cooperation, and the gradual realization of many of the objectives of the Helsinki Final Act with the liberation of Eastern Europe and the subsequent consolidation of democracy in many countries formerly under Communist rule has always been regarded as attributable in part to European solidarity. The Amsterdam Treaty added a new reference to the principles of the Helsinki Final Act on external borders. The Declaration on Principles Guiding Relations between Participating States lists among ten basic principles:

III Inviolability of frontiers

The participating States regard as inviolable all one anothers' frontiers as well as the frontiers of all States in Europe and therefore they will refrain now and in the future from assaulting these frontiers.

---

[8] Final Act of the Conference on Security and Cooperation in Europe (CSCE) August 1975, Cmnd 6198.
[9] Charter of Paris for a New Europe, November 1990, Cm 1464. See Hannay (2000) pp 276–7.

Accordingly, they will also refrain from any demand for, or act of seizure and usurpation of part or all of the territory of any participating State.

The final indent of paragraph 1, with its emphasis on democracy, the rule of law and on respect for human rights, is consistent with paragraph 1 of Article 6 (ex Article F), which provides that

1. The Union is founded on the principles of the liberty, democracy, respect for human rights and fundamental freedoms, and the rule of law, principles which are common to the Member States.

Although the reference to human rights as an objective of the common foreign and security policy was unchanged from the Maastricht Treaty, Article 6 paragraph 1 was a new provision added by the Amsterdam Treaty and may be regarded as bringing the Union's internal policy on human rights into line with its external policy.

Boundaries of the CFSP

Article 11 (ex Article J.1), setting out the objectives of the CFSP, must be read with Articles 1, 2, and 3 (ex Articles A, B, and C). These provisions make clear that the European Communities are the foundation of the Union and that the 'policies and forms of cooperation' established outside the Communities are supplementary in character. The Union has a single institutional framework, but the Council and Commission, in ensuring consistency of the Union's external activities, must do so each in accordance with their respective powers. To the extent that the European Community has external powers, the Council and Commission must use these powers. The Commission and the ECJ may police the boundaries of Community powers to ensure that their primacy is observed.

Beyond this subordination in cases where Community powers are available, and the requirement in Article 6 (ex article F) for the Union to respect the national identities of its Member States, there appear to be no limits to the powers of the Union to define and implement common foreign and security policy. The Union cannot of course proceed in any area of foreign or security policy in the absence of a defined policy, and the formation of policy in new areas requires the unanimous agreement of the Member States whether in the European Council or in the Council of Ministers. But there seems to be nothing in the text of Article 11 to limit the express scope of the words 'all areas of foreign and security policy', for example by leaving areas of external economic policy where Member States retain competence in a kind of no man's land between the European Community and the CFSP.[10] There seems to be nothing in the text of the Amsterdam

---

[10] Some doubt on this point is expressed by Dashwood (1999) at p 210.

Treaty to exclude CFSP action where there is a Community law obligation on the Member States to 'cooperate' in the context of international negotiations, since the EC Treaty does not provide any appropriate instrument or formal procedure for the purposes of such intergovernmental cooperation.[11]

Taking the Treaty of Amsterdam as a whole, and given in particular the importance attached to coherence of the external activities of the European Union, the general sense is that the overall policy approach or strategy towards a particular foreign State or group of States should be determined in the context of the Second Pillar. Consequential actions may then as a matter of law be for the Member States, may be taken under powers of one the European Communities, under the Second or under the Third Pillar. But no areas of external policy are excluded from consideration and possible determination under the Second Pillar.[12] Cross-pillar actions are considered more fully in Chapter 8 below.

The Legal Commitments on the Member States and the Council

The text of Article 11 (ex Article J.1) was re-formulated in the Treaty of Amsterdam so as to specify in paragraph 1 the task and objectives of the Union and in paragraph 2 the consequential legal commitments imposed on the Member States and on the Council. This distinction was not clear in the text of Article J.1 of the Maastricht Treaty—where the Member States, as well as the Union, were required to define and implement a common foreign and security policy. It is now clear that the objectives of the CFSP are Union objectives—even the reference in the earlier text to strengthening the security of the Member States has been omitted from the text in the Treaty of Amsterdam.

By contrast it is on the Member States, who have international legal personality, that quite strong international legal obligations are imposed. The obligations are both positive—to support the Union's external and security policy actively and unreservedly, and to work together to enhance and develop mutual political solidarity; and negative—to refrain from action 'contrary to the interests of the Union or likely to impair its effectiveness as a cohesive force in international relations'. Although the obligations are wide and general, they are hardly of a sufficiently precise nature to be justiciable before any international court. They are treaty obligations under international law and not Community law obligations—with all the

---

[11] A contrary view is advanced in relation to the Maastricht Treaty in editorial comment in [1995] CML Rev at p 385.

[12] See on this point Schmalz (1998) at pp 428 and 435–6. See also Smith (1998*b*) at p 82: 'The argument suggests that we should view the EU as the strategic framework for action in the world political economy, but the EC as the operational agent of the EU.'

attendant consequences which were explained in Chapter 1 above. Most importantly, they are not subject to the jurisdiction of the European Court of Justice and they entail no loss of national competence to take action, though any national action must not breach the obligations of loyalty and mutual solidarity which have been described.

Legal obligations notwithstanding, the obligations of loyalty and solidarity are on occasion publicly breached by one or more Member States. In March 2001, for example, President Mugabe of Zimbabwe was received by the Prime Ministers of Belgium and France and by the European Commissioner for Development—in spite of outraged objection from Members of the European Parliament and suggestions from the UK Government that the purpose of formal dialogue with Zimbabwe was to underline concern over deteriorating respect for human rights in that country and not to discuss peace in the Democratic Republic of Congo.[13]

The absence of any role for the ECJ in securing action by the Union to fulfil its objectives or compliance by the Member States with their obligations is to some extent balanced by placing on the Council, in the final indent of Article 11, the duty to 'ensure that these principles are complied with'. These words imply that the Council will have the responsibility of settling any disputes arising from the CFSP (given that it is unreal to suppose that such disputes would ever be referred to the International Court of Justice (ICJ) or to any other external form of arbitration). They also serve to emphasize at the outset of Title V the primacy of the Council in the institutional structure of the Second Pillar.

---

[13] *The Times*, 2, 6 and 7 March 2001.

Legal Instruments of the Common Foreign and Security Policy

ARTICLE 12 (EX ARTICLE J.2)

The Union shall pursue the objectives set out in Article 1 by:
—defining the principles of and general guidelines for the common foreign and security policy;
—deciding on common strategies;
—adopting joint actions;
—adopting common positions;
—strengthening systematic cooperation between Member States in the conduct of policy.

Article 12 is a new provision in the Amsterdam Treaty, drawing up a comprehensive list of the instruments whereby the CFSP is to be defined and implemented. It can be seen as the equivalent, for the Second Pillar, of Article 249 (ex Article 189) which lists the instruments available to the European Community. The following four Articles of the Treaty elaborate for each of these instruments the enabling powers and procedures as well as the legal consequences. Although among the instruments only common strategies were introduced by the Treaty of Amsterdam, the overall formulation as well as the detailed description of the instruments is much clearer.

Even from a first inspection of the language of Article 12 the different characters of the five instruments emerge. Principles and general guidelines, although they are published as part of the Conclusions of each European Council and commit the Member States and the institutions of the European Union, are not intended to have the precision of an instrument imposing direct legal obligations. This is apparent from their description, and from the fact that they are 'defined' by the European Council. Common strategies are 'decided' by the European Council—giving them a somewhat more legal character. But, although they bind the Council to take consequential implementing decisions and are also published, they also have more of the flavour of political obligations than of legal texts. Joint actions and common positions on the other hand are 'adopted' by the Council, befitting their character as legally binding instruments. 'Systematic cooperation between Member States in the conduct of policy' will not usually take the form of a published instrument. The European Council at Santa Maria da Feira referred expressly to the 'systematic cooperation' authority in Article 12 when setting up concrete targets for strengthening EU police capabilities for international crisis management operations.[14] The description which follows of what is intended is not drafted as a formal instrument.

[14] European Council Conclusions June 2000, Appendix 4 to Annex I.

The European Council Supervision of the CFSP

ARTICLE 13 (EX ARTICLE J.3)

1. The European Council shall define the principles of and general guidelines for the common foreign and security policy including for matters with defence implications.
2. The European Council shall decide on common strategies to be implemented by the Union in areas where the Member States have important interests in common.

Common strategies shall set out their objectives, duration and the means to be made available by the Union and the Member States.
3. The Council shall take the decisions necessary for defining and implementing the common foreign and security policy on the basis of the general guidelines defined by the European Council.

The Council shall recommend common strategies to the European Council and shall implement them, in particular by adopting joint actions and common positions.

The Council shall ensure the unity, consistency and effectiveness of action by the Union.

Article 13 sets out in a single provision the responsibilities of the European Council and defines the relations between the European Council and the Council in defining and implementing the CFSP. Very broadly it is for the European Council to define and for the Council to implement.[15] In this, Article 13 reflects Article 4 (ex Article D) which provides: 'The European Council shall provide the Union with the necessary impetus for its development and shall define the general political guidelines thereof.' European Council action is by its nature not confined to any one of the three Pillars. Many of its conclusions obviously straddle two or even three Pillars, and the same is true of the strategies which have been decided. This tends to reinforce the proposition suggested above—that although they are capable of imposing obligations on the Member States and now clearly impose obligations on the institutions they do not have the full character of legal instruments. Legal instruments by contrast must have a legal base within one of the Pillars. Although there are examples of instruments which straddle the Second and Third Pillars there are no Council instruments which straddle the First Pillar and either of the other two, for

---

[15] For a critical appraisal of the working of the European Council, the General Affairs Council and the relationship between them see Gomez and Peterson (2001).

the good reason that the legal and institutional consequences of such a hybrid would not be clear.

Article 13 provides two methods of European Council action—principles and general guidelines on the one hand, and common strategies on the other. The procedure for each form of action as well as the methods of implementation are different.

General Guidelines for the CFSP

In defining general guidelines for the common foreign and security policy, the European Council is unconstrained except by the general structure of the Treaties and by the objectives which have been defined in Article 11. There is no formal requirement for any prior 'proposal' from the Commission or from the Council of Ministers. In practice, of course, the Heads of State or Government of the Member States do not begin their meetings with a blank sheet of paper and it is the responsibility of the Sherpas (senior diplomats from the Member States) to prepare the ascent towards the summit under the direction of the current Presidency. European Council guidelines may be directed towards more specific action within any one or all of the three Pillars of the Union or towards action by some or all of the Member States. They may not be directed at immediate action of a legal or practical kind at all but may simply establish a policy framework or a common position of the European Union on a particular geographic area or substantive problem. By way of illustrating the width of European Council action within the common foreign and security policy one may quote from the summary account of the first European Council which followed the entry into force of the Treaty of Amsterdam, meeting in Cologne on 3 and 4 June 1999:

In the foreign policy sphere, the European Council adopted a declaration on Kosovo and reiterated the European Union's commitment to take a leading role in the reconstruction efforts in the region. Pursuant to the Amsterdam Treaty, it designated Mr Javier Solana Madariaga as High Representative for the common foreign and security policy and Secretary-General of the Council, and designated Mr Pierre de Boissieu as Deputy Secretary-General. It also adopted a declaration on security and defence, and decided upon a common European Union strategy with regard to Russia.[16]

More recently, the Extraordinary European Council which met in Brussels in response to the attacks on the US of 11 September 2001 formulated overarching conclusions and a plan of action set primarily in a foreign policy context:

[16] Bull EU 6-1999 point 1.1.

The European Council is broadly supportive of the American people in the face of the deadly terrorist attacks. These attacks are an assault on our open, democratic, tolerant and multicultural societies. They are a challenge to the conscience of each human being. The European Union will cooperate with the United States in bringing to justice and punishing the perpetrators, sponsors and accomplices of such barbaric acts. On the basis of Security Council Resolution 1368, a riposte by the US is legitimate. The Member States of the Union are prepared to undertake such actions, each according to its means. The actions must be targeted and may also be directed against States abetting, supporting or harbouring terrorists. They will require close cooperation with all the Member States of the European Union.

The European Council went on to call for the broadest possible global coalition against terrorism, and undertook to step up its action against terrorism 'through a coordinated and inter-disciplinary approach embracing all Union policies'. Subsequent elements of the plan covered actions across all three Pillars of the Union.[17]

The European Council has always operated on a basis of consensus and there has never been provision in the Treaties for it to take formal votes.[18] In the years before the European Council was even acknowledged in the Treaties it was sometimes suggested that it could, if it so wished, act as a Council of Ministers. But in practice it never did adopt legal instruments or take any form of decision under legal powers available to the Council of Ministers, and when it was given a formal identity (by Article 2 of the Single European Act) this was on the basis that it was separate from the Council of Ministers and not an institution with powers and jurisdiction. This reticence persists in the Treaty of Amsterdam. Article 23 (ex Article J.13) provides that 'Decisions under this Title shall be taken by the Council acting unanimously.' This cannot be regarded as implying that the European Council does not have power to take decisions—for example the appointment of the new High Representative for the common foreign and security policy was clearly a decision. Article 23 at a later point refers to the power of the Council to 'request that the matter be referred to the European Council for decision by unanimity'. The drafting of Article 23 may lack clarity, but it is clear that the Treaty of Amsterdam does not change the practice whereby the European Council acts by consensus. The limited exceptions to the unanimity rule which apply in the case of decision-making by the Council do not have any application to the European Council.

General guidelines defined by the European Council impose on the Council, by virtue of Article 13.3, the obligation to take 'defining and implementing' decisions. Decisions by the Council at a later date must as

[17] European Council Conclusions, Bull EU 9-2001 points 1.6 to 1.9.
[18] See Werts (1992) especially ch III Summit Meetings, the European Council and the institutional framework of the Community.

a general rule be taken on the basis of existing European Council guidelines. If however there are no relevant European Council guidelines for a particular region, policy area, or event, or a change of circumstances has made earlier guidelines inappropriate, can the Council nevertheless act? Under the Maastricht Treaty it was clear that the Council did not have power to adopt a joint action except on the basis of European Council authority. It could be argued that the Treaty of Amsterdam has generalized this restriction to all areas of CFSP decision by the Council.[19] Given that there may be a gap of six months between one meeting of the European Council and the next, such a limitation would be a significant limitation on the power of the Council to react promptly to important international events and changes. It seems unnecessary to read the words of Article 13.3 as imposing a straitjacket of this kind. There is no real institutional tension between the European Council and the Council both of which ultimately reflect the will of the Member States, and where new policy is to be made by the Council Article 23 retains the rule of unanimity.

As the common foreign and security policy develops and intensifies, a wider and wider spectrum of geographical and policy areas will be covered by European Council guidelines, and it should be noted that the guidelines are not limited to those established since the entry into force of the Treaty of Amsterdam. It will however never be possible for the Union—any more than it is possible for a single State—to have in existence a comprehensive system of European Council guidelines covering all possible external events. The provisions in the Treaty of Amsterdam for urgent convening of the Council (Article 22—ex Article J.12) and for meeting of the Political Committee 'at any time, in the event of international crises or other urgent matters' (Article 25—ex Article J.15 and accompanying Declaration) clearly presuppose the occasional need for urgent Council action, and they are not made subject to the pre-existence of relevant European Council guidelines. The European Council has emphasized the need for a capability of crisis management and urgent decision-making in its Declaration on strengthening the common European policy on security and defence made in Cologne immediately after the entry into force of the Treaty of Amsterdam.[20]

So long as the Council does not disregard existing European Council guidelines or the CFSP objectives spelt out in Article 11 it would appear to be entitled to adopt common positions or joint actions on its own initiative. This interpretation would seem to be confirmed by the way in which the Council in January 2000 reviewed and applied the guidelines on Russia

---

[19] This view is, somewhat doubtfully, put forward by Dashwood (1999) at p 211. Cameron (1998*b*) at p 70, on the other hand, says only that adoption by the Council of a qualified majority decision would not be possible without the blessing of the European Council.

[20] Bull EU 6-1999 points 1.58 and 1.59, Annex 3 to European Council Conclusions.

which the European Council had drawn up in December 1999 in the light of important changes of circumstances—in particular the resignation and replacement of President Yeltsin. These events are described below.

Common Strategies

As far back as 1995 the Council of Ministers had adopted a Strategy on EU/Russian Relations—described in Chapter 4 above. Common strategies under the Treaty of Amsterdam, however, differ in a number of important respects from this earlier 'strategy', which merely formed part of the Council conclusions.

1. The only precondition for deciding on a common strategy is that it should cover an area 'where the Member States have important interests in common'. As to content, a common strategy must specify 'objectives, duration and means to be made available by the Union and the Member States'.

2. Although the European Council is not formally limited to deciding on common strategies recommended by the Council, Article 13 clearly envisages that this should be the normal procedure.

3. Common strategies are legally binding, creating international legal rights and obligations for the Member States and for the institutions of the Union. As was suggested above, however, they have a somewhat political flavour and generally require implementation by more detailed legal instruments.

4. There is no Treaty requirement that common strategies should be published in the Official Journal. The first Common Strategy (on Russia)[21] however provided for its publication in this way, and the precedent has so far been followed in later common strategies.

5. The Council is required to implement common strategies, 'in particular by adopting joint actions and common positions'. Adoption of such joint actions and common positions may be subject to qualified majority voting under Article 23. Common strategies may, however, also require action by Member States or action by the Council under First or Third Pillar provisions of the Treaty. The first Common Strategy provided that such acts should be adopted 'according to the appropriate decision-making procedure provided by the relevant provisions of the Treaties', and this provision may be regarded as declaratory of the position under the Treaty.

The procedural constraints on deciding on a common strategy as well as the long-term and public commitments imposed and the possibility of the

---

[21] Bull EU 6-1999, point 1.3.97; OJ L157/1, 24.6.1999.

Council adopting implementing instruments by qualified majority voting all mean that the common strategy is likely to be limited to areas of the greatest significance for the Union's common foreign policy. This is borne out by the Common Strategy on Russia, adopted by the European Council at Cologne on 3 and 4 June 1999, one month after the entry into force of the Treaty of Amsterdam.

Common Strategy on Russia

At the outset it is instructive to glance back at the earlier Strategy on EU/Russian Relations of 1995 and to note that several of its objectives have been fulfilled—a substantial partnership between Russia and the EU, realized through the Partnership and Cooperation Agreement, free parliamentary and presidential elections, Russian accession to the Council of Europe, increased dialogue at the highest level. In other areas however—economic reform and respect for human rights—progress had been limited while expectations rose. The 1999 Common Strategy begins:

VISION OF THE EU FOR ITS PARTNERSHIP WITH RUSSIA
A stable, democratic and prosperous Russia, firmly anchored in a united Europe free of new dividing lines, is essential to lasting peace on the continent. The issues which the whole continent faces can be resolved only through ever closer cooperation between Russia and the European Union. The European Union welcomes Russia's return to its rightful place in the European family in a spirit of friendship, cooperation, fair accommodation of interests and on the foundation of shared values enshrined in the common heritage of European civilisation.

The two strategic goals for the EU are first stable, open, and pluralistic democracy in Russia, governed by the rule of law and underpinning a prosperous market economy, and secondly maintaining European stability, promoting global security and responding to common challenges through intensified cooperation. These grand ideals are followed by somewhat more precise objectives such as institutional reform, 'a comprehensive and sustainable economic programme approved by the IMF', a fair and transparent legislative and regulatory framework, and strengthening the climate for inward investment. 'Instruments and means' are largely a restatement of the institutional provisions of the Treaty, but they provide also for regular implementing work plans and for reviews by the Council of the Strategy, along with recommendation for its amendment. Part II of the Common Strategy lists areas of action which are specific, detailed, and comprehensive, ranging from Russia's World Trade Organization (WTO) accession through facilitating Russian participation in WEU missions within the Petersberg tasks to organising seminars on money laundering. Part III lists specific initiatives to be pursued by the Member States, the

Council or the Commission as appropriate. Overall, the structure proceeds from the strategic to the tactical and the drafting takes careful account of which provisions can properly be made binding and which are matters of aspiration or future implementation.[22]

Six months later, however, the European Council at Helsinki adopted a tough Declaration on Chechnya condemning the bombardment of Chechen cities, the threat to the residents of Grozny, and the treatment of internally displaced persons. While accepting the right of Russia to preserve its territorial integrity, they said that: 'The fight against terrorism cannot, under any circumstances, warrant the destruction of cities, nor that they be emptied of their inhabitants, nor that a whole population be considered as terrorist.' The European Council threatened a review of the Common Strategy on Russia as well as suspension of some provisions of the Partnership and Cooperation Agreement and transfer of technical assistance programme (TACIS) funds for Russia to humanitarian assistance.[23]

In January 2000 the Council reviewed the situation in Russia, concluding:

It welcomed the democratic conduct of the recent Duma elections and the smooth, constitutional transition of power after the resignation of President Yeltsin. It looks forward to a free and fair campaign leading up to the Presidential election on 26 March. The Council underlines Russia's importance as a major partner of the EU. To this end it is ready to continue its political dialogue with Russia in order to address questions of mutual interest, including issues of disagreement and concern such as the conflict in Chechnya . . .

No provisions of the Partnership and Cooperation Agreement were suspended, even though the Council complained of an increasing number of infringements by Russia. The Council did, however, invite the Commission to refocus TACIS funds to 'core areas directing promoting democratic values' and to humanitarian assistance.[24]

Common Strategy on Ukraine

In December 1999 the European Council adopted a second common strategy on Ukraine. Many of the long-term objectives were similar to those in the Common Strategy for Russia, but there were significant differences. The Common Strategy for Ukraine acknowledged Ukraine's European aspirations and welcomed Ukraine's 'pro-European choice', while making

---

[22] EU Common Strategy 1999/414/CFSP, OJ L157/1, 24.6.1999; Bull EU 6-1999 point 1.3.97.
[23] BQ Europe No 7612, 11 December 1999 pp 3, 8; Bull EU 12-1999 point 1, Annex II to European Council Conclusions.
[24] Council Conclusions in BQ Europe No 7640, 26 January 2000 pp 3–4.

no mention of the possibility of its eventual membership of the Union. There was also a greater emphasis on nuclear safety and the dismantling of the nuclear power station at Chernobyl was identified as a priority in EU–Ukraine relations. The European Union recognized that 'The geopolitical situation of Ukraine, situated along the North-South and East-West axes, gives it a unique position in Europe.'[25] As in the case of Russia, a comparison with the Union's Common Position on Ukraine adopted in 1994[26] shows that several of the objectives of the earlier instrument— democratic development, integration of Ukraine into the world economic order, nuclear disarmament, and accession of Ukraine to the Non-Proliferation Treaty (NPT) as a non-nuclear weapons State—had been achieved in the intervening five years.

Common Strategy on the Mediterranean

The third common strategy to be adopted, in June 2000, was on the Mediterranean region.[27] The aim was to build on the Euro–Mediterranean Partnership established by the Barcelona Declaration[28] and to work towards peace, security, and stability in the Middle East following a comprehensive peace settlement. This Common Strategy covered all EU partners in the Barcelona Process as well as Libya, but excluded States candidates for EU membership. It laid emphasis on promotion of human rights, democracy, good governance, transparency, and the rule of law, on strengthening cooperation in justice and home affairs as well as on cooperative security in the region. Some objectives were very specific to the region—better integrated water strategies and water management policies in the Mediterranean, improved education and vocational training for women, cooperation on illegal immigration as well as improving the legal status of Mediterranean partners' nationals who were long-term residents in the Member States. There has, however, been widespread criticism that in the case of this Common Strategy the framework is too wide and the range of countries too disparate for practical results to be achievable.

[25] 1999/877/CFSP OJ L331, 23.12.1999; Bull EU 12-1999 point 1.4.91; BQ Europe No 7614, 13 December 1999 p 10.
[26] 94/779/CFSP of 28 November 1994 OJ L313/1, 6.12.94, described in Chapter 4 above.
[27] Santa Maria da Feira European Council Conclusions, June 2000, para 58 and Annex V.
[28] For the Declaration and Work Programme see Bull EU 11-1995 or [1996] European Foreign Affairs Rev 125. See also Rhein (1996); Hakura (1997); Edwards and Phillipart (1997); Gomez (1998); Claire Spencer (2001); HL Select Committee on the European Union, 9th Report (2000–2001b).

Joint Actions

ARTICLE 14 (EX ARTICLE J.4)

1. The Council shall adopt joint actions. Joint actions shall address specific situations where operational action by the Union is deemed to be required. They shall lay down their objectives, scope, the means to be made available to the Union, if necessary their duration, and the conditions for their implementation.

2. If there is a change in circumstances having a substantial effect on a question subject to joint action, the Council shall review the principles and objectives of that action and take the necessary decisions. As long as the Council has not acted, the joint action shall stand.

3. Joint action shall commit the Member States in the positions they adopt and in the conduct of their activity.

4. The Council may request the Commission to submit to it any appropriate proposals relating to the common foreign and security policy to ensure the implementation of a joint action.

5. Whenever there is any plan to adopt a national position or take national action pursuant to a joint action, information shall be provided in time to allow, if necessary, for prior consultations within the Council. The obligation to provide prior information shall not apply to measures which are merely a national transposition of Council decisions.

6. In cases of imperative need arising from changes in the situation and failing a Council decision, Member States may take the necessary measures as a matter of urgency having regard to the general objectives of the joint action. The Member State concerned shall inform the Council immediately of any such measures.

7. Should there be any major difficulties in implementing a joint action, a Member State shall refer them to the Council which shall discuss them and seek appropriate solutions. Such solutions shall not run counter to the objectives of the joint action or impair its effectiveness.

The provisions in the Treaty of Amsterdam on joint actions are very similar to those in the Treaty of Maastricht. There are three changes:

1. In paragraph 1, the addition of the words 'Joint actions shall address specific situations where operational action by the Union is deemed to be required' distinguish clearly the character and purpose of joint actions. Joint actions are now clearly contrasted with common

positions—while the latter establish policy, the former involve a commitment by the Union of money and men.

2. There is no formal requirement, as there was in the Treaty of Maastricht, for the Council to 'decide, on the basis of general guidelines from the European Council, that a matter should be the subject of joint action'. The Council is of course bound by general guidelines as well as by common strategies decided on the by the European Council. But—as was suggested above—if there are no relevant guidelines or strategy, the Council may proceed to adopt a joint action. This change gives the Council a greater possibility of urgent action in emergency circumstances.

3. There is in paragraph 4 new provision enabling the Council to 'request the Commission to submit to it any appropriate proposals relating to the common foreign and security policy to ensure the implementation of a joint action'. This new provision does not give the Commission an independent right to propose, since the Council must first issue its request. It does however somewhat strengthen the role of the Commission within the Second Pillar and may be of assistance to the Commission in discharging its responsibility under Article 3 (ex Article C) to ensure consistency of the external activities of the Union. There is no requirement that the requested proposals should be proposals for Second Pillar instruments. They could, for example, be proposals for First Pillar measures on sanctions, on development cooperation or on visas.

In other respects, the provisions on joint actions are unchanged. Most proposals for joint actions will be made by the Presidency. Other Member States may suggest or elaborate proposals, but it is likely that they will try to persuade the Presidency to adopt or at least be associated with them, since otherwise their chances of progress will be limited. It is likely that proposals will increasingly originate with the Policy Planning and Early Warning Unit under the responsibility of the Secretary-General, High Representative for the CFSP. Again, however, the Declaration on the Establishment of a Policy Planning and Early Warning Unit makes clear that any such proposals are to be 'presented under the responsibility of the Presidency'.[29]

Joint actions impose international legal obligations on the Member States, committing them 'in the positions they adopt and in the conduct of their activity'. The obligations are however not within the jurisdiction of the European Court of Justice. The clear intention of the Treaty of Amsterdam is that disputes should be resolved within the Council, and in the nature of joint actions any disputes are likely to require urgent resolution. The

[29] Wessel (1999) pp 116–21.

Council may discuss national implementing actions (paragraph 5), national actions which fill any gap in the absence of Council decision (paragraph 6), changes in circumstances which affect a question subject to joint action (paragraph 2) and major difficulties in implementing a joint action (paragraph 7).

A number of the important joint actions adopted and implemented under the Treaty of Maastricht have been described and evaluated in Chapter 4 above. They covered, in particular, election monitoring in Russia and South Africa, the arrangements for the Stability Pact, prohibiting the export and transfer of landmines and working towards a worldwide Convention prohibiting their use, controlling export of dual-use goods, combating accumulation and spread of small arms and light weapons, resisting exorbitant jurisdictional claims from the US and the administration of the town of Mostar during the conflict in Bosnia.

A joint action under the Treaty of Amsterdam was adopted by the Council in December 1999 pursuant to the Common Strategy on Russia described above as well as the Partnership and Cooperation Agreement with Russia. This was to provide support for Russia's implementation of disarmament obligations by helping it to dismantle weapons infrastructure and industries in an environmentally friendly manner, and to convert former military sites. The programme would also provide a legal framework for an enhanced EU role in assisting with risk reduction activities in Russia.[30]

In March 2002, the Council adopted a Joint Action establishing a European Union Police Mission (EUPM) to follow up the UN International Police Task Force in Bosnia and Herzegovina. The mandate of the EUPM was to establish policing arrangements in accordance with best European and international practice, to assist with institution-building programmes, and to contribute to the overall peace implementation process in Bosnia. The Joint Action set out precise structures, staffing, and command arrangements for the EUPM, invited participation from non-European NATO members and candidates for accession, and made precise arrangements for financing through the Community budget.[31]

---

[30] Joint Action 1999/878/CFSP, OJ L331/1, 23.12.1999; Bull EU 12-1999 point 1.4.90. See in this context Hill (2001) at p 329: 'Nonetheless, the EU has an honourable record of having used its diplomacy to address the root causes of international conflict long before this became a fashionable discourse . . .'

[31] OJ L70/1, 13.2.2002.

Common Positions

ARTICLE 15 (EX ARTICLE J.5)

The Council shall adopt common positions. Common positions shall define the approach of the Union to a particular matter of a geographical or thematic nature. Member States shall ensure that their national policies conform to the common positions.

Like joint actions, common positions have their character and purpose more clearly identified under the Treaty of Amsterdam. Under the Treaty of Maastricht the Council had an open-ended power to define a common position 'Whenever it deems it necessary'. The second substantive change introduced by the Treaty of Amsterdam is that common positions are now *adopted* by the Council. The new wording emphasizes more clearly that they are formal legal instruments imposing public international law obligations on the Member States and on other institutions of the European Union.[32]

Examples of common positions of a geographical nature include the Council Common Positions on Angola,[33] Burundi,[34] and Nigeria.[35] Under the Treaty of Amsterdam the Council in October 1999 adopted a Common Position on support for democratic forces in the Federal Republic of Yugoslavia. The policy envisaged closer dialogue with democratically oriented local leaders and leaders of civic organizations, providing a forum for discussion on political and technical issues and intensified support for democratic needs.[36] A Common Position on Rwanda adopted in 2000 was carefully revised in 2001.[37]

In January 2000 the Council adopted a Common Position on Afghanistan. This begins by listing six objectives of the Union in Afghanistan: sustainable peace through support for the central role of the United Nations; stability of the region; respect for humanitarian law and human rights; effective humanitarian aid; fighting illegal drugs and terrorism; and reconstruction of the country after civil war. The later Articles set out in detail how the Union, through diplomatic methods and in conjunction with other organizations and agencies, must work towards these

---

[32] Wessel (1999) pp 121–30.
[33] Defined on 2. October 1995, 95/413/CFSP OJ L245/1, 12.10.95.
[34] Defined on 24 March 1995, 95/91/CFSP OJ L72/1, 1.4.95.
[35] Defined on 20 November 1995, 95/515/CFSP OJ L298/1, 11.12.95 and on 4 December 1995, 95/544/CFSP OJ L309/1, 21.12.95.
[36] 1999/691/CFSP OJ L273/1, 23.10.99, Bull EU 10-1999 point 1.5.57.
[37] OJ L236/1, 20.9.2000; OJ L303/1, 20.11.2001.

objectives. Contrasting this precise and well drafted instrument with the anodyne declarations and statements emerging from European Political Cooperation ten years ago brings out how far CFSP has advanced towards the reality of international legal obligation.[38] A revised Common Position on Afghanistan adopted a year later indicated rather less emphasis on reconstruction after civil war and more on the fight against terrorism. This instrument was soon followed by imposition of additional restrictive measures against the Taliban—a ban on arms supply, withdrawal of personnel, closure of offices in the country, a freeze on Afghan Government assets, prohibition of air services, and visa bans.[39]

A Common Position which had a geographical as well as a thematic nature concerned conflict prevention and resolution in Africa. This instrument stated in Article 1 that 'The policy of the Union is to facilitate African capacity and means of action in the field of conflict prevention and resolution, in particular through support for the OAU and subregional organizations and initiatives.' Article 2 provided that 'While recognizing the need to respond to existing crises, the Union's policy shall also focus on preventing the outbreak or recurrence of violent conflicts, including at an early stage, and on post-conflict peace-building.'[40] A later Common Position on the same theme, adopted in May 2001, extended the objectives to include management of conflicts at the acute stage, laid greater emphasis on enhancing African capabilities and covered the question of restricting export of arms (by then covered by the Union's Code of Conduct).[41]

An example of a common position on a matter of a 'thematic nature' adopted under the Treaty of Amsterdam was the Council Common Position on the European Union's contribution to the promotion of the early entry into force of the 1996 Comprehensive Nuclear Test Ban Treaty.[42] This Common Position, issued shortly before the first review conference of the Treaty, emphasized that the Treaty was an important step towards nuclear non-proliferation and disarmament which contributed to international confidence, stability, and peace in the world. It required the EU to support the convening of the forthcoming conference at political level and with the broadest participation, to support the presence of non-governmental organizations and to seek to identify and to promote measures to accelerate the ratification process. The strengthening of safeguards against proliferation of nuclear weapons had since the end of the Cold War been a central objective of the CFSP, and earlier efforts in the same direction were described in Chapters 2 and 4 above.

[38] 2000/55/CFSP OJ L21/1, 26.1.2000·

[39] OJ L21/1, 23.1.2001; OJ L 57/1, 27.2.2001; OJ L67/1, 9.3.2001 (implementing Council Regulation No. 467/2001). The 2001 Common Position was repealed in February 2002.

[40] 97/356/CFSP OJ L153/1, 11.6.97. See Hill (2001). [41] OJ L132/1, 15.5.2001.

[42] 1999/533/CFSP, adopted on 29 July 1999, OJ L204/1, 4.8.99. The Comprehensive Test Ban Treaty is published as Cm 3665, Misc No 7 (1997).

Common positions, like joint actions, impose international legal obligations on the Member States to 'ensure that their national policies conform to the common positions'. This wording implies that national policies coexist with common foreign and security policies. As was emphasized at the beginning of Chapter 4 above, the CFSP is a *common* foreign policy and not a *single* foreign policy. In areas where there is no common position in effect, Member States are at liberty to protect and pursue their separate national policies. Nor does a common position always impose any obligation on a Member State or institution of the EU to take further specific action. This distinguishes a common position from a joint action where the nature of the instrument imposes specific commitments in terms of money or of men.

Common positions on the imposition of sanctions—whether pursuant to or independently of a Security Council resolution—do however require implementing action by the Council to the extent that the subject matter falls within First Pillar powers to impose commercial or financial sanctions and by the Member States to the extent that the subject matter (for example an arms embargo) falls outside European Community competence. Although the EC Treaty, in Article 301 (ex Article 228a) speaks of action by way of a common position or a joint action, it has been consistent practice for the instrument determining the extent of EU sanctions to take the form of a common position. Sanctions are examined more fully in Chapter 8 below.

Decisions

The Treaty of Amsterdam does not make clear provision for decisions. Decisions are not among the instruments listed in Article 12. In Article 13 they are mentioned in paragraph 3: 'The Council shall take the decisions necessary for defining and implementing the common foreign and security policy on the basis of the general guidelines defined by the European Council.' Although the EC Treaty in Article 249 (ex Article 189) specifies that 'A decision shall be binding in its entirety upon those to whom it is addressed', this description relates to decisions within the First Pillar. The Council nevertheless adopts substantial numbers of Second Pillar decisions, and their legal purpose and effect must be inferred from Council practice.

Council decisions under the Second Pillar are given a CFSP number and are published in the legislative series of the Official Journal. From this it may be taken that the Council regards them as legally binding.[43] They are not in practice limited to decisions implementing general guidelines

---

[43] Koskenniemi (1998) at p 31, makes a similar point on common positions.

defined by the European Council, but they do have in common that, at least since the entry into force of the Treaty of Amsterdam, they are subordinate instruments. Their purpose is usually to implement details of common positions or of joint actions. Thus, for example, the Council by Decision appointed a Special Representative to act as Coordinator of the Stability Pact for South-Eastern Europe (though the appointment was later confirmed by a Council Joint Action).[44] On 15 November 1999 the Council adopted a common position on support for the implementation of the Lusaka ceasefire agreement and the peace process in the Democratic Republic of Congo. This was cast in general terms, referring back to earlier Common Positions on conflict prevention and resolution in Africa and on human rights, democratic principles, the rule of law and good governance in Africa.[45] Article 3 provided that 'The European Union will support the Joint Military Commission to allow it to fulfil its tasks as specified in its Rules of Procedure.' On the same day the Council adopted a Decision, drafted in clearly binding terms, committing the Union to contribute towards operational, non-military expenditure to enable the Joint Military Commission to deploy observers in the Democratic Republic of Congo for a six-month period. The Decision specified an amount, a procedure for disbursement and envisaged a further agreement with the Organization of African Unity (OAU) for accounting and auditing.[46]

Decisions are also used to amend, extend, or repeal other CFSP instruments. A Council Decision of 19 July 1999 repealed a Joint Action nominating a European Union Special Envoy for Kosovo, because following deployment of the UN Mission in Kosovo his mandate had been fulfilled.[47] Another Council Decision of 19 July 1999 amended a Common Position on arms exports to the former Yugoslavia—permitting transfers of small arms to police in Bosnia to take account of changes in the international military presence in Bosnia and the need to continue pacification in that country.[48] The Joint Action on the establishment of an assistance programme to support the Palestinian Authority in counter-terrorist activities in territories under its control was extended by a Council Decision.[49]

[44] Council Decisions of 2 July 1999, 1999/434/CFSP OJ L168/1, 3.7.99 and of 29 July 1999, 1999/523/CFSP OJ L201/1, 31.7.1999.

[45] 97/356/CFSP OJ L153/1, 11.6.97; 98/350/CFSP, OJ L158/1, 2.6.98.

[46] Common Position 1999/728/CFSP OJ L158/2; Council Decision 1999/729/CFSP, OJ L294/1, 16.11.99. A similar example is the Council Decision implementing the Council Joint Action on the European Union's contribution to combatting the destabilizing accumulation and spread of small arms and light weapons, OJ L318/1, 4.12.2001.

[47] 1999/524/CFSP OJ L201/1, 31.7.99.

[48] Council Decision 1999/481/CFSP, OJ L188/1, 21.7.99.

[49] Council Decision 1999/440/CFSP adopted on 6 July 1999 OJ L171/1, 7.7.99. The practice is not however consistent: the arms embargo on Ethiopia and Eritrea imposed by Common Position 1999/206/CFSP, OJ L72/1, 18.3.99, was extended by another Common Position 1999/650/CFSP OJ L257/1, 2.10.99. Joint actions have also been amended by further joint

By contrast, the mandate of Miguel Angel Moratinos as Special Representative for the Middle East peace process was extended in 2001 by a further Joint Action.[50] In this case the new instrument was not a simple extension, but contained a revised mandate, a financial reference amount for 2002, and a requirement for the Special Representative to conclude a contract with the Council.

Choice of Legal Instrument

Under the Treaty of Maastricht not only were the respective purposes of common positions and joint actions unclear, but the practice of the Council was not always consistent. Under the Treaty of Amsterdam the Council has developed a more consistent practice when selecting from the four kinds of legally binding instrument: common strategies, joint actions, common positions, and decisions. To summarize current practice:

1. Common strategies can be adopted only by the European Council and impose general obligations which require more specific legal implementation by the Council, the Commission, or the Member States.
2. Joint actions are adopted by the Council where 'operational action'— that is the commitment usually of money or men—is required.
3. Common positions are adopted by the Council to define a common approach to a specific area or subject, but somewhat exceptionally are used to prescribe sanctions.
4. Decisions are subsidiary instruments to implement, amend, or extend joint actions or common positions.

The distinction between common position and joint action was well illustrated by the Council Common Position concerning a Stability Pact for South-Eastern Europe.[51] The first Stability Pact, concluded under the Treaty of Maastricht and relating to European republics of the former Soviet Union, took the form of a comprehensive joint action.[52] The later Stability Pact by contrast, concluded under the Treaty of Amsterdam and setting out broad policy objectives of the European Union, took the form of a common position. More specific commitments such as the appointment of a Special Representative of the European Union to act as Coordinator of

---

actions—see for example Joint Action 1999/664/CFSP, OJ L264/1, 12.10.1999, amending Joint Action 96/676/CFSP OJ L315/1, 4.12.96. In this case the entry into force of the Treaty of Amsterdam between the original Joint Action and its amendment may have been a factor.

[50] OJ L303/5, 20.11.2001.

[51] 1999/345/CFSP OJ L133/1, 28.5.99, Bull EU 5-1999 point 1.3.71.

[52] 93/728/CFSP O L339/1, 31.12.1993; 94/158/CFSP OJ L70/1; 94/367/CFSP OJ L165/1, 1.7.1994. See Chapter 4 above.

the Stability Pact and the provision of financial aid and logistical assistance for the organization of a meeting of Heads of State and Government in Sarajevo on the Stability Pact were shortly afterwards adopted as Joint Actions.[53]

Statements and Conclusions without Legal Force

A very large part of the foreign policy output of a sovereign State consists of statements and documents which are not intended directly to create legal effects or legal relations—for example communiques, notes, aide-memoires, press releases, statements to the national parliament.[54] The same is true of the common foreign and security policy. In addition to the conclusions of the Foreign Affairs Council and press releases, the Council may issue formal statements which have political significance, and may as a matter of international law have certain legal effects. They are not, however, legally binding in the same sense as the four instruments described above.

The most weighty instruments are declarations—for example the Declaration on a new beginning for relations between the European Union and the Federal Republic of Yugoslavia (FRY) published on 1 October 1999.[55] In this Declaration the European Union 'undertakes' to pursue prescribed objectives on condition that the governments of Serbia and the FRY are democratically controlled and that all individuals indicted by the International Criminal Tribunal for the former Yugoslavia are 'removed from Federal and Republic offices'. Declarations were also published by the Council on 11 and 16 October 1999 on the entry into force of the Comprehensive Nuclear Test Ban Treaty. The first stressed the commitment of the Union to work for its early entry into force while the second deeply regretted the US Senate's decision not to ratify the Treaty.[56] On 21 May 2000 the EU issued a Declaration on the Middle East Peace Process noting the existence of a real opportunity to attain a 'just, lasting and comprehensive peace in the Middle East, based on the basic principles established within the framework of Madrid'. The Declaration appealed to Israel and the Palestinian authority to intensify efforts to conclude the Framework Agreement foreseen in the Sharm-al-Sheikh Memorandum of September 1999 as well as the Permanent Status negotiations. The Union also welcomed Israel's decision to withdraw from Southern Lebanon in accordance with Security Council Resolutions.[57]

---

[53] 1999/523/CFSP OJ L201/1, 31.7.99 and 1999/480/CFSP OJ L188/1, 21.7.99.
[54] See Satow (1979) ch 7 'The language and forms of diplomatic intercourse'.
[55] Bull EU 10-1999 point 1.5.20.   [56] Bull EU 10-99 point 1.5.22 and 1.5.23.
[57] Press Release 174, 8744/00-CFSP 73/00. On the legal nature of Declarations, see Wessel (1999) pp 185–9.

Much more frequent, but less formal, are presidency statements on behalf of the European Union.[58] These are not significantly different in content or effect from the declarations issued under European Political Cooperation or under the Treaty of Maastricht. They express condemnation, concern, regret and—rather less frequently—they welcome or congratulate.

Council conclusions—though never drafted in such a way as to suggest a legally binding character—may in certain contexts mark major policy shifts by the European Union and create expectations in non-Member States as well as in Europe. As an example in this category one may cite the Council Conclusions on Kosovo adopted on 21 June 1999, in which:

> The Council warmly welcomed the adoption of the UN Security Council Resolution (UNSCR) 1244, the full withdrawal of all Serb security forces, the end of NATO's air campaign, as well as the deployment of KFOR and the steps under way to establish an interim civil administration for Kosovo.

As well as calling for the creation of a democratic, multi-ethnic Kosovo, the return of refugees and the bringing of justice to the perpetrators of atrocities, the Conclusions stressed the importance of active and constructive Russian participation in the international community's efforts to restore stability and respect for human rights in Kosovo. They emphasized that the Union would participate fully in the UN Interim Administrative Mission in Kosovo, would appoint a Special Representative of the Secretary-General and welcomed reconstruction and humanitarian initiatives already undertaken by the Commission. These Conclusions may be regarded as marking the beginning of a much more pro-active policy by the European Union on Yugoslavia.[59]

The Conclusions of the European Council at Laeken drew together the results of a period of intense diplomatic and legal activity following the attacks in the US on 11 September 2001. Describing the Union's action in Afghanistan: 'The European Council welcomes the signing in Bonn on 5 December of the agreement defining the provisional arrangements applicable in Afghanistan pending the re-establishment of permanent State institutions. It urges all Afghan groups to implement that agreement.' The Conclusions welcomed the establishment of an international security force under United Nations mandate, and noted that participation by Member States in that force would 'provide a strong signal of their resolve to better assume their crisis management responsibilities . . .'. As well as noting specific pledges of humanitarian aid, the Conclusions declared 'The European Union will help the Afghan people and its new leaders rebuild the country and encourage as swift a return to democracy as possible.' The

---

[58] The Council made clear in a Decision of 8 November 1993, OJ L281/1, 16.11.93, that further statements under CFSP would be made in the name of the Union.

[59] Bull EU 6-1999 points I.26, 1.3.91, BQ Europe 25 June 1999 p 5, Cremona (1999).

European Council also reaffirmed its solidaarity with the American people and the international community in combating terrorism with full regard for individual rights and freedoms. It noted that the plan of action adopted on 21 September at an emergency European Council in Brussels was being implemented in accordance with the timetable set.[60]

[60] Conclusions of the European Council at Laeken, 14 and 15 December 2001, paras 13–18: The Union's action in Afghanistan.

Strengthening Systematic Cooperation
ARTICLE 16 (EX ARTICLE J.6)

Member States shall inform and consult one another within the Council on any matter of foreign and security policy of general interest in order to ensure that the Union's influence is exerted as effectively as possible by means of concerted and convergent action.

Adopting and publishing the declarations and statements described above is one form of the systematic cooperation envisaged by Article 16. The obligation of cooperation however goes wider than that. It covers not only the reflection in national foreign policy of political declarations and statements as well as legally binding instruments but also the whole process of actively working together to form, develop, and implement the Union's policy. It may be regarded as a somewhat weaker equivalent, in the Second Pillar, of Article 10 (ex Article 5) in the EC Treaty. Strengthening systematic cooperation by informing and consulting others within the Council is also reflected in the specific obligations in Article 19 (ex Article J.9) and in Article 20 (ex Article J.10) regarding coordination and cooperation in international organizations, conferences and through diplomatic and consular missions in third countries.

Security and Defence

ARTICLE 17 (EX ARTICLE J.7)

Security and defence are the subject of Chapter 11 below.

Representation of the Union

ARTICLE 18 (EX ARTICLE J.8)

1. The Presidency shall represent the Union in matters coming within the common foreign and security policy.
2. The Presidency shall be responsible for the implementation of decisions taken under this Title. In that capacity it shall in principle express the position of the Union in international organisations and international conferences.
3. The Presidency shall be assisted by the Secretary-General of the Council who shall exercise the function of High Representative for the common foreign and security policy.
4. The Commission shall be fully associated in the tasks referred to in paragraphs 1 and 2. The Presidency shall be assisted in those tasks if need be by the next Member State to hold the Presidency.
5. The Council may, whenever it deems it necessary, appoint a special representative with a mandate in relation to particular policy issues.

Paragraphs 1 and 2 of Article 18 set out the primary responsibility of the Presidency for the external representation and the implementation of the common foreign and security policy of the Union. The substantive responsibility of the Presidency to act as spokesman and coordinator in foreign policy matters goes back not only to Article J.5 of the Maastricht Treaty, but all the way to its original codification in the London Declaration of 1981.[61] The role of the Presidency as spokesman and marshal emphasizes the intergovernmental character of the CFSP and the continuing identities of the Member States—who are seen to appoint one of their number as agent on a rotating basis. It contrasts sharply with the position under the common commercial policy where the Commission, though acting within

---

[61] Described in Chapter 2 above.

Council directives, initiates and conducts external negotiations itself. (Special considerations apply in international organizations which are dealt with in Article 19 which is discussed below.)

It must be emphasized that in reality most significant dialogue and negotiations with non-Member States, as well as a high proportion of work in international organizations, straddle the boundary between First Pillar and Second Pillar matters. The theoretical position is that in such negotiations the Commission acts as spokesman where Community issues—in particular common commercial policy questions—are discussed and the Presidency acts as spokesman where the issue is one within the CFSP. In practice, given in particular the complex and shifting boundaries of Community competence, the question of representation may not be so clear cut and on the spot coordination is usually required. On issues which remain entirely within national competence, or where there are no CFSP guidelines or common position, the Member States are entitled to express their own national positions.

The disadvantages of representation of the Union's common foreign policy only by the rotating Presidency lay in the lack of continuity and the low level of visibility. Although in the Treaty of Maastricht the Member States sought to enhance the visibility of the Union on the international scene and to improve continuity through the troika system (assistance from the previous and succeeding Presidencies), it was generally believed that they had not succeeded. The Reflection Group had stressed that implementation of external actions required a high profile.[62] The additional provisions on external representation of the European Union—paragraphs 3, 4, and 5 of Article 18—are all designed to address these problems of continuity and of visibility.

High Representative for the Common Foreign and Security Policy

The appointment of a senior political figure as a long-term embodiment of the CFSP was widely supported by the Reflection Group and by the Member States at the Intergovernmental Conference. The first European Council after the entry into force of the Treaty of Amsterdam designated Javier Solana Madariaga as High Representative for the Common Foreign and Security Council and Secretary-General of the Council. Pierre de Boissieu was also appointed Deputy Secretary-General.[63] Javier Solana was a former Secretary-General of NATO and before that Foreign Minister of Spain. It was apparent before long that his appointment was indeed giving a higher profile as well as a greater degree of continuity and active

---

[62] Report SN 520/95 (REFLEX 21), described at p 125 above. See also Fink-Hooijer (1994) pp 186–8.
[63] Bull EU 6-1999 points 1.1, 1.3.4.

engagement to the Union's common policies. In the words of the UK Minister of State in the Foreign and Commonwealth Office: 'Frankly, I think he is worth his salary several times over because he has done such a good job in the very few months that he has been appointed and he has proved to be extremely effective at dealing with these very, very difficult and complicate issues.'[64]

The wording of Article 18: 'The Presidency shall be assisted by the Secretary-General of the Council . . .' emphasizes that the High Representative for the CFSP does not have an independent role or policy-making function. There was therefore some anxiety in London and Paris when in November 1999 it was widely reported that Mr Solana had pub-licly supported the idea that the European Union should have a seat in the UN Security Council additional to those of France and the UK. Ministers in those States were quick to point out that these remarks did not reflect agreed Union policy.[65]

The other functions of the High Representative for the common foreign and security policy are set out in Article 26, discussed below.

The New Troika

The old form of Troika, as formalized in Article J.5 of the Treaty of Maastricht comprised the Presidency 'assisted if need be by the previous and next Member States to hold the Presidency'. In practice however the provision that '[t]he Commission shall be fully associated in these tasks' was interpreted so as to include the Commission in any representation of the Union, so that the so-called Troika actually had four horses drawing it.[66]

The new formulation contained in Article 18 of the Treaty of Amster-dam gives greater emphasis to the participation of the Commission, some-what subordinates the participation of the next Member State to hold the Presidency (in that this State assists only 'if need be') and drops the previ-ous holder of the Presidency altogether. The new Troika may be composed of the Presidency, the High Representative of the Common Foreign and Security Policy, and the Commission. The regular involvement of the Commissioner for External Relations—since 1999 Mr Christopher Patten—has also raised the profile and the level of continuity in the exter-nal representation of the Union.

The changes in the allocation of Commission portfolios made when Mr Romano Prodi became President of the European Commission in 1999 resulted in the appointment of a single Commissioner and a single

---

[64] HL Select Committee on the European Union (1999–2000) at p 10.
[65] *The Times* 18 November 1999.   [66] See Fink-Hooijer (1994) at p 166.

Directorate-General for External Relations. These changes have helped to enhance the profile of the Commission in the external representation of the Union as well as to streamline relations with non-Member States and international organizations.

Special Representatives

Appointments of EU representatives for specific foreign policy tasks were made under and even before the Treaty of Maastricht. Examples include Lord Carrington and later Lord Owen as Chairman of the European Community Peace Conference on Yugoslavia and Hans Koschnick as European Union Administrator for Mostar. In March 1999 the Union appointed a Special Representative for Kosovo. This was a short appointment, terminated when his mandate was considered to be fulfilled when the United Nations Mission was deployed in Kosovo.[67] Under the express power conferred by the Treaty of Amsterdam, one early and important appointment was that of Mr Bodo Hombach as Special Representative of the European Union to act as Co-ordinator for the Stability Pact for South-Eastern Europe.[68] The 1997 appointment of Nils Eriksson as European Union Adviser to oversee the assistance programme to support the Palestinian authority in efforts to counter terrorist activity was extended in July 1999 until May 2002.[69]

These changes taken together provide for the Union a variety of possible forms of external representation, enhance the political weight and continuity of the Union's voice and image on the world stage, and help to differentiate EU policies and initiatives from those of the State holding the Presidency.

[67] Joint Action 1999/239/CFSP OJ L89/1 1.4.1999, repealed by Council Decision 1999/524/CFSP OJ L201/1, 31.7.1999.

[68] Under Joint Action 1999/523/CFSP OJ L201/1, 31.7.1999, extended by Joint Action 1999/822/CFSP OJ L318/40/1, 11.12.1999. The Joint Actions set out in detail the functions and responsibilities of the Special Representative: to chair the South-eastern Europe regional Table, promote achievement of the Pact's objectives among individual countries, participate in the High Level Steering Group coordinating donor countries.

[69] Joint Action 97/289/CFSP OJ L120/1, 12.5.1997, extended by Joint Action 99/440/CFSP OJ L171/1, 7.7. 1999.

International Organizations

ARTICLE 19 (EX ARTICLE J.9)

1. Member States shall coordinate their action in international organisations and at international conferences. They shall uphold the common position in such fora.

In international organisations and at international conferences where not all the Member States participate, those which do take part shall uphold the common positions.
2. Without prejudice to paragraph 1 and Article 14(3), Member States represented in international organisations or international conferences where not all the Member States participate shall keep the latter informed of any matter of common interest.

Member States which are also members of the United Nations Security Council will concert and keep the other Member States fully informed. Member States which are permanent members of the Security Council will, in the execution of their functions, ensure the defence of the positions and the interests of the Union, without prejudice to their responsibilities under the provisions of the United Nations Charter.

The wording of Article 19 is virtually unchanged from that in the Treaty of Maastricht. Each of its two paragraphs, however, originated in a different paragraph of Article J of the Treaty of Maastricht. Since both paragraphs relate to the conduct of the CFSP by Member States in the context of international organizations it was right to bring them together, but additional redrafting would have clarified the different obligations imposed on the Member States. These obligations are somewhat interwoven in the text of Article 19.

Essentially there are two obligations in Article 19. The first is to coordinate and—where not all Member States are represented—to inform. These functions have the purpose of ensuring the formation of a common foreign and security policy which takes full account of the interests of all Member States of the Union. The second obligation is to present and to defend the common policy of the Union—so far as it exists—in all international fora. An example of successful coordination among the Member States was the UN sponsored World Conference Against Racism, Racial Discrimination, Xenophobia and Related Intolerance in Durban, South Africa in 2001. Concerted efforts by the Member States avoided a Conference Declaration that slavery in the past was a crime against humanity calling for apologies and reparations from States involved. Instead there was acknowledgment that slavery and the slave trade were 'appalling tragedies in the history of humanity' because of their abhorrent barbarism, but no admission which might have founded vast claims for compensation.[70]

The second indent of Article 19(2) makes special provision for Member States which are also members of the UN Security Council. On the one hand it imposes an additional obligation—to ensure the defence of the *interests* of the Union as well as its common positions. It may be regarded as no more than a drafting anomaly that a similar obligation is not set out for other international organizations, since such an obligation can be inferred from other provisions of the Treaty such as Article 11(2). On the other hand, Security Council members are given a special safeguard in the final words: 'without prejudice to their responsibilities under the provisions of the United Nations Charter'. These words could be regarded as declaratory of Article 103 of the Charter which provides: 'In the event of a conflict between the obligations of the Members of the United Nations under the present Charter and their obligations under any other international agreement, their obligations under the present Charter shall prevail.' In the context of the Treaty of Amsterdam they serve however to highlight the fact that for the foreseeable future two Member States only of the Union will be permanent members of the Security Council and it will never be possible for all Member States of the Union simultaneously to be members of the Security Council.

The European Union and International Organizations

It must be borne in mind that whereas an increasingly large proportion of international diplomacy and law-making takes place within the framework of international organizations, it will for the most part be some or all of the Member States of the European Union who are members of these international organizations. Even the European Community which has had from the outset international legal personality acknowledged by non-Member States[71] has struggled for years to have full rights of membership, such as speaking and voting in most international organizations. Other States have been reluctant to embark on the constitutional revision required for admission of the European Community or have demanded unacceptable concessions as a price. In consequence it has usually been in the context of constitutional revision—as with the renewal of commodity agreements or the replacement of the informal GATT structures by the

---

[70] *Observer*, 9 September 2001; *Counsel*, December 2001, p 20; Bull EU 9-2001 point 1.2.1.

[71] The legal personality of the European Economic Community was not for many years accepted by the Soviet Union or by other Communist States.

World Trade Organization—that full membership has been accorded to the European Community. Where the European Community is to participate along with its Member States as a full member, special rules on speaking, voting, and financing must be agreed.[72]

The EU, by contrast, has no clearly defined international legal personality and is thus not even on the starting line to be accorded membership rights in any international organization. Even if international legal personality were to be expressly conferred by treaty revision or by some formal declaration by the Member States, the history of the European Community's emergence as an international entity suggests that treaty-making capacity would be accepted more readily than membership of an international organization. The formula used for the admittance of the European Community refers to 'a regional economic integration organization . . . to which its Member States have transferred competence over a range of matters within the purview of the Organization, including the authority to make decisions binding on its Member States in respect of those matters'.[73] As has been emphasized, the Member States have not in setting up the CFSP transferred competence or ultimate responsibility over foreign and security policy.

It does not therefore seem likely that the EU will be accepted in the near future as a full member of any other international organization. There would be little prospect of the UN—which obviously would be the organization of greatest interest to the Union—embarking on Charter revision in order to admit the Union while it did not claim to be a 'peace-loving state'. It follows that the obligations set out in Article 19 will remain of crucial importance for an indefinite period.

Practice in International Organizations

Much of what is said in commenting on Article 18 above applies equally in the context of international organizations. The principle that it is for the Presidency to take the lead in presenting common positions applies, but other Member States who are represented in the conference or international organization are also entitled to speak, provided that the substance of their proposal or intervention conforms to the common position of the Union. If the matter under discussion falls within Community competence and the Community does not have separate membership or representation, it will fall to the Presidency to take the lead in presenting the

---

[72] See *The European Community, International Organizations and Multilateral Agreements*; Denza (1996); Sack (1995). On practice in the UN, see Senni (2000).

[73] This is the wording used in the 1992 version of Article II of the Constitution of the Food and Agriculture Organization.

European Community's position and to ensure coordination among other Member States wishing to intervene.[74]

Where the Presidency Member State is not represented—most usually because it is not a member of the international organization in question— the duties of representation and coordination in accordance with Article 18 fall to the next Member State to hold the Presidency.

In the more important international organizations, practices have evolved in regard to Community coordination which take account of the extent to which the Member States are individually represented and the constitutional practices and procedures of the particular organization. If a dispute over procedure or representation cannot be resolved *sur place* in the light of the rules in the Treaty on European Union and the practices in the particular organization, instructions must be sought from the Council in Brussels.[75]

---

[74] For comment on the difficulties of effective formulation and presentation of an EU negotiating position where competence over the subject matter is divided, see Grubb and Yamin (2001) especially pp 274–6.

[75] On the growing experience of collective diplomacy in international negotiations, conferences, and organizations, see Ginsberg (1999).

Embassies and Consulates Abroad: Cooperation

ARTICLE 20 (EX ARTICLE J.10)

The diplomatic and consular missions of the Member States and the Commission Delegations in third countries and international conferences, and their representations to international organisations, shall cooperate in ensuring that the common positions and joint actions adopted by the Council are complied with and implemented.

They shall step up cooperation by exchanging information, carrying out joint assessments and contributing to the implementation of the provisions referred to in Article 20 of the Treaty establishing the European Community

One indication of their continuing independence in the conduct of their foreign relations is the fact that each Member State maintains diplomatic relations with close to two hundred non-Member States—and of course with all the other Member States. Each Member State is entitled to establish a permanent diplomatic mission in each State with which it has diplomatic relations, but for a variety of reasons may choose not to do so. The European Union, not being a State, has no power to enter into diplomatic relations and neither the Union nor the Council maintain representations in non-Member States.

The European Commission maintains delegations in a large number of non-member countries. These are often by courtesy named diplomatic missions, but they are not entitled to perform the full range of diplomatic functions. They are entitled to observe, report, and negotiate on questions which fall within Community competence. In practice most of their work relates to trade and aid.[76] By contrast, non-Member States send ambassadors to the European Union. These ambassadors are entitled to exercise the full range of functions of representatives of sovereign States, including those which fall within the common foreign and security policy, or the Third Pillar. How they carry out these functions, gather information, and negotiate will of course depend on the division of competence in the EU to which they are accredited.

[76] In 1995 the Commission had 121 missions in non-member countries: Hansard HL Debs 19 April 1995, WA 51. See also Hansard 1 May 1995, WA 100, Baroness Chalker: 'The European Commission has always maintained a network of offices in countries outside the European Community, to distribute aid under Community programmes, to monitor barriers to trade, to give economic and technical assistance, and to disseminate information.' For current information on activities of the Commission's Unified External Service see its annual General Report on the Activities of the European Union and Vacher's Companion.

Informal cooperation between the embassies and consulates of the Member States is as old as European Political Cooperation (EPC). Over the years it intensified in parallel with EPC until it was made a matter of legal obligation in the Treaty of Maastricht. The substance of the obligations is unchanged in the Treaty of Amsterdam. The first requirement is to cooperate in the implementation of Council common positions and joint actions. This could mean the delivery of an aide-memoire by a diplomatic representative of the Presidency or a common approach to such bilateral matters as contracts, official visits, or downgrading of relations. In the context of international conferences it could imply a prescribed approach by national representatives to amendments to a draft treaty, interventions in debate, and seeking support for EU initiatives contained, for example, in joint actions.

The second obligation is to exchange information and carry out joint assessments. This is an essential part of the formation by the Council in Brussels of a coherent and soundly based common policy. The information might be on compliance with human rights in a non-Member State, on immigration threats to the Union, on political developments affecting the stability of the government, or on evasion of an arms embargo. Information obtained which is of general interest or is jointly put together may be circulated on the COREU network so as to be received by those working in the Policy Planning and Early Warning Unit within the Council Secretariat and briefing members of the Political Committee.[77]

Specific mention is made of the implementation of Article 20 of the EC Treaty. Article 20 (ex Article 8c) of the EC Treaty—within the provisions on citizenship of the Union—provides that:

Every citizen of the Union shall in the territory of a third country in which the Member State of which he is a national is not represented, be entitled to protection by the diplomatic or consular authorities of any Member State, on the same conditions as the national of that State. Member States shall establish the necessary rules among themselves and start the international negotiations required to secure this protection.

The basic rules for extending such protection were defined in a Decision of the Representatives of the Governments of the Member States meeting within the Council on 19 December 1995.[78] Protection may cover assistance in case of death, accident or serious illness, arrest or detention, assistance to victims of crime, and relief and repatriation of distressed persons. More sensitive matters such as requests for pardon or early release and

---

[77] See Articles 25 and 26 pp 179–84 below. For an excellent account of how CFSP coordination works, based on interviews with Embassies of the Member States in Seoul, Commission officials and foreign ministries, see Stephanie Anderson (2001).

[78] OJ L314/73/1, 28.12.95. See Denza (1998) 36–7.

complaints of ill-treatment are taken in liaison with the Member State of which the detainee is a national. Non-Member States cannot under the general rules on diplomatic protection be required to accept representations based on these European Union obligations, but there is no public indication of resistance by other States.

Other Forms of Diplomatic Collaboration

In addition to the forms of cooperation specified in Article 20, the Member States show their closeness in foreign policy matters in other ways within the framework of the Vienna Convention on Diplomatic Relations. Where diplomatic relations are broken or a permanent mission withdrawn by one Member State alone, it is now standard practice for that State to ask another Member State, under Article 45 of the Vienna Convention, to protect its interests.[79]

A more recent development among Member States is the establishment of shared embassy premises. 'Shared embassies' do not imply that the ambassadors and diplomatic staff within them represent more than one Member State. Such multiple accreditation is compatible with individual sovereign status and is specifically permitted by Article 6 of the Vienna Convention on Diplomatic Relations. The option has not however been much used so far by European Union Member States, who insist on appointing only their own nationals as diplomatic representatives. Nor does the sharing extend to archives or communications—where national cypher facilities are extended to other Member States only in exceptional circumstances.[80]

For the avoidance of misunderstanding, shared embassies are often described as 'co-location of embassies'. It is the premises and, to some extent, the functions of observing, reporting, and protecting, which are shared. The most developed scheme is in Abuja, Nigeria, where almost all Member States participate. Other more limited projects are in Belarus, Iceland, Kazakhstan, and Zaire.[81] The UK and France at the St. Malo summit in December 1998 agreed to embark on shared embassies in Guinea, Mali, and Gabon—capitals where the UK had not previously maintained a permanent diplomatic mission.[82]

---

[79] Denza (1998) 400–1.

[80] It was reported in *The Times*, 13 January 1999, that the German Embassy in Freetown had allowed the exiled UK High Commissioner to Sierra Leone to send details of allegedly illegal arms supplies through German facilities to London.

[81] A list of co-location projects is in OJ C60/12/1, 26.2.1997.

[82] *The Times*, 31 December 1998.

The European Parliament

ARTICLE 21 (EX ARTICLE J.11)

The Presidency shall consult the European Parliament on the main aspects and the basic choices of the common foreign and security policy and shall ensure that the views of the European Parliament are duly taken into consideration. The European Parliament shall be kept regularly informed by the Presidency and the Commission of the development of the Union's foreign and security policy.

The European Parliament may ask questions of the Council or make recommendations to it. It shall hold an annual debate on progress in implementing the common foreign and security policy.

To the great disappointment of the European Parliament, the Treaty of Amsterdam left unchanged the provisions which set out the purely consultative role of the European Parliament in the CFSP. The duty on the Presidency to consult the Parliament and the duty on both Presidency and Commission to keep the Parliament regularly informed do not in practice give the Parliament any real power to make a substantive input into the instruments, declarations, and conclusions adopted by the Council and by the European Council.

In spite of its limited powers in the Treaty, the European Parliament makes vigorous efforts to contribute to the formation of common foreign policy. The extent of its success will be considered more extensively in Chapter 10 below on Parliamentary Control of the Pillars.

The Right of Initiating Action

ARTICLE 22 (EX ARTICLE J.12)

1. Any Member State or the Commission may refer to the Council any question relating to the common foreign and security policy and may submit proposals to the Council.
2. In cases requiring a rapid decision, the Presidency, of its own motion, or at the request of the Commission or a Member State, shall convene an extraordinary Council meeting within forty-eight hours or, in an emergency, within a shorter period.

The text of Article 22 is unchanged from the that in paragraphs 2 and 3 of Article J.8 of the Treaty of Maastricht. The effect of separating these provisions is to clarify the important matters of the right to make proposals and to set the Council machinery in motion.

The absence of an exclusive right of proposal for the Commission is one of the important distinguishing features of the inter governmental method of action. Not only does the Commission's near monopoly within the First Pillar of the power to propose provide a centralizing momentum for the Community and a continuity of approach resulting from the Commission's independent resources, it also ensures a degree of transparency for the proposal and its subsequent progress. Where the Commission makes a First Pillar proposal to the Council this is invariably published in the C series of the Official Journal. Member States are not required on the other hand to make their proposals public, and practice within the Second Pillar has tended to follow the traditional diplomatic practice whereby communications between friendly governments are not usually placed in the public domain.

In practice most proposals for decision or action within the Second Pillar are formally presented to the Council by the Presidency. The Commission secures input into the substance of the proposal, and in particular cross-pillar coordination, by virtue of its representation in the Policy Planning and Early Warning Unit. This is described in the commentary on Article 26 below.

Voting Procedures

ARTICLE 23 (EX ARTICLE J.13)

1. Decisions under this Title shall be taken by the Council acting unanimously. Abstentions by members present in person or represented shall not prevent the adoption of such decisions.

When abstaining in a vote, any member of the Council may qualify its abstention by making a formal declaration under the present subparagraph. In that case, it shall not be obliged to apply the decision, but shall accept that the decision commits the Union. In a spirit of mutual solidarity, the Member State concerned shall refrain from any action likely to conflict with or impede Union action based on that decision and the other Member States shall respect its position. If the members of the Council qualifying their abstention in this way represent more than one third of the votes weighted in accordance with Article 20(5)(2) of the Treaty establishing the European Community, the decision shall not be adopted.

2. By derogation from the provisions of paragraph 1, the Council shall act by qualified majority:

—when adopting joint actions, common positions or taking any other decision on the basis of a common strategy;
—when adopting any decision implementing a joint action or common position.

If a member of the Council declares that, for important and stated reasons of national policy, it intends to oppose the adoption of a decision to be taken by qualified majority, a vote shall not be taken. The Council may, acting by a qualified majority, request that the matter be referred to the European Council for decision by unanimity.

The votes of the members of the Council shall be weighted in accordance with Article 205(2) of the Treaty establishing the European Community. For their adoption, decisions shall require at least 62 votes in favour, cast by at least 10 members.

This paragraph shall not apply to decisions having military or defence implications.

3. For procedural questions, the Council shall act by a majority of its members.

Article 23 brings together in a single and clearly organized text all the provisions relating to Council decisions under the Second Pillar. It does not change the principles on voting which were agreed in the Treaty of Maastricht, but it clarifies some ambiguities and takes account of other changes to the Treaty Articles on the common foreign and security policy.

The fundamental principle remains that decisions establishing the common foreign and security policy of the Union are taken unanimously. Procedural questions may be determined by simple majority in the Council.

It would in theory be possible to reconcile the taking of binding policy decisions by majority vote with the retention by the individual Member States of ultimate independence in the conduct of their foreign relations. The Security Council of the UN is capable of adopting by majority vote decisions which may impose important and legally binding restrictions on all Member States—most of them not even represented on the Council. Membership of the UN has nevertheless been regarded as entirely compatible with sovereign statehood. It has been suggested in Chapter 2 above that if foreign policy were placed within the First Pillar of the European Union—with the loss of concurrent national autonomy which that would imply—it would by contrast not be possible to reconcile the position of the Member States with sovereign statehood as it has been defined by international law. But although the taking of policy decisions within the Second Pillar by majority vote would not in itself alter the constitutional character of the Union, there is no doubt that to national parliaments and national electorates the fact that a Member State cannot be outvoted on an issue of foreign policy is politically and symbolically of crucial importance.

At the end of Chapter 4 above it was suggested that the rule of unanimity had not proved a serious obstacle to the development of an effective CFSP and that it tended to lead to decisions which were solidly based on wide understanding of the issue and of the advantages and risks to the Union. Although there have been examples of obstruction based on a nationalist approach—Greece and Macedonia being the most obvious—the search for unanimity has more and more produced common understanding of national sensitivities over particular issues. Majority voting might sometimes lead to swifter decisions, but there is little evidence from within the Council that it would lead to better decisions.[83]

There are two exceptions in Article 23 to the general principle of adopting CFSP decisions by unanimity. These may be described as 'constructive abstention' and 'implementing decisions'.

---

[83] On this see Geoffrey Howe (1996): 'Douglas Hurd has claimed that, had qualified majority voting applied in CFSP, no significant decision would have been taken differently over the last five years, and that if it had—as in the case of recognising Macedonia—it might have led to a serious crisis between EU member states.'

Absence and Abstention

Paragraph 1 implies that, although abstention by a Member State does not prevent adoption of a decision by unanimity, this is not so if one or more Member States are absent. The rule is the same when the Council acts within the First Pillar (Article 205.4—ex Article 148.4). This precludes the majority of Member States from 'ganging up' on a recalcitrant State by fixing meetings without its knowledge or taking lightning votes in its absence. It does however imply that a Member State may by adopting the 'empty chair' practice indefinitely prevent the adoption of new CFSP decisions. While Article 23 falls short of requiring the 'concurring votes of all Member States' for adoption of a decision, it does not permit a Member State to be accidentally or deliberately overridden in the decision-making process.

This paragraph also provides a new possibility of 'constructive abstention'. Where an abstaining Member State makes a formal declaration, it is not obliged to accept the decision but must accept that the decision commits the Union. If constructive abstainers total more than one-third of weighted Council votes (calculated under European Community rules) the decision may not be adopted. Where a Member State abstains in the Council without this formal declaration it will be committed in the normal way by the decision adopted by the Council.

The likelihood is that constructive abstention will prove a useful option in the context of joint actions requiring commitment of money, men, or both. Denmark, for example, has already been given by Protocol 6 on the Position of Denmark the right not to participate in decisions and actions with defence implications, or to contribute to financing operational expenditure arising from them. Where a decision has been validly adopted, constructive abstainers may stand gracefully aside from its implementation, but are required to do nothing to undermine it.

Implementing Decisions

The second exception to the unanimity rule relates to what may be described as implementing decisions. Such decisions may be based on a common strategy adopted by the European Council or on a joint action or common position adopted by the Council. The common feature is that there has been a prior determination of the Union's policy made by consensus (which in practice is the basis of European Council decisions and of almost all Council decisions) or by unanimity.[84] It was pointed out above

---

[84] Nuttall (1996), commenting on the use of consensus, says that 'the consensus rule is not equivalent to a veto. There is strong peer pressure to reach a positive conclusion, and not to block a position held by a majority'.

that common strategies are general policy documents rather than precise legal instruments and it becomes clear from studying them that for their implementation they require legal instruments adopted under one of the three Pillars. The implementing decisions in the case of common strategies may be important and controversial, and to permit such decisions to be taken by qualified majority vote is an important inroad into the general practice of unanimity within the CFSP. Decisions implementing common positions or joint actions are generally less likely to be controversial. They may relate only to minor matters of detail which do, however, require to be determined quickly.

By way of safeguard, Article 23.2 provides in express terms for the equivalent of the so-called Luxembourg compromise. Since 1981 the 'Luxembourg compromise' has been limited within the European Community context to cases where the objecting State declares 'important and stated reasons of national policy'. This revised version was formally published in 1996.[85] The condition is intended to prevent the safeguard being invoked by a Member State for reasons which are frivolous or unrelated to the issue under discussion.[86] In the context of the Second Pillar, the Council instead of 'continuing discussion' indefinitely (as it does within the First Pillar) may by qualified majority vote refer the disputed matter to the European Council for decision by unanimity.

A further safeguard for Member States is that qualified majority voting may not be used under any circumstances for Council decisions with military or defence implications.

[85] Bull EC 3-96.
[86] On the Luxembourg Compromise see Nicoll (1984); Wyatt and Dashwood (1998) at p 44; Dashwood (1998) at pp 214–15; Horspool (2000) at 2.5 and 3.16.

Conclusion of International Agreements by the Council

ARTICLE 24 (EX ARTICLE J.14)

When it is necessary to conclude an agreement with one or more States or international organisations in implementation of this Title, the Council, acting unanimously, may authorise the Presidency, assisted by the Commission as appropriate, to open negotiations to that effect. Such agreements shall be concluded by the Council acting unanimously on a recommendation from the Presidency. No agreement shall be binding on a Member State whose representative in the Council states that it has to comply with the requirements of its own constitutional procedure; the other members of the Council may agree that the agreement shall apply provisionally to them.

The provisions of this Article shall also apply to matters falling under Title VI.

It was explained at the beginning of the Introduction above that the EU is not an international organization given legal personality under the law of its Member States and treaty-making powers under international law. Article 24—for which there is no precedent in the Treaty of Maastricht—has been invoked in order to qualify or even to cast doubt on the proposition that the Union does not have international legal personality in the full sense.

Within the context of the CFSP practical difficulties had arisen because of the Union's lack of international legal personality and therefore of treaty-making capacity. One particular example was the 1994 Memorandum of Understanding which formed the informal legal basis for the European Union Administration of Mostar—described in Chapter 4 above. This was signed on behalf of the Troika, the Commission, the Western European Union, and the Government of Bosnia. In the context of possible reform of the TEU the Commission argued strongly in favour of granting international legal personality to the Union, and 'a majority of members' of the Reflection Group also argued in favour of an explicit grant on the ground that the existing position was 'a source of confusion outside'.[87] In the negotiations which led to the Treaty of Amsterdam there

---

[87] Report, SN 520/95 (REFLEX 21) para 150.

were explicit proposals from some Member States to this effect. All were rejected.[88]

The UK Government, in the Explanatory Memorandum on the Treaty of Amsterdam which it submitted to its Parliament after the conclusion of the negotiations, said:

31. At UK insistence, the proposal to give the Union explicit, comprehensive legal personality was abandoned. Instead the Council has limited powers to authorise the Presidency to negotiate international agreements in the second and third pillars; the Council acting unanimously must agree separately both the mandate of the Presidency, and that the agreement should be concluded by the Council (Articles J.14 and K.10, TEU). A *Declaration* makes clear that such agreements will not imply any transfer of competence from the Member States to the Union.

The Council in a booklet based on a descriptive summary originally issued as a Conference document[89] says: 'The Union will have the capacity to negotiate and conclude international agreements to implement its common foreign and security policy.' Later Council information material is however more guarded and based closely on the text of Article 24.[90]

The text of Article 24 may be read as prescribing a procedure whereby the Council, represented in the usual way by the new style Troika which is described in Article 18, may negotiate international agreements as agent for the Member States. The Member States collectively will be bound in international law by the agreement negotiated and concluded on their behalf. The suggestion that it is the Member States who are to be the entities bound is supported first by the final sentence in the first indent of Article 24 which clearly contemplates—at least on an interim basis—that some Member States might be bound by an international agreement concluded under this procedure without all Member States being bound. Secondly it is supported to some extent by the contrasting wording of Article 300 (ex Article 228) of the EC Treaty which begins: 'Where this Treaty provides for the conclusion of agreements between the Community and one or more States or international organisations . . .' Article 24, by contrast, says nothing about agreements between the Union and one or more States or international organizations. Thirdly, the 'agency' interpretation is supported by the terms of Declaration 4, stating that the provision, the corresponding provision in Title VI 'and any agreements resulting from them shall not imply any transfer of competence from the Member States to the European Union'. Declaration 4 could be taken as referring only to the loss of national treaty-making autonomy—expressly

---

[88] For an account of the Conference proposals see Dashwood (1999) at p 219.

[89] CONF/4003/1/97 REV 1, published as *The Treaty of Amsterdam Challenges and Solutions*, at p 12.

[90] See *The Council of the European Union and the common foreign and security policy* on the Council website at http./ue.eu.int/pesc.

excluding the possibility that the *AETR* jurisprudence might be extended so as to exclude national treaty-making capacity in the relevant area.[91] It could, however, also be taken as underlining that this Treaty Article was not to be read as conferring by implication international legal personality on the Union.

Some commentators have suggested, on the basis of the judgment of the ICJ in the *Reparation for Injuries* case[92] that Article 24, in the context of the CFSP provisions as a whole, should be regarded as conferring international legal personality on the EU.[93]

There are however some strong objections to drawing any analogy from this judgment for the European Union. First, the Court based its attribution on quite narrow grounds:

In the opinion of the Court, the Organisation was intended to exercise and enjoy, and is in fact exercising and enjoying, functions and rights which can only be explained on the basis of the possession of a large measure of international personality and the capacity to operate on an international plane. It is at present the supreme type of international organisation, and it could not carry out the intentions of its founders if it was devoid of international personality.[94]

Although the founder members had not explicitly accorded international personality to the UN, they had expressly provided for it to conclude international agreements with its Member States[95] and it had already concluded several such agreements. Moreover given that the structure of the Union as well as its practice is based on the implementation of CFSP decisions and instruments through instruments adopted by one of the European Communities or by Member States, there are alternative ways in which the functions of the Union may be satisfactorily discharged. While it is clearly helpful from a presentational point of view that the Council should be entrusted with powers to authorize negotiation of and to conclude treaties, it would be difficult to argue that the Union could not carry out its functions without full international legal personality.

Secondly, the usual practice of States subsequent to the *Reparation for Injuries* case has been to avoid any similar difficulty by making express provision for international legal personality when setting up a new international organization. In the context of modern treaty practice it is difficult

---

[91] Case 22/70 *Commission v Council (AETR)* [1971] ECR 263, especially para 17: 'In particular, each time the Community, with a view to implementing a common policy envisaged by the Treaty, adopts provisions laying down common rules, whatever form these might take, the Member States no longer have the right, acting individually or even collectively, to undertake obligations with third countries which affect those rules.'

[92] [1949] ICJ Reports 174.

[93] Dashwood (1999) at p 220. See also Wessel (1997); Wessel (1999) ch 7, Wessel (2000a); Neuwahl (1998).

[94] *Reparation for Injuries* case [1949] ICJ Reports 174 at p 179.   [95] Articles 43 and 75.

to believe that the Member States—who were clearly divided on the issue—could be assumed to have by a sidewind, so to speak, conferred international legal personality on the European Union.

Thirdly, to assume that the Union has full international legal personality may place non-Member States who contract with it in difficulty. In the event of default, from which entity are they to obtain redress? The EU cannot be taken before the ICJ, and the TEU placed it beyond doubt that no Second Pillar matters are within the jurisdiction of the ECJ. While the express grant of legal personality to the European Community was accompanied by clear provisions for its contractual and its non-contractual liability—subjecting it to the applicable law for the contract in question and requiring it to make good any damage caused by its institutions or by its servants in the performance of their duties[96]—there are no comparable provisions ensuring that the European Union will accept responsibility for any obligations to be assumed or incurred. Non-Member States may find it convenient to have a single interlocutor, a single 'number for Europe', but in the event of default they would not wish to find some shadowy 'corporate veil' between themselves and the defendant Member States. Since the litigation which followed the collapse of the International Tin Council, States have been conscious of the potential pitfalls and the uncertain international legal position regarding the duty of Member States to pay compensation in respect of liabilities of international organisations which they have set up.[97]

The Member States may of course place the matter beyond doubt in a subsequent intergovernmental treaty. Alternatively they might by a consistent practice accepted by non-Member States show that the international legal personality of the European Union has been generally accepted. The difficulties faced by the European Community in establishing full membership of international organizations suggest, however, that this is unlikely to be a straightforward course. For the time being the safer view is to regard the Council as exercising a delegated treaty-making power on behalf of the Member States. It is the Member States who will ultimately enjoy the rights and be subject to the responsibilities set out in any international agreement concluded under the procedures of Article 24.

In April 2001, the Council concluded its first Agreement under the provisions of Article 24. This was an Agreement between the EU and the FRY on the activities of the European Union Monitoring Mission (EUMM) in the FRY.[98] The Council Decision on the conclusion of the Agreement

---

[96] Article 288 (ex Article 215).
[97] See *Re International Tin Council* [1988] 3 All ER 257; 81 ILR 670 and *Westland Helicopters Ltd v Arab Organisation for Development* [1995] 2 WLR 126, (1989) 28 ILM 687; Muller (1995) ch 3: 'Legal Personality of International Organizations'; Seidl-Hohenveldern (1987).
[98] OJ L125/1, 5.5.2001.

stated that it was 'approved on behalf of the European Union' and that the President was given power to designate the person 'empowered to sign the Agreement in order to bind the European Union'. While the naming of the EU as the Contracting Party to this Agreement strengthens the argument that the Member States have delegated treaty-making capacity to the Union, it does not in itself address the questions of enforcement and of liability addressed above.[99] There are a number of States—including the UK, Belgium, and Germany among the Member States of the Union—which have delegated or 'entrusted' treaty-making powers to constituent elements of the State while remaining ultimately responsible under international law for discharge of the relevant obligations.[100] The entities with such powers are not generally regarded as possessing full international legal personality.

The Treaty of Nice[101]—not yet in force—compounds the confusion and reinforces the view that the Member States are more concerned with questions of their own internal procedure than with their potential responsibilities under international agreements. It does not expressly confer legal personality on the Union. The version of Article 24 which would replace the text set out above replaces the rule that the Council, in authorizing negotiations or concluding an agreement, must act unanimously, by more complex rules. Under the Nice version the Council would act by qualified majority where it could by qualified majority adopt internal measures on the issue in question or where the agreement is envisaged in order to implement a joint action or common position. The revised version also provides expressly that

'Agreements concluded under the conditions set out by this Article shall be binding on the institutions of the Union.'

This might be assumed to be the position from the Treaty of Amsterdam version of Article 24, but it seems curious that the wording does not follow that of Article 300 (ex Article 228) of the European Community Treaty which says clearly that:

7. Agreements concluded under the conditions set out in this Article shall be binding on the institutions of the Community and on Member States.

Finally, the revised version of Article 24 retains the provision that no agreement shall be binding on a Member State whose representative in the

---

[99] In Wyatt and Dashwood (2000) the view is expressed (pp 184–7) that if agreements were to be concluded in the name of the Union it would be clear that the Member States and their partners had accepted the legal personality of the Union.
[100] For details and examples see Aust (2000) at pp 48–54.
[101] OJ C80/1, 10.3.2001; Cm 5090.

Council states that it has to comply with the requirements of its own constitutional procedure (which at least implies that for the other silent Member States *it will* be binding). In such circumstances:

the other members of the Council may agree that the agreement shall nevertheless apply provisionally.

The final words 'to them' in the Treaty of Amsterdam version have been omitted. Even though 'provisional application' is regarded as falling short of imposing legal obligations,[102] the change seems to suggest that a Member State which has given notice that it intends to submit an agreement to ratification or approval by its national parliament may be committed at least politically to implement it in advance of any parliamentary procedure or even if it is rejected by its national parliament.

---

[102] On provisional application generally, see Aust (2000) at pp 139–41.

Infrastructure: The Political Committee

ARTICLE 25 (EX ARTICLE J.15)

Without prejudice to Article 207 of the Treaty establishing the European Community, a Political Committee shall monitor the international situation in the areas covered by the common foreign and security policy and contribute to the definition of policies by delivering opinions to the Council at the request of the Council or on its own initiative. It shall also monitor the implementation of agreed policies, without prejudice to the responsibility of the Presidency and the Commission.

The Political Committee, composed of Political Directors from the diplomatic services of the Member States, is the longest established and most powerful part of the infrastructure of the CFSP. The 1970 Luxembourg Report which in response to a commission from Heads of State and Government first drew up procedures and practices for coordinating foreign policy formation was prepared by senior officials from the Foreign Ministries of the Six, and they themselves then formed the first Political Committee.[103] It was formally recognized in the 1981 London Report,[104] where it was placed immediately below Ministers of Foreign Affairs and above the Correspondents' Group and the Working Groups.

In the early years when EPC was organized quite separately from European Community institutions and Community action, the Political Committee had no formal relationship to COREPER which has always had primary responsibility for preparing the work of the Council of Ministers and implementing its decisions. Since the Treaty of Maastricht, however, the Council adopts measures and takes decisions on the CFSP and must also to an increasing extent implement them by means of European Community measures. There is a great emphasis on consistency across the three pillars, and the Council—with the assistance of COREPER in particular—is responsible for ensuring such consistency. The primary role of COREPER in relation to the Council was emphasized in the Treaty of Maastricht and again in the (largely identical) wording of Article 25. This is the significance of the opening words: 'Without prejudice to Article 207 of the Treaty establishing the European Community . . .'.

It is therefore necessary for the drafts and papers prepared by the Political Committee to be transmitted through COREPER to the Council. By convention, however, COREPER will not comment except—as is

---

[103] Nuttall (1992) p 51.   [104] Cmnd 8424. See Chapter 2 above.

increasingly the case—where a Second Pillar proposal raises cross-pillar questions either of consistency or of implementation under Community powers. In the words of Fink-Hooijer: 'COREPER's role is far from that of a letterbox for Political Committee decisions. COREPER is entitled to add its own observations or recommendations.'[105]

Declaration 5 to the Treaty, adopted by the Amsterdam Conference, requires the Member States to ensure that the Political Committee 'is able to meet at any time, in the event of international crises or other urgent matters, at very short notice at Political Director or deputy level'. Before the Treaty of Amsterdam, the Political Committee met only twice a month, one of these meetings being in the margins of the Foreign Affairs Council. It was generally believed that this was inadequate for the growing volume of business to be discussed and prepared for Ministerial decisions.

In February 2000 the Council, with the aim of strengthening CFSP and implementing the common European policy on security and defence, set up interim arrangements in the following terms:

1. The Political Committee established by Article 25 of the Treaty on European Union shall meet in Brussels under a separate formation, called the 'Interim Political and Security Committee', when it is not in session. This formation shall be composed of national representatives at senior/ambassadorial level within the framework of Member States Permanent Representations.
2. The Interim Political and Security Committee shall, in close contact with the Secretary-General/High Representative:

(a) prepare recommendations on the future functioning of the common European policy on security and defence;
(b) deal with CFSP affairs on a day-to day basis.[106]

This Decision in part, and the two related Decisions which are dealt with below in Chapter 11, were intended to provide infrastructure for the emerging decisions and actions on defence. Since, however, the new Interim Committee was mandated to deal with CFSP affairs on a day-to day-basis, it also achieved the long-standing objective of providing in Brussels a permanent body of Member States' representatives with the competence for regular oversight of the constantly enlarging Common Foreign and Security Policy.

In January 2001 the Council, implementing conclusions of the European Council at Nice, established the Political and Security Committee as a permanent body.[107] This Decision anticipated even the formal signature of

---

[105] The Common Foreign and Security Policy of the European Union [1994] European J of Intl L 173 at p 189. See also de Zwaan (1995) pp 174–80.

[106] Council Decision 2000/143/CFSP, OJ L49/1, 22.2.2000, Article 1.

[107] OJ L27/1, 30.1.2001. The functions of the Committee in regard to foreign policy were not substantially changed.

the Treaty of Nice in February 2001, which contained a new version of Article 25 and would (on its eventual entry into force) also establish a Political and Security Committee. Other additions to Article 25, which are most likely to be relevant in the context of defence, will be described in Chapter 11 below.

Below the Political Committee, but not mentioned in the Treaty, are the European Correspondents. Below the European Correspondents are the Working Groups composed mainly of representatives from national capitals. The Working Groups have responsibility either for subject areas such as arms control or the UN or for geographical areas. Since the entry into force of the Treaty of Maastricht these have gradually been merged with Council Working Groups with overlapping competences. It is, however, neither easy to divide the agenda for such groups cleanly into First, Second, and Third Pillar questions nor uncontroversial to determine the channel for further deliberation below the Council. In principle, the Working Groups will report to the Political Committee on Second Pillar issues and to COREPER on issues within Community competence. CFSP Counsellors, based within the Permanent Representations of the Member States in Brussels, are responsible not only for general oversight but also specifically for identifying issues with cross-pillar significance.

Infrastructure: The High Representative for the CFSP

ARTICLE 26

The Secretary-General of the Council, High Representative for the common foreign and security policy, shall assist the Council in matters coming within the scope of the common foreign and security policy, in particular through contributing to the formulation, preparation and implementation of policy decisions, and, when appropriate and acting on behalf of the Council at the request of the Presidency, through conducting political dialogue with third parties.

The High Representative for the CFSP, sometimes styled Mr CFSP, has two separate, but related functions. He plays a major role—though formally assisting the Presidency—in the external representation of the Union. His external function is also mentioned in Article 18 which sets out comprehensively how the Union is to be represented in CFSP matters. His second function is that of contributing within the Council to policy formation and implementation. With the help of the new Policy Planning and Early Warning Unit the High Representative can provide expertise, precedents, planning, and analysis for the benefit of the deliberation and decision-making by Ministers.

As Brian Crowe, Director-General for External Relations in the Council Secretariat, pointed out before the entry into force of the Treaty of Amsterdam:

> Much will depend on who he is, his level, his authority and skill. He will have a difficult task. He cannot challenge the authority of the Council whose servant he is, nor of the Presidency of the day, which will continue to be responsible under the Treaty for the management of CFSP.[108]

In appointing a single, high profile political figure to this key role in the making and implementing of policy, the EU for the first time seriously addressed one of the main weaknesses of CFSP—which was described at the outset of Chapter 4 above—the absence of continuous high-level professional support. The appointment of Mr Javier Solana, a former Secretary-General of NATO and Foreign Minister of Spain, ensures the political experience necessary to make certain that the advice of the High

---

[108] Crowe (1998) at p 322.

Representative will carry weight with the Foreign Ministers of the Member States.

Infrastructure: The Policy Planning and Early Warning Unit

The Policy Planning and Early Warning Unit set up on the entry into force of the Treaty of Amsterdam did not fill a vacuum. The 1981 London Report first set up a small team of officials from preceding and successive Presidencies who were based in the Presidency capital and provided continuity and support for the current Presidency along with its own Foreign Ministry officials. The Single European Act extended this to seconded diplomats from five Presidencies, and based the EPC Secretariat in Brussels. The Treaty of Maastricht, authorizing the Council for the first time to take decisions within the newly established CFSP, opened the way for the Council Secretariat to turn the EPC Secretariat into a CFSP Unit with stronger support and planning capabilities—working for the Council as a whole rather than for the current Presidency.[109]

A Declaration attached to the Treaty of Amsterdam on the Establishment of a Policy Planning and Early Warning Unit listed in paragraph 2 the tasks of the unit:

(a) monitoring and analysing developments in areas relevant to the CFSP;
(b) providing assessments of the Union's foreign and security policy interests and identifying areas where the CFSP could focus in future;
(c) providing timely assessments and early warning of events or situations which may have significant repercussions for the Union's foreign and security policy, including potential political crises;
(d) producing at the request of either the Council or the Presidency or on its own initiative, argued policy option papers to be presented under the responsibility of the Presidency as a contribution to policy formulation in the Council, and which may contain analyses, recommendations and strategies for the CFSP.

In themselves, these tasks were not entirely novel for the Council Secretariat, though the policy formulation element is now substantially greater. It is also conducive to greater understanding of the role of the Unit in the policy formation process to have its responsibilities clearly and publicly set out.

The change in the nature and role of the Unit emerges rather from other provisions in the Declaration which emphasize coherence with other external policies of the Union and cooperation with the other institutions involved in planning and executing CFSP. Paragraph 1 of the Declaration requires that 'Appropriate cooperation shall be established with the

---

[109] See Chapter 2 above.

Commission in order to ensure full coherence with the Union's external economic and development policies.' Paragraph 3 provides for the composition of the Unit, which 'shall consist of personnel drawn from the General Secretariat, the Member States, the Commission and the WEU'. Interinstitutional cooperation is thus ensured in the most effective way— by integration of professional staff with the traditions and direct working experience of the bodies with which the Council must work closely in order to form and implement common policy.

Instead of the Unit being solely at the disposition of the current Presidency, wide ranging input is guaranteed by the remaining paragraphs of the Declaration:

4. Any Member State or the Commission may make suggestions to the unit for work to be undertaken.
5. Member States and the Commission shall assist the policy planning process by providing, to the fullest extent possible, relevant information, including confidential information.

This provision should be seen as complementary to Article 22 of the Treaty, permitting any Member State or the Commission to refer any CFSP question or proposal to the Council. As was suggested above, the practice is still for formal proposals or agenda items to emanate from the Presidency, while the other potential players ensure their own input through the Policy Planning and Early Warning Unit. As Dashwood suggests: '. . . the unit will at least provide the raw material of a foreign policy conceived in the broader perspective of the Union'.[110] Clapham has suggested that, for example, the Unit should be given a specific focus on the UN Security Council, particularly with a view to ensuring that Security Council discussion is more closely linked to human rights issues and to devising solutions for post-conflict peace-building which take more account of work in the field by the Council's Working Group on Human Rights.[111]

The Policy Planning and Early Warning Unit can still not compete with the professional resources available to the larger Member States. But under strong political direction and with effective interinstitutional links it can begin to build a capacity for continuous monitoring and assessment of policy towards particular countries, regions and issues. It will no longer be the case that démarches, declarations, Presidency statements and common positions are no more than words in the wind. The CFSP now has its own men.

---

[110] Dashwood (1999) at p 218.   [111] Clapham (1999) at p 682.

Infrastructure: The Commission

ARTICLE 27 (EX ARTICLE J.17)

The Commission shall be fully associated with the work carried out in the common foreign and security policy field.

The text of Article 27 is unchanged from that in the Treaty of Maastricht and indeed from that in the Single European Act.[112] The way in which 'full association' is applied has however changed radically. The Commission is now a major player in the formation, representation, and implementation of the CFSP. It forms part of the new style troika (Article 18) and is almost always closely involved in the work of the Union in international organizations because of the increasing likelihood that the Community—if not actually a member—will have competence over some of the work of the organization. Article 24 provides for the Commission 'as appropriate' to assist in the negotiation of international agreements with non-Member States or with international organizations. The Commission may take an active role in coordination of action by diplomatic and consular missions of the Member States in third countries, provided that the issue involves a question within Community competence (such as aid, technical assistance, or assisting with the protection of citizens of the Union) so that the Commission delegation will also be involved.[113] Under Article 22 it has power to refer questions or proposals to the Council and to ask for an extraordinary Council meeting to be convened. Its staff are included in the personnel of the Policy Planning and Early Warning Unit.

By way of illustration of the extensive powers of implementation now conferred on the Commission, one may point to the Council Joint Action establishing a European Union Cooperation Programme for Non-proliferation and Disarmament in the Russian Federation.[114] The Joint Action—implementing objectives of disarmament and arms control in the Common Strategy for Russia—states in its Preamble that the Commission 'has agreed to be entrusted with certain tasks necessary for the implementation of this Joint Action'. These tasks include preparing projects, supervising their proper implementation with the assistance of a unit of experts,

---

[112] Article 30.3(b).

[113] The Commission has over 120 external delegations, representations, and missions to international organizations in Vienna, New York, Paris, Geneva, and Rome: Vacher's European Companion December 1999; Hansard HL Debs 19 April 1995, WA 51 and 1 May 1995, WA 100.

[114] OJ L331/11, 23.12.1999.

monitoring expenditure and reporting regularly to the Council and to the Presidency and the High Representative for the CFSP.

Under Article 3 of the Treaty the Commission, along with the Council, is responsible for the consistency of the Union's external activities as a whole and, within its powers, for the implementation of external policies. Fink-Hooijer argues that ensuring consistency between the three pillars in all the external activities of the Union is the most prominent general task of the Commission under the TEU.[115]

The Commission, however, lacks the institutional power which within the First Pillar flows from its near monopoly of the power to propose and formally to amend its own proposals and, in the external context, from its wide-ranging powers to negotiate alone on behalf of the European Communities.[116]

Since 1999 there has been a single Commissioner for External Relations (Mr Christopher Patten) and a single Directorate-General for External Relations. Within the structure of this Directorate-General there is no relegation of CFSP matters into a special compartment.

---

[115] The Common Foreign and Security Policy of the European Union [1994] European J of Intl L 173, at p 190.

[116] On this, see speech by Christopher Patten to the Institut Français des Relations Internationales, 15 June 2000: '. . . les États membres **n'ont pas** donné à la Commission un droit d'initiative exclusif; ils n'ont pas non plus accepte d'être liés par des décisions prises à la majorité; ils refusent que l'Europe "occupe le terrain" et réduise par la même leur marge de liberté. Il est essentiel de comprendre ceci et notamment que la Commission le comprenne. La politique étrangère demeure principalement l'affaire des gouvernements nationaux qui bénéficient d'une legitimité démocratique.'

The Single Institutional Framework

ARTICLE 28 (EX ARTICLE J.18)

1. Articles 189, 190, 196 to 199, 203, 204, 206 to 209, 213 to 219, 255 and 290 of the Treaty establishing the European Community shall apply to the provisions relating to the areas referred to in this Title.

. . .

Article 3 of the Treaty on European Union provides that:

> The Union shall be served by a single institutional framework which shall ensure the consistency and the continuity of the activities carried out in order to attain its objective while respecting and building upon the acquis communautaire.

Article 28.1 reflects this general requirement by providing that those provisions within the EC Treaty which give formal life to the European Parliament, the Council, and the Commission apply to the Articles in Title V (the Second Pillar) which confer functions on those institutions. The choice of Articles carried across from First to Second Pillar is made in such a way as to leave behind the provisions which give European Community powers and functions to the three relevant institutions.

Thus for the European Parliament the Articles which prescribe its composition and procedures are applied, but not the Articles relating, for example, to participation in Community legislation, investigating maladministration in the implementation of Community law or enabling the Parliament to adopt a motion of censure on the Commission. For the Council, the Articles on composition and procedure are applied, but not those regulating voting or Community powers. (Article 23 which deals with Council voting on CFSP matters contains some specific cross-references.) For the Commission also, the provisions on composition and procedures are applied, but not the legislative, executive, and watchdog functions which it has within the Community legal order.

The only addition of substance made in this context in the Treaty of Amsterdam is that the new Article 255 (ex Article 191a) conferring a right of access to Parliament, Council, and Commission documents (subject to principles, conditions, and limits on grounds of public or private interest to be determined) is extended to Second Pillar documents.

No provision is made in Article 28 in relation to those Community institutions—most notably the ECJ—which have no role or function within the Second Pillar.

Financing the Common Foreign and Security Policy

ARTICLE 28 (EX ARTICLE J.18)

...

2. Administrative expenditure which the provisions relating to the areas referred to in this Title entail for the institutions shall be charged to the budget of the European Communities.

3. Operational expenditure to which the implementation of those provisions gives rise shall also be charged to the budget of the European Communities, except for such expenditure arising from operations having military or defence implications and cases where the Council acting unanimously decides otherwise.

In cases where expenditure is not charged to the budget of the European Communities it shall be charged to the Member States in accordance with the gross national product scale, unless the Council acting unanimously decides otherwise. As for expenditure arising from military or defence implications, Member States whose representatives in the Council have made a formal declaration under Article 23(1), second subparagraph, shall not be obliged to contribute to the financing thereof.

4. The budgetary procedure laid down in the Treaty establishing the European Community shall apply to the expenditure charged to the budget of the European Communities.

In Chapter 4 above, the absence of automatically available funding for Council decisions was identified as a serious weakness in the provisions in the Treaty of Maastricht on the CFSP.[117] The need for Member States to agree on the method of funding, and then sometimes on the proportional allocation of the burden often delayed agreement on Council measures. Sometimes, inadequate financial provision meant that initiatives adopted were without practical benefit. In March 1995, for example, the Council adopted a Common Position on Burundi in which the Union expressed readiness to lend support to sending human rights experts within the framework established by the UN High Commissioner for Human Rights. The Common Position then continued, lamely:

---

[117] See pp 88–9, 122.

—the Commission intends to propose that the European Community contribute as soon as possible to the funding of this operation an approximate amount of ECU 3 million, which figure the Commission will reassess on the basis of the results of the Troika's visit and ongoing contacts.

The Commission was in this case able to find some funds, but it was not until June 1995 that the Council adopted a decision implementing its Common Position by placing a contribution of 1.5 million ECU at the disposal of the OAU to finance its efforts in sending observers to Burundi. The amount actually spent was certainly too little, too late.[118] The same criticism could be made in relation to Rwanda, where the Council's 1994 Common Position, in addition to giving priority to the return and humanitarian aid for refugees, stressed that it was 'important to increase as early as possible the number of human rights observers in Rwanda' and 'the importance of bringing to justice those responsible for gross violations of humanitarian law, including genocide'. The Union however offered neither money nor men to help secure these admirable objectives.[119]

The financing system established under Article 28 addressed the earlier weaknesses. Administrative expenditure is to be charged to the budget of the European Communities—as was already the case under the Treaty of Maastricht. Operational expenditure—which formerly required a unanimous vote of the Council to be charged to the Communities' budget—is now so charged automatically. There are two exceptions. The first relates to military or defence spending and the second is where the Council by unanimity—which will be hard to secure—decides to charge the Member States. Where Member States are to bear the burden, the proportions will follow the GNP scale, unless the Council unanimously decides otherwise. A Member State may however avoid paying its share where it has made the 'constructive abstention' declaration permitted under the voting rules in Article 23. But there is no provision for a Member State which has voted for a CFSP decision to withhold funding—the money must follow the mouth in the Council.

This system should avoid wrangling over finance delaying CFSP decisions by the Council or rendering them impotent. It considerably strengthens the bond between the Second and the First Pillar now that CFSP must use the money as well as the enforcing powers of the European Community to back its policies, and that the Budget itself—though still agreed under the institutional procedures of the First Pillar—is now the Budget of the European Union. The new system also gives the European Parliament through its powers in the budgetary process a somewhat more substantial base from which to question Council policies.

[118] Common Position 95/91/CFSP, OJ L72/1, 1.4.95; Council Decision 95/206/CFSP, OJ L130/1, 14.6.95; Clapham (1999) at pp 640, 651.
[119] Council Decision 94/697/CFSP, OJ L283/1, 29.10.94; Clapham (1999) at p 651.

By way of illustration of the more efficient way in which financial provision is now made, one may cite the 1999 Council Joint Action on the re-establishment of a viable police force in Albania, which contained specific provision for a financial reference amount to cover the necessary operational expenditure. The Joint Action was supplemented by later Joint Actions in 2000 providing additional specified financing.[120]

In the margins of the Amsterdam Conference, the European Parliament, the Council and Commission reached an Inter Institutional Agreement regarding financing of the Common Foreign and Security Policy.[121] They agreed that CFSP operational expenditure should be regarded as non-compulsory ('not necessarily resulting from the Treaty'), thus giving the European Parliament greater powers in the fixing of the CFSP annual budget.[122] The Council and European Parliament must annually agree on the amount and allocation of money, with a fall-back of the amount in the previous budget. The headings for allocation of funds could include observation and organization of elections, European Union envoys, conflict prevention, financial assistance for disarmament, contributions for international conferences, and 'urgent actions'. 'Urgent actions' may not exceed twenty per cent of the global amount of the CFSP budget chapter. There are provisions for systematic consultation of the Parliament by the Presidency on the main aspects and basic choices of the CFSP and for the Council to give the Parliament an estimate of costs each time a decision entailing expenses is adopted. The Commission is to provide quarterly information on execution of CFSP actions and financial forecasts.

Schmalz commented that the Inter Institutional Agreement on CFSP financing, formerly one of the most disputed fields of CFSP, indicated a change from ideological dichotomy to constructive pragmatism which was 'not only wishful thinking but can be a realistic vision for the future conduct of European external policy'.[123]

An Interim Balance Sheet of the CFSP after Amsterdam

It would be premature to evaluate the functioning and achievements of the new CFSP provisions in the way that was attempted for the Maastricht Treaty provisions at the conclusion of Chapter 4.[124] Clearly the greatest effort is now directed towards the construction of a new capability in terms of 'ships and men'—that is a directly available defence capacity.

---

[120] Joint Action 1999/189/CFSP, OJ L63/1, 12.3.1999, supplemented by Joint Actions 2000/388 and 798/CFSP, OJ L145/1, 20.6.2000 and OJ L324/1, 21.12.2000 respectively.
[121] CONF/4001/97. The Agreement was signed on 16 July 1997. See Bull EU 7/8-1997 points 1.4.1, 2.3.1.
[122] For the detailed implications, see Article 272 (ex Article 203) of the EC Treaty.
[123] Schmalz (1998) at p 440.   [124] See pp 120–2.

Simultaneously, in the area of foreign policy, the European Union is increasingly moving 'upstream'—into conflict prevention and promoting both by stick and by carrot democratic and responsible systems of government in neighbouring States—which it is hoped will make overt intervention or defensive measures on behalf of the European Union unnecessary.[125] This is particularly apparent in the efforts devoted to assisting the 1999 Stability Pact for South-eastern Europe.

It can however already be said that the new Treaty provisions build on the achievements under the Treaty of Maastricht which were singled out in Chapter 4. As to the four weaknesses there identified, the Treaty of Amsterdam has addressed the problem of the absence of independent financial resources and is building up the manpower to enable effective strategic planning by the Union to be carried forward. The legal personality problem remains, though it is suggested above that this may not be amenable to easy solution in the way which is often advocated. The problem of the need to borrow powers of action or enforcement also remains—but may be better tackled by growing familiarity with cross-pillar procedures and by institutional habits of cooperation than by pulling the Treaty provisions up by the roots.

[125] See Hill (2001) for a clear account of the record and potential of the EU in this area.

6

Achievements and Weaknesses of Justice and Home Affairs Cooperation

The Purpose and Scope of Cooperation in Justice and Home Affairs

There was less risk of misunderstanding arising from the title of the Third Pillar established by the Maastricht Treaty than there was in the case of the Second Pillar. The 'Common Foreign and Security Policy' suggested the formation of a comprehensive policy similar to the common policies of the European Community—the Common Agricultural Policy, the Common Fisheries Policy, the Common Transport Policy, and the Common Commercial Policy—which might in time replace the foreign policies of the Member States. 'Cooperation in the Fields of Justice and Home Affairs' by contrast suggested the much less ambitious objective of cooperation in making effective national policies which would remain essentially unchanged. Although, as was explained at the beginning of Chapter 3, the subject of cooperation in the enforcement of national criminal and immigration laws was so sensitive as to preclude extension of Community powers, it seems to have been well understood by the time that the Maastricht Treaty was ratified that such cooperation could make enforcement of national laws of each Member State much more effective while not radically threatening the differing substantive rules.[1]

The central purpose of the Third Pillar was set out in Article K.1 of the Maastricht Treaty as follows: 'For the purposes of achieving the objectives of the Union, in particular the free movement of persons, and without prejudice to the powers of the European Community, Member States shall regard the following areas as matters of common interest: . . .' This made clear that work in the listed areas, like the work which had progressed on parallel tracks under the Schengen process and in the Co-ordinators' Group on the basis of the Palma document, was directed mainly to achieving free movement of people. It might have seemed anomalous that a Community objective was to be pursued by intergovernmental rather than by Community law-making methods. But the real objective was the abolition of control of people at intra-Community borders, and not all Member States accepted that the removal of border control of people was a

---

[1] Hendry (1993) at p 298.

Learning Resources
Centre

Community objective at all. Moreover, even for those Member States which did regard removal of border controls as the logical corollary of free movement of people, the jealousy with which national criminal laws and immigration policies were guarded meant that they were ready at least to try to see whether the intergovernmental method could achieve adequate results. The greater national control of the law-making process under international legal methods, and the very limited role given to the ECJ meant that there was for a Member State little risk of unexpected loss of individual autonomy over its criminal law or immigration policy.

The scope of cooperation in justice and home affairs was set out precisely in Article K.1 which listed nine areas which were 'matters of common interest'. The implication was that these nine areas set the boundaries for Third Pillar powers, although of course nothing could prevent the Member States using intergovernmental procedures to formulate treaties among themselves which fell outside the framework of the Third Pillar. The formulation contrasts sharply with that in Article J.1 which provided that the common foreign and security policy should cover 'all areas of foreign and security policy'.

A description of what was achieved under the Third Pillar under the Maastricht Treaty may therefore follow these listed areas of cooperation. The first three areas fell under the remit of the Steering Group on immigration and asylum.

Asylum Policy

When the Treaty of Maastricht entered into force, all the Member States were already bound by numerous common international obligations on refugees, and their policies were also conditioned by non-binding recommendations. In 1946 the General Assembly of the UN laid down generally accepted principles providing that no refugee with valid objections should be returned to his country of origin, that the return of the displaced to their country of origin should be a priority and that an international body should be set up to deal with refugee problems.[2] The UN High Commissioner for Refugees (UNHCR) was established in 1950 as a subsidiary organ of the UN. The UNHCR remit is wide and non-political, but it has no powers to compel or to give binding interpretations of legal obligations. All European Union Member States were Parties to the 1951 Convention relating to the Status of Refugees[3] ('the 1951 Convention') and to the 1967 Protocol[4] which extended the application of the Convention to those who became refugees because of events *after* 1951.

---

[2] UNGA Resolution 8.   [3] 189 UNTS 150, UKTS No 39 (1954), Cmd 9171.
[4] 606 UNTS 267, UKTS No 15 (1969), Cmnd 3370.

Article 1 of the 1951 Convention—to which no reservation or derogation is permitted—defines refugees for the purposes of the Convention. The key elements are that refugees must be

(a) outside their country of origin;
(b) unable or unwilling to return there or to avail themselves of the protection of that country: where
(c) the inability or unwillingness is due to a well-founded fear of being persecuted; and
(d) the persecution is 'for reasons of race, religion, nationality, membership of a particular social group or political opinion'.

Article 33 of the 1951 Convention—to which any reservation is also prohibited—sets out the basic principle of protection (known as non-refoulement), providing that no Contracting State 'shall expel or return (*"refouler"*) a refugee in any manner whatsoever to the frontiers of territories where his life or freedom would be threatened on account of his race, religion, nationality, membership of a particular social group or political opinion . . .'.

Member States were also covered by a number of European Agreements and non-binding recommendations made by the Committee of Ministers or the Assembly of the Council of Europe. These sought to build on the minimal requirements of the 1951 Convention in regard to such matters as visas, acquisition of nationality, and harmonization of procedures for determining applications for refugee status. A 1981 Recommendation of the Council of Ministers, for example, recommended proper coordination between border control, local, and central authorities, that only the central authority should decide on a request, permission for the applicant to remain in the territory pending the decision on his request, and provision for appeals or review of decisions on requests.[5] Overlapping with these specific instruments on asylum were obligations of all the Member States under the European Convention on Human Rights. The European Commission on Human Rights in a series of decisions had confirmed that the prohibition of 'inhuman and degrading treatment' in Article 3 of the Convention was applicable to certain cases of expulsion or failure to admit potential refugees.

In spite of this common body of international law and practice, Member States retained a large measure of national discretion on asylum decisions. Neither the 1951 Convention nor the Council of Europe recommendations

---

[5] Recommendation R (1981) 16 on the Harmonisation of National Procedures relating to Asylum, printed in Plender (1988) p 147. Other Council of Europe instruments are also printed there, at pp 123 et seq. For a systematic description of the European instruments on the status of refugees see Plender (1988) pp 256–63.

contained any mechanism to resolve discrepancies in national interpretations or practices; there was no agreed assessment of the factual situation in individual third countries and there were no common requirements as to the procedure for determining asylum applications.[6] In consequence there was scope for a measure of political appraisal and for varying national responses to particular crises in other countries. By the end of the nineteen-eighties several factors—the collapse of barriers to travel from the formerly Communist States, the growth in relatively cheap air travel and the growth of specialist advisory services for prospective migrants—had led to a dramatic upsurge in applications for asylum within the EU.[7] Refugees became more sophisticated at selecting a European destination likely to be sympathetic to their case and when rejected by one Member State travelled to another to restart the application process.

The Dublin Convention

Against this background the Member States, acting within the framework of the Ad Hoc Group on Immigration, had adopted in 1990 the Dublin Convention determining the State responsible for examining Applications for Asylum lodged in one of the Member States of the European Communities,[8] described in Chapter 3 above. Although the Preamble to the Convention referred to concern 'that applications for asylum are left in doubt for too long as regards the likely outcome of their applications' and to continuation of 'dialogue with the United Nations High Commissioner for Refugees', the primary purpose of the Convention was to limit the extent to which asylum seekers could take advantage of the proposed 'area without internal frontiers' in order to shop for the most favourable forum within the Community. Article 3 provides that an application for asylum 'shall be examined by a single Member State, which shall be determined in accordance with the criteria defined in this Convention. The criteria set out in Articles 4 to 8 shall apply in the order in which they appear.' This is the principle of exclusive jurisdiction.[9] The criteria for identifying the single Member State, in order, are (i) that the applicant has a close family member already recognized as a refugee by and resident in that Member State, (ii) the applicant has a valid residence permit or visa from a particular Member State, (iii) the applicant has irregularly entered a par-

---

[6] For an outline of procedures in individual Member States see Rebecca Wallace (1980) pp 7–10, 83–120.

[7] For analysis of the increase in applications for asylum in Europe by year of application, between 1987 to 1997, broken down by country of destination, see Home Office White Paper *Fairer, Faster and Firmer—A Modern Approach to Immigration And Asylum* (1998) Cm 4018, 8–9. For numbers of asylum claims between 1992 and 1999 see Hailbronner (2000) at p 13.

[8] UKTS No 72 (1997), Cm 3806.   [9] Hailbronner (2000) pp 382 et seq.

ticular Member State, or (iv) the Member State is responsible for controlling the entry of the applicant into the Union (for example by issuing a visa). Where no Member State can be identified on these criteria, the first Member State with which the application is lodged in responsible for examining it.

The principles and criteria set out in the Dublin Convention are broadly similar, but not identical, to those in Articles 28 to 38 of the Schengen Implementing Convention,[10] which was negotiated at the same time and signed only four days later. Consistently with the central concept of the Schengen Implementing Convention as a spearhead towards measures applying to all EU Member States, the Parties to Schengen agreed that from the entry into force of the Dublin Convention the Schengen provisions on asylum would no longer be used.[11]

That the Dublin Convention took seven years to achieve the ratifications by all Member States necessary for its entry into force illustrates the most serious weakness of the international law method. The Convention was in fact applied from the date of its signature on an administrative basis, and was informally relied on by national courts, but it was not a source of legal obligation between the Member States. Moreover, since it was no more than a method of determining the Member State with jurisdiction to determine each application, it did nothing in itself to eliminate the differences in national practice which were the underlying cause of attempts by asylum seekers to make successive applications. Even less could it be said that it increased substantive or procedural protection or any other human rights of refugees.[12] Like the 1951 Convention it gave no rights to asylum seekers, and it imposed no duty on the 'responsible' Member State actually to examine the substance of individual applications. Article 3.5 of the Dublin Convention provided that: 'Any Member State shall retain the right, pursuant to its national laws, to send an applicant for asylum to a third State, in compliance with the provisions of the Geneva Convention, as amended by the New York Protocol.'

The Dublin Convention, however, set up requirements for Member States to conduct exchanges not only for the purposes of determining the responsible Member State under its provisions, but also in regard to national legislative measures and practices on asylum, on statistical data and new trends on applications, and on information on the situation in the countries of origin of applicants. Other exchanges on an intergovernmental basis

[10] (1981) 30 ILM 84. See Chapter 3 above.

[11] Protocol signed at Bonn on 26 April 1994, printed in *Statewatch texts* (1997) 134. An analysis of the differences in the provisions of the two Conventions and the effect of the Bonn Protocol is at pp 135–6.

[12] For criticisms by the UN HCR and others of the Dublin Convention see Michael Spencer (1995) at pp 94–5.

between Ministers for Immigration led to the adoption of Resolutions on manifestly unfounded applications for asylum and Conclusions on a harmonized approach to third countries posing generally no serious risk of persecution.[13] From the entry into force of the Maastricht Treaty these exchanges took place within the Third Pillar framework and laid the foundations for a common approach to the substance and procedure of determining applications. In June 1994, for example, some time before the formal entry into force of the Dublin Convention, the Council adopted principles on means of proof to be used in the context of the Convention system. The basic objective was that responsibility under the Convention should be determined on as few requirements of proof as possible, since otherwise determining responsibility might take longer than examination of the actual asylum request.[14]

At the same time, the Council adopted Guidelines for joint reports on third countries.[15] Under these guidelines the cooperation between diplomatic missions of Member States in non-Member States formalized under the Second Pillar[16] was applied for the benefit of Third Pillar policy. The central objective was that the reports should 'provide an accurate overall picture of the political, economic and social situation of the third country, without being over-detailed since it is vital that they be drawn up quickly.' The guidelines set out detailed points to be covered—such as whether the regime permitted free elections, a multi-party system, freedom of opinion and assembly, religious freedom, an independent judiciary, whether the country had acceded to instruments for protection of human rights, whether international organizations were permitted to monitor respect for human rights, actual practice on torture and on frequent use of the death penalty, on the possibility of avoiding persecution by fleeing within the State, and on the attitude of the regime to foreign asylum seekers and to nationals who lodged asylum applications elsewhere.

Since differences among Member States in their approach to asylum seekers stem in practice more from differing assessments of the factual situation in the country from which they are fleeing than from legal factors, provision for joint reports paved the way for a more uniform approach. A survey conducted under a 1997 Decision of the Council[17] revealed, however, that there remained wide variations between Member States in relation to the countries regarded as 'safe'. It has also been suggested, in

[13] The London Resolutions of 30 November 1992 and 1 December 1992, published in the UNHCR Collection (1995) and in Statewatch texts (1997) pp 64–6.
[14] Means of proof in the framework of the Dublin Convention, text adopted by the Council on 20 June 1994, OJ No C274/35, 19.9.1996.
[15] Adopted by the Council on 20 June 1994, OJ C274/52, 19.9.1996.
[16] Article 20 (ex Article J.10) of the TEU.
[17] Decision of 26 June 1997, OJ L178/6, 7.7.1997. For results of the survey see Commission Working Document, Towards common standards on asylum procedures, SEC (1999) 271.

particular by JUSTICE, that a source of objective information, independent both of Governments and of applicants, on the countries and circumstances from which asylum seekers come would expedite proceedings and ensure better decisions.[18]

A Common Approach to the 1951 Convention on Refugees

In 1995 the Council took some tentative steps towards approximating national laws and practices in regard to the 1951 Convention. A Resolution on minimum guarantees for asylum procedures,[19] carefully drafted to avoid the impression of binding legal effect, recommended that Member States should not expel asylum seekers pending a final decision on their application, that they should provide an examination of individual cases by a qualified authority, that asylum seekers should be given a fair hearing with adequate interpretation where required, an opportunity to communicate with the UNHCR and time to appeal. Applicants from another Member State of the EU were to be put on a fast track so that, while individual examination of the claim was not precluded, there was a presumption that they were manifestly ill-founded. The procedural guarantees did not relate to the application of the Dublin Convention.

A later Resolution on unaccompanied minors who are nationals of third countries[20] contained specific provisions acknowledging that these children had a right to apply for asylum on arrival, although Member States might reserve the right to require the appointment of a guardian. Such asylum applications were to be processed 'as a matter of urgency'.

Much more significant and carefully elaborated, however, was the 1996 Council Joint Position on the harmonized application of the definition of the term 'refugee' in Article 1 of the 1951 Geneva Convention.[21] This instrument referred back to successive European Councils which had endorsed the objective of harmonizing Member States' asylum policies and to the Commission communication on immigration and asylum policies of 23 February 1994.[22] It acknowledged the Handbook of the UNHCR as 'a valuable aid to Member States in determining refugee status'. It set out approved guidelines for the application of the 1951 Convention while making clear their very limited legal status: 'This joint position is adopted within the limits of the constitutional powers of the Governments of the Member States; it shall not bind the legislative authorities or affect decisions of the judicial authorities of the Member States.' The Joint Position

---

[18] JUSTICE (1999): JUSTICE comments on Commission working document 6072/99.
[19] OJ C274/13, 19.9.1996.
[20] Council Resolution on 26 June 1997, OJ C221/23, 19.7.1997.
[21] Joint Position 96/196/JHA, OJ L63/2, 13.3.1996; Nanz (1994) especially pp 127–30.
[22] COM(94)23 final.

also made clear that it did not affect the right of a Member State to give protection under domestic law to persons who did not qualify as refugees under the 1951 definition.

On substance the guidelines, *inter alia*, required examination of individual applications against the situation in the country of origin, provided that 'persecution is generally the act of a State organ . . . or of parties or organizations controlling the State' (including encouragement or tolerance of persecution by third parties) and permitted discriminatory prosecution and punishment to be classed as persecution under certain conditions. The guidelines elaborated the different grounds of persecution specified in the 1951 Convention—offering on the whole broad constructions of race, religion, and nationality. They were also generous on such questions as changes of circumstance since the departure of the asylum-seeker from his country of origin.

Most of the content of the guidelines reflected best practice in the Member States.[23] They had influence on national legislatures and administrative authorities and were cited in national courts,[24] though it was always correctly held that they had no more than persuasive authority. On controversial issues however, such as the crucial question of whether the fear of persecution by non-State agents brought applicants within the 1951 Convention, the Member States had been careful to leave their courts free, and national courts and legislatures continued to differ. More generous treatment for refugees could therefore result from national decisions,[25] or indeed from the developing jurisprudence of the European Court of Human Rights.[26] While the 1951 Convention was essentially a prohibition on the delivery of applicants to State persecutors, the 1950 European

---

[23] Some of the provisions of the Guidelines, and of the other European instruments described above, are reflected in the UK Asylum and Immigration Appeals Act 1993 (c 23) and the Asylum and Immigration Appeals Act 1996 (c 49). See Leigh and Beyani (1996); Harvey (2000).

[24] See, for example, *R v Secretary of State for the Home Department, ex parte Robinson* Times Law Reports 1 August 1997, CA, where Brooke LJ held that the Joint Position reflected a contemporary understanding of the obligations created by the Convention which was not confined to Member States of the EU. See also Peers (2000) p 125.

[25] In *R v Secretary of State for the Home Department ex parte Adan, Subaskaran and Aitseguer* [1999] AC 293, the English Court of Appeal held that the 1951 Convention offered protection against persecution by non-State agents, and that since France and Germany did not interpret the Convention in this wider sense, they were not 'safe countries' to which the asylum seekers could be returned. This approach to the construction of the Convention was confirmed by the House of Lords on 19 December 2000, [2001] All ER 593.

[26] See, for example, *Chahal v UK* [1996] 23 EHHR 413, where the ECtHR held that if the applicant, who had been refused asylum, were deported to India he was likely to suffer inhuman and degrading punishment and that the UK had violated Article 13, in conjunction with Article 3 of the Convention in failing to provide an effective remedy against this. The UK Government has assured Parliament that an asylum seeker whose application has been refused will be able to appeal also on the ground that his removal would breach the ECHR.

Convention on Human Rights and Fundamental Freedoms (ECHR) conferred rights on individuals to freedom from torture and inhuman or degrading treatment, to a fair trial and to private and family life. The incomplete nature of the harmonization of national interpretations of the 1951 Convention meant that the Dublin Convention, based on the assumption that the Member States shared common obligations, was seriously undermined.

Temporary Protection and Burden-sharing

The Council under the Maastricht Treaty also adopted some limited initiatives providing for burden-sharing with regard to admission and residence of displaced persons on a temporary basis and for related alert and emergency procedures.[27] A Joint Action in April 1999[28] established projects and measures to provide support for the reception and voluntary repatriation of refugees, displaced persons and asylum seekers. This was mainly intended to offer emergency assistance to those who had fled as a result of events in Kosovo. It followed earlier precedents where the Council had provided funds from the Communities' budget for projects giving protection or assisting voluntary repatriation of temporarily displaced persons.[29] More ambitious proposals from the Commission on temporary protection and on burden-sharing were not accepted by the Council.

Weaknesses of the Third Pillar Method for Asylum Policy

The above selection of instruments adopted by the Council under intergovernmental procedures either before or under Article K of the Treaty of Maastricht suggests that there was no overwhelming difficulty for the Council in reaching agreement at least on questions of jurisdiction and on limited clarification of pre-existing international obligations. The instruments, moreover, were generally responsive to democratic opinion on the question of asylum, that is, their primary objective was to achieve swifter and more reliable methods of excluding asylum seekers who did not qualify as refugees under the 1951 Convention as extended. While these policies were strongly criticized by liberal lawyers, politicians, and writers,[30] the Member States in the Council were firm in continuing to honour the

---

[27] Resolution of 25 September 1995, OJ C262/1, 7.10.1995; Decision 96/198/JHA of 4 March 1996 OJ L63/10, 13.5.1996.

[28] 1999/290/JHA. On the factual background, see Harding (2000) pp 33–42.

[29] See Peers (2000) p 124.

[30] See, for example, Shipsey (1997) ch 10 especially pp 175–6 and 178–80, and JUSTICE (1999).

letter at least of their obligations under the 1951 Convention as well as under the ECHR. Calls to restrict the 1951 Convention in the light of the surge in applications for asylum during the 1990s were resisted. There was little indication that the objective of excluding asylum-seekers was being met—more than 300,000 people sought asylum in the European Union in 2000—although it is likely that in the absence of deterrent measures the number would have been even higher.[31]

Burden-sharing was also an unrealized objective. States which were by reason of geographical position or for other reasons less likely to be responsible under the Dublin Convention criteria showed little inclination to accept a larger proportion of refugees on grounds of 'solidarity'. Nor was anything done at European Union level to ensure that those awaiting decisions, or granted refugee status, should be entitled either to work or to be supported or to have rights of free movement within the Union.

What was also inadequate was the legal character of the instruments employed. The only Convention in the field, the Dublin Convention, took seven years from its adoption in 1990 to its entry into force in 1997. Joint positions and joint actions were not sufficiently publicized or submitted to national parliaments in advance of their adoption. The Treaty of Maastricht did not give the Council a firm basis on which to make joint positions or joint actions legally binding and the instruments actually adopted were for the most part drafted so as not to impose legal obligations. Member States were divided on the nature and the legal effect of these new instruments,[32] and since any jurisdiction of the ECJ was excluded by the terms of the Treaty, there was no way to resolve the matter. The Council also adopted Decisions, Resolutions, and Conclusions which had no legal base in Article K of the Treaty of Maastricht and whose intended legal effect was even less clear. There was in consequence widespread uncertainty as to whether and to what extent the various instruments required implementation in national law.[33] There was little systematic monitoring of the national implementation of any of the instruments.[34]

The Treaty of Maastricht had scarcely entered into force when the Commission suggested that Article K.9—the passerelle provision enabling areas of the Third Pillar to be transferred into the First Pillar—should be invoked in regard to asylum policy. The Council considered the idea in

---

[31] *The Times* 26 January 2001.

[32] Report of the Council of Ministers on the Functioning of the Treaty on European Union, Cm 2866, para 80; Walker (1998) especially pp 235–6. See also discussion at p 78 above.

[33] See den Boer (1999) at pp 304–5.

[34] In 1997 the Council approved a decision providing for an annual questionnaire to Member States and for a Presidency report indicating any issues requiring further measures. This was to be 'submitted to the Council for examination'. See Minutes of JHA Council 26 and 27 May 1997, Council doc 8318/97.

June 1994 and concluded, unsurprisingly, that 'the time is not yet right'.[35] When the review of the Treaty of Maastricht began, there was widespread recognition that the Third Pillar was inadequate for the establishment of common rules for the entry, residence, and status of nationals from non-member countries. Instruments which worked well in the context of foreign policy were inappropriate for asylum, where for the Member States as well as for the thousands of asylum seekers arriving each year at the gates of Europe it was essential to ensure legal certainty. The Commission pointed out in its opinion on the holding of an intergovernmental conference in 1996 that in the context of establishing an area of freedom and security: 'The legal status of the joint action and the common position is obscure, while the entry into force of traditional international agreements may be delayed or uncertain: neither technique is suitable. The Union must have more effective legal instruments in this field.'[36]

The Reflection Group was divided, but according to their Report: 'many members agree in identifying, as an area which ought to be brought under Community competence, everything to do with the crossing of external frontiers: arrangements for aliens, immigration policy, asylum (ruling out asylum among citizens of the Union), and common rules for external border controls.'

This was also the view of the majority at the Conference of the Representatives of the Governments of the Member States which drew up the draft Treaty of Amsterdam. Asylum, together with the closely related areas of crossing of frontiers and immigration, was withdrawn from the Third Pillar and transferred into the First. Further elaboration of instruments on asylum under the Third Pillar came to a standstill while the Commission awaited the entry into force of its new powers to make proposals on asylum. An Italian Presidency proposal for a Convention establishing a EURODAC system for the identification of applications for asylum under Article 15 of the Dublin Convention—which would have involved compulsory fingerprinting of asylum seekers as young as fourteen and storing them on a centralized computer system—was among the projects set aside.[37]

The instruments adopted by the Council, however, remained in operation following the entry into force of the Treaty of Amsterdam, and the Commission accepted that they would form 'the starting point in

---

[35] Conclusions of 20 June 1994 OJ C274/34, 19.9.1996.

[36] COM (94) 23 final, paras. 15–18. See also Commission's Report for the Reflection Group paras 117–27, 1994 Communication on immigration and asylum policies, COM (94) 23 final, paras 86–90 and Working Document: Towards common standards on asylum procedures, SEC (1999) 271, para 2–3.

[37] See Council doc 11118/4/96 p 10; (1996) 6 Statewatch 4 (July–August) (2000); Commission Working Document SEC (1999) 271 para 5; Peers (2000) p 116.

preparing a proposal for a Community legal instrument'.[38] The slow progress in the Council even after new First Pillar powers were available seems to show that the failure to agree effective European measures cannot be ascribed entirely to the imperfections of the Third Pillar methods.[39]

Control of External Borders of the Member States

The second area to be regarded as a matter of common interest under Article K.1 was: '(2) rules governing the crossing by persons of the external borders of the Member States and the exercise of controls thereon; . . . '. This provision reflected the dispute during the negotiation of the Maastricht Treaty on whether visa and immigration policy should be placed within the European Community Treaty or dealt with on an intergovernmental basis. Under an unhappy and illogical compromise certain aspects only of visa policy were transferred by Article 100c of the EC Treaty into Community competence. The Council under Article 100c(1) was to determine the 'black list' of countries whose nationals required a visa to cross the external borders of the Member States. A country could be added to the 'black list' for six months only in the event of an emergency situation there posing a threat of sudden influx of its nationals into the Community(Article 100c(2)). By 1 January 1996 the Council was also required to adopt measures on a uniform format for visas (Article 100c(3)). Other aspects of visa policy and control of external borders, however, remained under national jurisdiction and might be dealt with under the Third Pillar provisions of Article K.1(2).

Underlying this curious division of visa policy between the First and Third Pillars was the dispute among the Member States described in Chapter 3 above—over whether the commitment in the Single European Act to establish the internal market as 'an area without internal frontiers in which the free movement of goods, persons, services and capital is ensured in accordance with the provisions of this Treaty' imposed an obligation on the Member States to eliminate border control of people. The United Kingdom took the firm view that there was no such obligation and was strongly opposed as a matter of policy to the lifting of internal border control of people. Regardless of their position on the underlying controversy, however, all Member States agreed that it was highly desirable to tighten control of the external borders of the Member States.

[38] COM SEC (1999) 271, especially at para 10. The Action Plan of the Commission and the Council adopted in December 1998, OJ C19/1, 23.1, 1999, at para 8 accepted that an 'impressive amount of work has already been carried out' but that the new Treaty provisions could remedy the weaknesses of the instruments adopted. See also O'Keeffe (1994*b*) at pp 272, 274; Kerse (2000/2001).

[39] On the likely effects of the transfer of asylum and immigration into the First Pillar, see Guild and Harlow (eds) (2001).

The link between the internal market and visa control of all those regarded as posing a threat in the context of free movement of people among Member States explains in part why the 'black list' of countries whose citizens would require visas was brought within the tighter regime of the European Community Treaty and in particular why it was placed within the internal market powers set out in Article 100.

Draft Convention on External Frontiers

In June 1991, well before the conclusion of the Maastricht Treaty, the Member States had within the framework of the Ad Hoc Group on Immigration agreed on the substance of a Convention among themselves for the purpose of strengthening external borders and regulating the issue of short-term national visas. This Convention was to cover common standards of border control, mutual recognition of visas and exchange of information on persons to be excluded.[40] The final provisions were however blocked over a dispute between the UK and Spain over how the Convention should apply to Gibraltar.

The entry into force of the Maastricht Treaty gave the Commission new powers of initiative and the Council new powers of decision in all the areas covered by the draft Convention. These powers were divided between the First Pillar—Article 100c—and the Third Pillar—Articles K.1 and K.3. In December 1993 the Commission presented to the Council a Communication containing two linked proposals—for a regulation based on Article 100c determining the third countries whose nationals would require a visa to cross the external borders and for a Council decision to establish a Convention on the crossing of the external frontiers of the Member States.[41] The Commission proposals split the substance of the Convention between the new First Pillar powers and the new Third Pillar powers available to the Council, but they did not otherwise materially change the substance of the draft Convention as it stood. The central purposes remained the same—to strengthen control of the external frontiers of the EU, to coordinate the grant of leave to enter the Union and to adopt a single form of visa for non-citizens of the Union which would be recognized in all Member States. This approach had been endorsed by Ministers for Immigration meeting in Copenhagen in June 1993. The Commission regarded swift adoption of these texts as a political priority to secure free movement of people and abolition of internal frontiers within the internal market.[42]

---

[40] See Chapter 3 above and COM (93) 684, paras 3 and 4.

[41] COM(93) 684; O'Keeffe (1994a) p 135.

[42] Commission evidence to House of Lords: see HL Select Committee on the European Communities, 14th Report (1993–94) para 14 and QQ 85–90.

The Commission proposals of course brought the draft Convention for the first time fully into the public domain and opened its terms to scrutiny. There was widespread criticism of the central concept of the Joint List under which a person whose name was placed on the List by one Member State would in principle be excluded from all the Member States. The grounds for inclusion on the List would include not only information that the person had committed a serious crime but also 'serious grounds for believing that he is planning to commit a serious crime or that he represents a threat to the public policy or national security of a Member State'.[43] The risk was that entries on the Joint List could originate from mistake or from personal malice with no adequate remedy for the person who might be wrongly excluded. The intention was for protection of personal data, including the right of access and correction of incorrect data, to be guaranteed under the entirely separate Convention on the European Information System.

Also criticized was the requirement for all Member States to adopt national legislation imposing on airlines, shipping, and international coach transport carriers responsibility to ensure that all persons carried from non-member countries possessed valid passports and visas. Carriers who failed were not only to be responsible for returning persons refused admission at the external frontiers but would also be subject to 'appropriate penalties'.[44] Most, but not all Member States, already had in place similar legislation on carriers' liability, and a similar requirement was contained in the Schengen Implementing Convention.[45] The European Parliament and other bodies such as the UK Immigration Law Practitioners Association argued that the draft provision, even if not actually contrary to the 1951 Convention on the Status of Refugees, was likely to hinder the ability of asylum seekers to escape from countries where they feared persecution as well as generally to obstruct free movement of travellers.[46]

Visa Lists and Boundary Demarcation

The division of visa policy between Article 100c of the EC Treaty and the Third Pillar also gave rise to disputes among the institutions which inhibited the development of a coherent strategy. The Commission's proposal

---

[43] Draft Article 10.   [44] Draft Article 14.   [45] Draft Article 27.

[46] See evidence in HL Select Committee on European Communities 14th Report (1993–94) at paras 40–47. Article 27 of the draft Convention gave primacy to the 1951 Convention on the Status of Refugees and to the European Convention on Human Rights. See Cruz (1995) and Nicholson (1987) especially pp 607–10, and conclusion at p 633: 'Under such circumstances States may hold that they are complying with the letter of the law but they are seriously undermining the spirit of their obligations under international law.'

for a Regulation under the new Article 100c determining the third countries whose nationals must be in possession of a visa when crossing the external frontiers of the Member States was based on an expansive interpretation of the enabling provision. The Commission took the view that Article 100c, as well as conferring power to draw up the 'black list' of countries whose nationals would require a visa, also enabled the Council to draw up a 'white list' of third countries to be exempt from the visa requirement. Its proposal also contained in Article 2 an obligation of mutual recognition among Member States of each others' visas, where such visas were valid throughout the Community. Member States, however, maintained that neither proposal was within the powers of Article 100c. In their view the mutual recognition of short-term visas and the introduction of uniform visas valid throughout the territory of the Member States were Third Pillar matters to be dealt with under Articles 17 to 25 of the draft External Frontiers Convention.

The Commission's draft was also criticized on the ground that the 'negative list'—based on the Schengen Convention list which comprised 130 countries—was unnecessarily long and capable of causing damage to relations with many non-member countries. The list of countries whose nationals would require visas included many Commonwealth countries for which the UK, which was their most likely destination, did not require visas.[47]

The Council therefore amended the Commission's draft Regulation on visas by deleting the provisions on establishment of a 'white list' and mutual recognition of visas. They also removed some Commonwealth countries from the 'black list'. They did not, however, reconsult the European Parliament, which had taken an even more expansionist interpretation than the Commission of the possibilities of Article 100c. The Parliament brought proceedings against the Council before the ECJ and the Court annulled the Regulation for failure to reconsult, while preserving its legal effects on an interim basis. The Council, nothing daunted, went through the prescribed hoops, ignored the Parliament's amendments, and adopted the Regulation a second time.[48]

There was a similar boundary dispute over the drawing up of common rules for airport transit visas, where the person was not intended to enter the territory of the transit State. For ten States on the 'black list' posing a

[47] See HL Select Committee on the European Communities, 14th Report (1993–94) paras 70–3 and 106–8. For a comparison of the different lists, with critical commentary on the complexity resulting from the differences, see [1995] Statewatch (October) 22–3.

[48] Council Regulation 2317/95, OJ L234/1, 3.10.1995; Case C-392/95 *European Parliament v Council* [1997] ECR I-3213; Council Regulation 574/1999, OJ L72/2, 18.3.1999 Peers (2000) pp 69–71 and Peers (1996b). Under powers available following the entry into force of the Treaty of Amsterdam, the Council later adopted a comprehensive measure on visa lists: Regulation 539/2001 OJ L81/1, 21.3.2001.

special threat, visas would be required, and Member States were permitted to require transit visas to persons from countries not on this list. The Council adopted a Joint Action on the basis of Article K.3, making clear that the objective of the measure was security and control of illegal immigration and that it did not relate to crossing external frontiers. The Commission however sought its annulment by the ECJ on the ground that it was essentially a measure related to the internal market which should have been adopted under Article 100c. This action the Council won.[49]

The laying down of a uniform format for visas was by contrast clearly placed within the EC Treaty, so that there was no controversy when in 1995 the Council, under Article 100c(3), adopted a Regulation.[50] The uniform format was to cover visas for less than three months' stay as well as airport transit visas. The Regulation stated in its Preamble that it was 'to be regarded as forming a coherent whole with measures falling within Title VI of the Treaty on European Union'.

Cooperative Measures on Visas

Although the adoption of key instruments on visa policy was thus bedevilled by disputes over Gibraltar and over legal base, there were some minor successes with confidence-building measures. These included a Council recommendation on local consular cooperation regarding visas, providing for the strengthened cooperation in overseas posts established under the Second Pillar to be used for exchange of information on national criteria for issuing visas, for common assessments of risks to national security, public order and of the threat of clandestine immigration.[51] In 1999 the Council made a further recommendation calling for 'uniform levels of expertise and equipment' in overseas posts and in visa offices of Member States in order to detect false or falsified documents.[52] The Council also strengthened the mandate of the Centre for Information, Discussion and Exchange on the Crossing of Frontiers and Immigration (CIREFT).[53] Significantly, all these measures avoided the difficulties described above over the legal status of Third Pillar measures since they were merely recommendations or Council conclusions.

---

[49] Joint Action 96/197 JHA OJ L63/8, 13.3.1996; Case C-170/96 *Commission v Council* (airport transit visas) [1998] ECR I-2763.
[50] Regulation 1683/95 of 29 May 1995, OJ L164/1, 14.7.95.
[51] Council recommendation of 4 March 1996 OJ C80/1, 18.3.1996.
[52] Recommendation of 29 April 1999, OJ C140/1, 20.5.1999.
[53] Conclusions of 30 November 1994 OJ C274/50, 19.9.1996.

Weaknesses of the Third Pillar Method for Control of External Borders and Visa Policy

In this area, even more than in regard to asylum policy, the structural weaknesses of the Third Pillar system were obvious. In the words of Hailbronner: 'The decision-making process was insufficient because of the clumsy procedure applied to decision-making, and the decisions lacked binding legal effect.'[54] By the time that the Treaty of Amsterdam was being negotiated there was a general perception that the need for coherent and binding rules on external borders and visas was pressing and that the Third Pillar method had shown itself inadequate to the task.[55] What progress was made towards strengthening the external frontiers of the Member States and providing at least sufficient coherence in visa policies to ensure exclusion of all those regarded by any one Member State as undesirable was achieved either through First Pillar instruments or through the Schengen Implementing Convention.[56] There was little evidence of development within the European Union of common criteria for the assessment of visa applications. The entire area of control of external frontiers was therefore transferred by the Treaty of Amsterdam from the Third Pillar into the new Title IV of the EC Treaty. The instruments which were adopted under the Third Pillar retained their validity pending their replacement by measures which may now be adopted under the EC Treaty.

Immigration Policy

The third area listed under Article K.1 as a matter of common interest was 'immigration policy and policy regarding nationals of third countries'. This area was divided into three parts: conditions of entry and movement; conditions of residence; combatting unauthorized immigration, residence and working. A brief glance at the list of instruments adopted shows that it was in the third of these parts that Member States cooperated with the greatest enthusiasm.

---

[54] Hailbronner (2000) at p 49.

[55] See, for example, Commission Opinion on the holding of an intergovernmental conference, paras 15–18 and Report for the Reflection Group, paras 117–27.

[56] For a more systematic account of law and policy formed by these various sources, see Hailbronner (2000) especially Parts B and C; Peers (2000) ch 4.

(a) conditions of entry and movement by nationals of third countries on the territory of Member States

Throughout the period when immigration was open to coordinated regulation under the Third Pillar, Member States generally shared a desire to limit immigration from non-Member States to the greatest possible extent. There were, of course many individuals with secondary rights under European Community law (such as family members of those with Community rights of free movement) or under international agreements with non-Member States (for example the Association Agreement with Turkey).[57] But in the absence of a claim to family reunification or to asylum the Member States sought to exclude from long-term residence all nationals of non-Member States other than those able to bring highly specialized skills or substantial investment potential to Europe.[58]

Three Council Resolutions of 1994 illustrated the unwelcoming face of Europe towards the tired and poor from the outside world. The Resolutions on admission of third-country nationals for employment and for the purpose of pursuing activities as self-employed persons, make clear even by their titles that their principal purpose is *limitation*.[59] In the first Resolution the Council pays lip service to the contribution of migrant workers to the economic development of host countries, but notes that at present 'no member State is pursuing an active immigration policy'. The principles set out—which were expressly declared not to be legally binding on the Member States—begin with the forbidding words: 'Member States will refuse entry to their territories of third-country nationals for the purpose of employment.' Nationals of non-Member States without special entitlements may be considered for admission only where vacancies cannot be filled by national and Community manpower or by lawful permanent residents. There are detailed exceptions where an employer seeks specialist qualifications and for temporary entrants such as seasonal workers, trainees, and business visitors.

A somewhat less wintry face is turned in the second Resolution to those seeking admission for self-employment. This is in part because the

---

[57] For details see Martin and Guild (1996); Cremona (1995); Peers (1996a) Marshall (2000) ch 4 'The European dimension'.

[58] See generally Harding (2000); Rasmussen (1996).

[59] Resolution of 20 June 1994 on limitation on admission of third-country nationals to the territory of the Member States for employment, OJ C274/3, 19.9.1996; Resolution of 30 November 1994 relating to the limitations on the admission of third-country nationals to the territory of the Member States for the purpose of pursuing activities as self-employed persons, OJ C274/7, 19.9.1996. For an account of the Council negotiations which made the Resolutions increasingly restrictive see Peers (1998b). For detail of the Resolutions see Hailbronner (2000) pp 260–73.

Council recognized that admission of such persons 'who add value investment, innovation, transfer of technology, job creation to the economy of
the host country is of benefit', but also because of the need to accommodate existing and future obligations under GATT, GATS, and OECD. The
principles for admission—which are again declared not to be legally
binding on Member States—are based entirely on benefit to the Member
States and on safeguards against any switching to paid employment. The
final principle allows Member States to lay down a special red carpet for
the rich 'who make very substantial investments in the commerce and
industry of that Member State'.

Only the third Resolution, on admission for study in a higher education
institution, is positive in its formulation, starting from the position 'that
the international exchange of students and academics is desirable'.[60] This
Resolution, however bars students from remaining after completion of
their studies as employed or self-employed persons, and also bars those
who entered to seek employment or self-employment from switching to
higher education. Although there are exceptions for those with separate
legal entitlements, the focus is on erecting barriers rather than on promoting social integration.

A Council Resolution of 1997 seeks to harmonize national measures
against marriages of convenience.[61] This Resolution on its face seeks to
operate within the framework of international obligations of the Member
States under Articles 8 and 12 of the European Convention on Human
Rights. The Preamble suggests that checks on a marriage already entered
into are to be made only where the authorities have 'well-founded suspicions' while advance checks are only a possibility. The test of a marriage
of convenience is that its sole aim is obtaining for a third-country national
a residence permit or authority to reside in a Member State. Seven criteria
are set out, including the lack of a common language, inconsistent
accounts by the spouses of their first meeting, the payment of money
(except where payment of dowry is traditional). Where suspicions are
aroused, Member States are to issue a residence permit only after a check,
but there is to be a right to review of any adverse decision. Within a framework of inescapable prior commitments, the central objective of the
Resolution, as with the earlier Resolutions described, is exclusion. Once
again the measure is not binding and Member States had only to 'endeavour' to bring their national legislation into conformity before 1999.

[60] Resolution of 30 November 1994 on the admission of third-country nationals to the territory of the Member States for study purposes, OJ C274/10, 19.9.1996; Peers (1998b) at
p 1252.
[61] Resolution of 4 December 1997 on measures to be adopted on the combatting of marriages of convenience, OJ C382/1, 16.12.1997. For negotiating history and criticism of the
Resolution see Peers (1998b) at pp 1258–62.

JHA Achievements and Weaknesses

Also in 1997 the Council agreed that Member States should exchange information on assistance for the voluntary repatriation of third-country nationals. National policies were to assist integration of non-citizens into society rather than actively to encourage their return.[62]

(b) conditions of residence by nationals of third countries on the territory of Member States, including family reunion and access to employment

Only one Third Pillar instrument sought to balance the wealth of Resolutions intended to exclude and to eject the uninvited with an attempt to integrate existing permanent residents into the EU. This was the 1996 Council Resolution on the status of third-country nationals residing on a long-term basis in the territory of the Member States.[63]

Under this Resolution Member States are to recognize as long-term residents those who provide proof that they have resided legally and without interruption for ten years. It is permissible for national legislation to extend the status more widely and in particular to apply a shorter period of time. Member States should grant to long-term residents a residence authorization for the maximum national period of validity and this is to be not less than ten years. A long-term resident and members of his family should enjoy access to the entire territory of the relevant Member State, as well as national treatment on working conditions, trade union membership, housing, social security, emergency health care, and compulsory schooling. He 'should be able to obtain authorization to engage in gainful activities, in accordance with the provisions of that Member State's legislation'. The Resolution is not legally binding, so that it confers no possible rights on individuals, and the Council does no more than 'call on' the Member States to notify it of the changes in their national law in the area of the Resolution.

(c) combatting unauthorized immigration, residence and work by nationals of third countries on the territory of Member States

Under this heading, the Member States adopted a series of Recommendations seeking to harmonize their means of controlling and combatting illegal immigration and employment, and of expelling or repatriating rejected third country nationals.[64] A Council Recommendation of 1996 for example specifies that prospective employees must have authorization for

---

[62] Council Decision 97/340/JHA OJ L147/3, 5.6.1997.   [63] OJ C80/2, 18.3.1996.
[64] OJ C5/1 10.1.1996; OJ C5/3; OJ C274/18, 19.9.1996; OJ C274/20, 19.9.1996; OJ C274/25, 19.9.1996. For details of policy and measures see Hailbronner (2000), pp 161–75.

a specific employment and any employment and its duration must correspond to that authorization. Member States are to impose appropriate criminal or administrative sanctions for breach of the requirements, on employers and traffickers as well as on employees. The Resolution provides for collaboration and exchange of information among Member States and for a review of compliance.[65] The only instruments however which sought to impose legal obligations on the Member States were two Decisions on monitoring Council instruments on illegal immigration and employment and on exchange of information on assistance for voluntary repatriation. These obligations related only to supply of information and not to application of the underlying rules.[66]

Weaknesses of the Third Pillar Method for Immigration Policy

As with asylum policy, there was no great difficulty for the Member States in reaching agreement on restrictive measures. The uncertainty already described as to the legal effect of Third Pillar instruments led to almost total reliance on explicitly non-binding instruments, but it also seems clear that Member States wished to cling to their national autonomy over immigration law and policy. In spite of the lack of effective monitoring, it seems that compliance with the restrictive measures agreed was good,[67] and Member States took full advantage of new opportunities to cooperate in the fight against illegal immigration and employment. Virtually nothing was done to make real improvements in the status of long-term residents, for example by giving them rights of access to employment or rights of free movement within the European Union. The body of arrangements generated lacked any legally binding effect, and it was nearly three years after the entry into force of the Maastricht Treaty before most of the measures already adopted were even published in the Official Journal.[68]

Immigration policy was transferred entirely by the Treaty of Amsterdam into the First Pillar, leaving the instruments already adopted intact pending their replacement. As with asylum, work under the Third Pillar came to a virtual standstill while the Treaty of Amsterdam was being ratified. The Commission in July 1997 submitted a draft Convention based largely on a consolidated and improved version of what had already been agreed on immigration, explaining that following the entry into force of the new Treaty this would be recast as a Directive.[69] It remains to be seen, however, whether for immigrants from non-Member States this

[65] Council Recommendation of 27 September 1996 on combatting the illegal employment of third-country nationals, OJ C304/1, 14.10.1996.
[66] OJ L342/5, 31.12.1996; OJ L147/3, 5.6.1997.
[67] See Peers (2000) at p 89.   [68] See OJ C274, 19.9.1996.
[69] COM(97) 387, OJ C337/9, 7.11.1997.

change will lead to early improvements in the level of freedom or justice to which they are entitled. History suggests that the slender achievements in this field are due to a lack of political enthusiasm among the Member States for integrating their national policies rather than to the weaknesses of the Third Pillar.[70]

Combatting Drug Addiction

The fourth area listed under Article K.1 as a matter of common interest was 'combatting drug addiction in so far as this is not covered by 7 to 9'. This wording immediately highlights the fact that measures to combat the use of and trafficking in drugs straddle a number of legal bases. Within the First Pillar, drug control measures are relevant to rules on the free movement of both goods and people, to the common agricultural policy, to indirect taxation, to the common commercial policy and to public health. As White says: 'However, regulation in the First Pillar is diffuse, with drug control measures found in diverse instruments, ranging from specific precursor control measures to punitive clauses in tariff preference agreements and measures to prevent money laundering.'[71]

Third Pillar measures may be directed at cooperation in criminal matters, between customs authorities and police (covered in Article K.1 (7)–(9)). Article K.1(4) is aimed at civil and administrative measures outside these areas of cooperation, but it is often not easy to separate them. Many of them, such as forfeiture and licensing restrictions, may be consequential on criminal conviction.[72]

A Joint Action adopted in 1996, for example, made provision for exchange of information among Member States on the chemical profiling of drugs (defined as including cocaine, heroin, LSD, amphetamines, and ecstasy-type derivatives). The European Drugs Unit (the embryo Europol) was given authority to act as clearing house for transmission of this information. The purpose of the exchange of information was to improve cooperation in combatting illicit drug trafficking.[73] The Council adopted shortly afterwards a Resolution on measures to combat and dismantle the

[70] For a call for a more enlightened policy, see Hakura (1998). See also Guild and Harlow (eds) (2001).
[71] Simone White (1999) ch 3 'European Community Drug Control: Internal economic regulation and external conditionality', at p 32.
[72] For a comprehensive account of the possible kinds of regulation see Simone White (1999). See also European Commission publication: *The European Union and the Fight Against Drugs* (1997).
[73] Joint Action 96/699/JHA OJ L322/5, 12.12.1996. See also Joint Action 97/396/JHA, OJ L167/1, 25.6.1997, concerning information exchange, risk assessment, and control of new synthetic drugs.

illicit cultivation and production of drugs within the EU.[74] This provided for exchange of intelligence, of skills and of detection equipment.

The Member States have widely differing policies on drug use and supply and in spite of study at the request of the European Council at Florence in June 1996 of the possibility of harmonization of national laws and of the impact which harmonization might have on reducing consumption and trafficking, there was no agreement on harmonizing substantive criminal laws or sentencing practices. A Joint Action adopted by the Council in December 1996 on the approximation of the laws and practices of the Member States to combat drug addiction and illegal drug trafficking was limited to requiring Member States to 'endeavour to approximate their laws to make them mutually compatible to the extent necessary to prevent and combat drug trafficking in the Union'.[75] The hard legal obligations in this Joint Action related only to operational cooperation and to combatting illicit cultivation of drugs and not to approximation of criminal laws. As the Council had made clear, the Joint Action was 'without prejudice to the general principle that a Member State may maintain or step up the national policy it pursues to combat drugs within its territory'.[76]

The main achievement of Third Pillar activity under this head was therefore to formalize and to enhance exchange of information and practical cooperation and, in the absence of any public clamour for a unified approach by Member States to the fight against drugs, there was no public dissatisfaction with this. The problem was rather with the institutional complexity of the arrangements under the Maastricht Treaty. By way of example one may point to the preparation of a Report requested by the European Council—requiring contributions from the Councils on Health and Education, from Second and Third Pillar bodies, from the European Drugs Unit, and from the European Monitoring Centre for Drugs and Drug Addiction.[77]

Combatting International Fraud

The fifth area of common interest was 'combatting fraud on an international scale, in so far as this is not covered by 7 to 9'. Since the overwhelming proportion of cooperation among Member States in the fight against fraud is carried out by judicial, customs, and police authorities which were specifically excluded from Article K.1(5), it is difficult to see why this head of common interest was listed separately. There seem to be no significant Third Pillar measures or initiatives based on it, although it

[74] OJ C389/1, 23.12.1996.   [75] 96/750/JHA OJ L342/6, 31.12.1996.
[76] Minutes of JHA Council 28 and 29 November 1996, Council doc 12104/96, p 13.
[77] Minutes of the JHA Council of 23 November 1995, Council doc 11720/95. The European Drugs Unit is described below pp 230–1.

may be regarded as providing a legal basis for ongoing administrative cooperation. Measures against fraud affecting the financial interests of the Community (other than those concerning application of national criminal law or administration of justice) were brought fully within the ambit of the Community Pillar by Article 280 (ex Article 209a) of the Treaty of Amsterdam.

Judicial Cooperation in Civil Matters

The sixth area of common interest under Article K.1 of the Maastricht Treaty, and the last to have been substantially absorbed into the First Pillar by virtue of the Treaty of Amsterdam was 'judicial cooperation in civil matters'.

Article 220 of the Treaty establishing the European Economic Community, which has survived unchanged through successive revisions of the Treaty up to and including the Treaty of Amsterdam, may be said to contain an embryo form of Third Pillar cooperation in this area. It provides:

Member States shall, so far as is necessary, enter into negotiations with each other with a view to securing for the benefit of their nationals:
—the protection of persons and the enjoyment and protection of rights under the same conditions as those accorded by each State to its own nationals;
—the abolition of double taxation within the Community;
—the mutual recognition of companies or firms within the meaning of the second paragraph of Article 48, the retention of legal personality in the event of transfer of their seat from one country to another; and the possibility of mergers between companies or firms governed by the laws of different countries;
—the simplification of formalities governing the reciprocal recognition and enforcement of judgments of courts or tribunals and of arbitration awards.

These four areas of legal cooperation were regarded as closely linked to the EEC, which explains why they were singled out. The Conventions which were adopted under Article 220 were not based on formal Commission proposals, were adopted by the Member States and not by the Council, required ratification by all the Member States for their entry into force. It was however assumed without controversy that their interpretation should be determined in case of dispute by the ECJ, although detailed Protocols were drawn up for this purpose. Overwhelmingly the most important Convention under Article 220 is the Brussels Convention on jurisdiction and the enforcement of judgments in civil and commercial matters, originally adopted in 1968 among the original Member States of the European Economic Community, but extended by successive amendments to permit the accession of all States which have subsequently joined the EEC.[78] The Brussels Convention is complemented by the Lugano Convention, opened for signature in 1988.[79] The Lugano Convention enables participation by European Free Trade Area (EFTA) States in an instrument which is substantially similar to the Brussels Convention, but its provisions are not subject to interpretation by the ECJ.

Under the second indent of Article 220 a Convention was adopted in 1990 on the arbitration of double taxation disputes.[80]

The success of the Brussels Convention in the field of private international law led to calls for further conventions among the Member States. These did not fall within the limited ambit of Article 220, but there was nothing to prevent the Member States drawing up free-standing international conventions in this area—just as in the area of asylum described above the Dublin Convention was adopted in advance of the establishment of the Third Pillar. The Member States took this course on a number of occasions—most notably with the Rome Convention on the Law applicable to Contractual Obligations, adopted in 1980 and opened to Austria, Finland, and Sweden in 1997.[81] There was considerable controversy about giving the ECJ jurisdiction to interpret the Contractual Obligations Convention, but this was ultimately agreed by special Protocols.

The entry into force of Article K of the Maastricht Treaty provided a specific procedure for the negotiation of conventions in the field of judicial cooperation, without alteration to Article 220 which continued to form the basis for conventions with a close link to the European Community such as the Bankruptcy Convention adopted in 1995.[82] There was however continuing debate about the appropriate relationship of future work within the Third Pillar and within other international organizations with a tradition of drawing up international conventions on private international law and judicial cooperation—in particular the Council of Europe, the Hague Permanent Conference on Private International Law, and the UN. Schutte spoke of 'a serious risk of duplication of work and unsound rivalries which would eventually be to the detriment of legal practice and security'. He stressed the importance of close links between the EU and other relevant international organizations, so that the objectives and goals of each could be taken into account in designing working programmes.[83]

In 1997 the Member States adopted under Article K.3 a Convention on the service in the Member States of the EU of judicial and extrajudicial

---

[78] Original text in OJ L299/32, 30.12.1972. The consolidated text, following accession by Denmark, Ireland, the UK, Greece, Spain, Portugal, Austria, Finland, and Sweden, is at OJ C27/1, 26.1.1998. On the legal character of the Convention, in particular that its provisions do not have direct effect, see Case C-336/96 *Gilly* [1998] ECR I-2793.

[79] OJ L319/9, 25.11.1988. For an account of the substantive rules of the Conventions see Dicey and Morris (1993) chs 11 and 14.

[80] OJ L225/10, 20.8.1990.

[81] OJ C15/10, 15.10.1997.

[82] (1996) 35 ILM 1223.

[83] Schutte (1994) especially pp 186–9.

documents in civil and commercial matters.[84] The purpose of the Convention was to improve mutual legal assistance in civil matters by simplifying and speeding up service of documents among Member States and thereby to facilitate citizens' access to justice.[85] Documents could be transmitted directly to the courts or to process servers without passing through the central authorities of the Member States. The role of the designated central bodies was limited to the supply of information, providing solutions to difficulties and forwarding documents in exceptional cases to the competent receiving agency. Although most Member States were not Contracting Parties to the 1965 Hague Convention on the service abroad of judicial and extrajudicial documents in civil and commercial matters, Article 19 of the 1997 Convention made explicit provision in order to avoid conflict between the Conventions.

The Convention on service of judicial and extrajudicial documents was accompanied by a Protocol providing for its interpretation by the ECJ.[86] The Protocol contained provisions based on Article 177 of the EC Treaty for references where a national court considers that a decision on a question of interpretation is necessary to enable it to give judgment. Provision was also made for a reference in the interests of clarifying the law at the instance of a competent authority of a Member State—a procedure which would not affect the result of cases which were already decided at national level. Following the outcome of the long-running dispute over giving the ECJ jurisdiction over Third Pillar Conventions, the Protocol will enter into force with the third ratification by a Member State, provided that the Convention (which requires ratification by all Member States) is already in force.

A Convention on Driving Disqualifications was adopted in 1998.[87] The purpose of the Convention was to ensure that a driving disqualification imposed in another Member State would be enforced in the Member State of the offender's residence. The Convention required a driving disqualification imposed on one of the grounds specified in the Annex to be notified to the Member State of residence, and required that State to give effect to it either directly or through one of two methods of conversion into a judicial or administrative decision of its own. Allowance was to be made for any period of disqualification already served in the Member State where the offence took place.

The most significant achievement in this area of the Third Pillar was the adoption in 1998 of the Convention on Jurisdiction and the Recognition

---

[84] OJ C261/1 (Council Act and Convention) and OJ C261/26 (Explanatory Report), 27.8.1997.

[85] Report by Council to European Council, Achievements in the field of Justice and Home Affairs during 1996, Council doc 11118/4/96 REV 4, 4.2.1.

[86] OJ C261/18 and OJ C261/38 (Explanatory Report), 27.8.1997.

[87] OJ C216/1, 10.7.1998 (Convention); OJ C211/1, 23.7.1999 (Explanatory Report).

and Enforcement of Judgments in Matrimonial Matters.[88] At an early stage of the negotiations, the Council held a public debate on the purposes and principles of the draft Convention—the first ministerial meeting in the field of justice and home affairs to be open to the media.[89] The Convention, known colloquially as Brussels II, establishes uniform grounds of jurisdiction in proceedings for divorce, nullity, or judicial separation. It also requires recognition of judgments given in such proceedings in all other Member States without any special procedure being required. Because the purpose of this Convention was similar to that of the Brussels Convention on jurisdiction and the enforcement of judgments in civil and commercial matters (Brussels I) and could be said to enhance the possibility of free movement of persons by increasing certainty as to their matrimonial status, it was argued by the Commission and by the Council Legal Service that it should like its predecessor be based on Article 220 of the EC Treaty. The Member States however decided finally that the provisions on Article K were more appropriate.[90] The Convention was accompanied by a Protocol for its interpretation by the ECJ.[91] This Protocol, like the Protocol to the Convention on service of judicial and extrajudicial documents described above, was to come into force after the third ratification by a Member State, provided that the Convention itself was already in force.

Although conventions were clearly the instruments of choice within the area of judicial cooperation, mention should also be made of the 1998 Joint Action which established the European Judicial Network.[92] This is intended to facilitate cooperation among judicial authorities and also to provide, through the Internet, practical information on mutual legal assistance. An earlier Joint Action of 1996 had already prepared the way by setting up and funding a programme of training incentives and exchanges for practitioners in the justice area, known as the Grotius programme.[93]

Assessment of Third Pillar Action on Civil Judicial Cooperation

It could not be said that Third Pillar methods and instruments were either inappropriate or inadequate for the task of improving mutual assistance and cooperation among the judicial authorities of the Member States or the

[88] OJ C221/1 (Council Act and Convention), OJ C221/27 (Explanatory Report by Dr Alegria Borras) 16.7.1998. For a critical analysis of the draft Convention at a relatively advanced stage of its negotiation see HL Select Committee on the European Communities, 5th Report (1997–98a).
[89] Minutes of the JHA Council of 25 and 26 September 1995, Council doc 9977/95, p 5.
[90] The Council acknowledged, however, that either legal base would have been possible when they approved the Explanatory Report prepared by Dr Alegria Borras and published in OJ C221/27, 17.7.1998.
[91] OJ C221/19 (Council Act and Protocol), OJ C221/65 (Explanatory Report) 16.7.1998.
[92] OJ L191/4, 7.7.1998.   [93] OJ L287/1, 8.11.1996.

substantive rules of private international law to be applied. On the other hand, Article 220 of the EC Treaty provided a happy precedent for integration into the First Pillar of aspects of judicial cooperation in civil matters and there seemed to be no overriding national objections to a wider application of the Community law method to the area. Many of the matters covered, such as extended recognition of judgments and judicial orders, were linked to improving the free movement of persons.

The entire area of judicial cooperation in civil matters was therefore transferred by the Treaty of Amsterdam to form a new Article 65 of the EC Treaty. Article 220 (now Article 293 EC) remains unchanged, so that problems of legal base—such as were raised by the Convention on Jurisdiction and Recognition and Enforcement of Judgments in Matrimonial Matters—may still arise. Article 65 EC does not widen the powers available under this heading of Article K.1 but it is more detailed in its description of the areas where measures may be taken 'insofar as is necessary for the proper functioning of the internal market'. During 2000, the Council replaced with EC Regulations the three most important of the Conventions described above—the Convention on Jurisdiction and the Recognition and Enforcement of Judgments in Matrimonial Matters, the Convention on service of judicial and extrajudicial documents, and finally the Brussels Convention on jurisdiction and the enforcement of judgments in civil and commercial matters.

Judicial Cooperation in Criminal Matters

The seventh area of 'common interest' listed in Article K.1 was: 'judicial cooperation in criminal matters'. Moves towards closer formal cooperation between Member States in criminal justice matters may be traced back to the abortive Dublin Agreement concluded within the framework of European Political Cooperation in 1979.[94] In 1977 the Member States of the Council of Europe adopted at Strasbourg the European Convention on the Suppression of Terrorism. The Strasbourg Convention was negotiated against a background of a marked increase in terrorism in Europe and a resulting interest among the authorities in cooperation in both formal and informal ways.[95] The key obligation set out in Article 1 was that: 'For the purposes of extradition between Contracting States, none of the following offences shall be regarded as a political offence or as an offence connected with a political offence or as an offence inspired by political motives.'[96]

---

[94] Cmnd 7823.

[95] See Chapter 3 above on the origins of the Trevi Group in 1975. In 1978 the UK Parliament was informed about the ongoing exchange of information on counter-terrorism, Hansard HC Debs 24 October 1978 WA col 870.

[96] UKTS No 93 (1978), Cmnd 7390.

The listed offences included hijacking, sabotage of aircraft, attacks on diplomats, taking of hostages, and the use of bombs endangering people. The Convention was ratified and in force quite quickly between most Member States of the Council of Europe, but contained a critical weakness in that it permitted, with qualifications, reservations to the provision set out above. The Dublin Agreement was an expedient among Member States of the EEC to remedy that weakness as regards extradition among themselves and was, in fact, tailored in order to overcome difficulties between the UK and Ireland (which did not ratify the Strasbourg Convention until 1989).[97]

Although the Dublin Agreement never entered into force, it was the first illustration of a concept which was later to be more generally applied under the Third Pillar—that mutual trust among the Member States and their common obligations to observe human rights should permit the withdrawal of safeguards for the individual which operated to bar or to slow down extradition and mutual assistance in criminal matters. Other examples of this kind, negotiated within European Political Cooperation before the entry into force of the Maastricht Treaty, include an Agreement on the simplification and modernization of methods of transmitting extradition requests.[98]

This would have permitted transmission of extradition requests and supporting documents, subject to safeguards, by fax. Perhaps unsurprisingly it was not signed by the UK or by Ireland. A 1991 Convention on the enforcement of foreign criminal sentences,[99] supplementing the Council of Europe's 1983 Strasbourg Convention on the Transfer of Sentenced Persons, also failed to attract the general support among Member States necessary for its entry into force.

Extradition

On the entry into force of the Maastricht Treaty, the Ministers of Justice declared improved extradition among Member States to be a priority and established a special working group. The first outcome was the 1995 Convention on Simplified Extradition Procedure between Member States of the European Union.[100] The purpose of this Convention was to speed up procedures where the person under arrest consents to extradition. Within ten days of receipt of a request for provisional arrest or, in the case of Parties to the Schengen Agreement, the making of an entry in the

---

[97] For a detailed account of the Strasbourg Convention and the significance of the related Dublin Agreement see Wood (1981).

[98] See Statewatch texts (1997) Vol I p 103.　　　[99] Statewatch texts (1997) Vol I p 104.

[100] OJ C78/1, 6.4.1995 For a full description of the Convention against the background of extradition law and practice see Mackarel and Nash (1997).

Schengen Information System, the requesting State should supply information about the identity of the person sought, the offence, and the consent to extradition. The person sought should be informed and have access to legal advice. He or she may consent not only to extradition but may waive the specialty rule (paving the way to trial in the requesting State on charges other than those specified for the purpose of the surrender).

In 1996 a much more far-reaching Convention relating to Extradition between the Member States of the European Union was adopted under Article K.3 of the Maastricht Treaty and signed in Dublin.[101] The 1996 Convention was intended to supplement and improve the functioning of the 1957 European Convention on Extradition[102] as well as the European Convention on the Suppression of Terrorism described above. In the Preamble the Member States stressed their 'interest in ensuring that extradition procedures operate efficiently and rapidly insofar as their systems of government are based on democratic principles and they comply with obligations laid down by the Convention for the Protection of Human Rights and Fundamental Freedoms'. Article 2 lowered the threshold for extraditable offences in the 1957 Convention to punishment by deprivation of liberty for at least twelve months under the law of the requesting State and at least six months in the requested State.

Other provisions made complex exceptions to the rule of double criminality in cases of conspiracy and association to commit offences, to the safeguards on not surrendering a suspect where the alleged offence is political or inspired by political motives, to the practice of non-surrender on fiscal offences, and to the practice of non-surrender of nationals of the requested State. Although the Convention required ratification by all Member States to enter into force, a novel exception permitted Member States making a declaration to that effect to apply it among themselves at an earlier date.

Substantive Criminal Law: Protection of the Communities' Financial Interests

Just as there was for many years great reluctance among the Member States to accept European Community competence over immigration from non-Member States, there was perhaps even greater reluctance to accept that the Community had any competence over the substance of national criminal laws. Such proposals as have been advanced for harmonization

---

[101] OJ C313/11, 23.10.1996, Cm 3533. A Press Release of 3 October 1996 on the Convention is in Council Doc 10262/96 Presse 250. For a summary and comment see Mackarel and Nash (1997). See also Minutes of Justice and Home Affairs Council (4 June 1996), Council Doc 7813/96, Presse\157 at pp 14–15.

[102] UKTS No 97 (1991), Cm 1762.

of substantive criminal laws have mainly originated from scholars and not from the governments of Member States.[103]

As emphasized in Chapter 1 above, the enforcement of European Community law, like that of international law, takes place through national authorities. Much directly applicable Community law can be effective only if it is enforced through criminal sanctions, but the Council practice was that a Regulation or Directive stopped short of imposing an explicit requirement on Member States to make breach of the Community rule a criminal offence. Instead the Member States were required to impose 'effective, proportionate and dissuasive penalties'. A Regulation on control of fishing, on prohibition of insider dealing, or on economic sanctions, would be supplemented at national level by a law creating penalties which might be civil, administrative, or criminal. In some cases it would be obvious that only criminal penalties would suffice. National law would then usually create the appropriate criminal offence and provide for jurisdiction and for penalties.

The extent to which the EEC could explicitly require Member States to impose criminal sanctions was hotly debated in 1990 in the context of the draft Council Directive on Money Laundering.[104] The Council, despite the advice of both the Commission and the Council Legal Services, adopted the Directive in the traditional form, without expressly requiring the creation at national level of a criminal offence of money laundering. Soon afterwards Advocate-General Jacobs said explicitly that while neither the Commission, the Court of First Instance (CFI), nor the ECJ had the function of a criminal tribunal, 'it should be noted, however, that that would not in itself preclude the Community from exercising, for example, powers to harmonize the criminal laws of the Member States, if that were necessary to attain one of the objectives of the Community'.[105]

The continuing sensitivity of Member States to potential European Community action affecting national criminal laws led the Commission, in formulating new proposals on the legal protection of the financial interests of the Community following the entry into force of the Maastricht Treaty, to split the administrative and the criminal aspects—placing the administrative aspects within the Community Pillar and the complementary criminal aspects in a draft Third Pillar Convention.[106] The long history of efforts to agree effective measures to counter fraud against the

---

[103] See Swart (1994) at p 197. For a comprehensive account of EC and Third Pillar measures affecting national criminal laws see Peers (2000).

[104] COM(90) 106, and see HL Select Committee on the European Communities, 1st Report (1990–91a) at paras 25–8 and 46–9.

[105] Case C-240/90 *Germany v Commission* [1992] ECR I-5383, ground 12 of Opinion. See also *Anklagemyndig Leden v Hansen* (Case C-326/88) [1990] ECR I-2911, where the ECJ made clear that the Member States had a discretion as to the type of sanction imposed.

[106] COM(94) 214 final. See Vervaele (ed) (1994) pp 161–202.

finances of the European Communities bore fruit in that relatively quickly—in July 1995—the Council adopted a Convention on the protection of the European Communities' financial interests.[107] The Convention contained a detailed definition of fraud affecting the Communities' financial interests (identical in the related Community framework Regulation). Intent is an element of this definition, but this 'may be inferred from objective, factual circumstances'. The Convention then requires each Member State to 'take the necessary and appropriate measures to transpose paragraph 1 into their national criminal law in such a way that the conduct referred to therein constitutes criminal offences'. The penalties are required to be 'effective, proportionate and dissuasive' and, at least in the case of serious fraud (defined) this should mean deprivation of liberty and the possibility of extradition. There is a duty to establish jurisdiction over the offences both on a basis of territoriality (including assisting or inducing the commission of fraud) and of nationality. Extradition under the European Convention on Extradition may not be refused on the ground that the request concerns a tax or customs duty offence. Where more than one Member State is concerned there is to be effective cooperation, prosecution, and punishment, and there are rules to preclude double jeopardy (*ne bis in idem*).

Over the next few years the Convention on the protection of the European Communities' financial interests was supplemented by two Protocols. The First Protocol was directed at corruption likely to damage the interests of the Communities and involving Community or national officials as well as members of Community institutions.[108] The Second Protocol deals with the responsibility of legal persons for fraud and corruption committed on their behalf, in the context of the protection of the Communities' financial interests.[109]

In 1997 a Convention was also adopted on the Fight against Corruption involving Officials of the European Communities or Officials of Member States of the European Union.[110] This was based on the First Protocol described in the previous paragraph, but was wider in scope in that it also covered corruption in cases where the European Communities' financial interests were not involved. The Convention required that both 'passive corruption' (action to solicit or receive advantage for acting or refraining from acting in accordance with his functions), and 'active corruption'

---

[107] OJ C316/48, 27.11.1995. Discussions on a draft Convention had taken place for about twenty years.

[108] OJ C313/1, 23.10.1996, and Explanatory Report in OJ C11/5, 15.1.1998.

[109] OJ C221/12, 19.7.1997 and Explanatory Report at OJ C91/8, 31.3.1999.

[110] OJ C195/1, 25.6.1997 and Explanatory Report in OJ C391, 15.12.1998. For an account of other international initiatives in the same direction see Sohmen (1999).

(promise or gift of an advantage for a similar act or omission) should be made criminal in the law of the Member States.

In their 1997 Action Plan to combat organized crime Member States undertook to implement the Convention and Protocols on the protection of the European Communities' financial interests.[111] By 1999 however, when the Treaty of Amsterdam entered into force, only a few States had done so, and there were doubts as to whether the Convention would ever enter into force. The general despondency seems to have encouraged the search for an entirely fresh approach in the form of the *Corpus Iuris*.[112]

Joint Actions

While the harmonization of criminal law was arguably not within the scope of Article K.1 at all and was therefore pursued by the laborious and uncertain route of international conventions requiring ratification of all Member States to enter into force, much more obvious practical results were being achieved through the adoption of joint actions. Among the most significant in the area of criminal justice cooperation were the 1996 Joint Action concerning action to combat racism and xenophobia,[113] the 1996 Joint Action establishing an incentive and exchange programme for persons responsible for combatting trade in human beings and the sexual exploitation of children,[114] the related Joint Action concerning action to combat trafficking in human beings and sexual exploitation of children,[115] and the 1998 Joint Action on corruption in the private sector.[116]

The 1997 Joint Action on action to combat trafficking in human beings and the sexual exploitation of children illustrates the capacity of the Council to come to rapid agreement where the necessary political will was focused in response to wide publicity given to a horrific case of paedophilia in Belgium.[117] The Joint Action sets out a common definition and requires Member States to review their existing laws and practices with a view to providing 'effective, proportionate and dissuasive criminal penalties'. There was in this no commitment to harmonize substantive laws, but the Joint Action required administrative penalties to be available against

---

[111] OJ C251/1, 15.8.1997, at point 14.

[112] See HL Select Committee especially paras 16–17, 32 and Q 269.

[113] 96/443/JHA, OJ L185/5 24.7.1996. See also minutes of Justice and Home Affairs Council of 19 and 20 March 1996, Council Doc 5727/96, Presse 63 for record of political agreement, with texts of Declarations by Greek, French, UK, and Danish Delegations.

[114] 96/700//JHA OJ L322/7, 12.12.1996.

[115] 97/154/JHA OJ L63/2, 4.3.1997.

[116] OJ L358/2, 31.12.1998. For a systematic account of Third Pillar measures affecting substantive criminal law, see Peers (2000) pp 149–53.

[117] See HL Select Committee on the European Communities, 15th Report (1997–98e) p 5 and QQ 7, 8.

legal persons involved in facilitating conduct of this kind and there were provisions on jurisdiction and on protection and assistance for victims.

Informal Cooperation

For those at the forefront of the battle against international crime, however, the greatest value of the Third Pillar framework lay in the informal exchanges through which information and analysis was shared and common approaches developed. Some of these exchanges led to non-binding Council Resolutions—for example the 1996 Resolutions on individuals who cooperate with the judicial process in the fight against international organized crime and on sentencing for serious illicit drug-trafficking.[118] The Council adopted successive Action Plans to combat organized crime which contained policy strategies as well as specific legislative targets. A 1998 Resolution focused on aspects of prevention rather than law enforcement—making provision, for example, for concrete projects to provide practical know-how and provide a basis for codes of good practice for preventing organised crime in specific areas.[119]

In the nature of things—and the same was shown to be true for the Second Pillar—the greatest successes attracted the least publicity. For a balanced assessment of the strength of the Third Pillar system for criminal justice cooperation one must take account of the assessments of those directly participating in the process whether as ministers or as officials. The UK Home Office in evidence to the House of Lords gave their view in these terms:

> It is also in the nature of such cooperation that it can advertise itself only through the adoption of high profile agreements, while much of the exchange of information and ideas on practical issues goes unseen and unremarked. The result can be a perception of a lack of results which may fail to do the Third Pillar full justice.[120]

Some commentators who accepted that the Third Pillar produced results were unhappy that these results were repressive, and in particular that they gave insufficient guarantees for the effective protection of human rights.[121] The concern was expressed mainly in terms of the absence of judicial and parliamentary accountability and oversight. These aspects of the process are addressed below, in Chapters 9 and 10.

---

[118] OJ C10/1 and 10/3, 11.1.1997. For a comprehensive list of instruments adopted by March 1995, mostly at that stage non-binding Resolutions, see OJ C270/5, 16.10.1995.

[119] Resolution of 21 December 1998 OJ C408/1, 29.12.98; see Peers (2000) pp 192–3.

[120] HL Select Committee on the European Communities, 15th Report (1997–98e) p 5 and Q 29. See also in that Report evidence from the Association of Chief Police Officers and National Criminal Intelligence Service (NCIS) and from Michael Howard QC, MP, former Home Secretary.

[121] See Walker (1998); Michael Spencer (1995); Statewatch texts (1997) passim.

Customs Cooperation

The customs union is at the heart of the European Community. The rules controlling the levying of customs tariffs and excise duties and prohibitions and restrictions on goods crossing frontiers were established by the Community, but their enforcement remained entirely for the Member States. Cooperation between customs authorities in administering the vast body of rules governing the movement of goods across internal and external frontiers of the European Union is long-standing and straddles the First and the Third Pillar. International action, or from 1993 onwards Third Pillar action, was required where cooperation related to the enforcement of criminal laws—in particular drug trafficking and the movement of prohibited or restricted goods. The EC Treaty also permitted national bans, restrictions, and controls under Articles 36 and 223. Before the entry into force of the Maastricht Treaty this work was within the remit of the Mutual Assistance Group. The completion of the single market in 1992 and the abolition of controls on goods at internal frontiers changed the way in which customs authorities operated to police the rules and greatly increased the need for cooperation among Member States.[122]

Cooperation between customs authorities on criminal enforcement matters was originally regulated under a 1967 Mutual Assistance Convention among the original Six known as the Naples Convention. Following the entry into force of the Maastricht Treaty and the need for more effective and sophisticated methods of policing, a further Convention on Mutual Assistance and Cooperation between Customs Administrations[123] (the Naples II Convention) was negotiated over a five-year period within the Third Pillar. On its entry into force following ratification by all Member States it will supersede the original Naples Convention.

The Naples II Convention lays down rules for modern forms of tracking crime such as controlled deliveries of illegal drugs (intended to lead to detection of dealers and organizers) and joint investigation teams among Member States. Hot pursuit and controlled deliveries are permitted for extraditable offences within the scope of the Convention, but Member States may limit or opt out of the relevant provisions.[124] The Naples II Convention is the first international agreement to make general provision for covert investigations outside national territory. Its provisions—no doubt reflecting practice developed without express legitimation—are flexible but give precedence to the law of the State where the actual investigation is taking place. As the Preamble to the Convention puts it: 'such

[122] See EP Working Paper *The Impact of the Amsterdam Treaty on Justice and Home Affairs Issues* Vol I ch 9 European Customs Cooperation.
[123] OJ C24, 23.1.1998.   [124] Articles 20 and 22; Peers (2000) pp 194–9.

cross-border actions must always be carried out in compliance with the principles of legality (conforming with the relevant law applicable in the requested Member State and with the Directives of the competent authorities of that Member State)'. Article 25 of the Convention contains safeguards for data protection in the context of exchange of data. The customs administrations are required to respect the 1981 Council of Europe Convention on data protection, but there are also specific commitments built into the Naples II Convention.

The Council in 1995 adopted under Third Pillar procedures a Convention on the use of information technology for customs purposes.[125] The Convention provided the framework and guarantees to permit the establishment of a joint automated system known as the Customs Information System (CIS). The purpose of the CIS was 'to assist in preventing, investigating and prosecuting serious contraventions of national laws by increasing, through the rapid dissemination of information, the effectiveness of the cooperation and control procedures of the customs administrations of the Member States'. As the Preamble to the Convention acknowledged, customs authorities 'have to implement both Community and non-Community provisions'. Enforcement of purely Community provisions is carried out under the Mutual Assistance Regulation,[126] or under other specific Community regulations and there was already in existence a database for Community purposes. The CIS is intended to provide assistance for the enforcement of rules remaining within the competence of Member States either under Article 36 or Article 223 of the EC Treaty. The First Pillar system, but not the Third Pillar system, is already covered by Community rules on data protection, and most of the detailed provisions of the Convention are intended to make specific provision for protection of the personal data to be entered. The objective was that the two systems should ultimately run in tandem. The standards provided for the CIS system are broadly those set out in the Council of Europe's 1981 Convention on the Protection of Individuals with regard to Automatic Processing of Personal Data[127] and a Committee of Ministers Recommendation on the use of personal data for law enforcement.[128]

In the field of customs cooperation there were few Joint Actions. In 1996, however, the Council adopted a Joint Action on cooperation between customs authorities and business organizations in combatting

---

[125] OJ C316/33, 27.11.95.
[126] Council Regulation 1468/81, OJ L144/1, 2.6.81, amended by Regulation 945/87 OJ L90/3, 2.4.1987. For an explanation of the relationship between First and Third Pillar activity in the customs field see Bavillard (1994) p 217.
[127] European Treaty Series 108.
[128] (87) 15. For explanation of the interrelation between the two systems see EP Working Paper *The Impact of the Amsterdam Treaty on Justice and Home Affairs Issues* Vol I pp 84–6.

drug trafficking.[129] This required the Member States to establish cooperative programmes with businesses at national level. The guidelines for the
matters to be covered in these national programmes included provision of
advance data on passengers and cargo, access by customs authorities to
business information systems, the making of security assessments, checking staff, and providing training for staff.

Because customs authorities already had a long tradition of cooperation
and of exchanges of liaison officers for training and experience, the establishment of formal Third Pillar structures for enforcement added less to
the level of mutual support than was the case for judicial and police
authorities.[130] Special joint enforcement operations, particularly in the
drugs field, intensified—with apparent success at least in terms of detec-
tions and convictions.[131]

Police Cooperation

The last of the nine areas of common interest was 'police cooperation for
the purposes of preventing and combatting terrorism, unlawful drug
trafficking and other serious forms of international crime, including if necessary certain aspects of customs cooperation, in connection with the organization of a Union-wide system for exchanging information within a
European Police Office (Europol). Police cooperation is generally regarded
as the jewel in the crown of the Third Pillar. Europol—whatever its defects
in terms of democratic and judicial control—was formally established by
an international convention ratified by all Member States and is operating
to the apparent satisfaction of the police authorities.

Europol resulted from an ambitious initiative taken by Chancellor Kohl
at the European Council meeting in Luxembourg in June 1991. This pro-
posal was for a body with operational powers, often described as a
European Federal Bureau of Investigation. For a majority of Member
States, however, this scheme was not politically acceptable. While in the
US the Federal Bureau of Investigation is responsible for the investigation
and prosecution of a body of federal criminal law, there exists no body of
European Community or European Union criminal law. The Member
States retain general competence over their national systems of criminal
law and their reluctance to accept any form of obligation to approximate
these national systems, which has already been described, was matched

[129] 96/698/JHA OJ L322/3, 12.12.1996.
[130] See Memorandum and evidence from HM Customs and Excise to House of Lords: HL
Select Committee on the European Communities, 15th Report (1997–98e) pp 48–57; EP
Working Paper *The Impact of the Amsterdam Treaty on Justice and Home Affairs* Vol I pp 86–90.
[131] Peers (2000) pp 203–4.

by immense reluctance to endorse anything going beyond European supervision of national enforcement.[132]

The German Chancellor's proposal was therefore merged with a separate UK initiative for a European Drugs Intelligence Unit, resulting in the Treaty provision set out above. A Declaration attached to the Maastricht Treaty specified the areas where the Member States envisaged further progress:

—support for national criminal investigation and security authorities, in particular in the combination of investigations and search operations;
—creation of data bases;
—central analysis and assessment of information in order to take stock of the situation and identify investigative approaches;
—collection and analysis of national prevention programmes for forwarding to Member States and for drawing up Europe-wide prevention strategies;
—measures relating to further training, research, forensic matters and criminal records departments.

Many of these activities were already taking place either on an entirely informal basis or within the framework of the Schengen Implementing Convention.[133]

In June 1993, before the entry into force of the Maastricht Treaty, the Member States still acting within the informal TREVI framework agreed to set up a Europol Drugs Unit. This Unit was a development of an existing European Drugs Intelligence Unit and would be a further step towards a full Europol organization. The Europol Drugs Unit began work in January 1994 in The Hague, and very quickly began to achieve useful results in terms of information exchanged between police authorities and resulting interceptions and arrests.[134] It was intended that Europol, once formally established by intergovernmental agreement, should have a wider remit in terms of the international crimes covered and wider powers which would involve analysis as well as simple exchange of factual data. The Member States however felt unable to wait so long before authorizing the European Drugs Unit to extend its activities to other crimes. By Joint Action in March 1995—drafted in apparently legally binding terms— they widened its remit to include illicit trafficking in radioactive and nuclear substances, crimes involving clandestine immigration networks, vehicle trafficking, and associated money laundering.[135] Although some

---

[132] See Nicoll and Salmon (2000) at p 391: 'The choice of model was unfortunate if not inappropriate, since there is no federal jurisdiction in Europe and federal is a word best avoided in debate.'
[133] See Anderson and den Boer (eds) (1994), especially Walker (1994) at pp 22–45.
[134] See evidence from Home Office and police in HL Select Committee on the European Communities, 10th Report (1994–95a) pp 10–11 and Q 466.
[135] 95/73/JHA, OJ L62/1, 20.3.1995.

limits were placed by this Joint Action on powers of the Europol Drugs Unit to analyse and to store personal data, there was criticism that the Joint Action was going a long way to setting up a full-scale Europol without proper scrutiny of the terms of the proposed Convention and without the safeguards for public accountability and individual remedies which were to be built into that Convention.[136]

The Europol Convention was adopted by the Council in July 1995.[137] Its objective is to improve

the effectiveness and cooperation of the competent authorities in the Member States in preventing and combatting terrorism, unlawful drug trafficking and other serious forms of international crime where there are factual indications that an organised criminal structure is involved and two or more Member States are affected by the forms of crime in question in such a way as to require a common approach by the Member States owing to the scale, significance and consequences of the offences concerned.

Initially, the competence of Europol was limited to drug trafficking, trafficking in nuclear and radioactive substances, illegal immigrant smuggling, trade in human beings, and motor vehicle crime. Terrorist crimes were to be added not later than two years from the entry into force of the Convention, and other specified crimes could also be added by unanimous decision of the Council.[138] Europol competence also extends to 'related criminal offences' and in particular to money-laundering connected with the above offences.

The methods to be used include exchange of information, analysis and intelligence, aiding investigations in the Member States, maintaining a computerized information system, and assistance in training, research, organization, and equipment of police authorities. Each Member State must establish or designate a single national unit for liaison between Europol and national authorities, and each national unit is to second at least one liaison officer to Europol.

Article 8 of the Convention sets out detailed controls of the nature of data which may be entered into the information system. The data may relate not only to those suspected of having committed a specified criminal offence but also to persons believed on serious grounds to be about to commit such offences in the future. Article 9 provides that only national

[136] See, for example, HL Select Committee on the European Communities, 10th Report (1994–95a) at p 25; [1997] Statewatch (March–April) 3–4.

[137] Cm 3050, OJ C316/1, 29.11.1995. For text and commentary see Bunyan: (1998); Hayes (2001).

[138] Extension to offences 'in the course of terrorist activities against life, limb, personal freedom or property' was by Council Decision, OJ C26/22, 30.1.1999. At the same time the Council extended the definition of 'traffic in human beings' to cover the sexual exploitation and assault of minors or trade in abandoned children, as well as child pornography OJ C26/21, 30.1.1999.

232   *JHA Achievements and Weaknesses*

units, liaison officers, and specified senior officials of Europol may have access to input, retrieve, correct, or delete such data. Data may be processed only for specified purposes and under safeguards linked to those in the 1981 Council of Europe Convention on Automatic Processing of Personal Data, and to the Recommendation on use of personal data in the police sector.[139] The Europol Convention also sets out specific safeguards on data protection such as right of access by the data subject, correction, and deletion of data. Each Member State must designate a supervisory body to monitor communication of data to Europol, and a Joint Supervisory Body is also established with overall responsibility to supervise the lawfulness and accuracy of the processing and use of personal data. Individual Member States are liable in their own courts under national law for damage to an individual occurring in their territory and resulting from Europol data processing errors. If the ultimate fault lies with another Member State the State paying compensation may reclaim on a State to State basis.

The Convention entered into force in October 1998, but Europol did not actually begin operating until July 1999 after agreement was finally reached by the Council on ancillary matters such as the confidentiality regime and the privileges and immunities to be accorded to the organization and its staff.[140] Of particular importance were the rules applicable to Europol analysis files. These rules provided that data might be processed 'to the extent that they are adequate, accurate, relevant and not excessive in relation to the purpose of the analysis work file in which they are included and provided that they are stored for no longer than necessary for this purpose'. Permissible data which may be listed include lifestyle, danger rating, drug abuse, and membership of criminal groups. Other rules adopted by the Council govern the entry of data received from entities outside the EU, providing for example that the reliability of the source must first be assessed and that information 'which has clearly been obtained by a third State in obvious violation of human rights' may not be entered in any Europol system. Separate rules limit transmission of Europol data outside the Union which may only take place within the framework of a specific agreement.

The politically sensitive question of the jurisdiction to be conferred on the ECJ—which will be considered below in Chapter 9—was also a major

[139] Recommendation No R (87) 15 of the Committee of Ministers of the Council of Europe of 17 September 1987. The 1981 Convention precludes storing of 'sensitive' information on racial, religious, political, health, and sexual matters.
[140] [1999] European Voice (20–6 May); Minutes of Justice and Home Affairs Councils 28 and 29 November 1996, Council Doc. 12104/96, Presse 346, pp 7–8 and 26 and 27 May 1997, Council Doc 8318/97, Presse 166 p 7. All the related decisions are published in OJ C26/1, 30.1.1999.

delaying factor.[141] Europol thus began to discharge the full range of its tasks just as the entry into force of the Treaty of Amsterdam radically altered the Third Pillar.

Assessment of Third Pillar Action on Judicial, Customs, and Police Cooperation

For these areas intimately bound up with criminal justice policy and the national enforcement of criminal law it is clear that the Third Pillar structures established by the Maastricht Treaty made possible a new level of both practical and formal legal cooperation. A wide range of agreements were drawn up without undue difficulty, and with a somewhat greater level of transparency than would otherwise have existed. Methods were found—some of them questionable—to open the way to an increasing degree of exchange of information and approaches to common problems while the inevitably slow procedures of formal ratification ground onwards.

It is particularly difficult to attempt an objective assessment of the strengths and weaknesses of Third Pillar action on justice and law enforcement. The information and comments publicly available are polarized. On the one hand stand the governments and the law enforcement agencies, jealous of national criminal laws but well pleased with the growing networks of information making it easier for them to fight international crime. They see secrecy as essential to their success, issue minimum amounts of information to the public on their policies and activities, aspire to minimum levels of parliamentary and judicial control of what is happening. In the nature of things they are not inclined publicly to ascribe successes in the detection of international criminals to international systems and to the cooperation of colleagues in other jurisdictions.[142]

On the other hand stand the national parliaments, the European Parliament, and civil liberties organizations. They struggle to comprehend on the basis of this limited information what is actually happening and to assess its positive value,[143] but they are well aware that the texts which they can study show weaknesses in accountability and in the availability of remedies for the individual who is unjustifiably accused, detained, or

---

[141] See [1996] Statewatch (March–April) 21.

[142] See O'Keeffe (1994*b*) at pp 273–4. O'Keeffe suggests that these 'technicians' are not necessarily imbued with a European vision but are largely concerned with operational efficiency.

[143] For an account of a Statewatch request for access to documents including a Report on the Europol Drugs Unit, January to June 1994 and on measures to combat drug-related crime and organized crime see [1996] Statewatch (March–April) 22–3. Denmark and the UK voted against the Council decision to reject the request. On later applications, also rejected, see [1996] Statewatch (May–June) 1, 21–2.

damaged. Spencer's assessment of the Maastricht Treaty, for example, is that:

like all its predecessors, it leaves too many matters affecting human rights to be decided in secret by representatives of national governments. There is then no possibility of democratic control beyond the notional responsibility of each government to its electorate. This is a quite inadequate safeguard where joint policies are agreed at an intergovernmental level.[144]

In comparison with the remedies available against police and other law enforcement officers at national level, the Third Pillar instruments are very limited in their provision for redress. The parliaments and the constructive critics have certainly by their sustained efforts improved the texts which are in force. They are however looking for safeguards for civil liberties, in particular higher standards of data protection, which are probably now unattainable.[145]

The questions of judicial and parliamentary control of the Third Pillar will be re-examined in later chapters.

[144] Michael Spencer at p 5.
[145] For a summary and criticism of data protection provisions in Third Pillar Conventions see Peers (2000) pp 216–19 and 224.

7

The Residual Third Pillar under the Treaty of Amsterdam

Calls for Reform

For each of the areas to be regarded as 'matters of common interest' for the purposes of the Third Pillar, the previous chapter has contained an assessment of its effectiveness. In the context of the 1996 revision of the Maastricht Treaty however there was little overall consensus as to how the provisions on Justice and Home Affairs Cooperation should be reformed. For the slow-moving legislative processes under the Third Pillar requiring for their entry into force completion of ratification by all Member States, it was particularly unfortunate that the review process began such a short time after the Maastricht Treaty had entered into force, when virtually none of its achievements were apparent in terms of binding law. As the Council said in its Report on the Functioning of the Treaty on European Union:

The initial results of the application of these provisions are inadequate although it is emphasized that the matters covered by this Title (asylum, border controls, immigration, combating international crime, and police cooperation) are very sensitive and time has been very short to allow a true assessment. The action plan approved by the European Council in Brussels in December 1993 has not yet been fully applied.[1]

The Commission in its Report for the Reflection Group[2] made some accurate observations on the inadequacy of Third Pillar legal instruments and working methods, saying:

Essentially, those instruments and methods are the same as for Title V (common foreign and security policy). Yet the two fields are utterly different. Foreign policy mainly has to deal with fluid situations, whereas justice and home affairs frequently involve legislative action which, because it directly affects individual rights, requires legal certainty.

The Report highlighted the disagreement over the effect of common positions and joint actions, the slow implementation of conventions, the absence of monitoring of implementation and the general requirement for

---

[1] Cm 2866, para 75.
[2] Intergovernmental Conference 1996—Commission report for the Reflection Group 1995, Part Two IB.

unanimity. In practice almost all initiatives came, as in the past, from the Presidency, and this led to inadequate transparency and failure to consult the European Parliament. The multi-tier negotiating structure was cumbrous and the interface between Third and First Pillar complicated decision-making, for example on visa policy.

In its formal Opinion on the holding of an intergovernmental conference, 'Reinforcing Political Union and Preparing for Enlargement', the Commission urged the need for clear objectives and appropriate instruments and methods. Its conclusion was that

> the best way of attaining all these objectives would be to transfer justice and home affairs to the Community framework, with the exception of judicial cooperation in criminal matters and police cooperation. The transfer of jurisdiction is particularly necessary in the fields most closely associated with the movement of individuals, such as rules on crossing borders, fighting drugs, immigration, policy on nationals from non-member countries, and asylum.
>
> Following the same logic, the content of the Schengen Agreement should be incorporated in the Treaty.[3]

The European Parliament in its Resolution[4] also argued that action on justice and home affairs should no longer be artificially distinguished from closely-related policies within the full Community domain. They identified the same areas as the Commission as requiring to 'be progressively brought within the Community domain' and also called for the Schengen Agreements to be integrated into Union policy.

While the Reflection Group in its Report[5] made a number of clear recommendations for the Second Pillar, which were accepted by the Intergovernmental Conference, for the Third Pillar there were no clear proposals. It was apparent that the Group were divided between members favouring transfer into the Community Pillar of asylum, control of external frontiers, visas and immigration and others who believed 'that the current separation of "pillars" is essential in order to respect intergovernmental management of these matters that are so closely linked with national sovereignty. For them, consequently, the principal way of improving the operation of Title VI is to find practical improvements which reinforce cooperation.' It may be assumed that the UK representative was among those arguing for limiting changes to Title VI to practical improvements alone.

The House of Lords Select Committee on the European Communities whose Report *1996 Inter-governmental Conference* was prepared in the light

---

[3] ibid paras 15–18.

[4] Resolution A4-0102/95 on the functioning of the TEU with a view to the 1996 Intergovernmental Conference—Implementation and development of the Union (Bourlanges-Martin Report), para 4.

[5] SN 520/95 (REFLEX 21) paras 45–55, First Part under Freedom and internal security and Second Part: An Annotated Agenda, paras 45–55.

of the Reports from the Institutions and from the Reflection Group described above, was also not persuaded that partial transfer of areas of justice and home affairs cooperation into the Community Pillar was the right course. They argued that 'the fact that third pillar instruments necessarily impinge on national criminal law and procedure and on immigration and asylum justified the reliance at this stage on commitments under international law, which offer more scope for variable geometry and for the safeguarding of particular national sensitivities.' The Committee however made recommendations on transparency for Third Pillar negotiations which will be considered below in Chapter 10.[6]

Changes Made by the Treaty of Amsterdam

In June 1997 the Intergovernmental Conference reached agreement in Amsterdam on the substance of a Treaty amending the Treaty on European Union and the three European Community Treaties. The new Treaty was signed in Amsterdam on 2 October 1997 and entered into force on 1 May 1999. The Third Pillar lost most of its content, was renamed and radically recast. The following points summarize the more significant changes of substance made to the Third Pillar:

1. A new Title IV, headed 'Visas, asylum, immigration and other policies related to free movement of persons' was added to the EC Treaty, effectively transferring into (somewhat modified) Community procedures the first six of the nine areas of 'common interest' described under Article K.1. of the Maastricht Treaty. This entire Title is subject to Protocols making special provision for the UK, Ireland, and Denmark which are described below.

2. Within five years from entry into force of the Treaty, the Council under the new Title must adopt measures to abolish controls on persons, whether citizens of the Union or nationals of third countries, when crossing internal borders.

3. A Protocol which explicitly reserved the special positions of Denmark, and of the UK and Ireland, effectively integrated of the entire Schengen acquis (defined in an Annex) into EU law. The Council, acting unanimously, was required to allocate the acquis between the new European Community Title IV and the Third Pillar.

4. Two Protocols for the benefit of the UK and Ireland explicitly entitled those States to continue control of persons at their frontiers with

---

[6] HL Select Committee on the European Communities, 21st Report (1994–95*b*). Evidence on Justice and Home Affairs is summarized in paras 188–95 and the Commission's Opinion on them is in paras 276–82. See also EP publication CIG 96: Sélection de références bibliographiques: articles de périodiques 1/96; Monar (1998), at pp 320–1; O'Keeffe (1995).

other Member States and safeguarded their Common Travel Area. Under circumscribed conditions the UK and Ireland may decide whether to participate in the negotiation of new measures on visas, asylum, and immigration, and may also decide to opt in to measures already adopted by the Council.

5. A Protocol excluded Denmark entirely from the negotiation of measures under the new European Community Title on visas, asylum, and immigration. Such measures when adopted have no legal or financial effect on Denmark. Denmark may decide within six months from adoption of an addition to the Schengen acquis to implement it in Danish law—if so this will create international law obligations between Denmark and the other Member States (including the UK and Ireland if they participate). Denmark may at any time divest itself of all or part of the special protection given by this Protocol.

6. The residual Third Pillar was retitled 'Provisions on police and judicial cooperation in criminal matters'. Its central objective is to provide citizens with a high level of safety within an area of freedom, security, and justice by developing common action in the fields of police and judicial cooperation in criminal matters. A new objective of preventing and combating racism and xenophobia was introduced.

7. For each of these two fields of cooperation, methods of common action were listed. The Council was given powers to enable Europol to initiate investigations coordinated between Member States. Common action on judicial cooperation in criminal matters now includes establishing minimum rules on constituent elements of crimes and penalties for terrorism and drug trafficking.

8. The instruments available to the Council—common positions, framework decisions for approximating national laws, other decisions, and conventions—were better differentiated and their legal effects clarified. Unless otherwise provided, conventions once adopted by at least half the Member States enter into force for those States.

9. Unanimity remains the rule for basic policy decisions, but measures implementing ordinary decisions may be adopted by a qualified majority and measures implementing conventions by a two-thirds majority of Contracting Parties.

10. The ECJ was given jurisdiction over Third Pillar questions and instruments, but with important exceptions. In particular, Member States may decide whether to accept for their own courts the jurisdiction of the European Court to give preliminary rulings.

11. The Council's new power under Article 24 to conclude CFSP implementing agreements with States or international organizations applies to Third Pillar matters.

12. The Council must consult the European Parliament before adopting framework decisions, other decisions, and conventions. A Protocol on the Role of National Parliaments in the European Union required Commission proposals and consultation documents to be sent to national parliaments. A six-week period must elapse between the availability in all languages of a proposal (whether legislative or Third Pillar) and its being placed for possible adoption on a Council agenda.

13. A new Title on closer cooperation entitles some Member States for the purpose of furthering European Union objectives to establish closer cooperation between themselves, making use from the outset of both Third Pillar and European Community institutions. The provisions on the Schengen acquis bypass these procedures since they are expressly incorporated into the TEU, subject to the exceptions described above for Denmark, the UK, and Ireland.[7]

The Vienna Action Plan and the Tampere Conclusions

In December 1998, some months before the entry into force of the Treaty of Amsterdam, the Justice and Home Affairs Council adopted an Action Plan of the Council and the Commission on How Best to Implement the Provisions of the Treaty of Amsterdam on an Area of Freedom, Security and Justice.[8] This was endorsed by the European Council meeting in Vienna on 11 and 12 December 1998, and hence became known as the Vienna Action Plan. This European Council also mandated the Council to start immediately (presumably with the implied proviso that it did not yet possess the powers contained in the new Treaty) to implement the priorities in the plan, and it decided that a special European Council would be convened by Finland as President in October 1999.

The Vienna Action Plan took as its starting point 'that one of the keys to its success lies in ensuring that the spirit of interinstitutional cooperation inherent in the Amsterdam Treaty is translated into reality'. It also stressed the importance of a balance between the concepts of freedom, security, and justice, saying that these 'three inseparable concepts have one common denominator "people" and one cannot be achieved in full without the other two'. Regarding security, however, the Plan recalled that the new Treaty provisions did not affect the responsibilities of the Member States to maintain law and order and safeguard national security. The new area of justice must respect 'the reality that, for reasons deeply

---

[7] For a general summary and comment on the Amsterdam changes to the Third Pillar see Walker (1998) at pp 236–8.

[8] OJ C19/1, 23.1.1999. For a general description and comment see European Union Law Reporter, 24 February 1999 [627].

embedded in history and tradition, judicial systems differ substantially between Member States'. The principle of subsidiarity was of particular relevance to the creation of an area of freedom, security, and justice. Procedural rules among the Member States should however incorporate the same guarantees, and the safeguards of the European Convention on Human Rights and Fundamental Freedoms should be complemented by common codes on such matters as interpretation, enforcement of criminal decisions, offender reintegration, and victim support.

The specific measures to be given priority by the Council and Commission were listed in Part II and insofar as they relate to areas within the Third Pillar will be described below.

The Special European Council convened at Tampere in 1999 by Finland as President was the first European Council to be devoted entirely to justice and home affairs policy. The objective was that following the entry into force of the Treaty of Amsterdam a high profile should be given to this area of increasing importance, that its relevance to the citizens of Europe should be demonstrated, and that strategy in novel areas should be established for some years ahead.[9] At the start of the proceedings the European Council held an exchange of views with the President of the European Parliament, Mme Nicole Fontaine, on the topics under discussion.

The Conclusions of the European Council at Tampere[10] set out the strategy for a Union of Freedom, Security and Justice in the following terms:

4. The aim is an open and secure European Union, fully committed to the obligations of the Geneva Refugee Convention and other relevant human rights instruments, and able to respond to humanitarian needs on the basis of solidarity. A common approach must also be developed to ensure the integration into our societies of those third country nationals who are lawfully resident in the Union.
5. The enjoyment of freedom requires a genuine area of justice, where people can approach courts and authorities in any Member State as easily as in their own. Criminals must find no ways of exploiting differences in the judicial systems of Member States. Judgments and decisions should be respected and enforced throughout the Union, while safeguarding the basic legal certainty of people and economic operators. Better compatibility and more convergence between the legal systems of Member States must be achieved.
6. People have the right to expect the Union to address the threat to their freedom and legal rights posed by serious crime. To counter these threats a common effort is needed to prevent and fight crime and criminal organisations throughout the Union. The joint mobilisation of police and judicial resources is needed to guarantee that there is no hiding place for criminals or the proceeds of crime within the Union.

---

[9] See HL Select Committee on the European Communities, 19th Report, (1998–99*b*), especially Opinion at pp 12–16.
[10] http://europa.eu.int/council/off/conclu/oct99.

To implement these political guidelines, the European Council set out concrete objectives under four headings: a Common EU Asylum and Migration Policy; a Genuine European Area of Justice; a Unionwide Fight against Crime; Stronger External Action. Like common strategies within the Second Pillar, these objectives straddled all three Pillars. Asylum and migration would require implementation under the new First Pillar powers, the area of justice would be implemented as regards civil judicial cooperation within the First Pillar and as regards criminal justice, recognition of criminal judgments, and extradition within the Third Pillar, the fight against crime would be carried out under the Third Pillar, while stronger external action would involve all three Pillars. In the words of the Conclusions:

The European Council underlines that all competences and instruments at the disposal of the Union, and in particular, in external relations, must be used in an integrated and consistent way to build the area of freedom security and justice. Justice and Home Affairs concerns must be integrated in the definition and implementation of other Union policies and activities.[11]

The specific initiatives, which will be described below insofar as their implementation falls within the revised Third Pillar, are indeed focused on highly practical needs of individuals. Examples include speeding small cross-border claims, mutual recognition of pre-trial orders for securing evidence and seizing assets and better protection against money laundering. Mutual recognition of orders in the criminal justice field, such as arrest warrants, warrants for search and seizure and witness summonses, was recognized at Tampere as central to a more effective enforcement of national criminal laws.

The overall aim of the reformed Third Pillar emerging from the Tampere Conclusions was to achieve a balanced development of collective measures against crime while protecting the freedom and legal rights of individuals and economic operators.

[11] Para 59.

THE NEW THIRD PILLAR: TEXT AND COMMENTARY

TITLE VI

Provisions on Police and Judicial Cooperation in Criminal Matters

ARTICLE 29 (EX ARTICLE K.1)

Without prejudice to the powers of the European Community, the Union's objective shall be to provide citizens with a high level of safety within an area of freedom, security and justice by developing common action among the Member States in the field of police and judicial cooperation in criminal matters and by preventing and combating racism and xenophobia.

That objective shall be achieved by preventing and combating crime, organised or otherwise, in particular terrorism, trafficking in persons and offences against children, illicit drug trafficking and illicit arms trafficking, corruption and fraud, through:

—closer cooperation between police forces, customs authorities and other competent authorities in the Member States, both directly and through the European Police Office (Europol), in accordance with the provisions of Articles 30 and 32;

—closer cooperation between judicial and other competent authorities of the Member States in accordance with the provisions of Articles 31(a) to (d) and 32;

—approximation, where necessary, of rules on criminal matters in the Member States, in accordance with the provisions of Article 31(e).

The central objective of the redefined Third Pillar lies in the establishment of an area of freedom, security, and justice. Under the Treaty of Amsterdam, the area of freedom, security, and justice straddles the First and the Third Pillars. Visas, asylum, immigration, and other policies related to free movement of persons have been transferred from the Third Pillar into Community competence,[12] but they remain closely linked to the

---

[12] The Treaty provisions incorporating the Schengen acquis provided a fail-safe mechanism which would have added to the Third Pillar elements whose incorporation in the

preventive and enforcement actions which remain in the Third Pillar.[13] The wording of Article 29 emphasizes this link, and also, with the words 'Without prejudice to the powers of the European Community' stresses the primacy of the Community Pillar. The link is also identified from the other end, in Article 61 of the EC Treaty. Problems of demarcation of competence will remain, but in any demarcation the powers of the European Community, effectively guarded by the ECJ, will take precedence.

Article 29 also responds to the frequently expressed criticism that the Third Pillar in its Maastricht Treaty form lacked any clearly formulated objective. The criticism was justified, although this was not an important reason for the inadequacy of its performance.

The common characteristic of the remaining Third Pillar powers is that they centre on the enforcement of criminal law. It is however crucial that criminal laws remain 'rules on criminal matters in the Member States'. Article 29 contains no hint of any general policy to unify national criminal laws, far less to create a supranational level of criminal law. Approximation of national criminal laws is a permissible method of cooperation only 'where necessary'. The implication—though this is not explicit—is that 'necessary' means 'necessary for the purpose of effective cooperation'. The most powerful constraint to any moves to unify, or even to approximate national criminal laws, is however likely to remain the jealousy with which the Member States guard their autonomy in the field of criminal law. There is nothing in the international legal method characteristic of the intergovernmental Pillars which imposes this constraint. Certain crimes—piracy, genocide, crimes against humanity—are said by some authorities to be crimes prohibited by international law and not merely crimes under national law in respect of which international law has established a common definition or required assumption of jurisdiction by national courts,[14] The history of the Third Pillar however—as set out in the previous chapter—shows that resistance to approximation in the EU context is deeply ingrained.

The three surviving 'matters of common interest' from Article K of the Maastricht Treaty have been compressed into two by amalgamating police and customs cooperation. This was a sensible move given that there are no inherent differences in the nature of their activities and the extent to which offences against customs laws are separately investigated and prosecuted is a matter within national competence. Article 29 also authorizes closer cooperation between 'other competent authorities'—wording which it has

European Community Pillar could not be agreed by the Council. In the event this mechanism was not needed.

[13] See Monar (1998) at pp 322–5.

[14] See, for example, the judgment of Lord Millett in *R v Bartle and the Commissioner of Police for the Metropolis, ex parte Pinochet* [1998] 4 All ER 897.

been suggested formalizes cooperation between state intelligence services.[15]

Article 29 highlights a number of specific crimes to be targeted by international cooperation. These are in fact crimes in respect of which joint actions or other measures had already been agreed under the Third Pillar.[16] They are crimes which are particularly likely to involve a transnational element and to require international assistance and common jurisdictional rules to ensure successful prosecutions. The Article now authorizes common action in 'preventing and combating racism and xenophobia'. The fact that 'racism and xenophobia' are not named as crimes was deliberate, reflecting the reluctance of some Member States to create crimes under these names and their preference for alternative approaches.

---

[15] den Boer (1999) at pp 315–16.   [16] For details, see previous chapter.

Police Cooperation

ARTICLE 30 (EX ARTICLE K.2)

1. Common action in the field of police cooperation shall include:

   (a) operational cooperation between the competent authorities, including the police, customs and other specialised law enforcement services of the Member States in relation to the prevention, detection and investigation of criminal offences;

   (b) the collection, storage, processing, analysis and exchange of relevant information, including information held by law enforcement services on reports on suspicious financial transactions, in particular through Europol, subject to appropriate provisions on the protection of personal data;

   (c) cooperation and joint initiatives in training, the exchange of liaison officers, secondments, the use of equipment, and forensic research;

   (d) the common evaluation of particular investigative techniques in relation to the detection of serious forms of organised crime.

2. The Council shall promote cooperation through Europol and shall in particular within a period of five years after the date of entry into force of the Treaty of Amsterdam:

   (a) enable Europol to facilitate and support the preparation, and to encourage the coordination and carrying out, of specific investigative actions by the competent authorities of the Member States, including operational actions of joint teams comprising representatives of Europol in a support capacity;

   (b) adopt measures allowing Europol to ask the competent authorities of the Member States to conduct and coordinate their investigations in specific cases and to develop specific expertise which may be put at the disposal of Member States to assist them in investigating cases of organised crime;

   (c) promote liaison arrangements between prosecuting/investigating officials specialising in the fight against organised crime in close cooperation with Europol;

   (d) establish a research, documentation and statistical network on cross-border crime.

Article 30 sets out the new framework for police cooperation. It is divided into two parts—a general paragraph and a paragraph on the powers of

Europol. In a number of important ways the first paragraph extends the police cooperation envisaged in Article K.1 of the Maastricht Treaty (described at the end of the previous chapter) although all the new activities were foreshadowed in the Declaration on Police Cooperation which was attached to the Maastricht Treaty. There is under the Amsterdam Treaty a more specific listing of techniques of cooperation—holding and exchange of data, joint training and research, common evaluation of techniques. On the other hand police cooperation is not limited to specified crimes but is quite general in character.

It should however be noted that all these forms of cooperation were taking place on an entirely informal basis before the Maastricht Treaty. They do not in practice require any authorization under international law because they give no specific powers to the police forces of any Member State and they impose no duty on any Member State to supply any information or to host specific visits, far less to accept intrusion into its territorial jurisdiction. Operation by one police authority in the territory of another, of course, does raise jurisdictional problems—but this is dealt with under Article 32 of the Treaty. Article 30 paragraph 1 is, however, useful from a presentational point of view: it is likely to encourage the development of cross-border police cooperation and it may have direct legal benefits in Member States where the powers of police authorities are narrowly circumscribed under national law.

An early example of an instrument adopted under Article 30 paragraph 1 (as well as under Article 31) was the Council Decision setting up a European crime prevention network.[17] The network consists of contact points designated by each Member State. Each State must designate at least one contact point from its national authorities with competence in the field of crime prevention, but others might be researchers, academics, or other actors in crime prevention such as non-governmental organizations. Contact points must be proficient in at least one other language of the EU. The Network was given a wide mandate to exchange information and experience and to develop cooperation on all aspects of crime prevention, but with a special focus on juvenile, urban, and drug-related crime. The Decision took effect immediately and the Network held its first meeting on 28 August 2001.

The formal Third Pillar acquis on police cooperation—which apart from the Europol Convention was rather limited and focused disproportionately on football matches[18]—was greatly enlarged by the incorporation of

---

[17] OJ L153/1, 8.6.2001.

[18] See, for example, Council Resolution of 21 June 1999 on a handbook for cooperative measures in connection with international football matches and Joint Action with regard to cooperation on law and order and security, OJ L 147/1, 5.6.1997. This Joint Action provided for exchange of detailed information, possible posting of liaison officers and cooperation

Articles 39 to 47 of the Schengen Implementing Convention.[19] The UK and Ireland are not bound by this incorporation, but have the option of participation. The general principle of cooperation in the prevention and detection of criminal offences, set out in Article 39, is subject to the proviso that 'the request or the implementation thereof does not involve the application of coercive measures by the requested Contracting Party'. Later Articles deal with cross-border surveillance, hot pursuit, and compensation for damage.

Declaration 7 on Article K.2 of the Treaty provides that 'Action in the field of police cooperation under Article K.2 of the Treaty on European Union, including activities of Europol, shall be subject to appropriate judicial review by the competent national authorities in accordance with rules applicable in each Member State.' This provision for judicial review by national courts of police action is of course without prejudice to the jurisdiction of the ECJ, which is described in Article 35 below. The jurisdiction of national courts to review action in the field of police cooperation is not limited by the exclusion imposed on the ECJ in regard to the maintenance of law and order and the safeguarding of national security. On the other hand, the Treaty imposes no common standards in regard to such crucial matters as immunity, admissibility of evidence, the extent of the duty owed by police officers, or the level of compensation.

Europol

Paragraph 2 of Article 30 sets out a five-year plan for Europol. It provides the powers which the Council must use to enhance the role of Europol from that of information and analysis exchange to facilitator of joint national police actions. It should be noted that Article 30 does not in itself add to the powers given to Europol by the Convention, which became fully operational in July 1999. It is for the Council to confer new powers on Europol and in doing so to provide the safeguards for Member States. It should also be noted that nothing in Article 30 comes close to giving Europol any powers of independent enforcement action within the territories of the Member States. Suggestions that Article 30.2 brings Europol closer to Chancellor Kohl's original concept of a European FBI are misconceived. Europol will be limited to facilitating, encouraging, and supporting actions which will continue to be actions 'by the competent

between central bodies on events attended by large numbers from more than one Member State, such as 'sporting events, rock concerts, demonstrations and road-blocking protest campaigns'.

[19] (1981) 30 ILM 84; Plender (1988) p 815; Statewatch texts (1997), Vol I, 110, and for general background see Chapter 3 above. For allocation of the Schengen acquis see OJ L176/1, 10.7.1999; Corrado (1999).

authorities of the Member States'. It cannot be given, as the Treaty stands, any powers of law enforcement independent of the inherent sovereign powers of the Member States to enforce their criminal laws within their territory. There is no 'federal' or 'supranational' layer of criminal law or of enforcement power such as exists in a federal State such as the United States of America.

Greater precision to this plan for Europol is provided by the Vienna Action Plan and the Tampere Conclusions described above. From the Vienna Action Plan the following emerge as the main priorities for the first two years:

(i) a possible database of investigations in Member States to avoid overlap;
(ii) making the fight against illegal immigration networks a priority;
(iii) reinforcing operational cooperation against terrorism and extending Europol's competence to other crimes, such as Euro forgery;[20]
(iv) general emphasis on operational activity, using joint actions by customs authorities as a model.[21]

A Council Recommendation of 30 November 2000 sets out the ways in which Europol should support joint investigative teams set up by the Member States—placing its knowledge of the criminal world at the disposal of the teams, assisting with coordination and advice and helping with the analysis of offences.[22]

The measures to be taken within five years are somewhat vaguer, but they include establishment of a research and documentation network on cross-border crime, examination of possible access by Europol to the Customs Information System (CIS) and of a system of electronic exchange of fingerprints between Member States.[23]

In the Tampere Conclusions, the European Council called in particular for:

(i) 'establishment of a European Police Chiefs operational Task Force to exchange, in cooperation with Europol, experience, best practices and information on current trends in cross-border crime and contribute to the planning of operative actions'; and
(ii) a European Police College for the training of senior law enforcement officials, to begin as a network of national training institutes.[24]

---

[20] On the embryo euro team preparing for the arrival of new notes and coins at the end of 2001, see Lister: Europol prepares to enter a wider arena, *The Times*, 19 January 2001: 'Along with the European Central Bank, the European Commission and Interpol, Europol will seek to ensure that the changeover does not turn into an unruly free-for-all for counterfeiters, robbers and money launderers.'

[21] Paras 42–4, OJ C19/11, 23.1.1999.   [22] OJ C357/7, 13.12.2000.

[23] Para 48, OJ C19/11, 23.1.1999.

[24] Paras 44 and 47. The Council agreed on 22 December 2000 on the creation of a European Police College (CEPOL) Decision of 22 December 2000 OJ L336/1, 30.12.2000; [2000]

Europol's competence, as described in the previous chapter, already extends to money laundering associated with the specific offences, such as smuggling of drugs, nuclear materials, and illegal immigrants, which are listed in the Convention. The Council may by unanimous decision extend the crimes within the Europol remit, and in the Tampere Conclusions the European Council invited the Council to use this power for money laundering in general. The Council took the necessary decision in September 2000, and in July 2001 adopted a Framework Decision on money laundering.[25]

Statewatch January/February. It will provide specialist training for police officers from Member States and accession candidates.

[25] OJ L182/1, 5.7.2001.

Judicial Cooperation in Criminal Matters

ARTICLE 31 (EX ARTICLE K.3)

Common action on judicial cooperation in criminal matters shall include:
 (a) facilitating and accelerating cooperation between competent ministries and judicial or equivalent authorities of the Member States in relation to proceedings and the enforcement of decisions;
 (b) facilitating extradition between Member States;
 (c) ensuring compatibility in rules applicable in the Member States, as may be necessary to improve such cooperation;
 (d) preventing conflicts of jurisdiction between Member States;
 (e) progressively adopting measures establishing minimum rules relating to the constituent elements of criminal acts and to penalties in the fields of organised crime, terrorism and illicit drug trafficking.

The focus of Article 31 is on practical measures to speed criminal justice in the Member States and to make it more effective. The five headings appear to be listed if not in order of importance at least so as to reflect the degree to which work was already well under way. While a great deal of progress had been made on the draft Convention on Mutual Legal Assistance in Criminal Matters, only a very few high profile areas such as fraud against the finances of the European Communities, corruption, and paedophilia had been subject to any attempts to agree on elements of a substantive offence.

Although Article 31 permits establishment of minimum rules relating to penalties for crime, this is qualified by Declaration 8 to the Treaty under which: 'The Conference agrees that the provisions of Article K.3(e) of the Treaty on European Union shall not have the consequence of obliging a Member State whose legal system does not provide for minimum sentences, to adopt them.' This Declaration considerably restricts the possible utility of the new power for the Council to establish minimum rules on penalties. The continued reticence over harmonizing sentencing policy was illustrated when the Council, in March 2001, declined to agree to a UK initiative to fix minimum sentences for trafficking in human beings.[26]

---

[26] *The Times*, 16 March 2001.

Other International Obligations

The conventions and other instruments adopted under the Third Pillar before the entry into force of the Treaty of Amsterdam, described in the previous chapter, were immediately enlarged by the incorporation of Articles 48 to 69 of the Schengen Implementing Convention.[27] dealing with mutual assistance in criminal matters, application of the *non bis in idem* principle, extradition, and transfer of the execution of criminal judgments.

The substantive criminal law applicable in the Member States is also extensively influenced by international conventions drawn up in the wider context of the Council of Europe or the UN. It is an essential part of EU decisions on future projects in the area of criminal law and judicial cooperation that they take account of this wider dimension. This may indeed be taken as an aspect of the principle of subsidiarity—that action should always be taken at the most appropriate and effective level. There are occasions when the tighter enforcement regime and closer political relations between EU Member States mean that a Third Pillar instrument—perhaps setting out a model for a convention of potentially wider application—will be best. On other occasions the achievement of worldwide participation will be the most important objective and this will point to a negotiating forum wider than that of the Third Pillar.

European Union Ministers, for example, worked closely to form a coordinated position in the UN negotiation of a Convention against Transnational Organised Crime.[28] The UN Convention contains provisions requiring, *inter alia*, criminalization of conspiracies, money laundering and corruption, on confiscation of proceeds of crime, on jurisdiction, extradition, and mutual legal assistance. In its Joint Position the Council stressed the need to ensure that the Convention would be consistent with the Action Plan on Organised Crime adopted by the European Council at Amsterdam in June 1997 and with existing EU instruments on participation in a criminal organization and on money laundering. There should also be 'appropriate safeguards for the protection of human rights'.[29] The Council later adopted a Common Position on a proposed Protocol against the illicit manufacturing of and trafficking in firearms, their parts and components and ammunition, one of three Protocols which now

---

[27] See n 19 above.
[28] For draft from Ad Hoc Committee in Vienna, July 2000, see UN Doc A/AC.254/L230/Add 1. The Convention was adopted in Palermo in December 2000: see [2001] Statewatch January/February. The final text is in UN Doc A/55/383.
[29] OJ L87/1, 31.3.1999.

supplement the Convention.[30] Coordination in the Conference thus followed closely the obligations under Article 37 to 'defend the common positions adopted under the provisions of this Title'.

The Work Programme

The Vienna Action Plan laid emphasis on implementing measures already in place—such as the European judicial network and the two Conventions on Extradition—or near agreement, as was the Convention on Mutual Assistance in Criminal Matters. New initiatives included work on mutual recognition of decisions (the Eurowarrant and Eurobail) and enforcement of judgments in criminal matters. Within two years there was to be identification of the offences in the field of organized crime, terrorism, and drug trafficking where agreed minimum rules were 'urgent and necessary'. The measures to be taken within five years included better coordination of criminal investigations to prevent duplication of proceedings or contradictory rulings, agreement on interception of telecommunications, and approximation of rules on compensation for victims of crime. This was the first time that the problems faced by victims of crime were addressed within the Third Pillar context.[31]

At Tampere the European Council called for integration of crime prevention aspects into further Third Pillar work on criminal justice. They also proposed establishment of a new unit— Eurojust—to be composed of 'national prosecutors, magistrates, or police officers of equivalent competence, detached from each Member State according to its legal system'. The task of Eurojust would be to coordinate national prosecuting authorities, support investigations into organized crimes (assisted by Europol's analysis) and cooperate with the European Judicial Network to simplify execution of letters rogatory.[32] In December 2000 the Council adopted a Decision setting up a Provisional Cooperation Unit in Brussels.[33] Article 2 of this Decision specified the objectives of the Provisional Unit in somewhat broader terms than those outlined at Tampere. Pending formal establishment of the new unit, national prosecutors were posted to permanent representations in Brussels to build the informal networks essential to efficient coordination.

The Treaty of Nice,[34] not yet in force, would place Eurojust on a formal institutional basis. It extends Article 31 by including under the heading of

---

[30] OJ L37/1, 12.2.2000, and see *Europe*, 4 February 2000. This Common Position was again based on an existing Council instrument.

[31] See the Council Framework Decision of 15 March 2001 on the standing of victims in criminal proceedings, OJ L82/1, 22.3.2001.

[32] Paras 41, 42 and 46.   [33] OJ L324/1, 21.12.2000.

[34] Cm 5090; OJ C 80, 10.3.2001.

'facilitating and accelerating cooperation between competent ministries and judicial or equivalent authorities of the Member States' a reference to 'where appropriate, cooperation through Eurojust', and by adding a new paragraph as follows:

2. The Council shall encourage cooperation through Eurojust by:
   (a) enabling Eurojust to facilitate proper coordination between Member States' national prosecuting authorities;
   (b) promoting support by Eurojust for criminal investigations in cases of serious cross-border crime, particularly in the case of organised crime, taking account, in particular, of analyses carried out by Europol;
   (c) facilitating close cooperation between Eurojust and the European Judicial Network, particularly, in order to facilitate the execution of letters rogatory and the implementation of extradition requests.

In February 2002, however, the Council—without awaiting the entry into force of the Treaty of Nice—used existing powers under Article 31 and 34(2)(c) of the TEU to adopt a Decision setting up Eurojust on a permanent basis 'with a view to reinforcing the fight against serious crime'. Eurojust was established 'as a body of the European Union with legal personality and financed from the general budget of the European Union, except as regards the salaries and emoluments of the national members and assisting persons, which are borne by their Member State of origin'. It is composed of one national member seconded by each Member State, 'being a prosecutor, judge or police officer of equivalent competence'. The Decision elaborated on the earlier mandates by setting out the objectives, competences, and tasks of Eurojust, drawing a distinction between tasks to be fulfilled through one or more national members and tasks to be fulfilled by Eurojust acting as a College. As with the Europol Convention, there are extensive provisions intended to guarantee a level of protection for personal data processed by Eurojust equivalent at least to that conferred by the 1981 Council of Europe Convention.[35]

The European Council also called for special action against money laundering. The Council and European Parliament should adopt as soon as possible the revised directive proposed by the Commission under European Community powers. Under Third Pillar powers there should be approximation of national criminal law and procedures to ensure that relevant offences were uniform and sufficiently broad in all Member States.[36]

[35] Council Decision 2002/187/JHA of 28 February 2002, OJ L63/1, 6.3.2002.
[36] Paras 51–8. For a more detailed account, appraisal and criticism of proposals on judicial cooperation in criminal matters see EP 2000 Working Paper The Impact of the Amsterdam Treaty on Justice and Home Affairs,LIBE 110 EN, Vol I pp 71–7.

There is thus an ambitious and practically oriented programme for the Council under its new Third Pillar powers. It is, however, open to the criticism that inadequate emphasis has been laid on checking implementation within national legal systems. The weakness of the Third Pillar under the Treaty of Maastricht was the uncertain legal status of most of the large number of instruments agreed by the Council. The Treaty of Amsterdam addressed some of the problems as regards new instruments, but neither the Commission nor the Council itself have been given serious powers to monitor implementation even of new instruments, far less those already agreed before the entry into force of the Treaty.

The European Council at Tampere expressed its determination to keep under constant review actual progress towards adopting the measures necessary for its objectives. It invited the Commission to propose 'an appropriate scoreboard to that end'. The Commission presented its 'Scoreboard to review progress on the creation of an area of freedom, security and justice in the European Union' in March 2000 and updated it in November 2000.[37] The measures listed straddled the First and Third Pillars as well as related external relations. Within the Third Pillar the Commission reported on the growing number of ratifications of the 1995 and 1996 Extradition Conventions and referred to its Communication on mutual recognition of final decisions in criminal matters which was adopted by the Council in November 2000.[38] In the area of the fight against crime the Scoreboard noted the Council decision to create a provisional unit of Eurojust (pending the entry into force of the Treaty of Nice which creates a formal Treaty basis for the new unit) and the preparatory work under way on the European Police College. The Customs Information System Convention had received a sufficient number of ratifications to enable it to enter into force provisionally.

Mutual Assistance in Criminal Matters

The most substantial achievement so far under the provisions of Article 31(a) of the Treaty is the Convention on Mutual Assistance in Criminal Matters adopted by the Council in May 2000.[39] Much of the preparatory negotiation took place earlier, but the entry into force of the Treaty of Amsterdam and the European Council initiatives described above gave impetus to the work, made it necessary formally to consult the European Parliament[40] and opened the way to participation by Iceland and Norway

---

[37] COM(2000) 167 and 782.   [38] Council doc 13750/1/00.

[39] OJ C197/1, 12.7.2000. The Explanatory Report on the Convention approved by the Council is at OJ C379/7, 29.12.2000.

[40] For a summary of the debate in the Parliament and amendments proposed to the draft Convention—mainly intended to improve protection of defendants' rights—see *Europe* 21 and 22 February 2000.

in some of the Convention provisions through their association with the development of the Schengen acquis. It also permitted adoption of Article 27 which provides that the Convention will enter into force after eight Member States (rather than all fifteen) have ratified it.

As with extradition, there is no requirement under international law for the existence of a treaty obligation before the judicial authorities in one State may assist criminal proceedings in another by gathering and transmitting oral or documentary evidence. But in the absence of a treaty, the assistance will depend on the vagaries and the unpredictable administrative obstacles of a foreign domestic legal system. With the increasing mobility of witnesses as well as in the international elements in many serious crimes there was throughout the twentieth century a growth both in bilateral and in multilateral schemes negotiated within the Commonwealth and the Council of Europe. In 1991 the UK finally ratified the 1959 European Convention on Mutual Assistance in Criminal Matters,[41] which had long been in force for all other Member States except Ireland and Portugal.[42]

The European Union Convention was negotiated against the background of several prior overlapping European instruments: the Council of Europe Convention and the 1979 Additional Protocol to it, the Naples II Convention (described in Chapter 6 above) and Articles 48 to 53 of the Schengen Implementing Convention, as well as a number of bilateral agreements. In 1998 the Council adopted a Joint Action on good practice on handling mutual legal assistance requests which required Member States to adopt and review national guidelines, examining in particular reasons for delays and other problems.[43] The new EU Convention, which resulted from a French initiative, consolidates, supplements, and updates these diverse provisions.

The Convention regime is general in character and not confined to specific offences such as drugs or customs offences. It will replace some of the relevant provisions of the Schengen Implementing Convention. It will be capable of applying to relations between Member States Parties and Iceland and Norway.[44] All Member States may become Parties, and no reservations are permitted other than those expressly provided in the text. This will in time greatly simplify the mutual assistance regime within the EU. New provisions include direct transmission of requests between courts in different Member States, interception of telecommunications

---

[41] UKTS No 24 (1992), Cm 1928. Domestic law powers were provided by the Criminal Justice (International Cooperation) Act 1990.

[42] Ireland and Portugal are now Parties.

[43] Joint Action 98/427/JHA, OJ L191/1, 7.7.1998.

[44] For an explanation of how this is permitted under the Agreement associating those two countries with the development of the Schengen acquis, see the Explanatory Report on the Convention, OJ C379/7, 29.12.2000, at p 9.

both terrestrial and satellite, hearings of witnesses in another Member State by videoconference or by telephone, temporary transfer of prisoners between Member States for the purpose of investigation, controlled deliveries within the framework of investigations into extraditable offences, and joint investigation teams.[45]

Equally significant are the omissions from the new Convention—a Member State may not refuse assistance on the ground that the offence is considered to be a political or a fiscal offence, or that it is not punishable under the law of the requesting Party and of the requested Party (the 'double criminality rule'). As the Preamble makes clear, dropping these safeguards reflects common obligations under the European Convention on Human Rights (ECHR) and 'confidence in the structure and functioning of their legal systems and in the ability of all Member States to guarantee a fair trial'. This confidence is, however, not shared by some of those who have commented on the new provisions.[46]

A Report to the Council in 2001 showed a considerable increase in the flow of requests for legal assistance in criminal matters. In Member States, 75 per cent to 95 per cent of their traffic was with other Member States. But despite this increased readiness to seek assistance for the purposes of criminal proceedings, the process of ratification of the relevant conventions remains much too slow and erratic, and the 2000 Convention has not yet received the eight ratifications necessary for its entry into force.[47]

The European Arrest Warrant

The most important instrument to be agreed under Article 31(b) of the Treaty, and the most controversial so far to emerge from the Third Pillar is the Framework Decision on the European Arrest Warrant and the surrender procedure between the Member States. The Framework Decision derives from the Conclusions of the European Council at Tampere, where it was agreed that

the formal extradition procedure should be abolished among the Member States as far as persons are concerned who are fleeing from justice after having been finally sentenced, and replaced by a simple transfer of such persons, in compliance with Article 6 TEU. Consideration should also be given to fast track extradition procedures, without prejudice to the principle of fair trial.[48]

---

[45] For critical analysis of the Convention in its draft form, see HL Select Committee on the European Communities, 14th Report (1997–98c).

[46] See evidence to House of Lords Committee in Report cited above; JUSTICE (2000) at p 22, and JUSTICE (2001) especially 4.3 at pp 8–10.

[47] Final Report on the first evaluation exercise—mutual legal assistance in criminal matters, OJ C216/14, 1.8.2001. See also Council Framework Decision on joint investigation teams, OJL 162/1, 20.6.2002.

[48] Bull EU 10-1999 point 1 at para 35.

Extensive consultations on a possible instrument had already taken place, enabling the Commission to make a formal proposal only eight days after the attacks of 11 September 2001 on the US.[49] Urgent discussions then continued within the Council, which reached political agreement as planned in December 2001. The need to re-consult the European Parliament, as well as several scrutiny reserves by national parliament, delayed formal adoption until 13 June 2002.

The Framework Decision will replace all extradition arrangements among the Member States by a system based on the concept of mutual recognition of court judgements. No ultimate political discretion over surrender will remain with the requested State. Most of the technicalities of extradition law which are intended to protect the human rights of the suspect, or the convicted person, but which greatly prolong and complicate the procedures, will no longer apply. Instead there will be reliance within the European Union on the fairness of the criminal justice systems of the other Member States, underpinned by common adherence to the ECHR and common acceptance of the right of individual petition. The rule of double criminality, for example, would no longer operate as a bar to extradition where the charge was any one of a list of thirty-two offences and was punishable in the requesting State by imprisonment for at least three years.

Many improvements were made to the text during these intensive negotiations in order to safeguard individual rights. These relate, for example, to the entitlements of a fugitive who has been convicted in his absence, or who is requested by a Member State which has been found to be in severe breach of human rights principles. Concerns however remain that the Framework Decision is not accopmpanied by guarantees of enitilement to bail on a non-discriminatory basis, of competent interpretation, and of adequate legal representation.[50]

[49] COM (2001) 522, OJ C332/305, 27.11.2001.
[50] HL Select Committee on the European Union, 6th Report (2001–02*a*); HL Select Committee on the European Union, 16th Report (2001–02*c*); Bull EU 12-2001, point 1.4.11; Jakobi (2002).

Joint Police Operations

ARTICLE 32 (EX ARTICLE K.4)

The Council shall lay down the conditions and limitations under which the competent authorities referred to in Articles 30 and 31 may operate in the territory of another Member State in liaison and in agreement with the authorities of that State.

Article 32 reflects the continuing sovereign status of the Member States and the basic rule of international law that no State may take enforcement action within the territory of another except with its consent. Although there already exists for the Parties to the Schengen Implementing Convention some carefully circumscribed degree of consent to such action under the provisions on hot pursuit, any further consent is made conditional on further action by the Council. It may be assumed that agreement giving operational powers to competent authorities of other Member States will be difficult to achieve and will be narrowly drawn.

Although Europol is mentioned in Article 30.2 it is not a 'competent authority' for the purposes of Article 32. The 'competent authorities' referred to in Articles 30 and 31 are 'the competent authorities, including the police, customs and other specialised law enforcement services of the Member States'. Article 32 does not enlarge the competence of Europol which, under Article 31, is limited to facilitating, supporting, and requesting operational action by the Member States.

The Vienna Action Plan lists among the measures to be taken within two years the implementation of Article 32, 'taking into consideration the Schengen acquis'. The most relevant provisions are Articles 40 and 41 of the Schengen Implementing Convention which provide for cross-border observation and hot pursuit of those suspected of a serious offence. These provisions are likely to be a starting point for proposals from a Member State or from the Commission.

Saving on Law, Order and Internal Security

ARTICLE 33

This Title shall not affect the exercise of the responsibilities incumbent upon Member States with regard to the maintenance of law and order and the safeguarding of internal security.

Article 33 reproduces exactly the wording of Article K.2(2) of the Maastricht Treaty. Its scope is however more likely to be called into question in consequence of the jurisdiction now conferred on the ECJ by Article 35 of the Treaty of Amsterdam. It may be said to serve two purposes. First, it avoids any argument of a loss of competence by the Member States in the field of law enforcement. The national legislative and executive authorities are not precluded from action on the basis that the European Union has 'occupied the field'. This entrenches the traditional international law approach, protecting it from infiltration by the more intrusive Community law doctrine which does, when the Council has acted, preclude parallel action by national legislatures. Secondly, it protects the individual complaining of unlawful police or judicial action, who might otherwise be met with the defence that the responsibility of the defendant Member State had been delegated to or taken over by the Council of the EU.

The provision has, more questionably, also been transported into the European Community Treaty to form Article 64.1 in the new Title IV (Visas, Asylum and other Policies related to Free Movement of Persons). In that context it cannot serve the first of the two purposes suggested in the previous paragraph, though it could appropriately serve the second.

Legal Instruments of Third Pillar Cooperation

ARTICLE 34 (EX ARTICLE K.6)

1. In the areas referred to in this Title, Member States shall inform and consult one another within the Council with a view to coordinating their action. To that end, they shall establish collaboration between the relevant departments of their administrations.

2. The Council shall take measures and promote cooperation, using the appropriate form and procedures as set out in this Title, contributing to the pursuit of the objectives of the Union. To that end, acting unanimously on the initiative of any Member State or of the Commission, the Council may:

(a) adopt common positions defining the approach of the Union to a particular matter;

(b) adopt framework decisions for the purpose of approximation of the laws and regulations of the Member States. Framework decisions shall be binding upon the Member States as to the result to be achieved but shall leave to the national authorities the choice of form and methods. They shall not entail direct effect;

(c) adopt decisions for any other purpose consistent with the objectives of this Title, excluding any approximation of the laws and regulations of the Member States. These decisions shall be binding and shall not entail direct effect; the Council acting by a qualified majority, shall adopt measures necessary to implement those decisions at the level of the Union;

(d) establish conventions which it shall recommend to the Member States for adoption in accordance with their constitutional requirements. Member States shall begin the procedures applicable within a time limit to be set by the Council.

Unless they provide otherwise, conventions shall, once adopted by at least half of the Member States, enter into force for those Member States. Measures implementing conventions shall be adopted within the Council by a majority of two-thirds of the Contracting Parties.

3. Where the Council is required to act by a qualified majority, the votes of its members shall be weighted as laid down in Article 205(2) of the Treaty establishing the European Community, and for their adoption acts of the Council shall require at least 62 votes in favour, cast by at least 10 members.

4. For procedural questions, the Council shall act by a majority of its members.

Article 34, which is largely self-explanatory, sets out comprehensively the methods of action, the instruments available and the legislative procedures under the new Third Pillar. It responds to the criticisms made of the Maastricht Treaty provisions on Third Pillar instruments which were one of the most important reasons for its inadequate performance.

Paragraph 1 sets out the basic obligation of informing and consulting among Ministries of Justice. No treaty authority is required for this cooperation to take place and self-interest rather than any form of supervision or coercion will ensure that links among those responsible for criminal justice are actively maintained.

Paragraph 2 lists the instruments which the Council may adopt, the purpose of each and whether it is legally binding. The instruments are:

(a) common positions, for the purpose of defining the policy approach of the Union. They are not legally binding.
(b) framework decisions, for approximation of laws of the Member States. They may be compared to directives within the European Community legal order. They are legally binding but not directly applicable.
(c) decisions, for any other purpose within the objectives of the Third Pillar. They may be compared to joint actions under the Treaty of Maastricht Article K. They are legally binding.
(d) conventions, the classical instruments of international law. Once they have entered into force in accordance with their own provisions they are legally binding on States which have signed and ratified them.

Legal Effects

Article 34 expressly excludes, for framework decisions and decisions, the possibility of direct effect. Under Article K of the Treaty of Maastricht it was not only uncertain whether joint positions and joint actions were legally binding but also whether they might be capable in certain circumstances of having direct effect.[51] The Treaty of Amsterdam, having given the ECJ some powers to interpret the revised Third Pillar, has forestalled the—admittedly somewhat remote—possibility that the Court might accord direct effect to Third Pillar instruments. There is no mention of direct effect for common positions, reflecting the fact that they will not create legal rights or obligations. Nor is potential direct effect mentioned for conventions—leaving national courts and the ECJ free to decide the question if it should arise.

---

[51] For discussion of this, see Meyring (1997) at pp 230–6.

What will not be possible in the case of conventions is that an individual should use the doctrine of direct effect to avoid the consequences of non-implementation by a national parliament or government. Although the Council may now prescribe a time limit for the beginning of national ratification requirements it may not prescribe a time limit for their conclusion. Third Pillar conventions remain treaties governed by the rules of international law and it remains a decision for each sovereign Member State whether to ratify each convention recommended to it by the Council.

The presumption will now be that a convention—though the negotiators may decide otherwise—will enter into force when half the Member States have ratified it. This eliminates one of the most serious weakness of the Maastricht version of the Third Pillar under which ratification by all Member States was required for a convention to enter into force. It also brings Third Pillar conventions more closely back in line with the position under general international law (explained in Chapter 1 above) whereby a certain critical mass of States is normally required for entry into force, after which a successful convention will begin to attract a gravitational pull for other States.

Legislative Procedures

Draft instruments under the revised Third Pillar may be proposed either by any Member State or by the Commission. This marks a change from the position under the Treaty of Maastricht, where the Commission in the areas of criminal justice, customs, and police cooperation had no right of initiative. Given however that the Commission is not at present extensively staffed with experts in national criminal laws, it is likely that most formal proposals to the Council for instruments to be adopted under Article 34 will be made by the Presidency. The position is similar under the Second Pillar—see commentary on Article 22 in Chapter 5 above. Within the Third Pillar, however, the Commission may exercise some control of the overall legislative timetable by drawing up the Scoreboard described in the commentary on Article 31 above or preparing the programme of measures to implement the principle of mutual recognition of decisions in criminal matters which the Council and Commission were required by the European Council to adopt by December 2000.[52] At an informal meeting of Ministers of Justice and Home Affairs in Lisbon in March 2000, Commissioner Antonio Vitorino stressed that Member States could not expect to rely entirely on the Commission, given its limited expertise and called for a partnership between Commission and Member States. Several

---

[52] Council doc 13750/1/00.

Member States then announced initiatives—for example France on money laundering and Belgium and the Netherlands on action against hooliganism.[53] France, Sweden, and Belgium together proposed a framework decision on the execution within the EU of orders freezing assets or evidence.[54] The Council Decision setting up a European crime prevention network, described in the Commentary on Article 30(1) above, was based on an initiative by France and Sweden.[55]

As regards voting, the general rule is that the Council acts unanimously. As with the Second Pillar however, there are exceptions for implementing measures, thus stopping possible blockages over minor details or over appointments after policy and substance have been agreed by all. In the case of decisions, implementing measures may be adopted by qualified majority (defined under European Community voting rules). It will no longer be necessary (as it was under Article K.3(2)(b) of the Maastricht Treaty version) for the Council first to take a unanimous decision in order to proceed to the 'qualified majority' stage. In the case of conventions implementing measures require a two-thirds majority of the Contracting Parties. The power given to Contracting Parties is a spur to early ratification.

Declaration 9 annexed to the Final Act of the Amsterdam Conference provides that:

The Conference agreed that initiatives for measures referred to in Article K.6(2) of the Treaty on European Union and acts adopted by the Council thereunder shall be published in the Official Journal of the European Communities, in accordance with the relevant Rules of Procedure of the Council and the Commission.

This is a welcome move towards transparency of the legislative process of the Third Pillar. As was noted in Chapters 3 and 6 above, it was only when the Maastricht Treaty by Article K.3 gave the Commission a new right of initiative in some of the Third Pillar areas that proposals began to be made public. It was in fact some considerable time after the entry into force of the Maastricht Treaty that even measures adopted by the Council— regarded by some as binding in international law—were published in the Official Journal. Publication of initiatives, most of which originate from the Presidency Member State, opens the way to constructive criticism of them by the European Parliament, by national parliaments and by specialist non-governmental organizations and groups before an instrument is adopted by the Council. The Declaration requiring publication of initiatives must be taken with the Protocol on the Role of National Parliaments in the European Union which requires a six-week period between a pro-

---

[53] *Europe* No 7669 (4 March 2000) p 7. [54] OJ C75/1, 3.3.2001.
[55] OJ L153/1, 8.6.2001.

posal for a Third Pillar measure and its being placed on a Council agenda for the adoption of an act. The question of parliamentary supervision of the Third Pillar is discussed in Chapter 10 below.

Jurisdiction of the European Court of Justice

ARTICLE 35 (EX ARTICLE K.7)

1. The Court of Justice of the European Communities shall have jurisdiction, subject to the conditions laid down in this Article, to give preliminary rulings on the validity and interpretation of framework decisions and decisions, on the interpretation of conventions established under this Title and on the validity and interpretation of the measures implementing them.

2. By a declaration made at the time of signature of the Treaty of Amsterdam or at any time thereafter, any Member State shall be able to accept the jurisdiction of the Court of Justice to give preliminary rulings as specified in paragraph 1.

3. A Member State making a declaration pursuant to paragraph 2 shall specify that either:

(a) any court or tribunal of that State against whose decisions there is no judicial remedy under national law may request the Court of Justice to give a preliminary ruling on a question raised in a case pending before it and concerning the validity or interpretation of an act referred to in paragraph 1 if that court or tribunal considers that a decision on the question is necessary to enable it to give judgment, or

(b) any court or tribunal of that state may request the Court of Justice to give a preliminary ruling on a question raised in a case pending before it and concerning the validity or interpretation of an act referred to in paragraph 1 if that court or tribunal considers that a decision on the question is necessary to enable it to give judgment.

4. Any Member State, whether or not it has made a declaration pursuant to paragraph 2, shall be entitled to submit statements of case or written observations to the Court in cases which arise under paragraph 1.

5. The Court of Justice shall have no jurisdiction to review the validity or proportionality of operations carried out by the police or other law enforcement services of a Member State or the exercise of the responsibilities incumbent upon Member States with regard to the maintenance of law and order and the safeguarding of internal security.

6. The Court of Justice shall have jurisdiction to review the legality of framework decisions and decisions in actions brought by a Member State or the Commission on grounds of lack of competence,

infringement of an essential procedural requirement, infringement of this Treaty or of any rule of law relating to its application, or misuse of powers. The proceedings provided for in this paragraph shall be instituted within two months of the publication of the measure.

7. The Court of Justice shall have jurisdiction to rule on any dispute between Member States regarding the interpretation or the application of acts adopted under Article 34(2) whenever such dispute cannot be settled by the Council within six months of its being referred to the Council by one of its members. The Court shall also have jurisdiction to rule on any dispute between Member States and the Commission regarding the interpretation or the application of conventions established under Article 34(2)(d).

Article 35 gives the ECJ a somewhat circumscribed jurisdiction over the binding instruments which may be adopted under the Third Pillar. It marks considerable progress in comparison with the Maastricht Treaty which gave the Court no jurisdiction over Council instruments but left the Member States free to determine for each convention the appropriate jurisdiction to be conferred on the Court. The decision proved to be extremely controversial—mainly due to the resistance by the UK on each occasion to giving the Court any jurisdiction whatsoever—and greatly delayed adoption of several conventions, particularly the Europol Convention. The question of jurisdiction, and the compromise solutions negotiated, are discussed more fully in Chapter 9 below.

There are three broad heads of jurisdiction given to the Court:

1. Jurisdiction to review legality of framework decisions and decisions on grounds which are the same as those on which European Community acts may be challenged under Article 230 (ex Article 173) of the EC Treaty. The two-month time limit runs from publication of the measure. A Member State or the Commission may bring proceedings for review, but individuals, legal persons, and the other institutions of the European Union have, by contrast with the position under the EC Treaty, no standing to do so.

2. Jurisdiction to rule on disputes between Member States on interpretation or application of any Third Pillar instrument—broadly parallel to the little used Article 227 (ex Article 170) of the EC Treaty. A Member State may bring these proceedings six months after referring the dispute to the Council. The Commission's power to bring proceedings regarding a dispute is limited to conventions. There is no requirement that the Council should first have tried to settle it, but the wording suggests that the dispute must be between Member States collectively and the Commission. This falls well short of the power given to the Commission by Article 226 (ex Article 169) of the EC Treaty.

3. Jurisdiction to give preliminary rulings to national courts on validity and interpretation of framework decisions, decisions, and implementing measures and on interpretation of conventions. Reflecting the continuing controversy over permitting the Court to give preliminary rulings regarding Third Pillar instruments, this is more limited than Article 234 (ex Article 177) of the EC Treaty. A Member State has four options:

   (a) to do nothing, thereby excluding references from its national courts;
   (b) by a declaration under paragraph 3(a) to permit only its national courts of last appeal to refer;
   (c) by a declaration under paragraph 3(b) to permit all its national courts to refer;
   (d) relying on Declaration No. 10 adopted by the Amsterdam Conference, to make a declaration under (b) or (c) above, reserving the right to make provision in national law requiring its courts of last appeal to refer.[56]

Declarations, with or without the reservation described, may be made on signature of the Treaty or at any time thereafter.[57] A Member State may intervene or make written observations in any case arising from a reference for a preliminary ruling, regardless of whether it has made any of these optional declarations. This provision will help to underline the authority of judgments of the Court in these cases for all Member States. It is significant that there is nothing in Article 35 to limit this binding character for Member States which have not opted in. The position may be contrasted with that under Article 2 of the Protocol on the Position of Denmark which provides that no decision of the Court interpreting a measure under the new Title IV 'shall be binding upon or applicable in Denmark'.

Paragraph 5 of Article 35 excludes for all Third Pillar cases the jurisdiction of the Court to review a wide range of national actions relating to law and order. There is concern that Member States could invoke this exclusion in a large proportion of the cases likely to arise under Third Pillar instruments, thus weakening the power of the Court to safeguard legality in areas—such as operations carried out by joint police teams of Member States—which are extremely sensitive.[58]

---

[56] Justice and the Standing Committee of experts on international immigration, refugee and criminal law in their Joint Briefing: The Treaty of Amsterdam: key issues on ratification, January 1998, at pp 7–8 urged that national governments should make declarations in this most extensive form in order to enable the ECJ to provide consistent judicial control particularly of human rights matters.

[57] Austria, Belgium, Germany, Greece, Luxembourg, and the Netherlands made declarations on signature, see OJ C340/308, 10.11.1997.

[58] See Monar (1998) at pp 331–2.

Article 35 does not extend the jurisdiction of the ECJ over Third Pillar instruments or conventions adopted before the entry into force of the Treaty of Amsterdam. The Court will—at least for the time being—be confined to the jurisdiction negotiated by the Member States in regard to individual conventions.

Infrastructure: The Coordinating Committee

ARTICLE 36 (EX ARTICLE K.8)

1. A Coordinating Committee shall be set up consisting of senior officials. In addition to its coordinating role, it shall be the task of the Committee to

—give opinions for the attention of the Council, either at the Council's request or on its own initiative;

—contribute, without prejudice to Article 207 of the Treaty establishing the European Community, to the preparation of the Council's discussions in the areas referred to in Article 29.

2. The Commission shall be fully associated with the work in the areas referred to in this Title.

Article 36, which is in substance unchanged from the Maastricht Treaty version, sets out the roles of the Coordinating Committee and of the Commission in preparing the work of the Council. The Coordinating Committee was previously known as the Article K.4 Committee and is now known as the Article 36 Committee. Below the Coordinating Committee are the Council Working Groups of national experts on specialized topics such as police cooperation, drug trafficking, customs cooperation, and cooperation in criminal matters.[59]

The relationship between COREPER and the Article 36 Committee is parallel to that between COREPER and the Political Committee monitoring the international situation and contributing to Council work on the common foreign and security policy. As noted in the commentary on Article 25 in Chapter 5 above, COREPER retains primary responsibility for preparing the work of the Council of Ministers and in particular for ensuring consistency between actions taken under different pillars of the EU. COREPER will not, however, intervene in the substance of what is submitted by the Article 36 Committee unless it raises an issue of cross-pillar coordination.[60]

By contrast with the Political Committee within the common foreign and security policy, the Article 36 Committee is not given an express responsibility to monitor the implementation of agreed policies. Recent

[59] For a complete organigram of Council bodies dealing with Justice and Home Affairs (including First Pillar matters) see EP Research Working Paper: The Impact of the Amsterdam Treaty on Justice and Home Affairs (2000, LIBE 110 EN) Vol II p 133.

[60] See de Zwaan (1995) at pp 181–7.

agreements and decisions by the Council show increasing awareness of the need for supervision of implementation of measures adopted. The Council may of course set up reporting or supervisory requirements in specific measures, but that is less effective than entrusting across-the-board supervision to a single body.

Another contrast with the Council infrastructure of the Second Pillar is the absence of any body comparable to the Policy Planning and Early Warning Unit. This absence reflects the fact that the subjects left within the Third Pillar are deeply grounded in national systems of criminal law enforcement. While policy and strategy for the Third Pillar may be formed at a general level by the European Council, translating this policy into acceptable instruments which take account of the legal constraints imposed by the Treaty on law-making measures is a task which can only be done by national experts. Because of the need for intensified contacts between Member States in preparation and application of Third Pillar commitments there has been a substantial strengthening of the permanent representations of the Member States in Brussels by prosecutors and other law enforcement officers.

Infrastructure: The Commission

The Commission's right to be 'fully associated' with Third Pillar activity is unchanged from the corresponding provision in the Maastricht Treaty. It still lacks the 'watchdog' functions characteristic of the European Community method—monitoring implementation and pursuing infraction by Member States (though it may now bring before the ECJ disputes with Member States on interpretation or application of conventions established under the new Third Pillar (Article 35.7). The Commission's powers are, however, substantially enhanced by its being given in the areas left in the Third Pillar a new right of initiative, shared with the Member States. This was discussed in the commentary on Article 34 above.

International Organizations and Conferences: Representation

ARTICLE 37 (EX ARTICLE K.9)

Within international organisations and at international conferences in which they take part Member States shall defend the common positions adopted under the provisions of this Title.

Articles 18 and 19 shall apply as appropriate to matters falling under this Title.

Article 37 sets out the rules requiring coordination by Member States within their agreed policy framework in external aspects of the Third Pillar. One important consequence of the international law character of Third Pillar legislation is that there is no transfer of external competence from the Member States to the European Community or to the EU. The Member States remain competent in these areas to conduct negotiations with non-Member States, to conclude international agreements, and to speak in international organizations. To the extent that they have assumed under the Third Pillar commitments which are binding in international law they are required not to assume later commitments towards other States which conflict with them. But this is an obligation limited to result—it does not automatically affect the method whereby they conduct international relations bilaterally or multilaterally.

As the content of Third Pillar instruments grew under the Maastricht Treaty, the importance of its external dimension also enlarged. It was impracticable for the EU to implement any kind of effective control of external frontiers and migration, of illegal drugs or transnational crime policy without cooperation from neighbouring States. Readmission agreements whereby illegal immigrants were repatriated to their States of origin became standard, and mixed agreements (to which the European Community and its Member States are Parties) increasingly contained elements relating to Third Pillar matters such as migration, transnational crime, and police cooperation. The Maastricht Treaty, however, although it required Member States to defend common positions in the context of international organizations and international conferences, did not contain general provisions relating to external representation of the Union on Third Pillar subjects.

The position is now clarified by the application of Articles 18 and 19 of the Treaty to Third Pillar matters. Article 18 sets out the general responsibility of the Presidency to represent the Union on common foreign policy and security matters, and Article 37 now enlarges this to include matters of police cooperation and judicial cooperation in criminal matters. The Presidency is to be assisted by the Secretary-General of the Council, exercising the function of High Representative for the common foreign and security policy. The title of the High Representative has not changed, but his remit now extends to Third Pillar matters. The representatives of the current Presidency and of the Commission together with the High Representative form the new style Troika.[61]

An important initiative under the external provisions of the new Third Pillar was the Action Plan with a view to common action between the European Union and Russia on combatting organized crime.[62] The plan envisages Russia's participation in international agreements drawn up within the Council of Europe and the UN on extradition, mutual assistance in criminal matters, money laundering, and corruption. It provides for training and assistance to Russia in developing best practices in judicial cooperation, and for exchange of information between law enforcement authorities with a view in particular to setting up controlled deliveries and strengthening border controls against drug trafficking.

A recent illustration of successful coordination in a major international conference was the preparatory work leading to the UN Convention against Transnational Organized Crime, described above in the commentary on Article 31.

For further commentary on Articles 18 and 19 and on practice in international organizations dealing with Second and Third Pillar matters see Chapter 5 above. The transfer of asylum, immigration, and other matters from the Third into the First Pillar of course means that the rules regarding the external competence and external representation of the European Communities now apply to those areas. The European Council at Tampere, acknowledging the new external Community competence in this area, called on the Council to conclude readmission agreements or to include standard clauses in other agreements between the European Community and relevant third countries or groups of countries.[63] Just as there is in practice constant overlap between First and Second Pillar matters in dialogue with non-Member States and in international organiza-

[61] See pp 158–9.

[62] OJ C106/5, 13.4.2000; *Europe* No 7707 (29 April 2000) p 6. The Action Plan derived from the Common Strategy on Russia endorsed by the European Council in Cologne in June 1999, as well as the Union's Action Plan on organised crime approved by the European Council in Amsterdam in June 1997.

[63] Para 27 of Conclusions. The Justice and Home Affairs Council in May 2000 worked on a draft mandate for a re-admission agreement with Morocco which could be used as a precedent for agreements with Pakistan, Sri Lanka, and Russia.

tions, there is increasingly overlap with Third Pillar matters. The division of home and justice affairs between First and Third Pillars has increased the likelihood of overlap. The rules on representation described in the commentary on Article 18 are therefore of importance for the external dimension of the Third Pillar.

Conclusion of International Agreements by the Council

ARTICLE 38 (EX ARTICLE K.10)

Agreements referred to in Article 24 may cover matters falling under this Title.

In Article 24 the Treaty of Amsterdam introduced a new procedure for the conclusion of international agreements with non-Member States or international organizations. It provided that agreements implementing the common foreign and security policy should be concluded by the Council. The commentary on Article 24 in Chapter 5 above explains the background to the provision and analyses its implications—arguing in particular that it does not by implication create full international legal personality for the European Union.

Article 38 extends the new procedure to agreements relating to Third Pillar matters. One context where it might be used concerns negotiations by the Director of Europol with non-Member States and with international organizations to strengthen the fight against organized crime. In issuing a mandate in March 2000 the Council suggested giving priority to cooperative arrangements with applicant States, with non-Member States associated with Schengen arrangements (Iceland and Norway) and with Interpol. Agreements may of course be concluded by Europol, which has the necessary international legal personality, or by its Director,[64] but a widening of their scope might make conclusion on behalf of the EU and ultimately on behalf of the Member States more appropriate. The Action Plan on common action for the Russian Federation on combatting organized crime, described above, also envisages an agreement under Article 38 with Russia for the purpose of its implementation.[65]

---

[64] See, for example, Council Decision of 27 March 2000 authorizing the Director of Europol to enter into negotiations on agreements with third States and non-EU-related bodies OJ C106, 13.4.2000. The non-EU bodies listed are Interpol, the UN Drugs Control Programme and the World Customs Organization.

[65] OJ C106/5, 13.4.2000, at p 12.

The European Parliament

ARTICLE 39 (EX ARTICLE K.11)

1. The Council shall consult the European Parliament before adopting any measure referred to in Article 34(2)(b), (c) and (d). The European Parliament shall deliver its opinion within a time-limit which the Council may lay down, which shall not be less than three months. In the absence of an opinion within that time-limit, the Council may act.
2. The Presidency and the Commission shall regularly inform the European Parliament of discussions in the areas covered by this Title.
3. The European Parliament may ask questions of the Council or make recommendations to it. Each year it shall hold a debate on the progress made in the areas referred to in this Title.

Article 39 gave the European Parliament for the first time a right to be formally consulted on Third Pillar instruments with binding effect. Although under the Maastricht Treaty the Presidency was required to consult the Parliament 'on the principal aspects of activities in the areas referred to in this Title' and was required to ensure that the Parliament's views were duly taken into consideration, there was in effect no sanction if the Presidency failed to carry out these obligations. Under Article 39.1, on the other hand, failure by the Council to consult will invalidate any instrument adopted without consultation.

The Parliament's new right to be formally consulted by the Council does not extend to non-binding instruments—collaborative arrangements among Member States and common positions adopted by the Council. They must be kept informed by the Presidency and the Commission of 'discussions' in all Third Pillar areas—although it must be open to question whether it would be realistic to inform them of direct contacts between Member States. In April 2000 the Commission, which had been consulted by the Council on the UK request to participate in some of the provisions of the Schengen acquis, passed the matter on to the Parliament. The Parliament however failed to adopt a report, and the Council, which had taken the view that consultation was not mandatory, went ahead.[66] The Parliament's right to ask questions of the Council and to make recommendations to it also extends to all Third Pillar areas.

It is however notable that the right to formal consultation extends to international conventions. Traditionally, treaties were negotiated in secret

[66] See *Europe* No 7705 (27 April 2000) p 12.

and revealed even to national parliaments only after their signature. But as was pointed out in Chapter 1 above, increased transparency in the negotiation at least of multilateral treaties of major significance is increasingly changing this. It is certainly preferable for any parliament—whether national or European—to have an opportunity to criticize or to suggest amendments to a treaty before its text is finalized rather than to delay or block its ratification afterwards. Article 39 does not, however, require formal consultation of the Parliament on agreements with non-Member States or with international organizations concluded by the Council under the powers of Article 38 (extending the Article 24 procedure). If, however, the Council approved an agreement by means of a 'decision' under Article 34(2)(c) this would trigger formal consultation of the Parliament.[67]

The Parliament was consulted on the draft Convention on Mutual Assistance in Criminal Matters soon after the entry into force of the Treaty of Amsterdam, though there is little indication that the amendments which it proposed in order to improve defendants' rights were accepted by the Council.[68]

The Parliament's new right to be consulted is somewhat circumscribed by the imposition of a three-month time-limit. In the absence of an opinion within that time the Council may act. The absence of a time-limit in the EEC Treaty provisions on consultation enabled the Parliament to try to increase its influence by delaying its opinion. When the Council proceeded to resist this tactic by adopting a Regulation without awaiting the opinion, the ECJ annulled the Regulation for failure by the Council to comply with an 'essential procedural requirement'.[69] The Member States in giving the Parliament its new right to be consulted on Third Pillar instruments have forestalled the possibility of any such delaying tactics. There is no corresponding time-limit imposed on the Council for the initiation of the consultation procedure, but Declaration 9, described in the commentary on Article 34 above, now requires publication in the Official Journal of initiatives by Member States as well as by the Commission on Third Pillar matters, so that there should be no difficulty for the Parliament in beginning consideration of its opinion at an early stage even if there has been no formal request from the Council.

The right to be formally consulted implies a right to be reconsulted if the Council radically alters the draft measure. As was said in *Parliament v Council*:[70]

---

[67] See EP Working Paper, The Impact of the Amsterdam Treaty on Justice and Home Affairs, 2000, LIBE 110 EN, Vol I at pp 123–4.

[68] See *Europe*, 22 February 2000, for account of amendments and debate.

[69] Cases 138/79 *Roquette Frères v Council* and 139/79 *Maizena v Council* [1980] ECR 3333 and 3393.

[70] Case C-65/90 [1992] ECR I-4593.

... the duty to consult the European Parliament in the course of the legislative procedure . . . includes the requirement that the Parliament be reconsulted on each occasion where the text finally adopted, viewed as a whole, departs substantially from the text on which the Parliament had already been consulted, except in cases where the amendments essentially correspond to the wishes of the Parliament itself . . .

Control of the Pillars by the European Parliament and by national parliaments is considered more fully in Chapter 10 below.

Closer Cooperation

ARTICLE 40 (EX ARTICLE K.12)

1. Member States which intend to establish closer cooperation between themselves may be authorised, subject to Articles 43 and 44, to make use of the institutions, procedures and mechanisms laid down by the Treaties provided that the cooperation proposed:

(a) respects the powers of the European Community, and the objectives laid down by this Title;

(b) has the aim of enabling the Union to develop more rapidly into an area of freedom, security and justice.

2. The authorisation referred to in paragraph 1 shall be granted by the Council, acting by a qualified majority at the request of the Member States concerned and after inviting the Commission to present its opinion: the request shall also be forwarded to the European Parliament.

If a member of the Council declares that, for important and stated reasons of national policy, it intends to oppose the granting of an authorisation by qualified majority, a vote shall not be taken. The Council may, acting by a qualified majority, request that the matter be referred to the European Council for decision by unanimity.

The votes of the members of the Council shall be weighted in accordance with Article 205(2) of the Treaty establishing the European Community. For their adoption, decisions shall require at least 63 votes in favour cast by at least 10 members,

3. Any Member State which wishes to become a party to cooperation set up in accordance with this Article shall notify its intention to the Council and to the Commission, which shall give an opinion to the Council within three months of receipt of that notification, possibly accompanied by a recommendation for such specific arrangements as it may deem necessary for that Member State to become a party to the cooperation in question. Within four months of the date of that notification, the Council shall decide on the request and on such specific arrangements as it may deem necessary. The decision shall be deemed to be taken unless the Council, acting by a qualified majority, decides to hold it in abeyance: in this case, the Council shall state the reasons for its decision and set a deadline for reexamining it. For the purposes of this paragraph, the Council shall act under the conditions set out in Article 44.

4. The provisions of Articles 29 to 41 shall apply to the closer coopera-tion provided for by this Article, save as otherwise provided for in this Article and in Articles 43 and 44.

The provisions of the Treaty establishing the European Community concerning the powers of the Court of Justice of the European Communities and the exercise of those powers shall apply to para-graphs 1, 2 and 3.

5. This Article is without prejudice to the provisions of the Protocol integrating the Schengen acquis into the framework of the European Union.

The provisions on closer cooperation within the Third Pillar framework probably have more political than practical importance. They could loosely be described as giving treaty authority for Member States to follow the precedent of the Schengen Agreement and Convention while using from the outset the institutions and procedures of the European Union. Progress whereby a number of States initiate a cooperation which gradu-ally exerts a gravitational attraction on others is characteristic of the inter-national method of law-making. The Schengen method whereby a small number of States bypassed the deadlock in the Council over lifting border control of people was regarded by the time of the conclusion of the Treaty of Amsterdam as a success, and the Member States sought to give this approach a certain respectability by building it into the TEU. At the same time it was made clear that the new Treaty provisions would not apply to the Schengen acquis itself—which in effect had bypassed the onerous con-ditions set out in Article 40 by being directly incorporated through Protocol 2 and the new Title IV.

The restrictions placed on closer cooperation are however so complex and restrictive that it is extremely difficult to imagine that the route will prove an attractive way of making progress. Paragraph 1 of Article 40 sets out the basic objective of more rapid development of the area of freedom, security, and justice and the self-evident requirement to respect European Community powers and Third Pillar objectives. Instead of the enthusiasts simply setting out by means of a separate agreement as happened at Schengen in 1985, they must now embark on a heavy authorization proce-dure permitting the Commission, the Parliament, and even the ECJ to question their intentions and allowing the Luxembourg compromise pro-cedure to block a Council decision and the matter to be referred to the European Council. For late joiners, paragraph 3 sets out another cumber-some obstacle course.

These restrictions are however not all. Paragraph 3 of Article 40 takes the enthusiasts across to new Title VII, which sets out Provisions on Closer Cooperation applicable to any part of the TEU. It is clear that the rules on

voting and on expenditure set out in Article 44 in Title VII take precedence, in case of Third Pillar closer cooperation over the rules on voting
and expenditure applicable to normal Third Pillar activity. It seems also—
though this is less clear—to be the case that the long list of restrictions on
closer cooperation set out in Article 43 are to be cumulated with the restrictions in Article 40. There is some overlap between the two sets of restrictions, but Article 43 goes further. It requires for example that closer
cooperation is 'only used as a last resort', that it 'concerns at least a majority of Member States' and that it 'does not affect the competences, rights,
obligations and interests of those Member States which do not participate
therein'. It could even be argued—though this is not at all clear—that
closer cooperation within the Third Pillar must comply with further criteria laid down in Article 11 of the EC Treaty which preclude closer cooperation which concerns citizenship of the Union or discriminates between
nationals of Member States.[71]

What is quite clear is that there is at the time of writing no apparent
interest in making use of these labyrinthine provisions. Instead what is
developing within the Third Pillar areas is a network of detailed bilateral
agreements on aspects of judicial cooperation. These are not concluded
among a sufficiently large number of Member States to attract the full
weight of the 'closer cooperation' provisions in Article 40, but they may
well serve the same purpose in that they set precedents which point the
way for other Member States either by extension of the network or
through a Third Pillar instrument.

The European Parliament in its opinion on the 2000 Intergovernmental
Conference, the Dimitrakopoulos/Leinen Resolution,[72] argued that closer
cooperation 'should constitute a force of attraction in order that the Union
may progress' and proposed a single set of provisions to apply to all three
Pillars. Pending the arrival of any such uniform provisions, the Member
States appeared to be proceeding on the basis that the Treaties have now
provided as much variable geometry as is compatible with comprehen-
sion and that their priority should be to exploit these existing powers.

In the Treaty of Nice, however, the Heads of State and of Government—
far from adopting a single set of provisions on closer cooperation or
indeed provisions likely to constitute a force of attraction in any sense—
added new provisions on enhanced cooperation within the Second Pillar
(Article 27a) and within the Third Pillar (Articles 40, 40a, and 40b) as well
as a new Title VI on enhanced cooperation generally. These provisions and
the relationship between them are of even more labyrinthine complexity

---

[71] Monar (1998) at p 333, assumes that Article 11 EC is carried across and comments that
this is 'rather surprising' since Third Pillar closer cooperation can certainly affect rights of
and non-discrimination between citizens of the Union.
[72] Printed in Europe Documents, 28 April 2000.

than those in force under the Treaty of Amsterdam. The conditions to be satisfied are so numerous and the obstacles to progress so formidable than it can only be supposed that the Articles were drafted as a deterrent to any actual attempt to invoke them. So far as the intergovernmental pillars are concerned, there is no legal obstacle to Member States setting up private schemes for progress towards a European Union objective—exactly what was done by the original Schengen Agreement. What is unlikely in the extreme is that the Treaty of Nice provisions on enhanced cooperation, even if they enter into force, will be chosen as the route for progress. On that basis they are not reproduced here.

The Single Institutional Framework

ARTICLE 41 (EX ARTICLE K.13)

1. Articles 189, 190, 195, 196 to 199, 203, 204, 205(3), 206 to 209, 213 to 219, 255 and 290 of the Treaty establishing the European Community shall apply to the provisions relating to the areas referred to in this Title.

...

Article 41 corresponds to Article 28 which implements for the Second Pillar the requirement of Article 3 of the Treaty on European Union that:

The Union shall be served by a single institutional framework which shall ensure the consistency and the continuity of the activities carried out in order to attain its objective while respecting and building upon the acquis communautaire.

The principle of the selection of institutional provisions is that those Articles giving formal life to the European Parliament, the Council, and the Commission are applied within the Third Pillar, while Articles giving European Community powers and functions to the institutions are omitted. The Commentary on Article 28 above gives examples of how this principle is applied.

A similar provision in the Maastricht Treaty applied most of the listed Articles within the Third Pillar context. There have however been some additions. The new Article 255 which gives a right of access to Parliament, Council, and Commission documents, subject to principles, conditions, and limits on grounds of public or private interest, is extended to apply to Third Pillar documents. The application of Article 195 (ex Article 138e) extends into the Third Pillar the powers of the Ombudsman appointed by the European Parliament to enquire into complaints of maladministration by EU institutions or bodies. Given the limitations on the powers of the Commission and on the jurisdiction of the ECJ under the Third Pillar, this could prove to be for the individual citizen an important source of redress. On voting, Article 205(3) is applied so as to provide that within the Third Pillar abstention by members of the Council will not prevent adoption of acts requiring unanimity.

Financing the Third Pillar

ARTICLE 41 (EX ARTICLE K.13)

. . .

2. Administrative expenditure which the provisions relating to the areas referred to in this Title entail for the institutions shall be charged to the budget of the European Communities.

3. Operational expenditure to which the implementation of those provisions gives rise shall also be charged to the budget of the European Communities, except where the Council acting unanimously decides otherwise. In cases where expenditure is not charged to the budget of the European Communities it shall be charged to the Member States in accordance with the gross national product scale, unless the Council acting unanimously decides otherwise.

4. The budgetary procedure laid down in the Treaty establishing the European Community shall apply to the expenditure charged to the budget of the European Communities.

The provisions on financing the Third Pillar follow generally those set out in Article 28 for financing the Common Foreign and Security Policy. While the provisions in the Maastricht Treaty for financing external operational expenditure proved so unworkable as to be a major weakness in the implementation of a European foreign policy, this was not so for Home and Justice Affairs. By contrast with foreign and security policy, justice and home affairs is directed not at the mounting of joint operations under an EU umbrella but at mutual assistance in the enforcement of policies on immigration, serious transnational crime, and preservation of public order whose substance remains national. Funding of operations or assistance not directly for the national benefit could easily be justified on grounds of reciprocity. The weaknesses of the Third Pillar method under the Maastricht Treaty also meant that there were few legally binding instruments calling for financial backing. Europol—to some extent an exception to these statements—had clear and detailed provisions governing the financing and auditing of its own budget.[73]

Under the Treaty of Amsterdam however, even though expenditure on border controls now falls within the First Pillar, it is likely that the amount of operational expenditure on police and judicial cooperation in criminal matters will increase. This is particularly the case in regard to the external

---

[73] Articles 35 and 36 of the Convention OJ C316/20, 27.11.1995, at pp 20–1.

dimension of the Third Pillar, which increasingly contains initiatives such as the Action Plan on common action with Russia on organized crime which involve a substantial element of financial support for training and exchanges of practitioners.[74] Clear provisions which presume that expenditure—both administrative and operational—is to be charged to the Communities' budget will ensure that policy decisions are not frustrated by failure by the Member States to allocate consequential expenditure. It will remain possible for the Council acting unanimously to reverse this presumption and charge operational expenditure to Member States in accordance with the gross national product scale. Much of the expenditure resulting from successful cooperation will in the ordinary course of events be carried without complaint by the Member States who derive direct benefit from the outcome.

The new financing system also has the advantages—already pointed out in the context of Article 28—that it strengthens the connection between the Third and the First Pillars and gives the European Parliament through its powers in the budgetary process a substantial base from which to question Council policies.[75]

---

[74] OJ C106/5, 13.4.2000.   [75] See Meyring (1997) at p 237.

The Bridge from Third to First Pillar

ARTICLE 42 (EX ARTICLE K.14)

The Council, acting unanimously on the initiative of the Commission or a Member State, and after consulting the European Parliament, may decide that action in areas referred to in Article 29 shall fall under Title IV of the Treaty establishing the European Community, and at the same time determine the relevant voting conditions relating to it. It shall recommend the Member States to adopt that decision in accordance with their respective constitutional requirements.

Article 42 forms the passerelle or bridge permitting transfer of areas of common action into the competence of the European Community. It replaces, with some changes, Article K.9 in the Maastricht Treaty. The original Article K.9 was never used under the conditions set out in the Maastricht Treaty. Instead these areas of common action were transferred into Community competence by the Treaty of Amsterdam. The overt reference in the Maastricht and the Amsterdam Treaties to a possible future transfer into the First Pillar underlines the concept of the Third Pillar as a way for the Member States to make practical progress in cooperation in sensitive areas and to build mutual confidence without the larger surrender of national autonomy implied by a transfer of competence to the European Community.

Article 42 differs in three ways from the corresponding provision in the Maastricht Treaty:

(a) all areas of common action under the Third Pillar may be transferred into the First Pillar;

(b) the European Parliament must first be consulted; and

(c) transfer would be into the new Title IV of the European Community Treaty, though the Council may prescribe voting conditions differing from those in Article 67.

On signature of the Treaty of Amsterdam, Denmark made a Declaration of which the Conference took note. This specified the constitutional requirements to be satisfied in the case of Denmark following a Council decision under Article 42. The terms are: 'In Denmark, such adoption will, in the case of a transfer of sovereignty, as defined in the Danish constitution, require either a majority of five sixths of members of the Folketing or both a majority of the members of the Folketing and a majority of voters in a referendum.'

In view of the requirement for ratification in all Member States of any Council decision on transfer of areas from Third to First Pillar, it must be regarded as unlikely that Article 42 will be used. Like Article 40 on closer cooperation its importance is political rather than practical.

An Interim Balance Sheet of the Third Pillar after Amsterdam

A great effort was made by the Member States in drawing up the Treaty of Amsterdam and afterwards at the European Council at Tampere to remedy the weaknesses in the structure of the Third Pillar established under the Treaty of Maastricht. In particular there are now clear objectives in the Treaty for police and judicial cooperation in criminal matters, given greater precision in the Conclusions of the European Council at Tampere. The Treaty has resolved the earlier uncertainty over the legal status of instruments—other than conventions—adopted by the Council under Third Pillar powers. Conventions, unless otherwise provided, will enter into force once ratified by half the Member States—which will enable them through effective operation in practice to exert gravitational force on late ratifiers in the way which is usual in the international community for multilateral treaties. The jurisdiction given to the ECJ, although in some respects optional for the Member States, will enable the Court to resolve significant disputes over interpretation and to safeguard the rights of individuals which are obviously vulnerable to exercise of the collective powers developing under the Third Pillar framework. The preparatory work by the Council is much more transparent and leaves significantly more room for constructive input from national parliaments and from national and international bodies concerned with justice and civil liberties.

The difficulty in making a fair evaluation of the Third Pillar which was identified at the conclusion of Chapter 6 nevertheless persists. Public assessments are polarized between the beneficiaries of better police and judicial cooperation—those in national authorities responsible for fighting international crime—and the protectors of potential victims whose human rights risk being marginalized. Both sides have gained as the Third Pillar has matured and its structures have been refined. The law enforcers actively engaged in international cooperation in The Hague, Brussels, and at national level have substantially increased their numbers and have continued to build up mutual confidence and trust. The benefits of this are greater than might appear from a study of texts adopted by the Council. Greater transparency and availability of legal remedies has to some extent alleviated earlier concern that the intergovernmental method was necessarily secret, unaccountable and unconcerned with individual human rights. What is beyond dispute is public support for the objectives of the Third Pillar. A Eurobarometer Report in 2000 showed that the European public regarded fighting organized crime and drug trafficking as the second equal highest priority for the EU.[76]

It is, however, apparent that there is no appetite among the Member States for a significant degree of harmonization of their national criminal laws or for the creation of a supranational or 'federal' layer of additional substantive criminal law. Nor is there any diminishing of the general wish to retain the sovereign right to enforce both national and European law. This being so, the international method remains appropriate for police and judicial cooperation among Member States. Other subjects might be added to the Third Pillar, but those already there are unlikely in the foreseeable future to be moved into the First Pillar. The structures put in place by the Treaty of Amsterdam for the Third Pillar seem to be well fitted for their purpose. They now need to be left alone for a sufficient time to prove themselves.

---

[76] Combatting unemployment was regarded as the highest priority (90%) and the other second equal (88%) was maintaining peace and security in Europe, *Europe*, 2 and 3 November 2000.

8

Cross-Pillar Action: The Struggle for Consistency

The Treaty Commitments

The Common Provisions set out in Title I of the Treaty on European Union, as amended by the Treaty of Amsterdam, lay far greater emphasis on integrated objectives and on consistency of action than they do on the separate pillars whereby these objectives are to be carried forward. Article 1 describes the structure of the Union and provides that: 'Its task shall be to organise, in a manner demonstrating consistency and solidarity, relations between the Member States and between their peoples.' None of the five primary objectives of the Union listed in Article 2 of the Treaty are explicitly linked to a particular method of decision-making and several of the objectives, such as the maintaining and development of an area of freedom, security, and justice, require implementing action under more than one of the pillars. Only the last of the five objectives underlines the primacy of the Community pillar and suggests that the two flanking pillars may be less permanent structures:

—to maintain in full the acquis communautaire and build on it with a view to considering to what extent the policies and forms of cooperation introduced by this Treaty may need to be revised with the aim of ensuring the effectiveness of the mechanisms and the institutions of the Community.'[1]

Article 3 sets out the central obligation to ensure consistency as follows:

The Union shall be served by a single institutional framework which shall ensure the consistency and the continuity of the activities carried out in order to attain its objectives while respecting and building upon the acquis communautaire.

The Union shall in particular ensure the consistency of its external activities as a whole in the context of its external relations, security, economic, and development policies. The Council and the Commission shall be responsible for ensuring such consistency and shall cooperate to this end. They shall ensure the implementation of these policies, each in accordance with its respective powers.[2]

---

[1] See Wessel (2000*b*) at pp 1145–9.
[2] Wessel (1999) at p 297, notes that other language versions of the Treaty use the term 'coherence' rather than consistency and says: 'Consistency in law is the absence of contradictions; coherence, on the other hand, refers to positive connections. Moreover, coherence

Article 4 defines the primary purpose of the European Council in the following way: 'The European Council shall provide the Union with the necessary impetus for its development and shall define the general political guidelines thereof.'

As policy-making under the Second and Third Pillars has developed since the entry into force of the Treaty of Maastricht, the cross-pillar aspects have become more apparent, and the Council and the Commission have become more practised at dealing with them. It has long been obvious that strategic decisions taken under the Common Foreign and Security Policy would require implementing action under European Community external commercial powers or development aid powers to be effective. Most joint actions and some common positions require financial resources for their implementation, and since the Second Pillar lacks its own financial resources, money has to be found from the budget of the European Communities using Community procedures.[3] The developments in the structure of the EU have all tended to make it easier for the Common Foreign and Security Policy to borrow powers and money from the First and from the Third Pillar rather than to depend on the Member States.

More recently it has become clear that external relations with many neighbouring States require the integration of those States into Union policies on fighting international crime, protecting external borders, and combatting illegal immigration. Transposing the greater part of the Third Pillar areas of common action into the First Pillar may have appeared to be a formula for clearer and more effective law, but it has left a messy interim situation in which a large number of instruments retain their original character, imposing international legal obligations only. The derogations granted to the UK, to Ireland, and to Denmark will for the foreseeable future make much of the Third Pillar acquis on immigration and asylum cross-pillar in nature.

Common Strategies

Common strategies, although introduced by the Treaty of Amsterdam into Articles 12 and 13 of the TEU as an instrument for the common foreign and security policy (CFSP), are in practice cross-pillar in character. Like 'principles and general guidelines for the common foreign and secu-

in law is a matter of degree, whereas consistency is a static concept.' The same distinction is drawn by Tietje (1997) and by Koutrakos (2001) at pp 39–40. None of these authors takes account of the fact that in English 'coherence' has the primary meaning of 'making sense', as opposed to 'incoherence'. In the English language, 'consistency' can indeed be used to indicate degrees of interconnection.

[3] Although the Budget is now styled 'Budget of the European Union', the fund-raising procedures and obligations remain entirely within the Community Pillar.

rity policy' they impose legal obligations on the institutions of the Union and on the Member States, but lack the formal and more precise character of joint actions and common positions which are 'adopted' by the Council under Second Pillar powers. They transcend the different law-making procedures in the Council and the different legal character of instruments adopted under the First, Second, or Third Pillars. They require to be given concrete legal form—usually under all three Pillars and also by the Member States.

The Common Strategy of the European Union on Russia[4]—the first to be adopted—sets out three principal objectives: consolidation of democracy, the rule of law and public institutions in Russia; integration of Russia into a common European economic and social area; cooperation to strengthen stability and security in Europe and beyond. The Council and the Commission are required to implement the Common Strategy 'by making appropriate use of all relevant instruments and means available to the Union, the Community and to the Member States'. Existing programmes, instruments, and policies are to be reviewed to ensure consistency with the Strategy and used as appropriate. The Partnership and Cooperation Agreement between Russia and the European Community and its Member States is singled out, but all relevant EU instruments and Member States' programmes are to be used.

The numerous areas of action listed straddle all three Pillars. Within the First Pillar there appears for example opening up the banking sectors to EU participation and promoting approximation of customs legislation. Within the Second Pillar there appear encouraging administrative reforms and an independent judiciary, as well as supporting Russian efforts to meet international human rights commitments. Within the Third Pillar is cooperation in the fight against organized crime, money laundering, and illicit traffic in human beings. On the basis of an inventory of existing instruments and an identification mission in Russia, the Commission was required to report by the end of 1999 and thereafter to submit proposals as appropriate.

It must be emphasized that although the Common Strategies give a high profile to the cross-pillar nature of European Union action towards particular States or regions, they reflect practice which was well established before the Treaty of Amsterdam. Chapter 4 above, in describing policies towards Russia in the years following the establishment of the Second Pillar, makes clear that a mixture of instruments under First and Second

---

[4] OJ L157/1, 24.6.1999; Bull EU 6-1999, point 1.3.97. The Russian Government responded to the Common Strategy by adopting its own Medium-Term Strategy for the Development of Relations between the Russian Federation and the European Union (2000–2010), which it submitted to the European Council in Helsinki in October 1999.

Pillar powers were deployed within a framework agreed with Russia in order to assist its political and economic reconstruction.

The Common Strategy on Ukraine[5] is equally cross-pillar in dimension. The Partnership and Cooperation Agreement—the first to be signed with a Newly Independent State—is again highlighted as is the financial assistance already being given by the European Community under the TACIS programme and under bilateral programmes financed by Member States. Support for the democratic transition process in Ukraine called for implementation through Second Pillar methods directed, for example, at training of the judiciary and close cooperation with the Organization for Security and Cooperation in Europe. Under the Third Pillar the emphasis is on cooperation to combat illegal immigration and trafficking in human beings. This dimension is given additional importance because, following enlargement, some future Member States will share an external border with Ukraine.

In the Common Strategy on the Mediterranean[6] the central objective of a common area of peace and stability points to implementation through Second Pillar methods such as arrangements for conflict prevention and encouragement of peaceful settlement of disputes and promotion of signature and ratification of international agreements on non-proliferation. Cooperation against terrorism, organised crime, and drug trafficking requires Third Pillar action, while the EU undertakes to 'ensure the integration into society of Mediterranean partners' nationals who have been lawfully resident in a Member State for a certain period of time and hold a long-term residence permit, aiming at approximating their legal status in that Member State to that enjoyed by EU citizens'. This latter undertaking may be given effect under powers within the First Pillar since entry into force of the Treaty of Amsterdam.[7]

Common strategies are not intended to be a substitute for precise decisions by the Council and the Commission. They have been criticized by the High Representative for the Common Foreign and Security Policy as being rhetorical and descriptive of existing instruments.[8] For the country or region concerned however, as well as for those working in a narrow area of the Council or Commission, an overview of existing and projected programmes is presentationally helpful and by formulating policy and objectives agreed unanimously by the Member States they open the way to

---

[5] 1999/877/CFSP OJ L331/1, 23.12.1999; Bull EU 12-1999, point 1.4.91.
[6] Santa Maria da Feira Conclusions, June 2000, para 58 and Annex V.
[7] Article 63(4) of the EC Treaty.
[8] The 'Solana Paper', intended to be a confidential assessment for the meeting of the General Affairs Council in January 2001, was published as No. 2228 of the Europe Documents series. See also BQ Europe 22 and 23 January 2001 and 1 February 2001.

coordinated implementing decisions which at least within the Second Pillar may be taken by qualified majority in the Council. The practice has been for each incoming Presidency to draw up a Work Programme for each Common Strategy, and in these documents the allocation between Pillars and specific legal bases is made clear.

Conclusions of the European Council on Freedom, Security, and Justice

The Treaty on European Union does not make provision for Common Strategies within the Third Pillar. The Conclusions of the European Council at Tampere in October 1999 on the creation of an area of freedom, security and justice did, however, have for the Third Pillar a similar importance to Common Strategies, and the Conclusions straddle all three Pillars in a similar way.

Under the heading of a Common EU Asylum and Migration Policy—on its face a First Pillar matter since the entry into force of the Treaty of Amsterdam—the European Council called for greater coherence of internal and external policies of the Union and for partnership with non-member countries of origin with a view to promoting codevelopment. The call for a common policy on visas—a subject which before the entry into force of the Treaty of Amsterdam was somewhat incoherently divided between First and Third Pillars—included 'closer cooperation between EU consulates in third countries and, where necessary, the establishment of common EU visa issuing offices'. Cooperation between overseas diplomatic and consular missions and the establishment of common overseas facilities takes place under the provisions of Article 20, within the Second Pillar of the EU. Action against illegal immigration, and in particular imposition of serious sanctions against trafficking in human beings and economic exploitation of migrants, would require use of powers under Article 31, within the Third Pillar. The related question of conclusion of readmission agreements with non-member countries of origin is however now a matter for the Community under new First Pillar powers, as the Conclusions themselves make clear. It is clear that a coherent and effective EU policy on asylum and immigration requires action under all three Pillars.

The Tampere Conclusions explicitly refer to the need for cross-pillar consistency in implementation in the section on Stronger External Action, which begins:

59. The European Council underlines that all competences and instruments at the disposal of the Union, and in particular, in external relations must be used in an integrated and consistent way to build the area of freedom, security and justice. Justice and Home Affairs concerns must be integrated in the definition and implementation of other Union policies and activities.

60. Full use must be made of the new possibilities offered by the Treaty of Amsterdam for external action and in particular of Common Strategies as well as Community agreements and agreements based on Article 38 TEU.

Human Rights

Article 6 of the TEU, as amended by the Treaty of Amsterdam, provides in its first paragraph that: 'The Union is founded on the principles of liberty, democracy, respect for human rights and fundamental freedoms, and the rule of law, principles which are common to the Member States.' This fundamental principle is explicitly reflected in the Second Pillar. The objectives of the common foreign and security policy include 'to develop and consolidate democracy and the rule of law, and respect for human rights and fundamental freedoms.'

Meaningful external action in pursuit of this objective requires constant cross-pillar action, so that common positions of the Council on violations of human rights in particular non-Member States are reflected in decisions to delay or to suspend commitments under international agreements to which the European Community, usually along with the Member States, is a Party or in positive measures to try to put an end to the violation.[9] Article 177 (ex Article 130u) of the European Community Treaty in setting out the objectives of Community development cooperation policy required that

. . .

2. Community policy in this area shall contribute to the general objective of developing and consolidating democracy and the rule of law, and to that of respecting human rights and fundamental freedoms.

In recent years, successive versions of the Lomé Convention and now the Cotonou Partnership Agreement have given greater legal strength to the efforts of the Community to respond swiftly and credibly to violations of human rights in African, Caribbean, or Pacific Parties to the Convention.[10]

One example of this integrated cross-pillar action is the European Union's response to the assassination of President Mainassara of Niger in 1999. Within the framework of the Second Pillar the Presidency issued a statement condemning the coup and announcing that cooperation with Niger would be assessed under the mechanisms set up under the Lomé IV

---

[9] See generally Cremona (1996); Brandtner and Rosas (1998).
[10] In particular, revised Article 5 and new Article 366a of the Fourth Lomé Convention, OJ L156/1, 29.5.1998. See Simma, Aschenbrenner, and Schulte (1999); McMahon (1999) especially p 615. Stronger provisions are contained in Articles 9, 96, and 97 of the Cotonou Partnership Agreement, OJ L317/1, 15.12.2000—see Martenczuk (2000) especially pp 469–72.

Convention. The Commission then entered into consultations under Article 366a of the Convention, claiming that the suspension of the Constitution of Niger, dissolution of its Government, national assembly, and Supreme Court and electoral irregularities violated the Convention obligations on respect for democratic principles and the rule of law. In response to both positive and punitive measures by the European Union, Niger undertook to re-establish democracy and the Commission proposed that cooperation should gradually be resumed.[11]

Neither the Lomé Conventions nor the Cotonou Agreement explicitly addresses a possible European Union response to involvement by ACP States in armed conflict. Within the Second Pillar, however, Article 3 of the Council's Common Position of 1997 concerning conflict prevention and resolution in Africa makes clear that:

In order to contribute better to the prevention and resolution of conflicts in Africa, the Union shall seek:

—to impose linkage between its efforts (policies and actions) and those of the Africans, and

—to use the various instruments available coherently to promote effective conflict prevention and resolution.

The Council notes that, in accordance with the relevant procedures, steps will be taken to ensure coordination of the efforts of the European Community and those of Member States in this field, including with regard to development cooperation and the support for human rights, democracy, the rule of law and good governance.[12]

While it cannot be claimed that the efforts by the European Union to encourage and to sanction human rights performance in non-Member States have been generally successful, there are at least coordinated cross-pillar mechanisms to ensure that financial and trading advantages are not uncritically continued where conditions in the recipient State make it unlikely that they could serve their intended purpose. Similar mechanisms have been built into recent agreements between the European Community and its Member States and individual non-Member States. National parliaments and the general public in Europe are extremely concerned that funds from their taxpayers and traders might be used to finance foreign conflicts or diverted by corrupt or unstable governments.[13]

---

[11] Bull EU 4-1999, points 1.4.12 and 104; COM(1999) 204; Bull EU 7/8-1999, point 1.4.165.
[12] OJ L153/1, 11.6.1997; Commission Communication on Cooperation with ACP Countries involved in Armed Conflict, COM(1999) 240 final.
[13] For a less positive appraisal, made a few years earlier, see Clapham (1999) especially pp 636–41, Quest for Consistency.

In the view of McGoldrick:

Evolution of the broader human rights dimensions of the EU now requires that the whole of the post-TEU constitutional structure be considered, and in particular the relationship between the different pillars. As the effect of human rights thinking has become clearer, and the institutional structure has been reformed, so Member States and Community institutions have been able to develop more precise strategies and practices in response.[14]

Sanctions

Imposition of political sanctions is the classic example of cross-pillar action by the Union. The ultimate purpose of such sanctions is to bring pressure to bear on a non-Member State in a foreign policy context, but many of the instruments which may be deployed for that purpose fall within the scope of the EC Treaty.[15] Even before the entry into force of the Maastricht Treaty, the practice was for a policy decision on collective sanctions to be taken by Ministers acting under European Political Cooperation and for the commercial aspects to be implemented under the old Article 113 of the EC Treaty.[16] The powers provided in Article 228a (later Article 301) of the EC Treaty by the Maastricht Treaty are on their face cross-pillar in character in that a condition precedent for their use is the existence of a Second Pillar common position or joint action requiring Community action to interrupt or to reduce economic relations with one or more third countries.[17]

Under modern practice, the Council must first adopt a common position or joint action determining the scope and the duration of the sanctions to be imposed by the European Union. The usual practice has been for the Council to adopt a common position, although given the specific and onerous obligations which follow for individuals and for business enterprises a joint action might be regarded as a more appropriate instrument. The Council common position will usually reflect the terms of a Security Council resolution which may be a decision imposing binding obligations

---

[14] McGoldrick (1994) at p 266.

[15] cf Opinion of Advocate-General Jacobs in Case C-120/94 *Commission v Greece* (Former Yugoslav Republic of Macedonia) [1996] ECR I-1513, paras 61–8, where he considers 'improper use' of the powers in the old Article 224 of the EC Treaty and says: 'It is difficult to identify a precise legal test for determining whether a trade embargo is a suitable means of pursuing a political dispute between a Member State and a third State. The decision to take such action is essentially of a political nature.' See also Opinion of Advocate-General Jacobs in Case C-124/95 *Centro-Com* [1997] ECR I-81 at p 99. For a general account of the nature of sanctions and the practice of the Member States, see Koutrakos ch 3 and 4.

[16] For details, see Chapters 2 and 4 above. For comments on EC practice before the Maastricht Treaty, see Fox and Wickremasinghe (1993) especially pp 951–5

[17] See Ryba (1995) at pp 21–2.

under international law on the Member States.[18] The existence of a Security Council decision is not, however, a requirement for the Council of Ministers. The Council may adopt a common position in the absence of a binding Security Council decision, and it will often clarify the terms of any Security Council resolution or go beyond it by imposing more extensive sanctions. It is, moreover, now increasingly frequent for a Council common position on sanctions to contain exceptions for humanitarian supplies as well as incentives for the non-Member State to return to normal constructive relations with the European Union.

The Member States will not, however, impose any sanctions going beyond the requirements of a Security Council decision unless they believe that these can be justified under general international law. The possible conflict with obligations of Members States under their bilateral air service agreements, for example, explained why in 1998 the Council delayed in adopting a Common Position imposing a flight ban on Yugoslav air carriers and revoking their operating authorizations.[19] In imposing restrictive measures on the US following the Helms-Burton and d'Amato legislation, the Council stressed both in its CFSP Joint Action and in the related Regulation that the extra-territorial application of the US measures violated international law and that their own counter-measures were intended to protect the Community and natural and legal persons within it from the adverse effects of this violation.[20] Other international obligations, in particular those arising under World Trade Organization (WTO) agreements, will also be taken into account before any Council decision.[21]

Once adopted by unanimity in the Council, the common position establishes policy and imposes binding international legal obligations on the institutions of the European Union and on the Member States.

The implementation of the Council's common position will then be fragmented between the Member States and the three Pillars of the Union. Some aspects, in particular any embargo on the supply of arms and other military equipment—which is outside European Community competence—will require implementation at national level. The common

---

[18] For an account of sanctions imposed by the Security Council since 1990, see Carver and Hulsmann (2000). See also Doxey (1987).

[19] Common Position 98/426 CFSP OJ L190/3, 4.7.1998, implemented by Regulation 1901/98, OJ L248/1, 8.9.1998. The flight ban was challenged by the Yugoslav national carrier Jugoslaevnski Aerotransport (JAT) before a Belgian court, which accepted that it satisfied international law requirements for countermeasures: *JAT v Etat belge*, Cour d'Appel de Bruxelles (9ème chambre), Journal des tribunaux, No. 5942 (30 October 1999) 699.

[20] OJ L309 and L309/7, 29.11.1996. The measures are described in more detail in Chapter 4 above.

[21] Any dispute as to whether compensatory measures taken by the EU violate WTO obligations may be, and has been in some recent cases, challenged under WTO dispute settlement procedures.

position under the Second Pillar imposes international legal obligations on the Member States but is not directly applicable,[22] so that implementing legislation under national powers controlling the export of arms will be needed in each Member State in order to make an embargo effective and impose penalties for its breach by individual traders. The Common Position by which the Council imposed an arms embargo on Sudan, for example, says in Article 2: 'Member States shall take the necessary steps to ensure that the embargo referred to in Article 1 is applicable from 16 March 1994.'[23]

Restrictions on the import and export of goods other than arms and other military equipment fall within Community competence and so require implementation by the Council. The Council acts by qualified majority on a proposal from the Commission under Article 301 (ex Article 228a) of the EC Treaty. Article 301 gives a general power 'to interrupt or to reduce, in part or completely, economic relations with one or more third countries' and may thus cover a ban on supply of services as well as goods. This general power has the advantage of bypassing any possible arguments in the Council as to the scope of the powers given by Article 133 (ex Article 113). The Council often adopts a Community regulation imposing a trade embargo immediately after the adoption of the enabling common position. Although the implementing regulation is directly applicable, it is likely to require further measures at national level—in particular to create criminal offences and appropriate penalties for breach of the sanctions by individual traders.

Restrictions on movement of capital and payments fall to be implemented by the Council acting by qualified majority on a proposal from the Commission under Article 60 (ex Article 73g) of the EC Treaty. In the case of financial sanctions, however, a Member State is entitled 'for serious political reasons and on grounds of urgency' to take unilateral measures against a third country, provided that it informs the Commission and the other Member States by the date of their entry into force. The Council acting by qualified majority on a proposal from the Commission may require the Member State to amend or abolish such unilateral measures. This power to impose unilateral financial sanctions does not explicitly require the existence of a Council common position, but it is declared to be without prejudice to Article 297 (ex Article 224) of the EC Treaty which requires Member States to consult to prevent the functioning of the common market being affected by measures which a Member State may be called upon to take in a number of circumstances, for example 'to carry out obligations it has accepted for the purpose of maintaining peace and international

[22] In the UK, legal obligations under the Second and Third Pillars are *not* given direct applicability by the European Communities Act 1972 as amended.
[23] OJ L75/1, 17.3.94.

security'. The more extensive powers given to Member States in the case of financial sanctions reflect the speed with which action may be needed to block transfer of liquid assets from their jurisdiction.[24] If criminal sanctions are required, pursuant to an obligation to impose effective and dissuasive penalties for breach of restrictions on financial movements, these must be imposed—as in the case of an embargo on goods—by national laws.

Finally, restrictions on movement of people, including imposition of visa requirements, could formerly be implemented under Third Pillar powers, although sometimes they were simply included in a Second Pillar common position.[25] Although provisions under the Community pillar are never combined in a single instrument with provisions under Second or Third Pillar powers (since the legal effects of such an instrument would be open to doubt), there is no objection to including in a single instrument provisions under the Second and Third Pillars. The Joint Action adopted in 1996 in response to the Helms-Burton and d'Amato legislation in the US (described in Chapter 4 above) was explicitly based on Articles J.3 and K.3(2)(b) of the TEU.[26] Since the entry into force of the Treaty of Amsterdam, however, the Council may adopt measures imposing visa restrictions under Article 62 of the EC Treaty.

A complex sanctions regime is thus likely to be implemented by several instruments adopted by the Council—some using intergovernmental powers and some using European Community powers—as well as by several instruments adopted at national level. If the regime is modified, some of these instruments will require amendment. The Treaty powers certainly open the way for a swift and uniform response by the EU and its Member States. There is however little possibility of any informed parliamentary debate, and the applicable law—which may be enforced by criminal procedures at national level and even by imprisonment—is likely to be scattered among a number of sources and poorly understood even by traders and other individuals affected.

Some of these complexities may be illustrated from the sequence of instruments imposing sanctions on the former Yugoslavia in the context of its failure to respect commitments under the Dayton Agreement and its conduct in Kosovo. In November 1995 the Security Council, welcoming the initialling of the Dayton Agreement which was to lead to a formal Peace Agreement, decided on a three-stage termination of its 1991 embargo on deliveries of weapons and military equipment.[27] In February

---

[24] Macleod, Hendry, and Hyett (1996) p 355.
[25] See Wessel (2000*b*) at p 1152, where it is suggested that this is an example of 'possible legal basis confusion'.
[26] 96/668/CFSP, OJ L309/1, 29.11.1996.
[27] Resolution 1021 (1995). The embargo was imposed by Resolution 713 (1991).

1996 the Council of the EU defined a Common Position whereby they would maintain their own embargo on arms, munitions, and military equipment towards Bosnia, Croatia, and the Federal Republic of Yugoslavia and would (subject to the provisions of the Security Council Resolution) consider export licence applications to Slovenia and the former Yugoslav Republic of Macedonia on a case-by-case basis.[28]

In March 1998, in a further Common Position, the Council of the EU noted that: 'Whereas recent events in the Federal Republic of Yugoslavia (FRY) and in particular the use of force against the Kosovar Albanian Community in Kosovo, represent an unacceptable violation of human rights and put the security of the region at risk; . . . ' They demanded that the Government of the FRY should take specific steps to stop the violence and commit itself to finding a political solution to the issue of Kosovo. In the absence of such steps they decided to confirm their arms embargo and to extend it to equipment which might be used for internal repression or for terrorism. They decided also to extend sanctions by imposing a moratorium on government-financed export credits for trade and investment, and by blocking issue of visas 'for senior FRY and Serbian representatives responsible for repressive action by FRY security forces in Kosovo'. The persons to be excluded were listed in an Annex.[29] A few days later the Security Council adopted a similar Resolution, condemning the use of excessive force by Serbian police against civilians and peaceful demonstrators in Kosovo as well as acts of terrorism by the Kosovo Liberation Army, calling on the FRY to take steps to achieve a political solution and in particular to offer political dialogue. The Security Council reimposed their embargo on sale or supply to the FRY of 'arms and related *matériel* of all types, such as weapons and ammunition, military vehicles and equipment and spare parts'.[30]

The extended sanctions covered by the European Union Council's 1998 Common Position fell within the scope of the EC Treaty. The Council therefore, acting under Articles 73g and 228a of the EC Treaty, adopted a Regulation prohibiting supply or sale to the FRY of equipment which might be used for internal repression or terrorism, such as that set out in the Annex. Items already covered by the arms embargo established by the Second Pillar Common Positions were expressly excluded. The Regulation also prohibited the grant of export credits for trade or investment in Serbia and provision or use of official financing for privatizations in Serbia in the absence of legally binding commitments. Article 5 of the Community Regulation required that: 'Each Member State shall determine the sanctions to be imposed where the provisions of this Regulation are infringed.'

---

[28] 96/184/CFSP OJ L58/1, 7.3.1996.   [29] 98/240/CFSP OJ L95/1, 27.3.1998.
[30] Resolution 1160 (1998). Later amendments were in Resolutions 1199 and 1203 (1998).

While this wording accepts that competence to impose penalties lies with the Member States, it implies that some form of sanction must be imposed for non-compliance.[31]

In the UK, the arms embargo imposed by the Security Council was implemented by the Federal Republic of Yugoslavia (United Nations Sanctions) Order 1998.[32] The Order prohibits export and supply of petrol, giving a wide construction to the words 'related *matériel*' in the Resolution. The Order also makes detailed provision for search of ships, aircraft, and vehicles suspected of carrying prohibited goods and for criminal proceedings and penalties.

This network of instruments is complex and scattered among a number of different legal sources, but it cannot be claimed that it lacks overall coherence.

Dual-use Goods

The legislative scheme adopted to control the export of dual-use goods—which may be used either for civil or for military purposes—was originally also cross-pillar in character. As with sanctions, the ultimate purpose of the measures, which are described in Chapter 4 above, is to prevent proliferation and diversion of weapons and to ensure compliance by Member States with international obligations on arms control and non-proliferation—a purpose clearly within the scope of the CFSP. The instrument employed however involves restriction on exports which notwithstanding their military and security uses have been held by the ECJ to fall within the scope of the common commercial policy.[33] The Court has also upheld the right of the Member States to control these exports under permitted exceptions in the EC Treaty relating to national security.

The dichotomy was clearly set out by Emiliou: 'On the one hand, export controls clearly fall within the sphere of commercial policy, a subject matter reserved to the Community's exclusive competence; on the other hand, effective protection of national security is primarily the responsibility of the Member States.'[34]

During the Cold War, uniformity among Member States was imposed by means of the informal but tightly monitored COCOM system. The winding up of COCOM following the end of the Cold War left Member States competent to impose national restrictions, but exposed the lack of a

---

[31] Regulation 926/98 of 27 April 1998 OJ L130/1, 1.5.1998.

[32] SI 1998/1065. See Canor (1998); Pavoni (1999). On French implementation, see Naud (1997).

[33] Case C-367/89 *Aimé Richardt* [1991] ECR I-4621; Case C-70/94 *Werner Industrie-Ausrüstungen v Germany* [1985] ECR I-3189; Case C-83/94 *Leifer* [1995] ECR I-3231.

[34] Emiliou (1996) at p 56. See also Koutrakos (2001) ch 5, 'The Community Regime on Exports of Dual-use Goods to Third Countries'.

Community system to ensure a uniform approach to what were potentially very lucrative as well as dangerous exports. The completion of the single market and the ending of border controls on goods also made the need for a Community-wide system obvious. In December 1994 the Council adopted a Second Pillar Decision and a Regulation under Article 113 (now 133) of the EC Treaty. The cross-pillar linkage between the two was made clear in Article 1 of the Decision in this way: 'This Decision and Council Regulation (EC) No. 3381 of 19 December 1994 setting up a Community regime for the control of exports of dual-use goods, constitute an integrated system involving, in accordance with their own powers, the Council, the Commission and the Member States.'[35]

The actual list of dual-use goods, permitted destinations (a 'white list' of allied and friendly States) and guidelines to be applied by national export control authorities were set out in the CFSP Decision. These guidelines included commitments under international agreements on non-proliferation, UN obligations to impose sanctions and criteria on export of conventional arms determined by the European Council. The items on the list, and the guidelines, not only required quite frequent modification (which did in fact happen) to take account of developments in military technology and new multilateral arms control agreements, but they also involved sensitive decisions on political, security, and defence matters within national competence, though within the potential scope of the CFSP.[36]

The uniform export control regime was set out in the related Council Regulation. National export licences—valid throughout the Community— were required for all items on the list, and for other items where the national authorities had grounds for suspecting that they might be used for development, production, or maintenance of chemical, biological, or nuclear weapons. Customs procedures and control measures were also prescribed. The Regulation was monitored by a Coordinating Group of national representatives and Member States were required to impose 'effective, proportionate and dissuasive penalties' for breach of the controls.

The need for cross-pillar action using two legal instruments was justified on the basis that, as in the case of sanctions, it reflected the difference between the foreign and security policy objective pursued by the Council and its implementation through a commercial policy instrument. It safeguarded from any possible claim to exclusive Community competence sensitive national decisions on the end uses of weapons and on the States to which they might be supplied.

---

[35] Council Decision 94/942/CFSP, OJ L367/8, 31.12.94; Regulation 3381/94 OJ L367/1, 31.12.94. See Stefanu and Xanthaki (1997); Emiliou (1996). On the background to the instruments see Eeckhout (1994) ch 7, 'The Community's Export Policy and the Case of Strategic Export Controls'.
[36] See Wessel (2000*b*) at p 1164.

The cross-pillar approach in this context, however, met with sustained criticism, not only on the basis that it was complex, but on the two grounds that it failed to achieve a uniform Community approach and was unnecessary in order to safeguard national autonomy over the sensitive decisions involved. The ECJ made increasingly clear that the fact that the ultimate objective of a measure lay in the field of foreign or security policy did not in itself exclude it from the Community's common commercial policy. Even though Member States retained ultimate competence over their national security policies, this did not exempt them from compliance with Community legal obligations or give them an increased margin of manoeuvre.[37] The criteria set out in the CFSP Decision were said to add nothing to constraints already obvious, and their vagueness left too much room for individual decisions by national export authorities which could distort competition among Community manufacturers. The Decision identified States which were permissible destinations, but contained no 'black list' list of prohibited destinations. It was not in substance a true Second Pillar decision formulating a common policy.

In June 2000 the Council, after prolonged argument as to the correct approach to regulating export of dual-use goods, adopted a new Regulation, based entirely on Article 133 of the EC Treaty. It repealed both the Regulation and the Second Pillar Decision of 1994.[38] The repealing Decision made clear that the Council's determination that the new system 'should be based solely on a European Community act' followed a review of the 1994 system and took into account the case law of the ECJ. The new Regulation stressed in its reasoning the need for 'an effective common system of export controls on dual-use items' both for the purpose of ensuring compliance with international commitments and responsibilities of the Member States and also to establish free movement of these goods within the Community. It also, however, allaying the fears of Member States, made it explicit that: 'The responsibility for deciding on applications for export authorisations lies with national authorities.' These national decisions were, however, to be taken in the framework of the common commercial policy and the common rules on exports. The common lists of dual-use items must conform to international obligations of each Member State in regard to non-proliferation. Member States would, pending further harmonization, retain rights to control transfer of certain items in order to safeguard public order or public security.

---

[37] See Case C-70/94 *Werner* (n 33 above), Case C-83/94 *Leifer* (n 33 above) and Case C-124/95 *R, ex parte Centro-Com Srl v HM Treasury and Bank of England* [1997] ECR I-81, especially Opinion of Advocate-General Jacobs. For sustained criticism of the two-pillar approach based on analysis of the Court's jurisprudence, see Koutrakos (2001) ch 5 and 6.

[38] Regulation 1334/2000 OJ L159/1, 30.6.2000 and Decision 2000/402/CFSP OJ L159/218, 30.6.2000. Regulation 1334/2000 was amended and updated by Regulation 2432/2001 OJ L338, 20.12.2001.

The final decision of the Council was therefore that the cross-pillar approach was inappropriate to the control of export of dual-use goods. To safeguard basic principles of the Community legal order and to ensure its uniformity and its effectiveness, it was necessary to rely on Community legislation alone. The international commitments of the Member States (including their commitments under the CFSP) could be safeguarded within this framework and national competence over security issues was expressly preserved.

Visa Policy

The Palma Document, which formed the starting point for intergovernmental cooperation among the Member States to tighten controls at external frontiers, listed the interrelated legal instruments to be agreed—a common list of countries whose citizens would be subject to a visa requirement, establishment of a common list of persons to be refused entry, harmonization of criteria for granting visas, and a European visa.

In the Maastricht Treaty, however, these areas were split between the First and the Third Pillars. A new Article 100c, placed among the internal market provisions of the EC Treaty, required the Council to 'determine the third countries whose nationals must be in possession of a visa when crossing the external borders of the Member States'. Within the Third Pillar, however, Member States were required by Article K to regard among areas of common interest appropriate for intergovernmental regulation 'rules governing the crossing by persons of the external borders of the Member States and the exercise of controls thereon'.

This division of competence resulted from a late compromise between those Member States who sought to integrate asylum and immigration policy fully into European Community competence and those who preferred to leave them for intergovernmental regulation under the new Third Pillar. The manner of the division reflected the fact that agreement on the States whose nationals should be excluded on a uniform basis was more closely related to the internal market objective of enhancing free movement of people by relaxing or lifting controls on intra-Community borders.

Soon after the entry into force of the Maastricht Treaty the Commission in a Communication to the Council and the European Parliament[39] made two closely connected proposals—a draft Regulation based on Article 100c of the EC Treaty determining the third countries whose nationals must be in possession of a visa when crossing the external borders of the Member States, and a draft Convention based on Article K.3 of the TEU establish-

[39] COM(93) 684.

ing a Convention on the crossing of the external frontiers. Taken together the two proposals reflected the substance of a draft Convention which the Member States had already negotiated, but which was blocked due to a dispute between Spain and the UK concerning its application to Gibraltar. The Commission emphasized that its two proposals were 'closely linked and need to be examined together'.

The Council did not dispute the need to consider the proposals together, but it did dispute the interpretation of Article 100c on which the Commission had based its draft Regulation. The Commission took a wide view, arguing 'that the objective of Article 100c is the total harmonisation of Member States' policies towards third countries in that area. Either there is a visa requirement for all Member States or there is not any visa requirement for any Member State, that is the final objective.'[40] Its proposal, therefore, not only set out a 'black list' of third countries whose nationals would require a visa to cross the external frontiers, but required the Council by 30 June 1996 to determine for all other countries whether they should be added to the 'black list' or in a 'white list' of countries whose nationals would be exempt from visa requirements. The proposal also required mutual recognition by Member States of national visas valid throughout the Community.

The resulting constitutional disputes between Council, Commission, and Parliament, described more fully in Chapter 6 above, considerably delayed agreement on a coherent European visa policy.[41] The failure to adopt the External Frontiers Convention was due to other factors, in particular the long running dispute over application to Gibraltar and the more general dispute as to the jurisdiction of the ECJ. But the cross-pillar allocation of competence over visa policy set out in the Maastricht Treaty could only have worked satisfactorily if the line between intergovernmental and Community action had been clearly drawn and logically defensible, and this was not the case. Whereas in the cases of sanctions and control of dual-use goods described above, cross-pillar action could be justified by the dichotomy between the foreign policy objectives and the commercial instruments for their implementation, this was not the case with visa policy. Visa policy called for integrated decision-making and legislation, and the artificial division set out in the Maastricht Treaty was not defensible. This was accepted when visa policy, along with all aspects of asylum and immigration, was transferred by the Treaty of Amsterdam into European Community competence.[42]

The difficulties over visa policy were not, however, attributable to any failure in consistency by the institutions.

---

[40] Commission evidence to House of Lords enquiry: HL Select Committee on the European Communities, 14th Report (1993–94) Q 130.
[41] See Peers (2000) pp 69–74.   [42] See O'Keeffe (1994*b*) at p 271.

A somewhat more successful example of cross-pillar action in regard to visa policy was the Council Recommendation relating to local consular cooperation regarding visas.[43] Although the Recommendation was adopted on the sole basis of Article K.1(3) within the Third Pillar of the TEU, it relied on the machinery of cooperation among overseas consular missions of Member States which was formalized under Article J.6 (now Article 20) within the Second Pillar. Consular posts of Member States are recommended to exchange information on national criteria for issuing visas and on national security, public policy, and illegal immigration risks. They should prepare joint reports on local issues affecting issue of visas, including reports on particular applicants, and measures to detect simultaneous or successive applications to consulates of different Member States. A later Recommendation aimed at collaboration among visa authorities in the detection of forged documents provides for lending and common use among consular posts of technical equipment and for opening training courses to consular officers and employees of other Member States.[44]

External Dimension of Third Pillar Actions

The external dimension of the First Pillar—which might initially have seemed limited to external commercial relations and development aid—has grown enormously as the areas of Community action have increased and the interconnection between the internal and the external has become apparent. The same is true for the Third Pillar. An effective immigration policy, for example, clearly required a degree of cooperation from the States from which most immigrants came. This related not only to the question of readmission of their nationals who were deported or excluded from European Member States but also to assistance in the control of illegal immigration at source and the pursuit of policies designed to make it a comparatively less attractive option. The Member States exchanged information about their policies on assistance for voluntary return of illegally resident third-country nationals. They also included in both Community only and mixed agreements with non-Member States standard clauses either requiring immediate admission, without further formalities, of nationals illegally present or in the alternative requiring the conclusion of specific agreements with individual Member States on request. All these aspects are brought together in the Common Strategy on the Mediterranean adopted by the European Council at Feira in June 2000 where under the heading of Justice and Home Affairs the Union says that it will

[43] OJ C80/1, 18.3.1996.   [44] OJ C80/1, 18.3.1996.

develop effective cooperation mechanisms to fight against illegal immigration networks, including trafficking in human beings, inter alia through the establishment of readmission arrangements relating to own and third country nationals as well as persons without nationality;

enter into dialogues with a view to setting up modern and effective border control systems, offering inter alia access to training programmes and exchanges of officials;

work with Mediterranean Partners to address the question of migration, taking into full consideration the economic, social and cultural realities faced by Partner countries. Such an approach would require combating poverty, improving living conditions and job opportunities, preventing conflicts, consolidating democratic states and ensuring respect for Human Rights;[45]

The transfer of asylum and immigration into Community competence has not lessened the need for an external dimension for the reduced Third Pillar. At Tampere, the European Council expressed its support for regional cooperation against organized crime involving the Member States and third countries bordering on the Union. The need for support from non-Member States to make internal cooperation against crime effective has become more apparent as organized crime has assumed an increasingly international character and as controls over people crossing internal borders between Member States have been eliminated or greatly reduced.

The cross-pillar dimension is also emphasized by Article 37 of the TEU as amended by the Treaty of Amsterdam, providing that 'Articles 18 and 19 shall apply as appropriate to matters falling under this Title.' Article 18 requires the Presidency to represent the Union on common foreign and security policy matters and makes provision for support from the Secretary-General of the Council and from the Commission. These three together form the new style Troika, and their responsibilities now expressly extend to Third Pillar matters. Article 19 imposes detailed duties to coordinate Member States' action in international organizations and conferences. This duty, as is now clear, applies not only to foreign policy but also to Third Pillar areas. Much of the collaboration between police, prosecutors, and others concerned with the fight against international crime is directed at the conclusion and enforcement of international agreements with wider participation. A recent example of successful collaboration of this kind, already referred to in Chapter 7 in the Commentary on Articles 31 and 37 concerned the negotiation of the United Nations Convention against Transnational Organized Crime.[46]

---

[45] Para 22. For a list of initiatives, many cross-pillar in nature, for the management of migration flows, see Commission Scoreboard on Home and Justice Affairs COM(2000) 782 at pp 10–11.

[46] Adopted in Palermo in December 2000. The final text is in UN Doc A/55/383. For a comprehensive account of programmes under way, particularly in the field of organized

The cross-pillar dimension is clearly evident in the European Union Action Plan on Common Action for the Russian Federation on Combating Organised Crime.[47] The Action Plan is designed to implement the Second Pillar Common Strategy on Russia endorsed by the European Council at Cologne in June 1999 and to take account of the Russian response—the medium-term strategy for development of relations between the Russian Federation and the Union. It is based in part on work undertaken within the framework of the Agreement on Partnership and Cooperation between the European Communities and their Member States and Russia, as well as on preparatory work by liaison officers from Member States based in Russia and international meetings between law enforcement officers from the two sides.

The Action Plan makes clear that effective judicial cooperation will require ratification and implementation by Russia of a long list of Council of Europe and UN Conventions and that priority should be given to the conventions on extradition, mutual assistance in criminal matters, money laundering, and corruption. The exercise of accession to and reviewing the implementation of these international conventions is already being given high priority in Moscow. The development of law enforcement cooperation would involve, *inter alia*, exchange of intelligence in the field of organized crime (subject to data protection and confidentiality requirements), training of Russian personnel and exchanges between liaison officers from the two sides which should also involve Europol and the European Commission. Implementation of the Plan might involve the Russian authorities being associated with programmes and instruments adopted within the European Union. The Union would also

urgently consider the question of developing an agreement under Article 38 TEU with the Russian Federation for the purpose of implementing this action plan. In addition EU Member States should examine closely the possibility of concluding appropriate multilateral and bilateral agreements with the Russian Federation to improve the fight against organised crime within the framework of the action plan.

Efficiency and Effectiveness of Cross-Pillar Action

Examination of recent practice by the institutions, suggests that where the need for cross-pillar action follows from a strategic overview of a subject or a geographical area or from a defensible division of powers set out in the TEU, the institutions are able to adopt consistent and coherent legislative instruments. Since the entry into force of the Treaty of Amsterdam

---

crime, see Eisl (1997). Eisl stresses that this cooperation must be seen not only in the context of potential EU membership but also as a benefit to the EU because of the indirect effects.

[47] OJ C106/5, 13.4.2000.

these preconditions have on the whole been met. Express provision for common strategies within the Second Pillar, accompanied by the possibility of implementation by qualified majority in the Council, opens the way to better coordination and to speedier implementation of policies unanimously agreed. The European Council at Tampere showed in its Conclusions that a similarly broad approach could provide cross-pillar coherence as well as impetus to decision-making on justice and home affairs. The division of powers between First and Second Pillars in regard to sanctions is defensible, and Council practice has been consistent. The fundamental reappraisal by the Commission and the Council of the system of controlling export of dual-use goods shows that the correct allocation of legislative powers between Pillars is constantly reviewed by the institutions. The Third Pillar has been given express provisions reflecting its need for an important external dimension. Generally speaking, the most obvious areas of continuing uncertainty flow from the special provisions for Denmark, Ireland, and the UK which were made in the context of transferring Third Pillar areas into the First Pillar.

If the pillar structure is accepted as an indefinite feature of the structure of the European Union, it is essential that it should result in efficient decision-making and effective legal instruments in those areas where cross-pillar action is necessary or appropriate. It may be too early to make judgments on the effectiveness of many of the actions described, but on the evidence of recent instruments, the institutions are becoming familiar with cross-pillar techniques and are now able to use their various powers in a consistent and convincing manner.[48]

[48] For recent assessments, see Schmalz (1998); von Bogdandy (1999); Curtin and Dekker (1999); p 83; Wessel (2000*b*) especially pp 1167–71.

9

Judicial Control of the Pillars

Limited Powers for the European Court of Justice

When the intergovernmental pillars were established by the Treaty of Maastricht, they were excluded almost totally from the jurisdiction of the ECJ. Article L gave the Court no jurisdiction whatsoever over Article J which formed the basis of the Second Pillar.[1] In regard to the Third Pillar, Article K, the jurisdiction of the Court applied only to:

'the third subparagraph of Article K.3(2)(c)'.

Article K.3(2)(c) gave the Council power, without prejudice to Article 220 of the European Community Treaty, to draw up conventions which should be recommended to the Member States for adoption in accordance with their constitutional requirements. The third subparagraph provided that

'Such conventions may stipulate that the Court of Justice shall have jurisdiction to interpret their provisions and to rule on any dispute regarding their application, in accordance with such arrangements as they may lay down.'

The European Court and the Second Pillar

To explain the exclusion of the ECJ from any jurisdiction over the Second Pillar it is important to recall that only with the Treaty of Maastricht did it become possible for the decisions and instruments which had long been drawn up under European Political Cooperation (EPC) procedures to be given any legal force whatsoever. Joint actions and common positions—if drafted in language appropriate to the creation of legal relations—would henceforth bind the Member States under international law. It is not of

---

[1] William Wallace and Helen Wallace (2000) p 524. Article L also excluded from the jurisdiction of the ECJ the whole of Title I of the TEU which sets out the Common Provisions on which the Union is based. This exclusion covers Article B which lists the common foreign and security policy, including the framing of a common defence policy, and development of close cooperation on justice and home affairs among the objectives of the Union. In Case C-167/94 *Criminal Proceedings against Grau Gomis* [1995] ECR I-1023, the Court said that it had no jurisdiction to interpret Article B of the TEU in the context of a reference for a preliminary ruling.

course characteristic of modern international law that compulsory settlement of disputes among States concerning the interpretation or application of legal obligations should be excluded. There were, however, two reasons for the Member States to keep the ECJ at a distance from the new Common Foreign and Security Policy (CFSP).

The first reason was that EPC, and CFSP instruments are essentially short-term in character, and potentially both wide-ranging and sensitive. Unlike treaties, the texts agreed by the Member States are not designed to establish a permanent framework of mutual legal obligations between Contracting Parties but to condition a collective approach to a specific overseas crisis, a catastrophe, or a change of regime or to impose collective discipline on a particular multilateral negotiation. They are often overtaken by events, and in this case the practice is for the Member States to renegotiate or even to ignore them. If an individual Member State steps out of line, there may be recriminations and a political price to pay—and this will be higher because the commitment is a legal one—but no question of any measures to enforce compliance. The insistence on the continuation of ultimately sovereign foreign policies, bound together by the CFSP but not replaced by it, together with the need for speed in the resolution of differences, mean that the conditions for judicial resolution of disputes do not really exist.

The second reason concerned the nature and the record of the ECJ. The judges appointed to the Court have not generally come to their task from a background of public international law, and they have over the years elaborated doctrines—particularly in the sphere of the external relations of the European Communities— which lay much more emphasis on the integrationist purpose of the Treaties and less on presuming a minimum derogation from individual sovereign powers than a tribunal of international lawyers would have done.[2] The UK was particularly sensitive to this fear that the ECJ might warm excessively to its task. While the Court, in considering the possible direct effect of GATT and WTO obligations, has shown itself sensitive to differences in meaning between the same expressions in the Community law and in the international law context, concern remained that certain ECJ doctrines—emphasizing for example the exclusive nature of Community external powers to the detriment of pre-existing national powers—might find their way into the CFSP.[3]

---

[2] For critical assessment of the 'legislative character' of some judgments of the Court see Hartley (1999) ch 2 (especially nn 71 and 72) and ch 3; Weiler (1999a) ch 5 The least-dangerous branch: a retrospective and prospective of the ECJ in the arena of political integration. See also Slaughter, Stone Sweet, and Weiler (1999), especially essay by Weiler and Haltern (1999) at p 331; Tesoka (1998).

[3] For a clear expression of UK determination to exclude the ECJ from jurisdiction over the CFSP, see evidence given to the House of Lords during negotiation of the Maastricht Treaty: HL Select Committee on the European Communities, 17th Report (1990–91b) QQ 64–75.

The European Court and the Third Pillar

In the case of the Third Pillar the first of the above reasons did not apply. Although the Third Pillar as designed by the Maastricht Treaty had a disappointing impact on national policies particularly on asylum and immigration, it was designed in part for the adoption of instruments which would not only have long-term effects on national laws, but would also have substantial impact on individual rights. In particular, the most important issues were to be addressed through international conventions which would be subject to national ratifications and be implemented in many cases through changes to national laws. The Member States were agreed that for these conventions at least some form of ECJ jurisdiction would be appropriate. The Maastricht Treaty, however, left the details of this jurisdiction to be determined in the context of each convention to be negotiated, as had been done with conventions under Article 220 of the EC Treaty such as the Brussels Convention on jurisdiction and the enforcement of judgments in civil and commercial matters.

In the event the latitude contained in Article K.3(2)(c)—set out above—proved to be a formula for deadlock. The adoption of a number of important conventions was delayed for months or years while the Member States wrangled over the jurisdiction to be given to the ECJ. The UK, while declining to be drawn in public as to its reasons, in effect refused to allow the ECJ any significant jurisdiction over any of the proposed Third Pillar Conventions. To understand its position one may turn to evidence given by Professor O'Keeffe in the context of the draft Convention on the crossing of the external frontiers of the Member States. He said:

However, in this case, the conferral of jurisdiction on the Court, once decided upon, is extremely important. As noted above, commentators expect that where such jurisdiction is attributed, Article K.3(2)(c) will in fact operate as a special sort of "passerelle" provision. The reason for this is that it is assumed that the Court will bring to the task of interpretation and dispute settlement of conventions concluded under this provision at least some of the features which have characterised its case-law when acting within the context of the Community Treaties. Thus, it might be expected that the Court could emphasise the rule of law, the pre-eminence of the general principles of law such as equality and non-discrimination, legal certainty, legitimate expectation, *ne bis in idem*, the right to a fair hearing, proportionality and the respect of the principles contained in human rights instruments to which the Community and/or its Member States are Parties, including the European Convention on Human Rights. An important role for the Court will be to see that the primacy of instruments set out in Article 27 is respected.[4]

---

[4] HL Select Committee on the European Communities, 14th Report (1993–94) at p 105.

Professor O'Keeffe was of course arguing in favour of jurisdiction for the ECJ, but his account of how the Court might approach the interpretation of Third Pillar Conventions articulates precisely why the UK—where at the time the ECJ was especially controversial—resisted it so strongly.[5]

The Europol Convention

The question of jurisdiction for the ECJ over Third Pillar Conventions came to a head over the Europol Convention. In this case the UK refused absolutely to permit resolution of disputes among Contracting Parties other than through the Council of Ministers and refused to give its courts any power to make references for preliminary rulings. It maintained that involvement of the ECJ would be contrary to the separate and inter-governmental nature of the Third Pillar. The then Home Secretary, Mr Howard, questioned in oral evidence by the House of Lords Select Committee on the European Communities as to the objection to involvement of the ECJ, replied: 'If there is no need for the European Court of Justice to be involved then it is undesirable for it to be involved.'[6] Although the majority of the House of Lords Select Committee favoured inclusion of the possibility of references to the Court and proceedings against a Member State for breach of the Convention, the issue was so controversial that the Committee divided for the first time in its twenty-year history.

The Europol Convention was adopted in July 1995 with a provision stating only that disputes between Member States on its interpretation or application should initially be discussed in the Council with the aim of finding a settlement. Article 40.2 further said that: 'When such disputes are not so settled within six months, the Member States who are parties to the dispute shall decide, by agreement among themselves, the modalities according to which they shall be settled.' All the Member States except the United Kingdom agreed in a Declaration that 'in such cases they will systematically submit the dispute in question to the Court of Justice of the European Communities.'[7] The question of preliminary references by national courts was left for further discussion. In the Justice and Home Affairs Council in November 1995 the UK rejected compromises under which only national courts of last resort would be permitted to make ref-

---

[5] See also Dehousse (ed) (1994) ch 1, especially p 10, where it is suggested that the exclusion of the Court was designed by the negotiators as a way of ensuring that 'the institutional bridges set up between the Community and the intergovernmental pillars should not lead to a complete absorption of the latter into the former'.

[6] HL Select Committee on the European Communities, 10th Report, (1994–95a) QQ 504–34, especially Q 515.

[7] Cm 3060; OJ C316/1, 27.11.1995.

erences, or the UK would be permitted to opt out.[8] In July 1996 a Protocol was finally agreed which enabled a Member State to 'opt in' by making a declaration. Such a declaration could permit only courts of final resort to make a reference, or it could permit any national court or tribunal to do so.[9]

The breaking of the deadlock over the jurisdiction of the ECJ over the Europol Convention also enabled agreement to be reached on two other Third Pillar Conventions, over which the UK was less intransigent. The Convention on the use of information technology for customs purposes contained an Article which required initial examination by the Council of any dispute between Member States, but provided that if no solution was found within six months, the matter might be referred to the ECJ by a party to the dispute. Any dispute between the Commission and one or more Member States on application of the Convention might also be submitted to the Court if it proved impossible to settle it through negotiation.[10] An identical provision was contained in the Convention on the protection of the European Communities' financial interests.[11] Later Protocols were also attached in 1996 to these two later Conventions, following the precedent of the Protocol to the Europol Convention.

The Court's Own View

In its 1995 Report on Certain Aspects of the Application of the Treaty on European Union, the Court drew the attention of the forthcoming Intergovernmental Conference to the long-term implications of the fact that it had, for all practical purposes, no jurisdiction over Second and Third Pillar activities of the Union. They argued that:

it is obvious that judicial protection of individuals affected by the activities of the Union, especially in the context of cooperation in the fields of justice and home affairs, must be guaranteed and structured in such a way as to ensure consistent interpretation and application both of Community law and of the provisions adopted within the framework of such cooperation. Further, it may be necessary to determine the limits of the powers of the Union vis-à-vis the Member States, and of those of each of the institutions of the Union. Finally, proper machinery should be set up to ensure the uniform implementation of the decisions taken.

The Court believed it essential, for uniform application of Community law and the conventions which were bound up with achievement of Treaty

---

[8] European Report, 25 November 1995; Council Minutes in Doc 11720/95 (Presse 332) p 8.
[9] Cm 3465; OJ C299/1, 9.10.1996.   [10] OJ C316/33, 27.11.1995, Article 27.
[11] OJ C316/49, 27.11.1995, Article 8.

objectives, to have a single judicial body such as the Court itself, able to give definitive rulings for the whole of the Union.[12]

Similar views were expressed by the Commission in its Report for the Reflection Group. The Commission emphasized that it was not possible for Third Pillar instruments to be reviewed by the ECJ for compatibility with general principles of law or with other conventions such as the European Convention on Human Rights (ECHR) or the Convention on the Status of Refugees, even though the TEU required the Union to conform to these other conventions. For common positions and joint actions the Court had no jurisdiction—even they might affect the rights and duties of individuals.[13]

The Treaty of Amsterdam

Chapter 7 above sets out the text of Article 35 (ex Article K.7) of the TEU as revised by the Treaty of Amsterdam, and comments generally on the limited jurisdiction which is now given to the ECJ over Third Pillar instruments. Although the revised Article marked significant progress over the terms of the Maastricht Treaty—in particular by providing provisions for conventions which are automatic rather than subject to controversial negotiation on each occasion—it bore the marks of the disputes and the uneasy compromises elaborated under the earlier Treaty. In particular, the scheme under Article 35.3 which (when taken with Declaration No 10 adopted by the Amsterdam Conference) leaves Member States with four options as to the extent to which they permit the ECJ to determine preliminary references from their national court, undermines the position of the Court as a uniform arbiter for all Member States and for all national courts and tribunals.[14]

Some encouragement may be taken from the fact that when the Treaty of Amsterdam entered into force, ten Member States stated that they would permit any of their national courts or tribunals to make preliminary references, and seven of these reserved the right to make such references obligatory for their highest courts. Spain permitted only its highest court to refer, while Denmark, France, Ireland, and the UK made no provision for references.[15] It is likely that the extent of acceptance will further increase.

---

[12] Report on Certain Aspects of the Application of the TEU 1995, paras 4 and 5.

[13] Commission Report paras 57–62.

[14] See Advocate-General Fennelly (2000) at pp 8–10.

[15] OJ C120/24, 1.5.1999. In spite of the declared intention of the European Council at Tampere to develop the Union as an area of freedom, security and justice, the Treaty of Nice made no increase in the powers of the ECJ in this context: Johnston (2001) at p 500.

The insistence by the UK on a provision of this optional kind must be regarded as a political gesture rather than a safeguard for its own legal order, for it must be regarded as unlikely in the extreme that a UK court would decline to follow a European Court interpretation of a Third Pillar instrument elaborated in the context of a reference from another jurisdiction. The UK Government would also be entitled, under Article 35.4, to influence the actual outcome by submitting observations to the Court. It is UK national courts, therefore, rather than the executive which will be excluded from contributing to the development of the legal principles which the Third Pillar may be expected to generate and to apply. Given the strong and consistent record of the UK in accepting the jurisdiction of the International Court of Justice, and indeed in promoting more generally the compulsory settlement of international legal disputes, it is greatly to be regretted that it has on this issue shown itself to be the most strongly opposed of all the Member States to permitting the ECJ realistic jurisdiction over Third Pillar instruments.[16] Some prospect of evolution in the Government's approach may be drawn from the statement by the Solicitor-General that the UK '. . . is a friend of the Court. . . . We value the contribution it has made to the development of the European Union.'[17]

Other aspects of Article 35 confine the ECJ in ways which underline the intergovernmental character of the Third Pillar. Article 35.5—excluding the Court's jurisdiction to review validity or proportionality of operations carried out by police or law enforcement services of a Member State, or the exercise of national responsibilities for law and order and the safeguarding of internal security—draw a line between the international instrument and national application of that instrument or enforcement action based on it. The provision is likely to exclude any substantial chance of individuals securing any practical remedy from the Court even where action by one or more Member States is based on a Third Pillar instrument. The same exclusion of individual remedies also results from the terms of Article 34.2(b) which provides that Third Pillar framework decisions 'shall not entail direct effect'.[18]

Individuals moreover are given no right under Article 35.6 to initiate review of framework decisions or decisions adopted under the Third Pillar regardless of whether they are directly affected. The responsibility for protecting individuals from breaches of human rights or from misuse

---

[16] See Arnull (1999) at pp 117–20; Albors-Llorens (1998).

[17] Dashwood and Johnston (eds)(2001) at p 5. See also, at p 25 in the same volume, 'A United Kingdom Perspective' the statement 'There is support for strong judicial institutions in the European Union and a readiness to support, in principle, measures to improve efficiency and effectiveness.'

[18] Hailbronner (2000) at pp 151–3, maintains, in the context of Schengen provisions, that nothing in the jurisprudence of the ECJ can be read as saying that obligations which do not derive from European Community legislation may be self-executing.

of powers will therefore lie with national courts—though of course there will be no exclusion of the review powers of the European Court of Human Rights. Member States, individually or collectively, remain accountable before the Strasbourg authorities—and that is one substantial benefit of the intergovernmental nature of the Third Pillar.[19]

In practical terms, probably the most important omission in Article 35 is that it gives the ECJ no jurisdiction over instruments already adopted under the Third Pillar. Where these instruments are replaced by instruments adopted under the new Title IV, the ECJ will not have the jurisdiction which it normally has over First Pillar treaty provisions and instruments but a more limited competence.[20] Third Pillar joint actions and joint positions which retain validity under the Third Pillar will not be subject to any form of judicial control from the ECJ, and conventions already adopted will be covered only by the compromise provisions described above. For the time being, therefore, it may be said that the substance of both the Second and the Third Pillar is beyond the judicial control of the ECJ. To the extent that instruments, including conventions, operate directly or have been transposed into national law, there may be forms of supervision available from national courts. What is altogether lacking is judicial control of national implementation or application of the instruments agreed. The emphasis on the intergovernmental approach has taken the form of almost total exclusion of international judicial supervision of how the law is being applied by the Member States.

It is also a curious omission that the ECJ is not given jurisdiction over the interpretation or application of the treaty provisions which constitute the residual Third Pillar. It may well prove impossible for the Court to review the legality of framework decisions and decisions without interpreting the treaty provisions under which they have been adopted, and it is probable that the Court will take the view that it has power to construe these enabling powers for the limited purpose of reviewing Third Pillar instruments. The treaty provisions do not themselves directly confer rights or obligations. Rather they establish a framework for Council action—and no power is provided in Article 35 to enable the Court to compel the Council to take action. The omission of ECJ jurisdiction over the treaty provisions themselves may therefore prove not to be of great significance.[21]

---

[19] Article 46(d) gives the ECJ jurisdiction to review any action of the institutions to test its compatibility with the requirement in Article 6(2) of the TEU that the Union shall respect fundamental rights, but only 'insofar as the Court has jurisdiction under the Treaties establishing the European Communities and under this Treaty'.

[20] Albors-Llorens (1998) at pp 1287–92.   [21] See Eeckhout (1999) at p 9.

Policing the Boundaries

Article 47 of the TEU (formerly Article M) provides that:

Subject to the provisions amending the Treaty establishing the European Economic Community with a view to establishing the European Community, the Treaty establishing the European Coal and Steel Community and the Treaty establishing the European Atomic Energy Community, and to those final provisions, nothing in this Treaty shall affect the Treaties establishing the European Communities or the subsequent Treaties and Acts modifying or supplementing them.

This Article is itself within the jurisdiction of the ECJ, so leaving the Court with the responsibility for ensuring that the primacy of the First Pillar is effectively safeguarded.

Where there is a dispute within or between the institutions of the EU as to whether legislation should be adopted or an international agreement concluded under the First Pillar or under one of the intergovernmental pillars, the Court has held that it is entitled to determine the question. Its task includes ensuring that acts adopted under the intergovernmental pillars do not encroach on the powers conferred by the EC Treaty. In challenging the legal base on which the Council had adopted a Development Cooperation Agreement with India for example, Portugal argued that provisions on cooperation in fighting drug abuse could not be adopted under Article 130u of the EC Treaty since internal measures in this area were adopted under the provisions of Article K within the Third Pillar. The ECJ, however, pointed to the somewhat general nature of the provisions in the agreement (which did not relate specifically to cooperation between criminal authorities), to the adoption of measures on control of drug abuse under First Pillar powers, and accepted that the terms of the agreement fell within the powers in Article 130u to foster economic and social development of the developing countries.[22]

In the *Airport Transit Visas* case[23] the European Commission sought the annulment of a Joint Position adopted by the Council on the basis of Article K.3 within the Third Pillar. Article K.3 gave the Council power to adopt joint positions contributing to the objectives of the Union which included drawing up 'rules governing the crossing by persons of the external borders of the Member States and the exercise of controls thereon'. The Commission argued that the legislation should have been adopted under Article 100c of the EC Treaty which gave power to the Council 'to determine the third countries whose nationals must be in possession of a visa

---

[22] Case C-268/94 *Portugal v Council* [1996] ECR I-6177 at pp 6224–6.
[23] Case C-170/96 *Commission v Council* [1998] I-2763. See comment in Peers (2000) pp 30–2.

when crossing the external borders of the Member States'. The UK, intervening, argued that the Court had no jurisdiction to decide the case, since Third Pillar measures were not among the measures which it was competent to annul under Article 173 of the EC Treaty. The Court recalled the terms of Articles L and M of the TEU and held that: 'It is therefore the task of the Court to ensure that acts which, according to the Council, fall within the scope of Article K.3(2) of the Treaty on European Union do not encroach upon the powers conferred by the EC Treaty on the Community.' It followed that the Court had jurisdiction to consider the Commission's application—although on the merits it held that the measure was not within the powers of Article 100c of the EC Treaty.

The ECJ has not so far had to determine any similar dispute regarding the boundary between Second Pillar and First Pillar powers. There have been a series of cases in which the Court, in order to construe Council legislation applying sanctions, have turned to the Security Council Resolutions which the Council intended to implement.[24] In the Centrocom case the Court specifically rejected the argument of the UK Government that national measures—even if derogating from Community measures—are covered by exclusive national competence in the field of foreign and security policy and in performance of national obligations under the United Nations Charter. The Court held that powers retained by the Member States must be exercised in a manner consistent with Community law and that it was entitled to determine whether this was the case. The background to Community legislation on sanctions must be examined to determine its objectives and context even if the background took the form of an international instrument or obligation which the Court was not directly entitled to construe.[25]

Given that the Member States may adopt Second Pillar measures which are not based on or which go beyond Security Council resolutions, it is likely that before long the Court well find itself having at least to examine the purpose and the content of a Second Pillar common position or joint action in order to interpret a Community Regulation giving effect to it. There may be a difficult line to draw between examining the Second Pillar instrument as essential background to implementing Community legislation and actually interpreting it. It is however unlikely that the Court will accept that it is precluded from taking the Second Pillar instrument into

---

[24] Case C-84/95 *Bosphorus Hava Yollari Turizm ve Ticaret AS v Minister for Transport, Energy and Communications, Ireland and the Attorney General* [1996] ECR I-3953, [1996] 3 CMLR 257; Case C-124/95 *The Queen v HM Treasury and Bank of England, ex parte Centro-com Srl* [1997] ECR I-81; Case C-177/95 *Ebony Maritime SA and Loten Navigation Co Ltd v Prefetto della Provincia di Brindisi and Ministero dell'Interno* [1997] ECR I-1111' [1997] 2 CMLR 24. For analysis of these cases and their implications see Koutrakos (2001) pp 131–52.
[25] See para 43 of Opinion of Advocate-General Jacobs in the *Centrocom* case (n 24 above).

account to the extent that this is necessary to enable it to fulfil the judicial tasks given to it by the EC Treaty.[26]

Access to Information

The Court has indirectly assisted control by others of the intergovernmental pillars by making clear in the case of *Svenska Journalistforbundet v Council*[27] that it is entitled to review the Community instrument on access to documents[28] even where the documents requested fall within the scope of the Third Pillar. This instrument on its face applies to all Council documents without exception. The case arose from a request by the Swedish Journalists Union—taken by way of a test case—for access to a number of documents relating to the setting up of Europol. Access to two Council documents was denied by the Council on the ground that they disclosed national negotiating positions, and passages in the documents provided had been deleted. The French Government argued that the Decision was not applicable to Third Pillar acts, while the UK Government contended that the Court of First Instance (CFI), since it had no general jurisdiction over the Third Pillar, had no jurisdiction to determine the question of access to documents concerning Third Pillar matters. The Court of its own motion examined the question of jurisdiction and, following its decision in *Carvel and Guardian Newspapers v Council*[29] emphasised that the Council Decision on access to documents, which contained no exclusion, applied to Third Pillar documents. It held further

'The fact that the Court has, by virtue of Article L of the EU Treaty, no jurisdiction to review the legality of measures adopted under Title VI does not curtail its juris-diction in the matter of public access to those documents. The assessment of the legality of the contested decision is based upon its jurisdiction to review the legal-ity of decisions of the Council taken under Decision 93/731, on the basis of Article 173 of the EC Treaty and does not in any way bear upon the intergovernmental cooperation in the spheres of Justice and Home Affairs as such.

The Court held that the fact that the documents were Third Pillar documents was relevant only when considering whether one of the permitted exceptions to disclosure—such as public security—might apply. But the fact that a document related to a Third Pillar matter could not in itself imply that it fell within the public security exception. The Council had failed when adopting its contested decision to make clear that it had car-ried out genuine balancing of the interests concerned, and the CFI annulled it on that ground alone.

[26] See Wessel (1999) pp 223–9.
[27] Case T-174/95 *Svenska Journalistforbundet v Council* [1998] ECR 2289. For critical com-ment see Peers (2000) pp 32, 37.
[28] Council Decision 93/731, OJ L340/43, 31.12.1993.
[29] Case T-194/94 [1995] ECR II-2765.

The reasoning of the Court applies equally in the context of access to Second Pillar documents. This was made clear in the case of *Kuijer v Council*[30] The applicant, a lecturer in asylum and immigration, applied for documents on the activities of CIREA, such as CFSP reports and evaluations on the situation in third countries and reports of joint missions of Member States in third countries. The request was rejected on the grounds that the documents contained sensitive information about the situation in the countries concerned and that disclosure might damage relations between the EU and the countries concerned. The Court held, however, that the Council had failed to give adequate, comprehensible, and clearly analysed reasons for rejection, or to give reasons why partial access could not be granted, and it annulled the decision to refuse access on those grounds.

Conclusion

Judicial supervision is more constrained than necessarily results from the intergovernmental character of the Second and Third Pillars. Although reference is sometimes made to the possibility to adjudication of disputes between Member States by the International Court of Justice, this is clearly not a realistic option for most disputes given the time scale required for the ICJ to reach a decision. The actual use by Member States of the ICJ to adjudicate on the intergovernmental provisions of the TEU would, moreover, certainly undermine the role of the ECJ as constitutional guarantor of the legal order of the European Union—in particular the requirement of unity and consistency.

It cannot, however, be expected that dramatic progress on this front will be made by the Member States. The Treaty of Amsterdam has opened up possibilities which the majority of Member States have embraced. What is needed now is a period in which some more actual cases relating to the intergovernmental pillars are decided by the ECJ in a manner which increases the confidence of the more reluctant Member States.

[30] Case T-188/98 [2000] ECR II 1959.

10

Parliamentary Control of the Pillars

The Nature of Parliamentary Scrutiny of the Intergovernmental Pillars

To assess whether the decisions taken and the instruments adopted under the Second and Third Pillar are subject to adequate democratic control it is first necessary to examine the nature and purpose of such control. If the purpose of control is taken as the exercise of a veto or revision of the detail of executive policy or a Council instrument, then it must be admitted that the results of scrutiny by national parliaments and by the European Parliament of intergovernmental cooperation are very meagre. Nicoll, for example, maintains that: 'National parliamentary scrutiny is not seriously influential. Ministers reporting back on EC/EU business are rarely harried on specifics. In the absence of a publicly available account of the meeting they attended, they can put "spin" on their own performance and achievement.'[1]

It may, however, be that the purpose of parliamentary supervision of the conduct of foreign policy—whether national or European—is not to harry Ministers on specifics (though there are examples where parliaments do indeed do this) but to carry out a public, transparent and continuous debate on the general lines of policies. The preparation within a Ministry of Foreign Affairs for a parliamentary debate or for an appearance before a committee involves careful reappraisal of past actions and future plans in terms of their merits, weaknesses, and likely criticisms. Except on broad and simple questions—of which there are not many—a parliament and even a specialist parliamentary committee will hold and express a range of views. The record of the debate or hearing will later be discussed among experts, analysed carefully within the Ministry, and Ministers' actions may be modified or refined. Ministers and the officials working with them think through the implications of their positions more carefully because they are about to present and justify them publicly. Ministers are strengthened in their positions in the Council or in other international bodies if these have been openly debated and broadly endorsed. They are constantly aware during any international or European Union negotiation that they are likely to have to defend the outcome, and in consequence of some form of continuous dialogue they are aware of what will be acceptable to their own parliaments.

[1] Nicoll and Salmon (2000) p 107.

If this analysis is accepted, it is not possible to evaluate the benefits of scrutiny of intergovernmental action by national parliaments and by the European Parliament simply in terms of occasions where a Minister was embarrassed or forced to change or publicly retract his views. The entire process if it is carried out conscientiously on both sides has inherent value even if no overt change in policy can be shown to flow directly from it. 'Conscientiously' means first that the governments of the Member States must ensure within the limits of necessary confidentiality that national parliaments and the European Parliament are supplied with proposals and draft instruments so that their deliberations are informed and relevant. For parliaments, 'conscientiously' means that they should use their best efforts to contribute to debate with regard to the importance and the urgency of what is proposed and that they should make constructive use of their own expertise as well as the expertise made available to them.[2]

Parliaments are generally limited in their scrutiny of foreign and security policy by the speed with which the most important events unfold and the frequent need for secrecy. Diplomatic documents and proposals are covered by an international practice of confidentiality. It is only recently that it has become common for drafts even of international agreements to enter the public domain before they are concluded among the governments concerned.[3] An important treaty will of course require ratification by national parliaments before it can enter into force—but at this stage parliament may only accept or reject it. Modification of the text is no longer possible, and the treaty may well limit or exclude reservations.[4]

International cooperation in justice and home affairs differs from foreign policy in that a much higher proportion of the output consists of instruments intended to take effect on a long-term basis through national laws. These instruments are also more likely to have direct consequences for individuals. Although decisions taken under the Second Pillar—particularly in the area of political sanctions—may have direct consequences for individuals, such decisions are likely to be implemented through a Community law instrument. Third Pillar instruments on immigration, asylum, and police cooperation, to the extent that they are legally binding, may constrain areas where national parliaments would normally expect to be in control of any legislative changes. If such instruments were to be adopted through a secret intergovernmental process and then presented

---

[2] For a general account and evaluation of scrutiny arrangements across Europe see European Parliament (1994) and European Parliament (1995a). On UK procedures see Denza (1993b) and Denza (1993a); Slynn (1993); Birkinshaw and Ashiagbor (1996); Cygan (1998) especially ch 10 on scrutiny of Intergovernmental Pillars.

[3] For some examples, see Chapter 1 above.

[4] On UK Parliamentary supervision of foreign affairs generally, see HL Select Committee on the European Communities, 28th Report (1992–93b) Part 2. On supervisory powers of other parliaments see Gosello Bono (1992).

to national parliaments as requiring unconditional implementation at national level, it would be clear that normal democratic processes of law-making had been by-passed. National parliaments are much less likely than in the case of foreign and security policy to accept that it was essential to maintain secrecy over the negotiation of these instruments or that generalized debate relating to broad trends of policy was an adequate method of democratic control.[5] The pressures for democratic accountability have therefore been significantly stronger in the context of the Third Pillar.

The Role of National Parliaments

For two reasons, national parliaments bear a heavier share of the responsibility for democratic control of the intergovernmental pillars than they do in the case of European Community measures. First, under the intergovernmental method of making law and policy, it is the Council which has the overwhelming power. Although under the Second Pillar the Commission is fully associated in the representation of the Union and in implementing its decisions and has powers to refer questions or make proposals to the Council, it lacks the monopoly powers of initiation and the enforcement powers which it has under the First Pillar. The European Parliament has deliberately been given only weak entitlements to be consulted, to make recommendations and to debate. The Member States have seen it as characteristic of the intergovernmental method that the European Parliament should be marginalized and unable effectively to control policy.[6] Ministers in the Council are on the other hand democratically accountable to their own national parliaments for their conduct of European Union as well as international affairs. The absence of proper accountability of the Council to the European Parliament throws the main burden of ensuring the democratic legitimacy of its decisions on to national parliaments.

Secondly, the most important decisions taken under the Common Foreign and Security Policy—such as commitments to action on security and defence matters—will ultimately have to be justified by individual governments to their national parliaments and through them to their electorates. Under the Third Pillar the most important long-term decisions will take the form of international conventions which will require ratification by national parliaments. So national parliaments do have the last word on policy under the intergovernmental pillars in a way which they do not have over European Community decisions. Constructive

---

[5] See Meyring (1997) especially p 243: 'Democratic control of measures in the field of JHA is therefore much weaker if the measures are adopted under the third pillar than it is in purely internal matters.'

[6] See Monar (1994) at p 75.

involvement by national parliaments should not take the form only of rejection of important commitments or conventions, but should rather involve an open dialogue in which the views of the parliaments contribute to the political process at an earlier stage.[7]

Declarations on the Role of National Parliaments

It is not possible for an international agreement such as the TEU to pre-scribe duties or procedures for the parliaments of the individual Member States. How individual parliaments carry out scrutiny of the activities and the instruments adopted under any of the three pillars of the EU is a matter for national constitutional law and practice. All that may be done on a collective basis by an Intergovernmental Conference of the Member States is to require the provision by the governments of the Member States of the relevant information to their parliaments, and to issue exhortations which serve to encourage at national level the development of appropri-ate procedures.

The first such call was Declaration No. 13 attached to the Maastricht Treaty which read:

The Conference considers that it is important to encourage greater involvement of national Parliaments in the activities of the European Union.

To this end, the exchange of information between national parliaments and the European parliament should be stepped up. In this context, the governments of the Member States will ensure, inter alia, that national Parliaments receive Commission proposals for legislation in good time for information or possible examination.

Similarly, the Conference considers that it is important for contacts between the national parliaments and the European Parliament to be stepped up, in particular through the granting of appropriate reciprocal facilities and regular meetings between members of Parliament inter-ested in the same issues.

Following this was Declaration No 14 on the Conference of the Parliaments, in the following terms:

---

[7] See evidence by Douglas Hurd, then UK Foreign Secretary, to HL Select Committee on the European Communities, 28th Report (1992–93*b*) Q 111. See also Observations by the Foreign Secretary and the Home Secretary responding to the Report, Cm 2471 at p 3: 'The Government believe that it is an important feature of the intergovernmental process that national governments of member states should be accountable to national parliaments, not to the European Parliament, on business under these pillars.' See also Cygan (1998) pp 188–90.

The Conference invites the European Parliament and the national parliaments to meet as necessary as a Conference of the Parliaments (or 'Assises').

The Conference of the Parliaments will be consulted on the main features of the European Union, without prejudice to the powers of the European Parliament and the rights of the national parliaments. The President of the European Council and the President of the Commission will report to each session of the Conference of the Parliaments on the state of the Union.

Within the loose framework provided by these Declarations intensification of scrutiny across the board by national parliaments did in fact take place. National parliaments which did not already have a specialist committee dedicated to European affairs established such a committee. The specialist European Affairs Committees had already begun to meet informally but regularly within a Conference known by its French acronym of COSAC, to exchange views at a general level and to exercise pressure for more information to be supplied to them and for a bigger consultative role. The key to effective scrutiny was the supply of proposals and documents in time for informed discussion in the light of evidence as to their implications, and this was found to be particularly difficult in the case of Second and Third Pillar proposals. In the first years, Third Pillar instruments were not published in the Official Journal even after their adoption by the Council far less in draft form.

The UK House of Lords Select Committee on the European Communities embarked at the outset on scrutiny of the intergovernmental pillars as extensive as circumstances permitted. In a Report published on the day after the Maastricht Treaty entered into force they stated that:

It is essential that work under the inter-governmental pillars of the European Union should be supervised by national parliaments. We intend to be vigilant in holding ministers to account in these areas. The key to effective and constructive supervision is to obtain documents in draft.

Documents should be provided to Parliament if they qualify under any one of three tests—significance, eventual need for United Kingdom legislation or imposition of legal commitments on the United Kingdom.[8]

The Committee also maintained that there should be consultation between national parliaments and the European Parliament to ensure that a document available to one was available to all. But there was no need for coordination of subsequent national procedures which depended on individual constitutions and traditions.

---

[8] HL Select Committee on the European Communities, 28th Report (1992–93*b*) paras 65 and 66.

The UK Government fully supported the view that accountability for work under the intergovernmental pillars should be to national parliaments. When it came to practical arrangements however they were more guarded, arguing that the vast majority of Second Pillar documents would usually be non-legislative and short-term and would have to remain confidential until agreed and published for diplomatic and security reasons. Third Pillar documents they would supply, though on a more limited basis than requested by the House of Lords, but they refused to withhold agreement in the Council until Parliament had scrutinized a document.[9] Although the availability of documents remained a recurrent source of friction, the House of Lords began intensive scrutiny at least of the Third Pillar with an enquiry into Europol[10] and followed with many other influential reports. In the House of Commons, Third Pillar documents were at the outset examined by the Home Affairs Select Committee, since they did not fall within the terms of reference of the Select Committee on European Legislation.[11]

Other national parliaments also developed procedures for scrutiny of intergovernmental proposals and instruments. The Netherlands Parliament, in particular, already practised detailed scrutiny of treaties before their ratification by the Government and of decisions of international organizations which where they are binding prevail over Netherlands domestic legislation. Their scrutiny focused on Third Pillar instruments as well as decisions taken within the framework of the Schengen Convention. The Parliament required draft texts to be submitted to them, and approval of the States General had to be obtained before a Netherlands representative could participate in the taking of any binding Schengen Committee or Third Pillar decision. They also discussed Second Pillar policy with the Government on the basis of Council agendas and minutes of Council meetings.[12]

---

[9] Response by the Secretary of State for Foreign and Commonwealth Affairs and the Secretary of State for Home Affairs, Cm 2471.

[10] HL Select Committee on the European Communities, 10th Report (1994–95*a*), discussed in Chapters 6 and 9 above. See Cygan (1998) at pp 178–9 and Chapter 10, especially pp 192–9. For evaluation and suggestions for reform see HL Select Committee on the European Communities, 6th Report (1997–98*b*).

[11] Cygan (1998) pp 119–25. Proposals for change were set out in HC Select Committee on European Legislation, 27th Report (1995–6). See also the same Committee's 24th Report HC Select Committee on European Legislation (1994–95) Norton (1995); Pratt (1999); Carter (2000).

[12] Besselink, Hins, Jans, de Reede, and van der Vlies (1997) pp 125–50; Wessel (1999) pp 230–2; Soetendorp (1999) pp 55–6; Rideau (ed) (1997); evidence from both Chambers of the States-General and from the Netherlands Meijers Committee on Netherlands procedures in HL Select Committee on the European Communities, 6th Report (1997–98*b*) pp 85–6 and 110–12. At pp 74–90 and p 101 of this Report there is evidence from the national parliaments of most of the other Member States on their individual arrangements for scrutiny of the Third Pillar.

Finland, on its accession to the European Union, amended its Constitution so as to include provision for scrutiny by its Parliament of the affairs of the Union and detailed procedures for this purpose. The Grand Committee considers draft acts, agreements and measures within the First and Third Pillars while the Foreign Affairs Committee has competence in regard to the Second Pillar. Ministers are required to submit to Parliament any proposals within their remit and documents relating to them, and it is for the Grand Committee to determine the degree of confidentiality to be accorded to the information they have received. Ministers are constrained from taking a position before completion of Parliamentary scrutiny and there are frequent hearings of Ministers and officials by the Grand Committee, the Foreign Affairs Committee and their specialized committees.[13]

The Reflection Group's Report in 1995 recommended an improved process of prior consultation and transparency, 'the central pivot of which must be respect for the role played by each national parliament in shaping the will of each Member State in regard to Union matters'. They were opposed to adding to institutional structures—for example by setting up a chamber of members of national parliaments—and commented that experience of the Conference of the Parliaments (referred to in Declaration No. 14 set out above) had shown that this was not a practical arrangement. On the other hand they praised the practical results of COSAC and of meetings between specialist committees such as those dealing with Foreign Affairs or Justice and Home Affairs.[14] Such meetings were also strongly recommended by the European Parliament in the 1993 Robles-Piquer Report.[15]

The Treaty of Amsterdam

Under pressure from the UK Government, the legal status of the earlier Declarations was enhanced.[16] A Protocol on the Role of National Parliaments in the European Union was annexed to the Treaty on European Union and to the Treaties establishing the three Communities. The Protocol was designed to encourage greater involvement of national parliaments in the activities of the Union and enhance their ability to express views on matters of particular interest to them. The binding provisions, so far as they relate to the intergovernmental pillars, state

[13] HL Select Committee on the European Communities, 6th Report (1997–98*b*) pp 75–7.
[14] Paras 91–5.   [15] EP Doc A3-0215/93.
[16] The Government made its intentions clear in its White Paper: *A Partnership of Nations*, Cm 3181, para 33, where they stated: 'National parliaments remain the primary focus of democratic legitimacy in the European Union, holding national Ministers in the Council to account. The Government is keen to develop this role and is considering a range of ideas, some of which have been suggested by Parliamentary Committees . . .' The ideas listed were later adopted in the Treaty.

'1. Information for national parliaments of Member States

1. All Commission consultation documents (green and white papers and communications) shall be promptly forwarded to the national parliaments of the Member States.

. . .

3. A six-week period shall elapse between a legislative proposal or a proposal for a measure to be adopted under Title VI of the Treaty on European Union being made available in all languages to the European Parliament and the Council by the Commission and the date when it is placed on a Council agenda for decision either for the adoption of an act . . . subject to exceptions on grounds of urgency, the reasons for which shall be stated in the act . . .

2. The Conference of European Affairs Committees

4. The Conference of European Affairs Committees, hereinafter referred to as COSAC, established in Paris on 16–17 November 1989, may make any contribution it deems appropriate for the attention of the institutions of the European Union, in particular on the basis of draft legal texts which representatives of governments of the Member States may decide by common accord to forward to it, in view of the nature of their subject matter.

5. COSAC may examine any legislative proposal or initiative in relation to the establishment of an area of freedom, security and justice which might have a direct bearing on the rights and freedoms of individuals. The European Parliament, the Council and the Commission shall be informed of any contribution made by COSAC under this point.

6. COSAC may address to the European Parliament, the Council and the Commission any contribution which it deems appropriate on the legislative activities of the Union, notably in relation to the application of the principle of subsidiarity, the area of freedom, security and justice as well as questions regarding fundamental rights.

7. Contributions made by COSAC shall in no way bind national parliaments or prejudice their position.

The principal significance of the Protocol to the Treaty of Amsterdam lay in establishing a direct channel from the Commission to national parliaments as well as a binding requirement to supply Commission proposals. Although on its face the Protocol applies to the intergovernmental pillars, its value in that context is limited by the fact that it covers only Commission documents and proposals and not documents originating from the Presidency or any other Member State, which constitute the majority of working drafts. Availability to national parliaments of

Member State initiatives is therefore still dependent on the goodwill of governments and the readiness of national parliaments and the European Parliament to exchange documents which come into their hands. The Protocol moreover does not cover Commission proposals under the Second Pillar (though there are few of these).[17]

The Code of Conduct

National parliaments were also able to take advantage of information which became publicly available through reliance on the 1993 Code of Conduct concerning public access to Council and Commission documents.[18] The Code contained important exceptions to the basic principle of wide access, including public security and protection of international relations. The Netherlands Government in fact opposed the adoption of the Code on the ground that it could undermine more generous national arrangements regarding supply of documents to national parliaments, and secured a statement in the Council minutes to the effect that the Code would not alter existing practices or obligations of governments towards their national parliaments.[19]

The Treaty of Amsterdam contained new provision in Article 255 on access to documents, as follows:

1. **Any citizen of the Union, and any natural or legal person residing or having its registered office in a Member State, shall have a right of access to European Parliament, Council and Commission documents, subject to the principles and the conditions to be defined in accordance with paragraphs 2 and 3.**
2. **General principles and limits on grounds of public or private interest governing this right of access to documents shall be determined by the Council, acting in accordance with the procedure referred to in Article 251 within two years of the entry into force of the Treaty of Amsterdam.**
3. **Each institution referred to above shall elaborate in its own Rules of Procedure specific provisions regarding access to its documents.'**

A Declaration on this Article however stated that:

The Conference agrees that the principles and conditions referred to in Article 191a [now Article 255] of the Treaty establishing the European Community will allow a Member State to request the Commission or

---

[17] For criticisms of Protocol when in draft, see HL Select Committee on the European Communities, 6th Report (1997–98*b*) at paras 138–45.

[18] OJ L340/41, 31.12.93, with implementing Council Decision at [1993] OJ L340/43.

[19] Wessel (1999) at pp 237–9. For critical appraisal of the Code see Bunyan (1999); HL Select Committee on the European Union, 16th Report (1999–2000*b*).

the Council not to communicate to third parties a document originating from that State without its prior agreement.

This Declaration substantially limited the utility of Article 255 in the context of the Third Pillar, where most proposals for binding instruments emanate from the Presidency or a Member State. The UK Government, along with others committed to transparency in a domestic context, have sought to discourage extensive reliance on it by Member States.

A revised Code on public access to European Union documents was adopted, following prolonged argument, in May 2001 and came into force on 3 December 2001.[20] In the Preamble, the Council made it explicit that the right of access applied also to documents relating to the intergovernmental pillars. Article 13 also provided that 'as far as possible' initiatives presented to the Council by Member States under Article 34 of the TEU as well as common positions adopted under Article 34 would be published in the Official Journal.

A further narrowing of possible access to Second Pillar documents was set out in a Council Decision of 14 August 2001 where defence and military documents having a Top Secret, Secret, or Confidential classification were comprehensively excluded from any access by the public.[21] The decision was justified on the ground of the need for effective cooperation with NATO, but its lawfulness has been challenged before the ECJ by the Netherlands and by the European Parliament.[22]

In the UK itself, parliamentary powers to scrutinize the intergovernmental pillars were substantially enhanced by the establishment by the House of Lords on 6 December 1999 of a European Union Committee as successor to the European Communities Committee. At the same time control by the House of Lords was improved by the adoption of a Resolution which formalized for the Lords the scrutiny reserve precluding a Minister from giving agreement in the Council to Community legislation or to adoption of a binding intergovernmental instrument until parliamentary scrutiny was complete. The reserve had previously been based on a Resolution adopted by the House of Commons in 1980 and applied to the House of Lords on an informal basis. On the following day the European Union Committee appointed six Sub-Committees—adding to the Sub-Committee already engaged in the supervision of the Third Pillar a new Sub-Committee to cover the Common Foreign and Security Policy.[23]

---

[20] OJ L145/43, 31.5.2001.

[21] OJ C239, 23.8.2000. See HL Select Committee on the European Union, 8th Report, (2000–01a).

[22] Case C-369/00 *Netherlands v Council* and Case 387/00 *European Parliament v Council*.

[23] HL Select Committee on the European Union Special Report (1999–2000a).

Prospects for Improved Supervision by National Parliaments

It may be argued that successive amendments to the TEU have at multilateral level opened the way as far as is legally possible to better accountability of the intergovernmental pillars to national parliaments. The key elements which are now in place are early access to proposals, a requirement that the taking of decisions should await completion of a minimum period to permit parliaments to contribute their views and informal exchanges of documents and views among national parliaments. Once these requirements are effectively applied—and this requires constant pressure by national parliaments—the onus falls on the parliaments themselves to make a constructive contribution.

There are in principle three ways in which a national parliament may influence the substantive content of EU policy. The first—which is generally accepted as the most important—is by exercising pressure on the national government. Probably the most successful in exercising power in this way is the Danish Parliament, which binds the Minister in the Council by a formal mandate. The exchanges which lead to the mandate are confidential—enabling the Minister to divulge more about his negotiating position and the pressures he is likely to encounter.[24] The view of the Folketing do not however have any wider influence within the European legislative process. The inflexibility of the mandate is also an argument against extension of the Danish system more generally. The greater the number of Member States negotiating in the Council, the more important it becomes that at least on matters of detail each retains a margin of discretion.

The second method of control is by the initiation of a wide and public debate, followed by the public dissemination of views which are largely based on a synthesis of informed contributions to that debate. This method has been most successfully practised by the House of Lords, although other chambers establishing more recent systems of scrutiny have also published valuable reports. It has been successfully applied to scrutiny of intergovernmental instruments and policies—mainly under the Third Pillar. The influence of House of Lords reports has depended in part on the contribution to their deliberations made by the Community institutions themselves and on a deliberate effort to make sure that their views are brought to the attention of those taking the critical decisions.[25] Wide

[24] Soetendorp (1999) pp 53–5.

[25] See HL Select Committee on the European Communities, 28th Report (1992–93*b*) at paras 56–8; Cygan (1998) at pp 226–7; Dutheil de la Rochère and Jarvis (1997) at pp 424–8; Birkinshaw and Ashiagbor (1996) especially at p 527: 'On occasion, Select Committees can work superbly well. But to do the work thoroughly is time-consuming, onerous and politically unrewarding.'

debate and informed report is appropriate to instruments of major significance—and Third Pillar conventions are a good example of those. It must be admitted, however, that the House of Lords reports could not have had such influence if similar exercises had been conducted by a large number of other national parliaments. There is a limit on the capacity of those directly involved in the legislative process to read and absorb the results of public debate.

The third method of control lies in the power to ratify or to refuse ratification of conventions, which is of major importance in the context of the Third Pillar. One powerful argument for more transparent and considered debate on conventions before they are adopted is that a national parliament which has carefully considered and endorsed the underlying policy while a convention was still in draft form ought then—unless its expressed wishes have been flouted—to complete the ratification process promptly. There is evidence that such a link does exist. The early years of Third Pillar activity—when instruments were still negotiated in secrecy— were characterized by the adoption of a number of important conventions which lay unratified for years.[26] It was also noticeable that the UK, where the House of Lords had held an intensive enquiry into the draft Europol Convention, was the first Member State to ratify the Convention.[27] If national parliaments are unable to complete ratification procedures in a more timely manner—and the fault may lie with governments where implementing domestic legislation is first required—the result is likely to be an increase in the use of framework directives by the Council. Thus, for example, the Extradition Conventions of 1995 and 1996, which have failed to secure the ratification by all Member States necessary for their entry into force, will be superseded by the Framework Decision on a European arrest warrant described in Chapter 7 above.

Improvements in democratic accountability, however, continue to pre-occupy the leaders of Europe. In Declaration 23 on the Future of the Union attached to the Treaty of Nice, the Conference agreed, with somewhat misplaced optimism, that they had opened the way for enlargement of the EU and that ratification of the Treaty would complete the institutional changes necessary for this. The Declaration then envisaged a further 'deeper and wider debate about the future of the European Union', and included among the items to be debated:

The Role of National Parliaments in the European Architecture

[26] In a written answer to a question from the European Parliament in April 1997, the Council listed five Third Pillar Conventions and four related Protocols—each of which required fifteen ratifications for its entry into force. Three of the Conventions and one Protocol then had only one ratification each while there were no ratifications at all of the others: OJ C217/77, 17.7.97.

[27] The Convention was adopted on 26 July 1995 and the UK ratified on 10 December 1996.

The purpose of the debate was 'to improve and to monitor the democratic legitimacy and transparency of the Union and its institutions, in order to bring them closer to the citizens of the Member States'.[28]

There has been a resurgence in recent years of proposals for a second parliamentary chamber within the EU, whose members would be mandated by the national parliaments of the Member States and perhaps also by regional assemblies. A range of functions have been proposed for this second chamber, including oversight of the Common Foreign and Security Policy (CFSP). The HL Select Committee on the European Union reported on the various proposals in 2001 and concluded that they did not provide a practical answer to the real difficulties of scrutiny.[29]

Rather than embarking on a grand debate about restructuring the European architecture, national parliaments should in the immediate future concentrate on the ratification of important conventions and instruments—for example on extradition and mutual assistance in criminal matters—which are useless until they have been ratified and effectively implemented in national laws.[30] They should also ensure that the promises in the Treaty of Amsterdam about transparency and a proper period for scrutiny by national parliaments are kept and that they themselves take full advantage of the opportunities now open to them.[31] To treat the architecture of Europe as a perpetual building site is not conducive to effective democratic scrutiny of the practical policies and instruments being developed under intergovernmental procedures.

The Role of the European Parliament

Under the Maastricht Treaty, the European Parliament was assigned a very limited role in the Second and Third Pillars. Although the drafting of Article J.7 and Article K.6 was not identical the substance was the same. The European Parliament was entitled:

1. to be consulted by the Presidency. Consultation was however limited to 'the main aspects and the basic choices of the common foreign and security policy' and to 'the principal aspects of activities in the areas

---

[28] For sceptical comment on Declaration 23 see editorial comments: Preparing for 2004, The Post-Nice process, in [2001] CML Rev 493–7.

[29] HL Select Committee on the European Union, 7th Report (2001–02*b*).

[30] The Justice and Home Affairs Council on 20 September 2001, a few days after the terrorist attacks in the US, called on Member States to step up ratification of these Conventions and of the 1999 UN Convention for the Suppression of the Financing of Terrorism.

[31] cf Finland Prime Minister Paavo Lipponen in Jean Monnet Lecture, Florence, 12 April 2001. He suggested that creating new layers in the institutional structure of the Union might not be the best solution for increasing democracy. Instead each Member State should improve its own system for providing information and involve its national parliament more closely in policy-making.

referred to in [the Third Pillar]'. The implication was that the Parliament need not be consulted on specific proposals for action or for decision. The Presidency had to ensure that the views of the Parliament were 'duly taken into consideration';

2. to be kept regularly informed by the Presidency and the Commission;
3. to ask questions of the Council or make recommendations to it;
4. to hold an annual debate on progress in each Pillar.

It was therefore unsurprising that the European Parliament took a poor view of the effectiveness of the Second and Third Pillars and pressed, during the preparation of the 1996 Intergovernmental Conference, for their integration into the First Pillar. The Parliament's Report on the functioning of the Treaty argued for 'a more effective EU foreign policy within the framework of the Community pillar, integrating the common commercial policy, development cooperation policy, humanitarian aid and CFSP matters' as well as better defined security and defence policies within the EU framework. Justice and home affairs policies should no longer be artificially distinguished from closely-related policies within the Community domain. The Report accepted that accountability for matters outside the Community Pillar was shared between national parliaments and the European Parliament.[32]

There was little support even within the Reflection Group for such radical proposals. The Report of the Reflection Group concluded that the role of the European Parliament in the Second Pillar could not be the same as in Community legislation 'since national parliaments do not use the same mechanisms of participation in framing and monitoring foreign policy as in their legislative work or in domestic control'. As regards the Third Pillar there was more sympathy for the Parliament's suggestions, though this was based more on appraisal of the limited results of the early years of intergovernmental cooperation on asylum and immigration.[33]

The Treaty of Amsterdam left unchanged the powers of the European Parliament under the Second Pillar. Within the Third Pillar, however, new provision was added requiring the Council to consult the Parliament in a more meaningful way. Article 39 now provides:

1. The Council shall consult the European Parliament before adopting any measure referred to in Article 34(2)(b), (c) and (d). The European Parliament shall deliver its opinion within a time limit which the

---

[32] Bourlanges-Martin Report: European Parliament (1995*b*) paras 3 and 4. See also EP Resolution on the CFSP OJ C21, 25.1.1993 and EP working document on the Common Foreign and Security Policy, 16. January 1996, DOC_EN\DT\287\287673. For an account of the European Parliament's powers before the Treaty of Maastricht see Bieber (1990).

[33] Report SN 520/95 (REFLEX 21) paras 45–55, 163–4.

Council may lay down, which shall not be less than three months. In the absence of an opinion within that time limit, the Council may act.

The institutional implications of this new right to formal consultations are described in the Commentary on Article 39 in Chapter 7 above. The introduction of formal consultation provisions—even with a built-in time limit—recognizes the legislative character of those binding instruments which the Council may adopt under Third Pillar procedures.

The European Parliament have not been discouraged by the limited powers given to them under the TEU from making wide-ranging and constructive reports. These have ranged from the future relationship between the EU, WEU, and NATO, the strengthening of the Conference on Security and Cooperation in Europe (where they regretted their exclusion from the CSCE Parliamentary Assembly), conflict prevention in Europe and the role of the proposed Stability Pact, neutrality in the context of enlargement to more detailed proposals on landmines and blinding laser weapons. Looking at some of these reports and resolutions from the European Parliament in the early years of operation of the intergovernmental pillars, it is striking how many of the views and recommendations of the Parliament on specific matters of policy have been followed (though of course not necessarily as a direct consequence).[34] This contrasts sharply with their recommendations on reforming the institutional architecture of the EU, which seem to have had no effect.

Disappointment has generally been expressed by the Parliament with the results of the CFSP and with their own role in forming it. This has been because they have had unrealistic expectations of the speed at which major changes can take place and also because—even where their recommendations were in fact followed—the Council did not acknowledge this.[35] More recently, however, the October 2001 European Parliament resolution on the progress achieved in the implementation of the common foreign and security policy adopts a more positive and constructive attitude to achievements of Union policy as well as to initiatives in progress. In the operative part of the resolution the European Parliament:

1. Recognises, now that the CFSP bodies and tools have finally been put in place in accordance with the Treaty of Amsterdam, that the EU is, for the first time, trying to give effectively expression to the political will to develop a distinctive foreign policy profile and the ability to act on its own initiative in crisis situations;
2. Acknowledges that, as the crises have intensified in the western Balkans and the Middle East, the EU has assumed a diplomatic mediation role with the aim of linking short-term operational crisis management measures to long-term prospects;

---

[34] For description of EP action in relation to the Gulf War and Yugoslavia, see Viola (2000).
[35] For an example, see European Parliament (1996). On the Third Pillar see Monar (1994) at p 78: '. . . until now the Member States have never made any reference whatsoever to the resolutions of the European Parliament in their declarations and decisions on JHA'.

3. Applauds the personal commitment of Javier Solana, High Representative for CFSP and of Chris Patten, Commissioner for External Relations, to the reform of the EU's external relations now under way and, although the pillar structure is still in place, their joint efforts to provide consistency and coherence in European foreign and security policy; continues nevertheless to support its goal of consolidating the office of high representative within the Commission by requiring the High Representative to be accountable to both the Council and the European Parliament;

The resolution makes a number of procedural proposals—for example the establishment of a standing delegation from the Parliament's Committee on Foreign Affairs, Human Rights, Common Security and Defence Policy to handle relations with the NATO Parliamentary Assembly, and joint meetings with the foreign affairs and defence committees of national parliaments. There are also, of course, many recommendations on foreign policy issues ranging from Afghanistan, the Middle East peace process, priorities in conflict prevention to dialogue with Russia, and these are well informed and realistic.

The Committee on Civil Liberties and Internal Affairs[36] as early as 1996 declared that it was encouraged by the Council's increasing practice of consulting it on draft conventions. Its criticisms at that time of the working of the Third Pillar were made on grounds which were more generally shared.[37] Consultation of the Parliament became more regular following the political agreement in June 1997 on the draft Treaty of Amsterdam and even before the new provisions on formal consultation had entered into force.[38]

It is too early to assess the impact of the new right of the European Parliament to be consulted on draft Third Pillar decisions and conventions. Study of the Parliament's activities in September 2001 shows, however, that it has already contributed its views on a number of draft instruments—for example on the draft Council framework decision on the execution in the European Union of orders freezing assets or evidence.

Conclusion

There are many welcome signs that both national parliaments and the European Parliament are making increasing use of the possibilities for constructive dialogue with Member States in the Council on Second and Third Pillar policies. National parliaments are more actively engaged in

[36] Now the Committee on Citizens' Freedoms and Rights, Justice and Home Affairs.
[37] EP Working Document with a view to the annual debate on justice and home affairs, 16 October 1996, DOC_EN\DT\305\305711.
[38] See EP Working Paper on The Impact of the Amsterdam Treaty on Justice and Home Affairs, LIBE 110 EN, 2000, Vol I pp 119–25.

making contributions on specific issues and insisting on their treaty rights of timely access to documents. It is, however, disappointing that they seem unable to discharge in a more energetic fashion their responsibility to take timely decisions on the ratification of conventions drawn up within the Third Pillar, since this is their main source of real power in intergovernmental negotiations. The European Parliament is moving on from its preoccupation with dismantling the intergovernmental pillars and is instead producing well-informed and narrowly focused reports on complex issues of foreign policy and criminal justice. Networks of interchange between all the parliaments, particularly on methods of scrutiny and on access to documents and information have been set up and operate with increasing effectiveness. Both national parliaments and the European Parliament are exploiting their respective strengths to greater effect.

There is no prospect that national governments will accept a democratic veto over action in the areas within the Second and Third Pillars—except for long-term legislation such as international conventions. But the more realistic and detailed contributions now emerging both from national parliaments and from the European Parliament have more influence than may appear from the Treaty provisions or from the texts adopted by the Council.

11

Security and Defence Policy

The Nervous Approach to Security and Defence

The right to self-defence against armed attack is of course a fundamental attribute of a sovereign State. This has not however precluded States from entering into defensive alliances or collective security arrangements with other States. It has never been suggested that the delegation to the UN of basic powers over peace and security threatened the sovereign status of its Members. Article 2 of the Charter in setting out the Principles of the United Nations begins by asserting that: 'The Organization is based on the principle of the sovereign equality of all its Members.'

The European Community, however, was for the first thirty years of its existence rigorously excluded from any action or even discussion of defence questions. The old Article 223 ringfenced the powers of a Member State to resist disclosure of information which it considered contrary to the essential interests of its security, and to protect essential security interests 'which are connected with the production of or trade in arms, munitions and war material'. The old Article 224—a provision debated more often than it was invoked—provided that:

Member States shall consult each other with a view to taking together the steps needed to prevent the functioning of the common market being affected by measures which a Member State may be called upon to take in the event of serious internal disturbances affecting the maintenance of law and order, in the event of war, serious international tension constituting a threat of war, or in order to carry out obligations it has accepted for the purpose of maintaining peace and international security.[1]

This provision made it quite clear that powers to maintain peace and international security were entirely reserved to the Member States. In the exercise of these powers they were not constrained by any direct legal obligation to safeguard the common market—their only legal obligation was the weak requirement to consult.

Overwhelmingly the most important reason for excluding the Community from any competence in the field of security and defence was

---

[1] See Stefanou and Xanthaki (1997). For a historical account of the evolution of European defence policy see Hottiaux and Liponska-Laberou (2000).

the acceptance that the responsibility for the collective defence of Europe lay with NATO. The NATO Handbook begins

The North Atlantic Treaty is the political framework for an international alliance designed to prevent aggression or to repel it. It provides for continuous co-operation and consultation in political, economic and military fields. It is of indefinite duration.[2]

The North Atlantic Treaty

The North Atlantic Treaty, signed in Washington in 1949[3] established an alliance for collective self-defence within the framework of the UN Charter. In 1993, the NATO Member States included eleven of the twelve original European Union, Member States as well as three other European States—Iceland, Norway, and Turkey—and the US and Canada. The core obligations are set out in Articles 3 to 7, in particular Article 5 which begins:

The Parties agree that an armed attack against one or more of them in Europe or North America shall be considered an attack against them all, and consequently they agree that, if such an armed attack occurs, each of them, in exercise of the right of individual or collective self-defence recognised by Article 51 of the Charter of the United Nations, will assist the Party or Parties so attacked by taking forthwith, individually, and in concert with the other Parties, such action as it deems necessary, including the use of armed force, to restore and maintain the security of the North Atlantic area.

Article 5 was formally invoked for the first time by the NATO Alliance in response to the terrorist attacks of 11 September 2001 against the US.[4]

The North Atlantic Treaty Organisation, NATO, is the international organization established to provide the structures for political and military cooperation for the purposes of the North Atlantic Treaty. NATO's policy, formed during the Cold War years, was based on the principle that its Members must maintain adequate defence to deter aggression and, should this deterrence fail, to preserve their territorial integrity and restore peace.[5] Complementary to this were undertakings to settle international disputes by peaceful means and a policy of searching for progress towards a stable East–West relationship. The principal organ of NATO is the North Atlantic Council which may meet at the level of Foreign Ministers or of Permanent Representatives of ambassador rank. At Summit meetings, Member States are represented by Heads of State or

---

[2] NATO (1989).   [3] 34 UNTS 243, 1949 AJIL Supp 159.
   [4] Statement to the Press by NATO Secretary-General, 4 October 2001; NATO Press Release (2001) 138, on http://www.nato.int/docu.
   [5] NATO (1989) p 22.

Government.[6] Below the North Atlantic Council is an extensive structure of Committees and planning groups.

Each Member of NATO is responsible for maintaining and equipping its military forces. Within NATO, however, there is extensive cooperation and coordination on arms and military equipment, with the object of improving the defensive strength of the Alliance and avoiding duplication in such matters as research, production, and procurement of weapons and systems. NATO Members assign some of their forces to come under the operational command or control of a NATO Commander when required, and other forces may be earmarked for assignment to NATO at a later date. Alyson Bailes described the position thus: 'The Alliance's most characteristic achievements are the exchange of absolute mutual defence guarantees and the creation of an unparalleled multinational, integrated military structure.'[7]

When the Cold War came to an end, NATO embarked on a process of enlarging its objectives. It aspired to contribute to building structures for a more united Europe and to enhance the political component of the Alliance. The Conference for Security and Cooperation in Europe (CSCE), which derived from the first efforts to construct links across the Iron Curtain,[8] was to contribute to the development of common European security structures. CSCE was later established more formally as the Organization for Security and Cooperation in Europe (OSCE)). In January 1994, the NATO Summit launched a Partnership for Peace Programme, with a framework document, a Declaration and an invitation to former members of the Warsaw Pact to participate. Each partner—and by 1995 there were twenty-five—was invited to draw up with NATO a programme appropriate to its capabilities. These programmes might include joint exercises in peacekeeping or humanitarian operations, and in some cases they were to lead to some of the States which had only recently returned to democracy—Poland, the Czech Republic, and Hungary—becoming Members of NATO.[9]

The Individual Partnership Programme for Ukraine, for example, formally agreed in 1995, set out general principles for NATO–Ukraine relations. This was elaborated in 1997 by a Charter for a Distinctive Partnership between NATO and Ukraine and by a number of specific agreements, understandings, and military collaboration arrangements.

---

[6] See the list at the summit in Brussels in June 2001, which now includes the leaders of the Czech Republic, Hungary, and Poland, The Times 14 June 2001.

[7] Bailes (1996) at p 28.

[8] From the Helsinki Final Act, 1975, Cmnd 6198 and the Charter of Paris for a New Europe 1990, Cm 1464. See Article 11.1 of the TEU as amended by the Treaty of Amsterdam.

[9] Hansard HC Debs 12 January 1994, cols 177–80. The Declaration is in *NATO Review*, February 1994. See Light, Lowenhardt, and White (2000); Weller (1998) at pp 70–8.

Ukraine contributed to the NATO-led Implementation Force (IFOR) in Bosnia set up after the Dayton Agreement and later to the Stabilisation Force (SFOR) which replaced it. It was a contributor also to the Kosovo Force (KFOR).[10]

Western European Union

Western European Union (WEU), like NATO, is based on a treaty commitment to collective self-defence within the framework of UN obligations. Article IV of the Treaty of Economic, Social and Cultural Collaboration and Collective Self-Defence[11] signed at Brussels in 1948 provided that

If any of the High Contracting Parties should be the object of an armed attack in Europe, the other High Contracting Parties will, in accordance with the provisions of Article 51 of the Charter of the United Nations, afford the Party so attacked all the military and other aid and assistance in their power.

When it proved impossible to reach agreement on the creation of a European Defence Council, the Brussels Treaty was amended in 1954 by the conclusion of Protocols[12] which opened the way to entry by the Federal Republic of Germany and by Italy and laid down obligations on armed forces and on the manufacture and control of armaments. The security guarantee was modified so that Contracting Parties were required to 'afford assistance to each other in resisting any policy of aggression . . .'. The organization was renamed the Western European Union (WEU) and the 1954 Protocols defined its relationship to NATO. Spain and Portugal became members of WEU in 1989 and Greece in 1995. The remaining five Member States of the EU—Denmark, Ireland, Sweden, Finland, and Austria—are observers in WEU. In addition WEU has three associate members who are not EU Members, Turkey, Norway, and Iceland.

WEU has seen itself as 'a bridge between the process of European Integration and the Atlantic Alliance.'[13] It is a European organization based on a mutual defence commitment, with no geographical restrictions on its competence and committed to cooperation with NATO. For many years it lay largely dormant, but during the 1980s it began to extend its activities, particularly in the field of arms control. As the process of negotiation of the Maastricht Treaty and forming the Common Foreign and Security Policy gained momentum, WEU began to adapt its practices and

[10] NATO Handbook, 2001 version, at www.nato.int/docu/handbook/2001.
[11] UKTS No 1 (1949) Cmd 7599.
[12] UKTS No 39 (1955); William Wallace and Helen Wallace (2000) pp 463–4.
[13] Extraordinary meeting of the WEU Council of Ministers, 22 February 1991, Presidency conclusions para 10; Wallace and Wallace (2000) p 472. A less kind metaphor is offered by Lenzi when he refers to a 'spaghetti junction of institutions': Lenzi (1998) at p 107.

policies to open the way to practical collaboration with the emerging EU. Such moves, however raised the obvious problem of the position of those States which were members of the EU, or of NATO, but were not also members of WEU. They were also open to legal question in that the new functions could not even on a generous construction be brought within the constituent Treaties.

The Treaties Break the Taboo

The first tentative mention of European security in the Community Treaties was Article 30, paragraph 6 of the Single European Act, in which the Member States—in carefully non-committal language—stated their readiness to coordinate more closely on the political and economic aspects of security. With a rather firmer voice they declared their determination to maintain the technological and industrial conditions necessary for their security. But in a clear indication that reality lay elsewhere, they made clear that: 'Nothing in this Title shall impede closer cooperation in the field of security between certain of the High Contracting Parties within the framework of the Western European Union or the Atlantic Alliance.'

Article J.4 of the Maastricht Treaty provided that 'the common foreign and security policy shall include all questions related to the security of the Union, including the eventual framing of a common defence policy, which might in time lead to a common defence'. The Union 'requested' WEU, declared to be 'an integral part of the development of the Union' to elaborate and implement decisions and actions of the Union with defence implications. Article J.4, however, expressly safeguarded 'the specific character of the security and defence policy of certain Member States' (a veiled reference to the neutrals) and also the obligations of other Member States under the North Atlantic Treaty. Closer cooperation was permitted within the framework of the WEU or of NATO. In a Declaration attached to the Treaty, the nine Member States who were then also members of WEU, elaborated on how

WEU will be developed as the defence component of the European Union and as the means to strengthen the European pillar of the Atlantic Alliance. To this end it will formulate common European defence policy and carry forward its concrete implementation through the further development of its own operational role.

The Declaration also made clear that WEU would develop close working links both with the EU and with NATO. WEU's operational role would be built up in such matters as logistics, transport, training, and surveillance and the WEU Council and Secretariat would be transferred to Brussels.

In another Declaration the ten Member States, also members of WEU, invited the other Member States to accede to, or become observers in WEU and invited other European Members of NATO to become associate members of WEU. Greece did become a full Member of WEU in 1995 and Denmark and Ireland became observers. The other European Members of NATO—Turkey, Norway, and Iceland—became associate members.[14]

Changes in the Purpose of Security and Defence Policy

By the time the Maastricht Treaty entered into force the Cold War was over and it was clear that international stability was threatened no longer by the prospect of a Soviet armed attack but instead by a proliferation of conflicts and disintegration of States. There was a general recognition, particularly in the light of events in Yugoslavia, that military forces were required to fulfil quite different tasks. Many called for a gradual fusion of the European Union and WEU, with Denmark and Ireland as well as Greece becoming full members of WEU.[15]

In June 1992 the Foreign and Defence Ministers of the WEU Members drew up at Petersberg a Declaration under which they would create a military force capable of being used at the request of the CSCE or of the UN Security Council. The Declaration stated that WEU forces could be used for humanitarian and rescue tasks, peacekeeping tasks and for tasks of combat forces in crisis management, including peacemaking.[16] These were to become known as the 'Petersberg tasks'. WEU already had some practical experience of carrying out these tasks during the Kuwait conflict. Following the Petersberg meeting a WEU military planning cell was established, Chiefs of Defence Staff began to meet regularly, and national governments placed certain military units at the disposal of WEU, including the Franco-German Corps which became Eurocorps, and the Anglo-Dutch Amphibious Force. A WEU naval task force monitored the enforcement of UN sanctions against Serbia. NATO had also undertaken to perform similar tasks, and a NATO task force was also engaged in this task—monitoring different zones.[17] WEU contributed to the police component of the EU Administration of Mostar set up in 1994.[18]

NATO for its part expressed full support for these developments and at its Brussels Summit meeting in January 1994 had stated that 'the emer-

---

[14] On the background to these provisions, see Wyn Rees (1996).

[15] The Committee on Institutional Affairs of the European Parliament, for example, drew up precise plans for gradual integration in a Report on the future relations between the European Community, WEU and the Atlantic Alliance, PE 202.482.

[16] The text of the Declaration is in Europe Documents No. 1787. For a helpful clarification of the terminology of security tasks such as 'peace enforcement', 'peace-building', 'peace-making', and 'peace-keeping' see Wouters and Naert (2001).

[17] House of Commons Research Paper No 93/27, The Maastricht Debate: The Common Foreign and Security Policy, March 1993; Kintis (1998).

[18] Described in Chapter 4 above.

gence of a European Security and Defence Identity will strengthen the European pillar of the Alliance while reinforcing the transatlantic link and will enable European Allies to take greater responsibility for their common security and defence'. At the same time NATO also offered to lend its assets for the purposes of WEU operations and to consider Combined Joint Task Forces.[19]

The Neutral Member States

These uncertainties as to the purpose of European security and defence and institutional complexities were compounded by the fact that by the time review of the Maastricht Treaty began in 1996 there were as a result of enlargement of the Union four Member States committed to a policy of neutrality. The historical and legal reasons for neutrality differed as between Ireland, Austria, Finland, and Sweden, and in each of these cases there would now be no legal or external political obstacle to the State itself modifying its policy.

In classical international law a neutral State was one which did not participate in a war being fought by other States. Precise duties were laid on neutral States and duties were also laid on belligerent States regarding their conduct towards neutral States and their nationals. Because of the provisions of the UN Charter it is now very rare for war to be formally declared, and the rules on neutrality have had to be adapted for armed conflicts which would colloquially be described as wars but have not been characterized as such by the participating States.[20]

Distinct from neutrality in a particular conflict was the status of being permanently neutralized. Where a State was permanently neutralized there was a collective agreement by States generally that the independence and political and territorial integrity of the neutralized State would be guaranteed subject to two conditions. The first was that the neutralized State would not take up arms against another State except in self-defence. The second was that it would not enter into treaties of alliance or other obligations (such as accepting military bases on its territory) which might compromise its impartiality or lead it into war. The first of these obligations now binds all Member States of the UN, so that only the second remains peculiar to States committed to a policy of neutrality.[21]

---

[19] Declaration of the Heads of State and Government, paras 4, 6, and 9, published in *NATO Review*, February 1994. See Holbrooke (1995); Kintis (1998) at pp 546–8; Lenzi (1998).

[20] Neff (2000).

[21] Oppenheim (1996) pp 319–23; Subedi (1993) especially pp 241–5.

Ireland

Irish neutrality had its origins in the ambition of Irish Republicans to establish Ireland as a neutralized independent State under international guarantees. This was seen as a visible sign of full sovereignty and independence from the quarrels of the European powers and in particular Britain. Neutrality was not included in the 1921 Treaty nor in the Constitution of Ireland but became a national policy during the 1930s. During the 1939–45 War Ireland pursued a policy of 'benevolent neutrality' towards the Allies. Ireland's initial application for UN membership was vetoed by the Soviet Union ostensibly on grounds of her wartime neutrality and she did not become a member until 1955. An informal invitation to Ireland to join NATO was rejected on the ground that participation along with the UK might imply acknowledgment of Britain's sovereignty over part of Ireland.[22]

Ireland has, however, often contributed forces to UN peacekeeping operations and has been willing (with the possible exception of the 1982 measures against Argentina following its invasion of the Falkland Islands) to implement sanctions imposed by the European Community or the Union. It has never joined NATO and is an observer only within WEU. Its neutrality has been of a flexible and idiosyncratic character, but its persistence was shown when it became a factor in the June 2001 Referendum vote against the Treaty of Nice.

Austria

Austria's neutral status was established by the State Treaty signed in 1955[23] for the Re-establishment of an Independent and Democratic Austria. Under its terms the Four Powers guaranteed the independence and territorial integrity of Austria, prohibited any political or economic union with Germany and imposed restrictions on Austria's military capacity. Following the State Treaty Austria enacted a Constitutional Law in fulfilment of a prior bilateral agreement with the Soviet Union, under which it declared that it would never accede to any military alliance or permit establishment of foreign military bases on its territory. This Law was notified to all States with which Austria had diplomatic relations, and those States either expressly or by acquiescence recognized Austria's neutrality. Austria became a Member of the UN without special provision but sometimes reserved its neutral status in the context of Security Council sanctions.[24]

[22] Salmon (1982).   [23] UKTS No 58 (1957).   [24] Kunz (1956).

In the context of Austria's accession to the EU its neutral status was carefully considered and the view was taken that it posed no impediment to fulfilment of EU obligations relating in particular to sanctions. Austria has never joined NATO and is an observer only within WEU.

Finland

Finland's neutrality was to some extent based on its 1948 Treaty of Friendship, Cooperation and Mutual Assistance with the Soviet Union, where Finland declared its desire to remain 'outside the conflicting interests of the Great Powers'. This Treaty was terminated in 1991, leaving Finland's policy unequivocally a matter of political choice.[25] Finland has not joined NATO and is an observer within WEU.

Sweden

Sweden's neutrality evolved during the nineteenth century in response to the loss of major power status following the War of the Swedish Succession. Sweden remained neutral during the Second World War but was admitted to the United Nations on its first application in 1946. It has used its neutral status for political bridge building and mediation and protected the interests of many other States following a breach of diplomatic relations. Sweden was non-aligned during the Cold War, and with its ending the policy has been closely re-examined. Like the other three States discussed above it is not a member of NATO and is an observer within WEU.[26]

Denmark

Denmark is in no sense neutral. It is a Member State of NATO, but has always been reluctant to accept that European Community and later the Union should become involved in defence. This reluctance was one factor in the initial rejection by the Danish people of the Maastricht Treaty.[27] The Decision negotiated by the European Council in Edinburgh in December 1992, which opened the way to a second successful referendum in Denmark, provided that

Nothing in the Treaty on European Union commits Denmark to become a member of the WEU. Accordingly, Denmark does not participate in the elaboration and the

---

[25] Subedi (1993) at pp 247–8.
[26] Subedi (1993) at pp 246–7. For a comprehensive account of the policies of Finland and Sweden see Ojanen, Herolf, and Lindahl (2000).
[27] See Chapter 2 above.

implementation of decisions and actions of the Union which have defence implications, but will not prevent the development of closer cooperation between
Member States in this area.[28]

Since 1992, however, Denmark has become an Observer within the WEU
and in the context of the fighting in Bosnia undertook some active involvement in military aspects of crisis management.

The reservations of the four neutrals and of Denmark explain in part
why the first steps taken by the EU towards a defence policy were carried
out through WEU. At first sight the building up of WEU institutional and
military capacities appeared redundant, but it helped to enable the
European States to acquire some sort of experience of collaboration on
defence matters without cutting across the primacy of NATO or the need
for open consultation among all Members within the North Atlantic
Council, and without directly raising for the neutrals the question of the
EU's competence in defence. What was sought during the early 1990s was
a relationship which avoided duplication of NATO but enabled Europe to
build a capacity for complementary tasks—in particular the Petersberg
tasks.

The position was explained by the Reflection Group in its 1995 Report
in the following way:

Apart from the classic collective defence of territorial integrity, the cooperation on
security and defence matters which the new challenges require is also directed at
preventing conflicts and managing regional crises. While both types of task may
become intertwined in practice, it must also be pointed out that, as we shall see
below, some Member States of the Union, which are not members of military
alliances, wish to contribute to European security by participating in humanitarian, peacekeeping and other crisis management operations (the so-called
Petersberg tasks) but without entering into collective defence commitments such
as those defined in Art. 5 of the Brussels and Washington Treaties. These two facts
will have to be taken into account when considering future arrangements for
European security and defence cooperation.[29]

At the 1996 Intergovernmental Conference there remained deep divisions among the Member States as to the best way forward on defence.
Although some argued for a merger of WEU and the EU, a majority were
against—the four neutrals and Denmark were supported on this by
Luxembourg, Portugal, and the UK.[30]

---

[28] Bull EC 12-1992, 1.2, 1.3 and 1.37. When defence is discussed in the Council during the
Danish Presidency, Denmark cedes the chair to Greece.

[29] SN 520/95 (REFLEX 21) para 168.

[30] Nicoll and Salmon (2000) p 366. For analysis of individual approaches at this period, in
particular France, Germany, Italy, the Netherlands and the UK, see Howorth and Menon
(1997).

The Treaty of Amsterdam

ARTICLE 17 (EX ARTICLE J.7)

1. The common foreign and security policy shall include all questions relating to the security of the Union, including the progressive framing of a common defence policy, in accordance with the second subparagraph, which might lead to a common defence, should the European Council so decide. It shall in that case recommend to the Member States the adoption of such a decision in accordance with their respective constitutional requirements.

The Western European Union (WEU) is an integral part of the development of the Union providing the Union with access to an operational capability notably in the context of paragraph 2. It supports the Union in framing the defence aspects of the common foreign and security policy as set out in this Article. The Union shall accordingly foster closer institutional relations with the WEU with a view to the possibility of the integration of the WEU into the Union, should the European Council so decide. It shall in that case recommend to the Member States the adoption of such a decision in accordance with their respective constitutional requirements.

The policy of the Union in accordance with this Article shall not prejudice the specific character of the security and defence policy of certain Member States and shall respect the obligations of certain Member States, which see their common defence realised in the North Atlantic Treaty Organisation (NATO) under the North Atlantic Treaty and be compatible with the common security and defence policy established within that framework.

The progressive framing of a common defence policy will be supported, as Member States consider appropriate, by cooperation between them in the field of armaments.

2. Questions referred to in this Article shall include humanitarian and rescue tasks, peacekeeping tasks and tasks of combat forces in crisis management, including peacemaking.

3. The Union will avail itself of the WEU to elaborate and implement decisions and actions of the Union which have defence implications.

The competence of the WEU to establish guidelines in accordance with Article 13 shall also obtain in respect of the WEU for those matters for which the Union avails itself of the WEU.

When the Union avails itself of the WEU to elaborate and implement decisions of the Union on the tasks referred to in paragraph 2 all

Member States of the Union shall be entitled to participate fully in the tasks in question. The Council, in agreement with the institutions of the WEU, shall adopt the necessary practical arrangements to allow all Member States contributing to the tasks in question to participate fully and on an equal footing in planning and decision-taking in the WEU.

Decisions having defence implications dealt with under this paragraph shall be taken without prejudice to the policies and obligations referred to in paragraph 1, third subparagraph.

4. The provisions of this Article shall not prevent the development of closer cooperation between two or more Member States on a bilateral level, in the framework of the WEU and the Atlantic Alliance provided such cooperation does not run counter to or impede that provided for in this Title.

5. With a view to furthering the objectives of this Article, the provisions of this Article will be reviewed in accordance with Article 48.

Article 17 makes the following changes from Article J.4 of the Maastricht Treaty:

1. Instead of 'the eventual framing of a common defence policy, which might in time lead to a common defence' there is a specific commitment to 'progressive framing of a common defence policy' and a specific mechanism for establishing a 'common defence'. The mechanism is a European Council Decision, taken of course by unanimity and requiring ratification by national parliaments under their constitutional requirements.

2. There are to be closer institutional relations with WEU, but full integration of WEU into the European Union would again require a European Council Decision followed by national ratifications. Meanwhile WEU supports the Union in framing the common defence policy.

3. The Petersberg tasks are expressly brought within the competence of the EU.

4. When the Union uses WEU to implement defence aspects of the Petersberg tasks, all EU Member States (including the neutral non-members of WEU) are entitled to take part in the planning, the decision taking and the action.

5. There is in paragraph 1 presentational strengthening of the deference to NATO. Article 17 contains no collective commitment to defence of the territory of the Member States such as forms the foundation of the North Atlantic Alliance and of WEU. Taken as a whole the Article makes clear that for the foreseeable future the EU's defence role will be directed towards the Petersberg tasks, which relate essentially to underpinning the Common Foreign and Security Policy (CFSP).

6. There is a reference to cooperation between Member States in the field of armaments, but it is tentative and non-binding, probably due to the need to avoid trespass into NATO competences.

Declarations on Western European Union

Attached to the Treaty of Amsterdam were two relevant Declarations. In the first the Conference invited the Council to put in hand security clearance for Council Secretariat personnel—an apparently technical matter which foreshadowed the way in which before long uniformed officers would be seen in the Council corridors as defence policy moved from language into reality.

In the second Declaration the Conference noted a parallel Declaration by the WEU Council. This pointed out that:

Today the WEU Council brings together all the Member States of the European Union and all the European Members of the Atlantic Alliance in accordance with their respective status. The Council also brings together those States with the Central and East European States linked to the European Union by an Association Agreement and that are applicants for accession to both the European Union and the Atlantic Alliance. WEU is thus establishing itself as a genuine framework for dialogue and cooperation among Europeans on wider European security and defence issues.

A Protocol spelt out the practical details of participation by WEU Observer States in planning and decision taking and of cooperation between WEU and the European Union. It also dealt with relations between WEU and NATO in the framework of development of the European Security and Defence Identity (ESDI) within the Alliance. In this context WEU undertook to perform its role to the full, 'respecting the full transparency and complementarity between the two Organisations'. ESDI was to be grounded on sound military principles and 'permit the creation of militarily coherent and effective forces capable of operating under the political control and strategic direction of WEU'. This aspiration was translated into specific commitments in the fields of principles for the use of armed force, defence planning, and intelligence.[31]

Ships and Men

Even before the Treaty of Amsterdam was in force there were signs that the progressive framing of a common defence policy in the framework of the Common Foreign and Security Policy was at last under way. For different reasons, the UK and France were in the vanguard. The Labour

[31] Vignes (1999). See also Bailes (1999).

Government elected in the UK was anxious to position itself in the fore-front of some aspects of European cooperation, to offset its refusal to end border control of people or to participate in the initial establishment of a single currency. The need for some autonomous capacity to use credible military force to underpin the CFSP was becoming increasingly obvious. NATO had made it clear that it was time for Europe to shoulder a greater responsibility for its own security and that—so long as it retained the first choice over whether it would become involved—this was entirely com-patible with maintenance of the new-style Atlantic Alliance. France had lost its earlier suspicions of NATO as an instrument of US dominance of Europe, and accepted its primacy on questions of territorial defence. It was eager to see WEU transformed into an agency of the European Union for the purposes of its Second Pillar.[32]

In December 1998 the Heads of State and Government of France and the UK issued at St Malo a Joint Declaration aimed at making a reality of the defence provisions in the new Treaty, emphasizing that: 'To this end, the Union must have the capacity for autonomous action, backed up by cred-ible military forces, the means to use them, and a readiness to do so, in order to respond to international crises.' This would not prejudice existing collective defence commitments or differing positions regarding NATO membership. The key commitments were

3. In order for the European Union to take decisions and approve military action where the Alliance as a whole is not engaged, the Union must be given appropri-ate structures and a capacity for analysis of situations, sources of intelligence, and a capability for relevant strategic planning, without unnecessary duplication, tak-ing account of the existing assets of the WEU and the evolution of its relations with the EU. In this regard, the European Union will also need to have recourse to suit-able military means (European capabilities pre-designated within NATO's European pillar or national or multinational European means outside the NATO framework).

4. Europe needs strengthened armed forces that can react rapidly to the new risks, and which are supported by a strong and competitive European defence industry and technology.[33]

Responding to this initiative in April 1999, the Washington Summit of NATO—which was celebrating its own fiftieth birthday—offered consul-tations with the EU which would address European access to NATO planning capabilities and to common assets for EU-led operations. The

---

[32] See Soetendorp (1999) ch 8, 'The impotence in former Yugoslavia: setting up the miss-ing military capability', especially pp 131–7; Wyn Rees (1996) at pp 241–2.

[33] *The Times*, 5 December 1998. See also [1999] European Foreign Affairs Rev 125. For com-ment see Biscop (1999). The terms of the St Malo Declaration gave rise to the informal description 'Rapid Reaction Force'. This is not used in formal documents—perhaps because it suggests a single standing force, which is not intended.

concept of a European Security and Defence Identity (ESDI) within NATO was explicitly acknowledged.[34] This access to real military capability and integrated equipment was essential if the EU's fledgling security and defence policy was to be taken seriously.

When the European Council met in Cologne in June 1999, the Treaty of Amsterdam had just entered into force, and the Heads of State and Government were determined to give the Union the means and capabilities for autonomous action. In Annex II to its Conclusions, a European Council Declaration set in hand the development of more effective European military capabilities, in particular for EU-led crisis management. It would be open to NATO members as well as neutral and non-allied members of the European Union to participate on an equal footing in such operations. The aim was to take the necessary decisions by the end of 2000.

For decision-making, there might be meetings of the General Affairs Council including Defence Ministers, a Political and Security Committee with relevant expertise, a European Union Military Committee, Military Staff including a Situation Centre and other resources such as a Satellite Centre. It was emphasized that: 'Member States will retain in all circumstances the right to decide if and when their national forces are deployed.'[35]

In December 1999 the European Council in Helsinki put more flesh on these plans and agreed in particular that 'cooperating voluntarily in EU-led operations, Member States must be able, by 2003, to deploy within 60 days and sustain for at least one year military forces of up to 50,000 to 60,000 persons capable of the full range of Petersberg tasks; . . . ('the Headline Goal')'. The Helsinki European Council also declared that 'a non-military crisis management mechanism will be established to coordinate and make more effective the various civilian means and resources, in parallel with the military ones, at the disposal of the Union and the Member States.'[36] The Council set up an Interim Political and Security Committee in February 2000 and gave it a mandate to prepare recommendations on the future functioning of the common European policy on security and defence. At the same time it set up an Interim Military Body to give military advice to the Political Committee, including in its formation

[34] NATO Press Releases NAC-S(99) 64 and 65 (24 March 1999); Nicoll and Salmon (2000) pp 378–84; Teunissen (1999).

[35] Bull EU 6-1999. In its annual review of global armed forces, published in October 1999, the Institute of Strategic Studies emphasized the need for Europe to spend much more on defence and procurement in order to acquire a credible military capability: *The Times* 22 October 1999.

[36] Bull EU 12-1999, I.9. In the UK there was at this time intense controversy over European plans—attacked in particular by Baroness Thatcher as a threat to NATO and a drive towards a single European superstate: *The Times* 8 December 1999. The Chief of the Defence Staff denied this and emphasized that there were no plans to create a European army: *The Times* 10 December 1999.

as Interim Political and Security Committee. The Council also decided that national experts in the military field would be seconded to the Council Secretariat.[37] In April 2000 the Eurocorps took over from NATO command of the peacekeeping operation in Kosovo.[38]

At Santa Maria da Feira in June 2000, the European Council added to this growing machinery a commitment by Member States to provide up to five thousand police officers for international missions across the range of conflict prevention and crisis management operations. A thousand police would be able to be deployed within thirty days. This would form part of the work under way to enhance the Union's capability in civilian aspects of crisis management. There was to be a Capabilities Commitment Conference at the end of 2000 which would draw together the emerging military promises, including those from non-Member States—Turkey, Poland, the Czech Republic, and Norway. The European Council noted that Treaty amendment was not essential for what had already been agreed, but they kept the question open. An Appendix set out principles and recommendations for EU/NATO relations.

The Capabilities Commitment Conference took place in Brussels in November 2000 and issued a Declaration. This made clear that it was 'essential to the credibility and effectiveness of the European security and defence policy that the European Union's military capabilities for crisis management be reinforced so that the EU is in a position to intervene with or without recourse to NATO assets.'[39] The commitments made—set out in a 'Force Catalogue'—satisfied the requirements established by the Helsinki European Council, though it was acknowledged that there was a need for quantitative and qualitative improvements to maximize the capabilities available to the European Union. The Conference noted that restructuring of defence industries in some Member States would increase capabilities in terms of such items as transport aircraft, helicopters and sea transport vessels. The exemption of the armaments industry from Community rules under the Treaties has meant that these enterprises have only recently begun to be exposed to competition or to merge with a view to improving economic efficiency. Following the Conference there were ministerial meetings with non-European Union Members of NATO and with accession candidate States which led to pledges of additional contributions from these States in the context of their possible participation in EU-led operations.

The US remained publicly supportive. US Secretary of State Madeleine Albright and the British Foreign Secretary Robin Cook in a joint statement said:

---

[37] OJ L49, L49/2 and L49/3, 22.2.2000.   [38] *The Times*, 15 April 2000.
[39] Council Press Release No 13427/2/00 of 20 November 2000.

Europe's security and defence policy is not and will not become a European army run from Brussels. Any military operation organised by the EU will require the consent of every Member State. Any national deployment will be a matter for that nation to decide.

Nor is this a blueprint for dividing Europe or the Atlantic alliance. NATO remains the foundation of the collective defence of its members. An important part of this initiative is the crafting of new arrangements to link the EU and NATO in unprecedented ways, laying the foundation for a true strategic partnership between the two key institutions of the West.[40]

President Bush later offered support in somewhat more guarded terms— the EU's forces must be 'properly integrated with NATO', undertake only those operations which NATO opted not to lead and avoid waste and duplication.[41]

The Treaty of Nice

The European Council at Nice in December 2000 had before it a French Presidency Report on the European Security and Defence Policy which summarized the results of the Cologne, Helsinki, and Santa Maria da Feira Councils. The Report emphasized that:

In response to crises, the Union's particular characteristic is its capacity to mobilise a vast range of both civilian and military means and instruments, thus giving it an overall crisis-management and conflict-prevention capability in support of the objectives of the Common and Foreign Security Policy.

The Report was explicit on the fact that the European Union would launch and conduct military operations 'where NATO as a whole is not engaged'. The commitment of national resources by Member States to such operations would be 'based on their sovereign decisions'. European Security and Defence Policy would 'lead to a genuine strategic partnership between the EU and NATO in the management of crises with due regard for the two organisations' decision-making autonomy'. The European Union would itself assume the crisis-management function of the WEU.

As well as the Political and Security Committee, already established on an interim basis, the proposed Military Committee and Military Staff would be set up as soon as possible. Detailed work was in hand to establish permanent arrangements for consultation and cooperation with NATO—dealing with such practical matters as exchange of documents, frequency and level of contacts in times of crisis and at other times and

---

[40] *Observer*, 26 November 2000.
[41] NATO Summit meeting in Brussels: *The Times*, 14 June 2001. See also Duke (2001) at pp 171–4.

access by the EU to NATO assets and capabilities.[42] Turkey, however, a Member of NATO and now accepted as a long-term candidate for accession to the Union, has blocked the conclusion of an agreement which would ensure such access and has agreed to access only on an ad hoc basis.[43]

The Treaty of Nice, signed on 26 February 2001, replaced Article 17 of the TEU with yet another version. The text is identical with that established by the Treaty of Amsterdam except that all the references in paragraphs 1 and 3 to the WEU have disappeared. This reflects the intention of the European Council that the European Union should itself take political decisions on crisis management and on fulfilment of the Petersberg tasks and should henceforth obtain access to full operational capability through NATO. Paragraph 3—which in the Amsterdam version set out elaborate provision for the use by the EU of WEU capabilities—was replaced by a short paragraph providing that

3. Decisions having defence implications dealt with under this Article shall be taken without prejudice to the policies and obligations referred to in paragraph 1, second subparagraph.

The change in the residual Article 17, paragraph 3 is no more than a drafting amendment consequential on the deletion of the second subparagraph in the Amsterdam version of the paragraph.

The Treaty of Nice does not, however, expressly effect the 'integration of the WEU into the Union'—the possibility envisaged by the Treaty of Amsterdam. WEU continues its increasingly shadowy existence—and the new version of Article 17 paragraph 4 continues to refer to the possibility of closer cooperation between two or more Member States in the framework of the WEU.[44]

Declaration No 1 adopted by the Nice Conference, on the European Security and Defence Policy, emphasized that the objective for the EU was for that policy to become operational quickly. A decision to that effect would be taken by the European Council as soon as possible in 2001 on the basis of the existing provisions of the TEU. Entry into force of the Treaty of Nice was not a precondition.

---

[42] Annex VI to Nice European Council Conclusions, Bull EU 6-2000. Detail of the Standing Arrangements for Consultation and cooperation between the EU and NATO is in Annex VII to Annex VI. For a savage attack on the scheme see *The Times* leader, 18 January 2001. More balanced, though critical assessments are in Duke (2001); Missiroli (2001).

[43] Yesson (2001) at pp 207–12.

[44] It is of course not possible by amendment of the TEU to wind up WEU, in view of the participation in WEU on non-EU States. All the EU can do is to terminate its reliance on WEU. A full absorption would require the consent of all observers as well as members of WEU. See comment by Teunissen (1999) at p 331.

The Political and Security Committee

The other change relevant to security and defence in the Treaty of Nice was the replacement of Article 25 describing the functions and duties of the Political Committee by a new Article which reads:

ARTICLE 25

Without prejudice to Article 207 of the Treaty establishing the European Community, a Political and Security Committee shall monitor the international situation in the areas covered by the common foreign and security policy and contribute to the definition of policies by delivering opinions to the Council or on its own initiative. It shall also monitor the implementation of agreed policies, without prejudice to the responsibility of the Presidency and the Commission.

Within the scope of this Title, this Committee shall exercise, under the responsibility of the Council, political control and strategic direction of crisis management operations.

The Council may authorise the Committee, for the purpose and for the duration of a crisis management operation, as determined by the Council, to take the relevant decisions concerning the political control and strategic direction of the operation, without prejudice to Article 47.

The Political and Security Committee had already been established on an interim basis,[45] but the new Article 25 would go beyond a renaming of the Political Committee. The important feature is the new power to exercise political control and strategic direction of military operations. The provision of a facility for day-to-day supervision of crisis management at a level below the Council is essential to effective crisis management and therefore to proper performance of the Petersberg tasks. The new Article 25 continues to make clear that ultimate responsibility for political supervision remains with the Council, and that there is no change to the rules giving legal primacy to the Community Pillar in any case of overlap or conflict. But it also underlines the new determination of the Heads of State and Government to provide men for the new security and defence policy—not only in terms of paper battalions but also in terms of effectiveness in deployment and control of resources.[46]

---

[45] By Council Decision 2000/143/CFSP OJ L49/1, 22.2.2000, Article 1. See Commentary on Article 25 in Chapter 5 above.

[46] For assessment of the existing and proposed structures for crisis management see Missiroli (2001).

In January 2001 the Council, without awaiting the entry into force of the new Article 25, set up the Political and Security Committee on a permanent basis.[47]

A Practical Exercise: Afghanistan

The peacekeeping force mandated by the UN for deployment in Afghanistan under UK leadership was not legally authorized by the EU, but those fourteen countries selected to participate were, with the sole exception of New Zealand, European, and only Turkey, Romania, and Norway among the remainder were not EU Member States. Attempts in Europe to present the force as an embryo Euro-army met with a cold response in the UK.[48]

German participation was constrained by a 1994 ruling of the Federal Constitutional Court which stated that the German constitution permitted its armed forces to take part in action abroad only in the context of a system of mutual collective security (the UN, NATO, and the European Union) and then with specific authority from its parliament. Participation by German forces in the collection of weapons from Albanian rebel groups in Macedonia in 2001 was politically controversial, and the vote to authorize deployment in Afghanistan—the first outside Europe since 1945—was won by only three votes. There were, subsequently, public disagreements between German and British authorities over the UN mandate, the command structure, the number of soldiers from each country and the period of British leadership. The differences illustrate how difficult it will be to assemble a credible European force—even when all the legal structures are in place and the promised miitary capabilities have been supplied.[49]

Conclusion

Only three years after the beginning of the construction of a serious capacity in terms of money and men to underpin the CFSP it is premature to evaluate its potential. The construction has required skilled navigation of fundamental political differences between many of the Member States of the European Union—including the key players in terms of military potential. The co-existence of so many organizations with overlapping competence over European security and defence has added legal impediments.[50] The structures now being assembled have not yet been put to the

---

[47] OJ L27/1, 30.1.2001.   [48] *The Times*, 24 December 2001 and 9 January 2002.
[49] [2001] *Statewatch* November–December, *Frankfurter Allgemeine Zeitung* 15 and 18 December 2001; *The Times* 14 January 2002.
[50] See Wouters and Naert (2001).

test, and the overall success of CFSP may well be demonstrated if it proves unnecessary to have frequent recourse to them. What is needed is stability in the Treaty structures coupled with determination by the major military players among the Member States to provide long-term political and financial support to make them effective.[51]

Politically, the European Union is treading a fine line. The European Council in December 2001 declared the European Security and Defence Policy operational, and at Seville in June 2002 reaffirmed that the Union was in a position to take charge of crisis management operations in Bosnia and in the former Yugoslav Republic of Macedonia. On the other hand, noting a National Declaration by Ireland and seeking to reassure the Irish people who must approve the Treaty of Nice in a second referendum before it can enter into force, it stressed that recent developments do not constitute a decision to move to a common defence. The Treaty on European Union 'does not impose any binding mutual defence commitments. Nor does the development of the Union's capacity to conduct humanitarian and crisis management tasks involve the establishment of a European army'.[52]

It is clear that for the foreseeable future security and defence will be based on the intergovernmental method. Flexibility and individual choice on commitment of the military forces of the Member States to the support of specific policies have been essential in persuading governments to go as far as they have on matters so close to the heart of national sovereignty. The new defence capacity is intimately linked with the CFSP and there are no good reasons for removing it from the Second Pillar. Greater coordination with the Commission to as to ensure overall coherence will best be achieved in the context of practical experience of collective management of particular external events.

[51] See Solana (2002).
[52] Presidency Conclusions, Seville, June 2002, paras 10–17 and Annexes III and IV.

Bibliography

AKEHURST [1979] 'Withdrawal from International Organizations', Current Legal Problems 143.

ALLEN (1998), 'Who speaks for Europe?', in Peterson and Sjursen (eds), *A Common Foreign Policy for Europe?* (Routledge) 41.

ALBORS-LLORENS [1998] 'Changes in the Jurisdiction of the European Court of Justice under the Treaty of Amsterdam', CML Rev 1273.

ALSTON (ed) (1999) *The EU and Human Rights* (OUP).

ANDERSON, Stephanie [2001], 'The Changing Nature of Diplomacy: The European Union, the CFSP and Korea' European Foreign Affairs Rev 465.

ANDERSON and DEN BOER (eds) (1994) *Policing across National Boundaries* (Pinter).

——ET AL (eds) (1995) *Policing the European Union* (OUP).

ARNULL (1999), 'Taming the Beast? The Treaty of Amsterdam and the Court of Justice' in O'Keeffe and Twomey (eds), *Legal Issues of the Amsterdam Treaty* (Hart) 109.

AUST (2000), *Modern Treaty Law and Practice* (CUP).

BAILES [1996] 'NATO: Towards a New Synthesis', Survival 27.

——[1999] 'European Defence: what are the convergence criteria?', RUSI Journal 60.

BANN (1996), *An Imperfect Union, The Maastricht Treaty and the New Politics of European Integration.*

BARKER (2001), *International Law and International Relations* (Continuum).

BARRETT (ed) (1997), *Justice Cooperation in the European Union* (Institute of European Affairs, Dublin).

BAVILLARD (1994) 'Customs Cooperation in the Context of Title VI of the Treaty on European Union', in Monar and Morgan (eds), *The Third Pillar of the European Union* (European Interuniversity Press) 217.

BESSELINK, HINS, JANS, DE REEDE and VAN DER VLIES (1997) *Europese Unie en nationale soevereiniteit* (Deventer).

BETHLEHEM (1998), 'International Law, European Community Law, National Law: Three Systems in Search of a Framework' in Koskenniemi (ed), *International Law Aspects of the European Union* 169.

BIEBER [1990] 'Democratic Control of European Foreign Policy' European J of Intl L 148.

——' "(1994) The K.9 procedure establishes in fact a one-way street."— Links between the "Third Pillar" (Title VI) and the European Community (Title II) of the Treaty on European Union' in Monar and

Morgan (eds), *The Third Pillar of the European Union* 37 (European University Press).

BIRKINSHAW and ASHIAGBOR [1996], 'National Parliaments in Community Affairs: Democracy, the UK Parliament and the EU', CML Rev 499.

BISCOP [1999] 'The UK's Change of Course: a New Chance for the ESDI', European Foreign Affairs Rev 253.

BLUM [1967], 'Indonesia's Return to the United Nations', ICLQ 522.

BLUMANN (1994), 'La ratification par la France du traité de Maastricht', Revue du Marché Commun 393.

BOURLANGES-MARTIN Report. *See* EUROPEAN PARLIAMENT.

BRANDTNER and ROSAS [1998], 'Human Rights and the External Relations of the European Community', European J of Intl L 473.

BRITISH INSTITUTE OF INTERNATIONAL AND COMPARATIVE LAW (1996), *The Role and Future of the European Court of Justice*, Report of the EC Advisory Board of the British Institute chaired by Lord Slynn of Hadley.

——(1997), *Human Rights as General Norms and a State's Right to Opt Out: Reservations and Objections to Human Rights Conventions* (British Institute Publication).

BUNYAN (1993), *Statewatching the New Europe: a Handbook on the European State* (Statewatch).

——(1998), *The Europol Convention* (Statewatch).

——*Secrecy and Openness in the EU*.

——(ed) (1997), *Key texts on justice and home affairs in the European Union* [cited as 'Statewatch texts' (1997)'].

BUTTERWORTHS (1996), *Butterworths Expert Guide to the European Union*

CAFRUNY (1998), 'The European Union and the war in the former Yugoslavia: the failure of collective diplomacy' in Cafruny and Peters (eds) *The Union and the World: The Political Economy of a Common European Foreign Policy* (Kluwer) 133.

CAFRUNY and PETERS (eds) (1998), *The Union and the World: The Political Economy of a Common European Foreign Policy* (Kluwer).

CAMERON (1998a) 'CFSP Reform: A Commission Perspective', in Koskenniemi (ed) *International Law Aspects of the European Union* (Kluwer) 45.

——(1998b) 'Building a common foreign policy: do institutions matter?', in Peterson and Sjursen (eds) *A Common Foreign Policy for Europe?* 59.

CANOR [1998] 'Can Two walk together except They Be Agreed? The Relationship Between International Law and European Law: the Incorporation of United Nations Sanctions against Yugoslavia into European Community Law through the Perspective of the European Court of Justice', CML Rev 137.

CARRINGTON (Lord)(1981/82) 'European Political Co-operation: America should welcome it' 58 International Affairs 1.

CARTER (2000), 'Democratic Governance Beyond the Nation State: Third-Level Assemblies and Scrutiny of European Legislation' 6 European Public Law 429.

CARVER and HULSMANN [2000], 'The Role of Article 50 of the UN Charter in the Search for International Peace and Security', ICLQ 528.

CASSESE (1980), *Parliamentary Control over Foreign Policy* (Alpen aan den Rijn, Sijthoff & Noordhoff).

CLAPHAM [1990], 'A Human Rights Policy for the European Community' Yearbook of European Law 309.

——(1999), 'Where is the EU's Human Rights Common Foreign Policy, and How is it Manifested in Multilateral Fora? in Alston (ed), *The EU and Human Rights* (OUP) 627.

CLOSE (1985), 'Subordination Clauses in Mixed Agreements' ICLQ 382.

COOK and SANDS [1995], 'Current Developments in EC External Relations', ICLQ 225.

CORNISH (1979), 'Joint Action, The "Economic Aspects of Security" and the Regulation of Conventional Arms and Technology Exports from the EU', in Holland (ed) *Common Foreign and Security Policy: The Record and Reforms* (Pinter) 73.

CORRADO [1999], L'Intégration de Schengen dans l'Union Européenne: Problèmes et Perspectives, Revue du Marché Commun 342.

CRAIG and HARLOW (eds)(1998), *Lawmaking in the European Union* (Kluwer).

CRAWFORD (1997), *The Creation of States in International Law* (OUP).

CREMONA [1995] 'Citizens of Third Countries: Movement and Employment of Migrant Workers Within the European Union', Legal Issues of European Integration 87.

——(1996), 'Human Rights and Democracy Clauses in the EC's Trade Agreements' in Emiliou and O'Keeffe (eds) *The European Union and World Trade Law after the GATT* (Wiley) 62.

——[1998], 'The European Union as an International Actor: The Issues of Flexibility and Linkage' European Foreign Affairs Review 67.

——(1999) 'Creating the New Europe: The Stability Pact for South-Eastern Europe in the Context of EU-SEE Relations' 2 CYELS 463.

CROWE [1998], 'Some Reflections on the Common Foreign and Security Policy' European Foreign Affairs Rev 319.

CRUZ (1995), *Shifting Responsibility: Carrier Liability in the Member States of the European Union and North America* (Trentham and the School of Oriental and African Studies).

CURTIN [1993], 'The constitutional structure of the Union: A Europe of bits and pieces', CML Rev 17.

——and DEKKER (1999), 'The EU as a "Layered" International Organization: Institutional Unity in Disguise' in Craig and de Burca (eds), *The Evolution of EU Law* (OUP) 83.

CURTIN and VAN OOIK (1994), 'Denmark and the Edinburgh Summit: Maastricht without Tears' in O'Keeffe and Twomey (eds), *Legal Issues of the Maastricht Treaty* (Chancery Law Publishers).

CYGAN (1998), *The United Kingdom Parliament and European Union Legislation* (Kluwer).

DASHWOOD [1998], 'States in the European Union', ELR 201.

——and JOHNSTON (eds)(2001), *The Future of the Judicial System of the European Union* (Hart).

——(eds)(1999) 'External Relations Provisions of the Amsterdam Treaty' in O'Keeffe and Twomey (eds), *Legal Issues of the Amsterdam Treaty* 201. (This article can also be found at 1998 CML Rev 1019.)

DEHOUSSE (ed)(1994), *Europe after Maastricht: An Ever Closer Union?* (Law Books in Europe).

DE LOBKOWICZ (1994) 'Intergovernmental Cooperation in the field of Migration—from the Single European Act to Maastricht', in Monar and Morgan (eds) *The Third Pillar of the European Union* (European Interuniversity Press) (1994).

DEN BOER (1998), *Taming the Third Pillar: Improving the Management of Justice and Home Affairs Cooperation in the EU* (European Institute of Public Administration).

——(1999),'An Area of Freedom, Security and Justice: Bogged Down by Compromise' in O'Keeffe and Twomey (eds), *Legal Issues of the Amsterdam Treaty* (Hart) 303.

DENZA [1993a], 'Parliamentary Scrutiny of Community Legislation', Statute Law Review 56.

——(1993b),'La Chambre des Lords: Vingt Années d'Enquêtes Communautaires', Revue du Marché Commun 740.

——[1994a] 'La ratification du traité de Maastricht par le Royaume-Uni', Revue du Marché Commun 172.

——(1994b) 'Groping towards Europe's Foreign Policy' in Curtin and Heukels (eds), *Institutional Dynamics of European Integration, Essays in Honour of Henry Schermers* Vol II p 575 (Kluwer).

——(1996) 'The Community as a Member of International Organizations', in Emiliou and O'Keeffe (eds) *The European Union and World Trade Law after the GATT Uruguay Round* (Wiley). 3.

——(1998), *Diplomatic Law* (2nd edn) (OUP).

DE SCHOUTHEETE (1980), *La Co-opération Politique Européenne* (Editions Labor, Brussels).

——[1986], 'Le rapport Tindemans dix ans après', Politique étrangère 527.

DE WITTE [1994], 'Rules of change in International Law: How Special is the European Community' Netherlands Yearbook of International Law 299.

DE ZWAAN (1995), *The Permanent Representatives' Committee* (Elsevier).

DICEY and MORRIS (1993), *The Conflict of Laws* (12th edn and Supplements)(Collins).

DORN (ed)(1999), *Regulating European Drug Problems* (Kluwer).

DOXEY (1987), *International Sanctions in Contemporary Perspective* (St Martin's Press).

DUKE (2001), 'CESDP: Nice's Overtrumped Success' European Foreign Affairs Rev 155.

DURAND (1992), 'Le traité sur l'Union européenne—Quelques réflexions' in Mégret (ed), *Le droit de la CEE* p 359 (2nd edn) Vol I.

DUTHEIL DE LA ROCHÈRE and JARVIS (1997), 'C. XIV Royaune-Uni', in Rideau (ed) Les Etats Membres de L'Union Européenne (LGDI). p 409

EDWARDS [1993], 'Common Foreign and Security Policy', Yearbook of European Law 497.

——[1994], 'Common Foreign and Security Policy', Yearbook of European Law 541.

——and PHILLIPART (1997), 'The Euro-Mediterranean Partnership: Fragmentation and Reconstruction', European Foreign Affairs Rev 465.

EECKHOUT (1994), *The European Internal Market and International Trade: A Legal Analysis* (OUP).

——(1999), 'The European Court's New Competences: Challenges and Problems', presented at the Bar European Group Brussels Seminar on 6 November 1999.

EISL [1997], 'Relations with the Central and Eastern European Countries in Justice and Home Affairs: Deficits and Options', European Foreign Affairs Rev 351.

EMILIOU [1996], 'Strategic Export Controls, National Security and the Common Commercial Policy', European Foreign Affairs Rev 55.

——and O'KEEFFE (eds)(1996), *The European Union and World Trade Law after the GATT* (Wiley).

EUROPEAN COMMISSION *The European Community, International Organizations and Multilateral Agreements*.

EUROPEAN COMMUNITY (1991), Guidelines on the recognition of new States (1992) 31 ILM 1486–7; [1993] EJIL 72.

EUROPEAN PARLIAMENT (1994), *The European Parliament and the Parliaments of the Member States: Parliamentary Scrutiny and Arrangements for Co-operation* (European Parliament).

——(1995a), *European Affairs Committees of the Parliaments of the Member States* (European Parliament).

——(1995b), Resolution A4-0102/95 on the functioning of the TEU with a view to the 1996 Intergovernmental Conference—Implementation and development of the Union (Bourlanges-Martin Report).

EUROPEAN PARLIAMENT (1996), Report of the Committee on Foreign Affairs, Security and Defence Policy on progress in implementing the common foreign and security policy in 1995, 5 February 1996, DOC_EN\ PR\291\291192.

EVANS (ed) (1996), *Aspects of Statehood and Internationalism in Contemporary Europe* (Ashgate).

EVERLING [1994], 'The Maastricht Judgment of the German Federal Constitutional Court and its Significance for the Development of the European Union', Yearbook of European Law 1.

FENNELLY (2000), 'The Area of "Freedom, Security and Justice" and the European Court of Justice—A Personal View' ICLQ 1.

FINK-HOOIJER [1994], 'The Common Foreign and Security Policy of the European Union', European J of Intl L 173.

FOX and WICKREMASINGHE (1993), 'UK Implementation of UN Economic Sanctions', ICLQ 945.

FREEDMAN (1994) 'Why the West Failed' Foreign Policy 54.

FREESTONE [1993], 'The Development of the CSCE after the Helsinki Conference', ICLQ 411.

——[1994], 'The Road from Rio: International Environmental Law after the Earth Summit', inaugural lecture printed in Journal of International Environmental Law 193.

GARDINER [1997], 'Treaties and Treaty Materials: Role, Relevance and Accessibility, ICLQ 643.

GÉRARD [1987] 'La Coopération politique européenne: Méthodes et résultats' Revue du Marché Commun 466.

GILLESPIE (ed) (1996), *Britain's European Question: the Issues for Ireland* (Institute of European Affairs, Dublin).

GINSBERG [1999], 'Conceptualizing the European Union as an International Actor: Narrowing the Theoretical Capability-Expectations Gap' JCMS 429.

GLAESNER [1986] 'L'acte unique européen', Revue du Marché Commun 307.

GLISTRUP (1994), 'Le traité sur l'Union européenne: la ratification du Danemark' Revue du Marché Commun 9.

GOMEZ (1998), 'The European Union's Mediterranean Policy' in Peterson and Sjursen (eds), *A Common Foreign Policy for Europe?* (Routledge) 133.

——and PETERSON [2001] 'The EU's Impossibly Busy Foreign Ministers: No One is in Control' European Foreign Affairs Rev 53.

GOSELLO BONO [1992], 'The International Powers of the European Parliament, the Democratic Deficit and the Treaty on European Union', Yearbook of European Law 85.

GRUBB and YAMIN [2001], 'Climatic collapse at the Hague: what happened, why, and where do we go from here?' International affairs 261.

GUILD (1998), 'The Constitutional Consequences of Lawmaking in the Third Pillar of the European Union' in Craig and Harlow (eds), *Lawmaking in the European Union* (Kluwer).

GUILD AND HARLOW (eds) (2001), *Implementing Amsterdam: Immigration and Asylum Rights in EC Law* (Hart).

HAILBRONNER [1992], 'Perspectives of a Harmonization of the Law of Asylum after the Maastricht Summit' CML Rev 917.

——(2000), *Immigration and Asylum Law and Policy of the European Union* (Kluwer).

HAKURA [1997], The Euro-Mediterranean Policy: The Implications of the Barcelona Declaration, CML Rev 337.

——[1998], 'The External EU Immigration Policy: The Need to Move beyond the Orthodoxy', 1998 European Foreign Affairs Rev 115.

HANNAY (2000), 'Europe's Common Foreign and Security Policy: Year 1', European Foreign Affairs Rev 275.

HARDING (2000), *The Uninvited: Refugees at the Rich Man's Gate* (Profile Books).

HARRIS (1998), *Cases and Materials on International Law* (6th edn).

HARTLEY [1993] 'Constitutional and Institutional Implications of the Maastricht Agreement', ICLQ 213.

——(1999), *Constitutional Problems of the European Union* (Hart).

HARVEY (2000), *Seeking Asylum in the UK—Problems and Prospects* (Butterworths).

HAYES (2001), The activities and development of Europol: 1993–2001 (Statewatch).

HENDRY [1993], 'The Third Pillar of Maastricht: Cooperation in the Fields of Justice and Home Affairs', German Yearbook of International Law 295.

HIGGINS (1991), 'International Law and the Avoidance, Containment and Resolution of Disputes' 230 Recueil des Cours (1991-V), also published as *Problems and Process: International Law and How We Use It* (1994) ch 1: 'The Nature and Function of International Law'.

HILL (1998), 'Closing the Capability-Expectations Gap?' in Peterson and Sjursen (eds), *A Common Foreign Policy for Europe?* (Routledge).

——[2001] 'The EU's Capacity for Conflict Prevention', European Foreign Affairs Rev 315.

——(ed)(1983), *National Foreign Policies and European Political Cooperation*.

HOLBROOKE [1995], 'America, a European power', Foreign Affairs 47.

HOLLAND [1995], 'Bridging the Capability-Expectations Gap: A Case Study of the CFSP Joint Actions on South Africa', JCMS 555.

——(1997a) 'The Joint Action on South Africa: a Successful Experiment?' in Holland (ed) *Common Foreign and Security Policy: The Record and Reforms* (Pinter).

——(ed) (1997b), *Common Foreign and Security Policy: The Record and Reforms* (Pinter).

HORSPOOL (2000), *European Union Law* (2nd edn)(Butterworths).

HOTTIAUX and LIPONSKA-LABEROU (2000), *La Politique Européenne de Défense* (L'Harmattan, Paris).

HOUSE OF COMMONS SELECT COMMITTEE ON EUROPEAN LEGISLATION (1994–95) *The 1996 Intergovernmental Conference: The Agenda, Democracy and Efficiency, the Role of National Parliaments*, 24th Report, (HC Paper 239 I + II).

HOUSE OF COMMONS SELECT COMMITTEE ON EUROPEAN LEGISLATION (1995–96), *The Scrutiny of European Business*, 27th Report, (HC Paper 51-xxvii).

HOUSE OF LORDS SELECT COMMITTEE ON THE EUROPEAN COMMUNITIES (1988–89) *1992: Border Control of People*,22nd Report, HL Paper 90.

——(1989–90), *Economic and Monetary Union and Political Union*, 27th Report, HL Paper 90.

——(1990–91*a*) *Money Laundering*, 1st Report, HL Paper 6.

——(1990–91*b*) *Political Union: Law-making Powers and Procedures*, 17th Report, HL Paper 80.

——(1992–93*a*), *Human Rights Re-examined*, 3rd Report, HL Paper 10.

——(1992–93*b*), *House of Lords Scrutiny of the Inter-governmental Pillars of the European Union*, 28th Report, HL Paper 124.

——(1993–94), *Visas and Control of External Borders of the Member States*, 14th Report, HL Paper 78.

——(1994–95*a*), *Europol*, 10th Report, HL Paper 51.

——(1994–95*b*), 1996 Inter-governmental Conference, 21st Report, HL Paper 105 and 18th Report, HL Paper 88, Minutes of Evidence.

——(1997–98*a*), *Brussels II: The Draft Convention on Jurisdiction, Recognition and Enforcement of Judgments in Matrimonial Matters*, 5th Report, HL Paper 19.

——(1997–98*b*), *Enhancing Parliamentary Scrutiny of the Third Pillar*, 6th Report, HL Paper 25.

——(1997–98*c*), *Mutual Assistance in Criminal Matters*, 14th Report, HL Paper 72.

——(1997–98*d*), *Evidence by the Minister of State, Home Office, on the United Kingdom Presidency Work Programme on Justice and Home Affairs*, 12th Report, HL Paper 65.

——(1997–98*e*), *Dealing with the Third Pillar: the Government's Perspective*, 15th Report, HL Paper 73.

——(1998–99*a*), *Prosecuting Fraud on the Communities' Finances - the Corpus Iuris*, 9th Report, HL Paper 62.

——(1998–99*b*), *Prospects for the Tampere Special European Council*, 19th Report, HL Paper 101.

HOUSE OF LORDS SELECT COMMITTEE ON THE EUROPEAN UNION (1999–2000*a*) Special Report, HL Paper 12.

——(1999–2000*b*), *Public Access to EU Documents*, 16th Report, HL Paper 102.

——(1999–2000c), *Evidence by the Minister of State, Foreign and Commonwealth Office in the Helsinki European Council*, 3rd Report, HL Paper 22.

——(2000–01a) *Access to Documents: The Council Decision of 14 August 2000*, 8th Report, HL Paper 31.

——(2000–01b), *The Common Mediterranean Strategy*, 9th Report, HL Paper 51.

——(2001–02a), *Counter Terrorism: The European Arrest Warrant*, 6th Report, HL Paper 34.

——(2001–02b), *A Second Parliamentary Chamber for Europe, An Unreal Solution to some Real Problems*, 7th Report, HL Paper 48.

——(2001–02c), *The European Arrest Warrant*, 16th Report, HL Paper 89.

HOWE, GEOFFREY [1996], 'Bearing More of the Burden: In Search of a European Foreign and Security Policy' The World Today 23.

HOWORTH and MENON (1997), *The European Union and National Defence Policy* (Routledge).

HURD [1981], 'Political Co-operation', 57 International Affairs 383.

——(1994), 'Developing the Common Foreign and Security Policy', 70 International Affairs (No 3) 421.

JACQUÉ [1986], 'L'acte unique européen', Revue Trimestrielle de Droit Européen 575.

JAKOBI [2002], 'Tattered Justice', *Counsel* (April) 18.

JOHNSTON [2001], 'Judicial Reform and the Treaty of Nice', CML Rev 499.

JUSTICE (1999), *Towards Common Standards on Asylum Practice*.

——[2000] 'EU Co-operation in Criminal Matters, a Human Rights Agenda', August 22.

——[2001] 'Response to Specific Proposals', February.

KERSE [2000/2001], 'Converting Conventions into Regulations', The European Advocate, (Winter) 2.

KINTIS (1997), 'The EU's Foreign Policy and the War in Former Yugoslavia' in Holland (ed), *Common Foreign and Security Policy: The Record and Reforms* (Pinter) 148.

——(1998), 'NATO–WEU: An Enduring Relationship' European Foreign Affairs Rev 537.

KISSINGER (1994), *Diplomacy* (Simon & Schuster).

KOSKENNIEMI (1998), 'International Law Aspects of the Common Foreign and Security Policy' in *International Law Aspects of the European Union* (Kluwer) Koskenniemi (ed) 27.

——(ed)(1998), *International Law Aspects of the European Union* (Kluwer).

KOUTRAKOS (2001), *Trade, Foreign Policy and Defence in EU Constitutional Law* (Hart).

KUNZ [1956], 'Austria's Permanent Neutrality', AJIL 418.

KUYPER [1984], 'European Community Law and Extraterritoriality: Some Trends and New Developments', ICLQ 1013.

——(1982), 'Community Sanctions against Argentina: Lawfulness under Community and International Law' in O'Keeffe and Schermers (eds) *Essays in European Law and Integration* (Deventer) 141.

——(1993), 'Trade Sanctions, Security and Human Rights and Commercial Policy' in Maresceau (ed) *The European Community's Commercial Policy after 1992: The Legal Dimension* (Nijhoff) 387.

LANG AND WEBER [2000], 'Ten Years of Economic Reforms in Russia: Windows in a Wall', The International Lawyer 179.

LEIGH AND BEYANI (1996), *Blackstone's Guide to the Asylum and Immigration Act 1996* (Blackstone).

LENZI (1998), 'Defining the European Security Policy' in Zielonka (ed) *Paradoxes of European Foreign Policy* (Kluwer) 103.

LEVITT (1988), *Democracies against Terror*.

LIGHT, LOWENHARDT and WHITE [2000] 'Russian Perspectives on European Security', European Foreign Affairs Rev 489.

LIVINGSTONE [1965], 'Withdrawal from the United Nations—Indonesia' ICLQ 637.

LOUIS [1990], *The Community Legal Order* (2nd edn)(European Communities).

LOWE [1984], 'The European Response to the US Export Administration Regulations', ICLQ 515.

——[1985], 'Extraterritorial Jurisdiction: Economic Sovereignty and the Search for a Solution' ICLQ 724.

——[1997], 'US Extra-territorial Jurisdiction: The Helms-Burton and d'Amato Acts', ICLQ 378.

McGOLDRICK (1994), 'The European Union after Amsterdam: An Organisation with General Human Rights Competence?' in O'Keeffe and Twomey (eds) *Legal Issues of the Amsterdam Treaty* (Chancery Law Publishers) 249.

MACKAREL and NASH [1997], 'Extradition and the European Union', ICLQ 948.

MACLEOD, HENDRY, and HYETT (1996), *The External Relations of the European Communities* (OUP).

McMAHON [1999], 'Negotiating in a Time of Turbulent Transition: the Future of Lome' CML Rev 599.

MANCINI (2000), *Democracy and Constitutionalism in the European Union* (Hart).

MARSHALL (2000), *The New Germany and Migration in Europe* (Manchester University Press).

MARTENCZUK [2000], 'From Lome to Cotonou: The ACP–EC Partnership Agreement in a Legal Perspective' European Foreign Affairs Rev 461

MARTIN and GUILD (1996), *Free Movement of Persons in the European Union* (Butterworths).

MATHESON [1997], 'The Opinions of the International Court of Justice on the Threat or Use of Nuclear Weapons', AJIL 417.

MEIJERS (1991), *Schengen, Internationalization of Central Chapters of the Law on Aliens, Refugees, Privacy, Security and the Police* (Kluwer).

MEYNELL [1981], 'Annual Survey of External Relations of the European Community' Yearbook of European Law 347.

MEYRING [1997], 'Intergovernmentalism and Supranationality: Two Stereotypes for a Complex Reality', ELR 221.

MISSIROLI (2001), 'European Security Policy: The Challenge of Coherence' European Foreign Affairs Rev 177.

MONAR (1994), 'The Evolving Role of the Union Institutions in the Framework of the Third Pillar' in Monar and Morgan (eds), *The Third Pillar of the European Union* (European Interuniversity Press).

——(1997), 'The Financial Dimension of the CFSP' in Holland (ed), *Common Foreign and Security Policy: The Record and Reforms* (Pinter) 34.

——[1998], 'Justice and Home Affairs in the Treaty of Amsterdam: Reform at the Price of Fragmentation' European Law Rev 320.

——and MORGAN (eds)(1994), *The Third Pillar of the European Union* (European Interuniversity Press).

MORGAN (1994), 'How Common Will Foreign and Security Policies be?' in Dehousse (ed), *Europe After Maastricht, An Ever Closer Union?* (Law Books in Europe, 1994) 189.

MULLER (1995), *International Organizations and their Host States* (Kluwer).

——and VAN DASSEN (1997), 'From Cacophony to Joint Action: Successes and Shortcomings of the European Nuclear Non-Proliferation Policy' in Holland (ed) *Common Foreign and Security Policy: The Record and Reforms* (Pinter) 52.

MÜLLER-GRAFF [1994], 'The Legal Bases of the Third Pillar and its Position in the Framework of the Union Treaty', CML Rev 493.

MURPHY [1999], 'Democratic Legitimacy and the Recognition of States and Governments', ICLQ 545.

NANZ (1994), 'The Harmonization of Asylum and Immigration Legislation within the Third Pillar of the Union Treaty—a Stocktaking' in Monar and Morgan (eds), *The Third Pillar of the European Union* (European Interuniversity Press) 123.

NATO (1989), NATO Handbook (NATO Information Service, Brussels).

——(2001), NATO Handbook (NATO Information Service Brussels).

Nato Review (1994) February.

NAUD [1997], 'L'Embargo: Une Valse à Trois Temps, Nations Unies, Union Européenne et Etats Membres', Revue du Marché Commun 25.

NEFF (2000), *The rights and duties of neutrals, A general history* (Juris Publishing, Manchester University Press).

NEUWAHL [1998], 'A Partner with a Troubled Personality: EU Treaty-Making in Matters of CFSP and JHA after Amsterdam', European Foreign Affairs Rev 177.

NEVILLE-JONES [1983], 'The Genscher/Colombo Proposals on European Union', CML Rev 657.

NICHOLSON (1987), 'Implementation of the Immigration Carriers' Liability Act 1987: Privatising Immigration Functions at the Expense of International Obligations', ICLQ 586.

NICOLL [1984], 'The Luxembourg Compromise' 23 JCMS 35

——[1993], 'Note the Hour and File the Minute', Journal of Common Market Studies 559.

——and SALMON (2000), *Understanding the European Union* (Longman).

NORTON [1995], 'National Parliaments and the European Union' Journal of Legislative Studies 92.

NUTTALL [1985*a*], 'European Political Co-operation and the Single European Act' Yearbook of European Law 203.

——[1985*b*], 'Interaction between European Political Cooperation and the European Community' Yearbook of European Law 211.

——(1992), *European Political Co-operation* (OUP).

——[1994], 'The EC and Yugoslavia, *Deus ex Machina or Machina sine Deo?*', 32 Journal of Common Market Studies (Annual Review) 12.

——(1996), 'Common Foreign and Security Policy' in *Butterworths Expert Guide to the European Union*.

——(2000), *European Foreign Policy* (OUP).

OJANEN, HEROLF and LINDAHL (2000), *Non-Alignment and European Security Policy: Ambiguity at Work* (Ulkopolittinen Institutti & Institut für Europäische Politik, Helsinki and Bonn).

O'KEEFFE [1991], 'The Schengen Convention: A Suitable Model for European Integration?', Yearbook of European Law 185

——(1994*a*) The New Draft External Frontiers Convention and the Draft Visa Regulation in Monar and Morgan (eds) *The Third Pillar of the European Union* (European Interuniversity Press).

——(1994*b*) 'Can the Leopard Change its Spots? Visas, Immigration and Asylum—Following Amsterdam' in O'Keeffe and Twomey (eds), *Legal Issues of the Amsterdam Treaty* 271.

——[1995] 'Recasting the Third Pillar' Common Market Law Rev 893.

——and SCHERMERS (eds) (1982), *Essays in European Law and Integration* (Deventer).

——and TWOMEY (eds)(1994), *Legal Issues of the Maastricht Treaty* (Chancery Law Publishers).

——and——(eds)(1999) *Legal Issues of the Amsterdam Treaty* (Hart).

Oppenheim (1996), *International Law* Jennings and Watts (eds)(9th edn) (Longman).

Osieke [1993], 'The Legal Validity of Ultra Vires Decisions of International Organizations' AJIL 239.

Pavoni [1999], 'UN Sanctions in EU and National Law: The *Centrocom* Case', ICLQ 582.

Peers [1996a], 'Towards Equality: Actual and Potential Rights of Third-Country Nationals in the European Union', CML Rev 7

——[1996b], 'The Visa Regulation: Free Movement Blocked Indefinitely?', 1996 ELR 150.

——[1996c], 'Common Foreign and Security Policy 1995–6' Yearbook of European Law 611.

——[1998a], 'Common Foreign and Security Policy 1998', Yearbook of European Law 659.

——[1998b], 'Building Fortress Europe: The Development of EU Migration Law', CML Rev 1235.

——(2000), *EU Justice and Home Affairs Law* (Longman).

Pellet [1992], 'The Opinions of the Badinter Arbitration Committee: A Second Breath for the Self-Determination of Peoples', EJIL 178.

Peterson and Sjursen (eds)(1998), *A Common Foreign Policy for Europe?* (Routledge).

Piris [1999] 'Does the European Union have a Constitution? Does it need one?', ELR 557.

——[1990], Competence, European Community Law and Nationals of Non-Member States, ICLQ 599.

Plender (1988), *Basic Documents in International Migration Law* (2nd edn) (Nijhoff).

Pratt (1999), 'The Role of National Parliaments in the Making of European Law', Cambridge Yearbook of European Legal Studies 217.

Rasmussen (1996), *NO ENTRY–Immigration Policy in Europe* (Handelshojs-kolens Forlag)(English version 1997).

Regelsberger and Wessels [1996], 'The CFSP Institutions and Procedures: A Third Way for the Second Pillar' European Foreign Affairs Rev 29.

Rhein (1996), 'Europe and the Mediterranean: A Newly Emerging Geopolitical Area' European Foreign Affairs Rev 79.

Rideau (ed)(1997) *Les États Membres de l'Union Europénne* (LGDI).

Riesenfeld and Abbott (eds)(1994), *Parliamentary Participation in the Making and Operation of Treaties: A Comparative Study* (Nijhoff).

Ryba [1995], 'La politique étrangère et de securité commune (PESC), Mode d'emploi et bilan d'une année d'application' Revue du Marché Commun 14.

SACK [1995], 'The EC's Membership of International Organizations', CML Rev 1227.

SALMON [1982], 'Ireland: A Neutral in the Community?', JCMS 205.

SANDS (2000), 'International Law, the Practitioner and non-State Actors' in Wickremasinghe (ed), *The International Lawyer as Practitioner* (British Institute of International and Comparative Law) 103.

SAROOSHI (1999), *The United Nations and the Development of Collective Security* (OUP).

SATOW (1979), *Guide to Diplomatic Practice* (5th edn)(Longman).

SCHMALZ [1998] 'The Amsterdam Provisions on External Coherence: Bridging the Union's Foreign Policy Dualism', European Foreign Affairs Rev 421.

SCHUTTE [1991] 'Schengen, its Meaning for the Free Movement of Persons in Europe', CML Rev p 549.

——(1994), 'Judicial Cooperation under the Union Treaty', Monar and Morgan (eds), *The Third Pillar of the European Union* (European Interuniversity Press, 1994) 181.

SCHWARZE (1994), 'La ratification du traité de Maastricht en Allemagne, l'arrêt de la Cour constitutionnelle de Karlsruhe' Revue du Marché Commun 293.

——[1999], 'Concept and Perspectives of European Community Law', EPL 22.

SEIDL-HOHENVELDERN (1987), 'Responsibility of Member States of an International Organization for Acts of that Organization' in *International Law at the Time of its Codification, Essays in Honour of Robert Ago* 415.

SENNI (2000), 'La Partecipazione della Communità Europea al Sistema delle Nazioni Unite' (thesis submitted to Università Cattolica del Sacro Cuore Milano).

SHIPSEY (1997), Asylum Policy and Title VI of the Treaty on European Union, in Barrett (ed) *Justice Cooperation in the European Union* (Institute of European Affairs, Dublin).

SIMMA, ASCHENBRENNER and SCHULTE (1999), 'Human Rights Considerations in the Development Cooperation Activities of the European Community' in Alston (ed), *The EU and Human Rights* (OUP) 571.

SINCLAIR (1987) *The International Law Commission* (Grotius Publications).

SLAUGHTER, STONE SWEET, and WEILER (1999), *The European Court and National Courts* (Hart).

SLYNN, (Lord) of Hadley [1993], 'Looking at European Community Texts', Statute Law Review 12.

SMIS and VAN DER BORGHT [1999], 'The EU–US Compromise on the Helms-Burton and d'Amato Acts' AJIL 227.

SMITH (1998a), 'The Instruments of European Union Foreign Policy', in Zielonka (ed.), *Paradoxes of European Foreign Policy* (Kluwer) 67.

——(1998*b*) 'Does the flag follow trade?' in Peterson and Sjursen (eds): *A Common Foreign Policy for Europe?* (Routledge) 77.

SOETENDORP (1999), *Foreign Policy in the European Union* (Pearson).

SOHMEN [1999], 'Critical Importance of Controlling Corruption', The International Lawyer 863.

SOLANA [2002], 'La Politique européenne de sécurité et de défense (PESD) est devenue opérationnelle' Revue du Marché Common et de l'Union Européenne 213.

SPENCER, Claire (2001), 'The EU and Common Strategies: The Revealing Case of the Mediterranean', European Foreign Affairs Rev 31.

SPENCER, Michael (1995), *States of Injustice: A Guide to Human Rights and Civil Liberties in the European Union* (Pluto Press).

STATEWATCH *See* BUNYAN (ed)(1995).

STEFANU and XANTHAKI (1997), *A Legal and Political Interpretation of Articles 224 and 225 of the Treaty of Rome* (Dartmouth).

STEIN (1994), 'Musings at the Grave of a Federation', *Institutional Dynamics of European Integration, Essays in Honour of Henry Schermers*, Vol II (Kluwer) 619.

SUBEDI [1993] 'Neutrality in a Changing World: European Neutral States and the European Community', ICLQ 238.

SWART (1994) 'Cooperation in the field of Criminal Law: Some Comments', Monar and Morgan (eds) *The Third Pillar of the European Union* (European Interuniversity Press) 193.

TEMPERLEY and PENSON (1938), *Foundations of British Foreign Policy from Pitt (1792) to Salisbury (1902)* (CUP).

TEMPLE LANG [1987], 'The Irish court case which delayed the Single European Act: *Crotty v An Taoiseach and Others*', CML Rev 709.

TESOKA (1998), 'Judicial Politics and EC external relations: the role of the European Court of Justice' in Cafruny and Peters (eds), *The Union and the World: The Political Economy of a Common European Foreign Policy* (Kluwer) 35.

TEUNISSEN [1999], Strengthening the Defence Dimension of the EU: An Evaluation of Concepts, Recent Initiatives and Developments, European Foreign Affairs Rev 327.

TIETJE [1997], 'The Concept of Coherence in the Treaty on European Union and the Common Foreign and Security Policy' European Foreign Affairs Rev 211.

TIMMERMANNS [1999], 'The EU and Public International Law', European Foreign Affairs Rev 181.

TWOMEY (1994), 'Title VI of the Union Treaty: "Matters of Common Interest" as a Question of Human Rights' in Monar and Morgan (eds), *The Third Pillar of the European Union* (European University Press).

UETA (1997), 'The Stability Pact from the Balladur Initiative to the EU Joint Action' in Holland (ed), *Common Foreign and Security Policy: The Record and Reforms* (Pinter) 92.

UNITED NATIONS HIGH COMMISSION FOR REFUGEES (1995), *Collection of International Instruments and other Legal Texts Concerning Refugees and Displaced Persons* (Geneva).

USHER [1997], 'Variable Geometry or Concentric Circles: Patterns for the European Union', ICLQ 243.

VERVAELE (ed)(1994), *Administrative law application and enforcement of community law in the Netherlands* (Deventer-Boston).

VIGNES, (1993), 'Communautés Européennes et Union Européenne, Trinité des Structures et Unité des Institutions Établies par le Traité de Maastricht' in *International Law in an Evolving World, Liber Amicorum Eduardo Jimenez de Arechaga)* 1329.

——[1999], 'Et si Amsterdam avait fait encore une autre chose de bien: permettre de realiser la politique de défense commune?', Revue du Marché Commun et de l'Union européenne 77.

VIOLA (2000) *European Foreign Policy and the European Parliament in the 1990s: An Investigation into the Role and Voting Behaviour of the European Parliament's Political Groups* (Ashgate).

VON BOGDANDY [1999], 'The Legal Case for Unity: The European Union as a Single Organization with a Single Legal System', CML Rev 887.

WALKER (1994), 'European integration and European policing: a complex relationship', in Anderson and den Boer (eds), *Policing across National Boundaries* (Pinter) 22.

——[1998], 'Justice and Home Affairs, in Current Developments in EC Law,' ICLQ 231.

WALLACE, REBECCA (1980), *Refugees and Asylum: A Community Perspective* (Butterworths).

——, William and WALLACE, Helen (2000), *Policy-making in the European Union* (4th edn) (OUP).

WARBRICK [1993], 'Recognition of States Part 2', ICLQ 433.

——(1996), 'Recognition of States: Recent European Practice' in Evans (ed) *Aspects of Statehood and Internationalism in Contemporary Europe* (Ashgate) 9.

WEBER-PANARIELLO (1995), *Nationale Parlamente in der Europäischen Union* (Nomos).

WEILER (1999*a*) *The Constitution of Europe* (Cambridge University Press).

——(1999*b*), 'The External Legal Relations of Non-Unitary Actors: Mixity and the Federal Principle', in Weiler, *The Constitution of Europe* 130.

——and HALTERN (1999) 'Constitutional or International? the Foundations of the Community Legal Order and the Question of Judicial Kompetenz-Kompetenz' in Slaughter, Stone Sweet, and Weiler, *The European Court and National Courts* (Hart).

WELLER [1992], 'The International Response to the Dissolution of the Socialist Federal Republic of Yugoslavia', AJIL 569.

——(1998), 'The European Union within the "European Security Architecture" ' in Koskenniemi (ed), *International Law Aspects of the European Union* (Kluwer) 57.

WERTS (1992), *The European Council* (North Holland).

WESSEL [1997], 'The International Status of the European Union', European Foreign Affairs Rev 109.

——(1999), *The European Union's Foreign and Security Policy: A Legal Institutional Perspective* (Kluwer).

——[2000a], 'Revisiting the International Status of the European Union', European Foreign Affairs Rev 507.

——[2000b], 'The Inside Looking Out: Consistency and Delimitation in EU External Relations, CML Rev 1135.

WHITE, BRIAN (2001), *Understanding European Foreign Policy* (Palgrave).

WHITE, N.D. (1996), *The Law of International Organizations* (Manchester University Press).

WHITE, SIMONE (1999), 'European Community Drug Control: Internal economic regulation and external conditionality' in Dorn (ed) *Regulating European Drug Problems* (Kluwer).

WOOD [1981], 'The European Convention on the Suppression of Terrorism', Yearbook of European Law 307.

WOUTERS and NAERT [2001], 'How effective is the European Security Architecture? Lessons from Bosnia and Kosovo', ICLQ 540.

WYATT [1982], 'New Legal Order, or Old?', ELR 147.

——and DASHWOOD (1993) *European Community Law* (3rd edn) (Sweet & Maxwell).

—— ——[2000], *European Union Law* (Sweet & Maxwell).

WYN REES [1996], 'Constructing a European Defence Identity: The Perspectives of Britain, France and Germany', European Foreign Affairs Rev 231.

YESSON [2001], 'NATO, EU and Russia: Reforming Europe's Security Institutions', European Foreign Affairs Rev 197.

ZIELONKA (1998a), Policies without Strategy: the EU's Record in Eastern Europe, *Paradoxes of European Foreign Policy* (Kluwer) 131.

——(ed) (1998b), *Paradoxes of European Foreign Policy* (Kluwer).

Index